Calvin's Theology and Its Reception

Calvin's Theology and Its Reception

Disputes, Developments, and New Possibilities

EDITED BY

J. TODD BILLINGS
AND I. JOHN HESSELINK

WESTMINSTER
JOHN KNOX PRESS
LOUISVILLE · KENTUCKY

© 2012 Westminster John Knox Press

First edition
Published by Westminster John Knox Press
Louisville, Kentucky

12 13 14 15 16 17 18 19 20 21—10 9 8 7 6 5 4 3 2 1

Scripture quotations from the New Revised Standard Version of the Bible are copyright © 1989 by the Division of Christian Education of the National Council of the Churches of Christ in the U.S.A. and are used by permission.

Excerpts from J. Todd Billings, "John Calvin's Soteriology: Key Issues in Interpretation and Retrieval," *International Journal of Systematic Theology* 11:4 (October 2009): 428–47, have been used by permission of Blackwell Publishing.

Book design by Sharon Adams
Cover design by Lisa Buckley

Library of Congress Cataloging-in-Publication Data

Calvin's theology and its reception : disputes, developments, and new possibilities / edited by J. Todd Billings, and I. John Hesselink.
    p.   cm.
  Includes index.
  ISBN 978-0-664-23423-2 (alk. paper)
  1. Calvin, Jean, 1509–1564.   2. Calvinism—History.   I. Billings, J. Todd.
  II. Hesselink, I. John, 1928–
  BX9418.C3855   2012
  230'.42092—dc23

                                                                2012011908

Contents

Acknowledgments

As editors, we have many to thank for the work in putting together this volume of essays on Calvin's theology, which is distinctive in its scope and approach.

First and foremost, we are grateful to the scholars who contributed to this volume. Focusing on both the theology and reception history of key themes in Calvin's theology, this volume includes scholars with a wide range of disciplinary specialties, including historical theology, social history, liturgical theology, and systematic theology. Moreover, the contributors are scholars at seminaries, universities, and Christian colleges from a very wide range of ecclesial locations. So, we thank these scholars for their willingness to engage in this corporate project together, for receiving editorial feedback, and for integrating their work into the framework of this volume on Calvin's theology and its reception history. While we appreciate the distinctive perspective offered by each scholar, we also appreciate their willingness to adopt the shared methodological approach of this volume (which is outlined in the introduction).

We are also grateful to Don McKim and his fine editorial staff at Westminster John Knox for their enthusiasm about this project and their support along the way. It is no small challenge to coordinate a multiauthor volume with ten essays, and the road has not been without bumps. But it has been a pleasure to work with the WJK staff.

Finally, we express our gratitude to two exceptionally gifted assistants at Western Theological Seminary: Ms. Dustyn Keepers and Mr. Andrew Mead. These student assistants helped in the editorial process, taking on multiple tasks with energy and competence.

J. Todd Billings and I. John Hesselink

Introduction

J. TODD BILLINGS AND I. JOHN HESSELINK

There are many books available on the theology of John Calvin. Why is there a need for a book like this one? There is a short answer and a long answer to that question. The short answer is that this book is positioned to be a useful resource for students and scholars of both historical and systematic theology. It exposits key points in Calvin's theology, gives an account of the reception history of these ideas, and then offers a series of reflections on the contemporary possibilities and limitations in developing Calvin's thought. What is usually separated into many different journal articles or monographs is brought together in one book: readers receive both a careful reconstruction of Calvin's thought and an introduction to the disputes, controversies, and developments of that thought. This can help readers to become critically reflective as they read Calvin's work. On the one hand, readers should distinguish between Calvin's thought and its use in later controversies. Calvin should not be read as the expositor of the five points of Calvinism (from the seventeenth-century Synod of Dort) or of evangelical revivalism (of the eighteenth and nineteenth century). Yet, by combining a contextually sensitive account of Calvin's theology with the history of reception, readers can become aware of the ways in which their own approach to Calvin may share assumptions with past moments in the history of reception. Readers come to see Calvin's thought in its otherness while also becoming self-aware about the way in which the history of reception shapes their own disposition in reading Calvin's works.

For students who are using this book as a textbook, this short answer may be sufficient. But there is a longer answer as well—an answer which suggests that this is not "just another textbook" on Calvin, but a novel scholarly enterprise.

This longer answer probes a more basic question: why is there a need for any more books on Calvin's theology at all? The last century has seen a score of monographs, edited collections of essays, and conferences on the theological,

political, and social thought of John Calvin. What stone has been left unturned
in his writings? What new insights can be brought to this profoundly influential writer and leader in the continental Reformation?

Perhaps it would be best to start with an analogy to another collection of
writings that have been probed in historical scholarship, but continue to produce new reflection: the Christian Bible. To say that it constitutes one book—
Holy Scripture, the Old and New Testament—is already to receive these
writings in a particular way. There is nothing intrinsic in these writings that
demands that they be read through a canonical lens that unites them together
into one book. In light of this, for over two centuries, critical scholars have
sought to contextualize and reconstruct the origin, authorship, and significance
of these writings apart from the canonical framework of Christian reception.
These approaches have led to significant insights and advances in our reception
of the Bible as ancient literature. But from a historiographic standpoint, these
historical critics have not eliminated the "interests" and prejudices that readers
bring to the Bible so much as changed them. Rather than looking for how a
particular passage in Isaiah points to the Messiah (or to Jesus Christ specifically), the textual history of the passage is probed, along with the social and
political circumstances of its origin. The historical critic is not interested in *all*
questions about a text any more than is a "precritical" reader of the Christian
canon. Certain questions are privileged over others in the inquiry, as the texts
are put to different uses.

Ultimately, both precritical and critical readers of the Bible bring interests to the texts that illuminate some features of the text while placing other
textual features into a shadow. Thus, readers of the Bible are in a somewhat
paradoxical position: The texts themselves are never exhausted of meaning
after two thousand years of reading; yet, some readings do better justice to
the features of the text than others. Moreover, some readings of the text are
more useful for particular purposes than others. Some readings of a text may
be historically insightful but profoundly ineffective for receiving a word from
God through the text to be proclaimed to a congregation. Other readings
may be useful for congregational edification but not useful if one is seeking
to use the text as a piece of evidence to reconstruct a historical event behind
the text.

In the late twentieth and early twenty-first century, the history of Scripture's
reception has been making a significant comeback.[1] Reading Scripture in light
of its history of reception was a common practice until the rise of historical

---

1. There are many signs that this is the case: from the publication of numerous commentaries
from the history of biblical interpretation to changes in courses and curricula at universities,
seminaries, and colleges. Recent anthologies of commentaries from the history of biblical exegesis
include the *Ancient Christian Commentaries on Scripture* (InterVarsity), *The Church's Bible*
(Eerdmans), and *Reformation Commentary on Scripture* (InterVarsity). For a general account of how
and why precritical exegesis has met with renewed interest in recent scholarship, see Brian E. Daley,
"Is Patristic Exegesis Still Usable?" *Communio* 29 (Spring 2002): 185–216.

criticism during the Enlightenment. Now it is being revived—frequently as a supplement to, rather than a replacement of, historical critical approaches to the biblical text.[2] Some of this revival reflects a renewed interest in ecclesiology—reading Scripture with the people of God throughout history. But its origins also have hermeneutical roots related to the meaning and significance of texts and how they are received into our horizons of understanding. Some would follow the approach of Hans-Georg Gadamer who suggests that understanding a text always involves a fusion of horizons. The reader's prejudices are never left behind, but they shape (and are reshaped by) the encounter with the text. "Not just occasionally but always, the meaning of a text goes beyond its author. That is why understanding is not merely a reproductive but always a productive activity as well."[3] We cannot remove ourselves from the history-of-effects of a particular work; applied to the present book, there is no tradition-free location from which to interpret Calvin's writings. For we must "understand in a different way, if we are to understand at all."[4]

Whether or not we follow a Gadamerian rationale for the renewal of interest in the history of reception, the fruit of such inquiry often has surprising and illuminating results. We discover new things about the texts of Scripture—as well as about ourselves—when we read exegetes from other times and cultures.[5] And just as examining the history of scriptural interpretation can illuminate and supplement historical-critical approaches, the same is the case for studying of the work of John Calvin, whose corpus of writing has exercised great influence over a long period of time. For many generations, the writings of Calvin have been used as a type of authority to justify—or disqualify—particular theological proposals as being "orthodox" or "Reformed" or "Protestant" or "evangelical." These receptions are always selective: whether positive, negative, or ambivalent, they always draw on certain parts of Calvin's corpus, while setting aside others. Usually they draw on certain genres (like the *Institutes*) and sideline others (like the sermons or polemical pieces). There are no disinterested readers of Calvin, and each act of reception says a great deal about the receiver. Moreover, these varied forms of reception carry the potential for drawing out dormant features in Calvin's writings themselves.

In the early to middle twentieth century, scholarship on Calvin's theology was frequently energized by Barthian dogmatic concerns. This movement

2. See the "supplementing" approach advocated in various ways by John L. Thompson, *Reading the Bible with the Dead: What You Can Learn from the History of Exegesis That You Can't Learn from Exegesis Alone* (Grand Rapids: Eerdmans, 2007); Jason Byassee, *Praise Seeking Understanding: Reading the Psalms with Augustine* (Grand Rapids: Eerdmans, 2007); Frances Young, "The 'Mind' of Scripture: Theological Readings of the Bible in the Fathers," *International Journal of Systematic Theology* vol. 7, no. 2 (April 2005): 126–41.

3. Hans-Georg Gadamer, *Truth and Method*, 2nd ed., trans. Joel Weinsheimer and Donald Marshall (New York: Continuum, 1993), 296.

4. Ibid., 297.

5. For a set of examples demonstrating the hermeneutical illumination that can come from the history of interpretation, see John L. Thompson, *Reading the Bible with the Dead.*

rightly recognized that many of the nineteenth- and early twentieth-century construals of Calvin's thought were caricatures—Calvin's theology used as a foil for pursuing other agendas. In the last decades of the twentieth century and the first of the twenty-first century, the trend has swung to "historical" rather than "dogmatic" readings of Calvin's work. These approaches have brought us a much more highly contextualized account of Calvin—not only in terms of his relation to his late medieval and early modern theological sources but also to the social and political context of his work. This scholarship has often functioned as a corrective to the Barthian gloss which earlier scholars gave to Calvin's theology. The sympathetic Barthian readers of Calvin brought to light features of Calvin's thought that countered the earlier caricatures; but they often framed Calvin's project in terms that would make more sense in a twentieth-century systematic theology classroom than in sixteenth-century Geneva. In the course of that, their own dogmatic interests sometimes blinded them to the historical otherness in Calvin's writings—the ways in which Calvin's writings resist playing into a neo-orthodox agenda. Late twentieth- and early twenty-first-century scholarship on Calvin has sought to correct this with a thoroughly historical portrait of Calvin's project and theology.[6]

While these historical readings of Calvin serve as a healthy corrective to earlier portraits of his theology, they are not without their dangers as well. In particular, for anyone who inhabits a tradition that is in some way indebted to Calvin (whether "Protestant" or "Reformed" or "evangelical" or other), a historical account of Calvin's theology only gives part of the picture. The other necessary part of the portrait is to reflect on how Calvin's writings have been—and continue to be—received in different contexts and used for different purposes. From the standpoint of one inhabiting a tradition like this, Calvin's writings cannot simply "mean" for the tradition what a reconstruction says they "meant" in the sixteenth century. The meanings of Calvin's writings are tied to the history of the effects that they have helped to produce.

For example, it is not unusual for one to hear talk of "Calvin's doctrine of total depravity."[7] On the one hand, this way of speaking about Calvin needs to be qualified and corrected: Calvin never speaks about "total depravity" per se; thus, he cannot have a doctrine of it. But stopping with that correction is somewhat flatfooted. Whether one inhabits a tradition that is seeking to exposit or attack a doctrine of total depravity, there is still something to be considered about the validity of talk about total depravity. In light of the history of reception, these issues can be clarified. For example, one could consider the question of the

6. For an overview of this shift in Reformation studies, see J. Jeffery Tyler, "What Happened to the Reformation? The Contentious Relationship between History and Religion," in *A Goodly Heritage* (Grand Rapids: Eerdmans, 2007), 201–24. For a documentation of this shift in Calvin studies, see Richard Muller, *The Unaccommodated Calvin* (Oxford: Oxford University Press, 2000), 3–17.

7. For an example that uses "total depravity" as a technical term for Calvin's thought, see Serene Jones, *Feminist Theory and Christian Theology* (Minneapolis: Fortress, 2000) 102–8.

relative continuity between Calvin's doctrine of sin and the Canons of Dort's five points. Just because Calvin does not speak in the exact terms of the Canon does not mean that the Canons are radically discontinuous with Calvin's thought. Or, one could consider Calvin's doctrine of sin in relation to the twentieth-century development of the English acronym TULIP (Total depravity, Unconditional election, Limited atonement, Irresistible grace, Perseverance of the saints).[8] It could be that the person speaking about "Calvin's doctrine of total depravity" is not seeking to speak about a specific aspect of Calvin's thought at all, but the particular development of Calvin's thought into a TULIP formula. Critically reflecting upon the history of receiving Calvin's thought increases our awareness of the dynamics that are at work when we "receive" his thought in the context of a tradition. Whether one's particular tradition tends to treat Calvin as a great teacher or a dangerous sophist is not the point. The point is that there have been many previous receivers of Calvin's thought, and awareness of the history of reception opens our eyes to the particularity of our own norms and questions brought to Calvin's texts.

By combining historical, contextualized accounts of Calvin's theology with key episodes in the history of reception, this book brings together the best of both worlds in contemporary scholarship on Calvin's theology. In addition, after having reflected upon how Calvin's texts have been received in the past— along with the works that have been emphasized, neglected, or forgotten—each doctrinal topic ends with reflections from a theologian on the contemporary possibilities in the reception of Calvin's thought. As such, this book intentionally blurs the strict boundaries between theology and history, reconstruction and reception. It does so not in order to give yet another "dogmatic portrait" of Calvin, but to reflect on the content and significance of Calvin's writing in a way that is cognizant of the reasons why so many have read Calvin in the past and the ends toward which his writings have been used.

This general approach could be fruitfully employed for a number of dimensions of Calvin's thought— social, economic, rhetorical, etc. But this volume narrows the scope to key topics (*loci*) of Christian doctrine because that is a category native to Calvin himself as well as many of his historical and contemporary readers. This is not to assume that Calvin was doing "systematic theology" in a contemporary sense. Rather, with his general method of articulating the *loci communes* ("common places") of biblical and theological teaching, the loci approach in this book can be seen as an extension of that part of his project. For reasons of space, we have limited our inquiry to five doctrinal topics. These particular topics have been chosen because they receive special emphasis in Calvin's theology and because they have a lively history of reception.

---

8. On the history of the English acronym TULIP, which does not predate the twentieth century, see Kenneth J. Stewart's "The Points of Calvinism: Retrospect and Prospect," *Scottish Bulletin of Evangelical Theology* 26, no. 2 (Autumn 2008): 187–203.

Here is the general format of the book:

DOCTRINAL TOPIC

Essay A

First section of Essay A—reconstruction of Calvin's thought on the topic

The first portion of this essay contains a contextually sensitive account of Calvin's thought on this particular locus of doctrine. This part of the essay will briefly engage the historical sources and influences that are relevant, but the central goal will be to provide a sketch of the material content of Calvin's thought on this point of doctrine.

Second section of Essay A—highlights in the history of reception up through Protestant Orthodoxy

The second part of this essay addresses a different question: in what significant ways was Calvin's thought on this point of doctrine received by later theological thinkers and/or ecclesial movements? The response to this question cannot be a comprehensive reception history of Calvin on this point but will point to some key illustrative debates, movements, or other means of "reception" of this point in Calvin's thought. In terms of historical periodization, this essay explores the reception history of Calvin in the period of confessionalization and Protestant Orthodoxy.

Essay B

First section of Essay B—highlights in the history of reception in the modern period

While Essay A ends with the reception history of Calvin's thought on the topic, this is where Essay B begins: a reception history of Calvin's thought on this point of doctrine in the modern era. This essay addresses the question, In what significant ways was Calvin's thought on this point of doctrine received by later theological thinkers and/or ecclesial movements in the modern and late modern periods? The response to this question will not be a comprehensive reception history of Calvin on this point but will point to some key illustrative debates, movements, or other means of "reception" of this point in Calvin's thought.

Second section of Essay B—contemporary promise and challenges in the contemporary reception of Calvin on this topic

In light of the historical sketch about how Calvin's "archive" has been utilized and developed in certain ways, as well as ignored in others, what are the distinctive possibilities for drawing upon this part of Calvin's thought in our contemporary context? This portion of the essay points to areas of promise and challenge in our context for retrieving, developing, or otherwise dialoguing with Calvin's thought on this point of doctrine.

Within this broad framework, the contributors to this volume have a number of different approaches. But for all of the theological topics of focus in this volume, readers receive a careful contextual account of Calvin's thought, an illustrative overview of key points in the history of reception, and reflection upon the contemporary possibilities for receiving Calvin's thought on this point.

This format makes the present volume both useful for classroom use and novel in scholarly terms. It is useful for classes in historical theology, especially classes focused on the Reformation, Calvinism, and the Reformed tradition. Unlike other studies, it gives concentrated attention to key theological ideas in Calvin's thought and then extends into the history of reception from that strong starting point. It is also useful for systematic theology classes. Systematic theologians frequently draw on historical thinkers like Calvin in an ad hoc manner, with appreciation (or denigration) of Calvin's particular theological thoughts, but with little self-awareness as to how and why the "Calvin" they draw on is being used. Particularly for theologians who inhabit a tradition in which Calvin's writings have been significant, awareness of the history of reception is indispensable for perceiving how Calvin's writings have been used and for seeing the possibilities for retrieving Calvin's thought today. Overall, this book models the insight that the contemporary development or repudiation of a feature in Calvin's theology should be done very carefully. It needs to be done in careful dialogue with Calvin's writings in their historical context and within the context of their history of reception, which influences our own horizon whether we are aware of it or not.

Before closing, it is necessary to correct a possible misunderstanding of the book's title and project—a misunderstanding that several essays within this volume also seek to counter. By focusing on Calvin and the reception history of his writings, we are not implying that Calvin is the sole "progenitor" of the Reformed or "Calvinist" tradition. As editors of this volume, we are not seeking to frame Calvin as a unique and distinctive thinker who becomes the single measure of what is later called "Reformed." Indeed, it is no accident that when we speak of various traditions appropriating Calvin above, "Reformed" is listed as only one of several.

This point is particularly significant in considering Calvin's theology in its sixteenth- and seventeenth-century context. In the modern era, Calvin often is interpreted as a Reformer quite separately from Bullinger, Bucer, Farel, and others. As such, this is worthy of examination in the modern reception history. But in his sixteenth-century context, Calvin was not "unique" or particularly "distinctive" in relation to other early theologians of the Reformed tradition. As Richard Muller has recently documented by examining the letters of various Reformers, Calvin was part of a "network of Reformers writing to one another concerning the conduct of the Reformation on theological, political, and organizational issues, in which Calvin appeared quite clearly as a central figure, but not as an authority to whom the others appeal."[9] Moreover, while Calvin certainly has influence on the Reformed tradition in the late sixteenth and seventeenth century, his positions are generally not used as a strict measuring stick of what it means to be "Reformed." Rather, he is drawn on with a collection of other Reformers, including Luther, Bullinger, Bucer, Vermigli, and others.

Nevertheless, when this qualification is fully granted, Calvin's writings have exercised considerable influence—in his day with the influential and active printing presses of Geneva, in Reformed Orthodoxy, and in the modern period as well. This book offers a distinctive window into Calvin's theology by combining a concern to contextualize Calvin's thought in the sixteenth century with an exploration of the ways in which his theology has been received in many other contexts as well. Moreover, Calvin's thought continues to be retrieved for theological purposes by Christians around the world today. To understand and assess contemporary efforts at retrieval, readers should seek to understand Calvin's writings in their sixteenth-century context as well as the various ways in which they have been received in the past.

9. Richard A. Muller, "Demoting Calvin: The Issue of Calvin and the Reformed Tradition," in *John Calvin, Myth and Reality: Images and Impact of Geneva's Reformer*, Papers of the 2009 Calvin Studies Society colloquium, ed. Amy Nelson Burnett (Eugene, OR: Wipf and Stock, 2011), 9.

SECTION 1
CALVIN'S THEOLOGY
OF SCRIPTURE
AND REVELATION,
AND ITS RECEPTION

Chapter 1

The Revelation of God in Creation and Scripture

Calvin's Theology and Its Early Reception

I. JOHN HESSELINK

In this chapter, I first discuss Calvin's understanding of revelation, broadly conceived. Then I turn to its early reception, examining the Reformed confessions of the latter half of the sixteenth and seventeenth centuries. In addition, I examine the reception of Calvin's thought on the revelation of God in creation and Scripture in John Owen and Thomas Watson as seventeenth-century Puritan theologians and Francis Turretin as a prominent Reformed Orthodox theologian.

PART I—CALVIN ON THE REVELATION OF GOD IN CREATION AND SCRIPTURE

Introduction
I. God's Revelation in Creation

When the topic of revelation is discussed, the normal approach is to turn immediately to the Bible since this is "our only rule of faith and practice."[1]

1. This, or some variant thereof, is the language commonly used in Presbyterian and Reformed confessions.

3

In the case of Calvin, however, this is to ignore the special place he gives to God's revelation in creation. No other reformer exulted in the beauties and wonders of the creation as much as Calvin.[2] Peter Wyatt may overstate the case, but he expresses an important truth when he says, "If Spinoza has been called 'the God-intoxicated philosopher,' then Calvin surely must be "the creation-intoxicated theologian."[3]

For Luther, by way of contrast, "God preserves his holiness and inviolability in creation by veiling himself as the hidden God."[4] Luther is so afraid of a theology of glory[5] that he believes "the knowledge of God from his works and knowledge of God from his sufferings are opposed to each other."[6] Calvin simply does not think in these terms.[7] As we shall see shortly, for Calvin the creation is an evident manifestation of God's glory, particularly to believers. For unbelievers, however, this general revelation only results in idolatry and renders them inexcusable. Calvin argues in this way not only in the *Institutes* and in his commentary on Romans 1:18–23, but also in his exposition of the second part of Psalm 19 where David declares in verse 7 that "the law of the LORD is perfect, reviving the soul." Calvin comments: "While the heavens bear witness to God, their testimony does not lead men so far that they thereby learn well true godliness." It only serves to render them inexcusable. The problem is that by nature we are so "dull and stupid" that "the signatures and proofs of Deity which are to be found in the theatre of the world" are not sufficient to move us to acknowledge and revere God. "Without the aid of the Word" and the "special grace," which God gives to those whom he "calls to salvation," we are blind even though "we are surrounded by so clear a light."[8]

Calvin wrote these lines toward the end of his career (1557). The argument that the knowledge of God in creation only leaves the natural man without excuse was already taken up in the second (1539) edition of the *Institutes*. In book 1, chapters 3 and 4, Calvin states that there is "an awareness of divinity" (*Divinitatis sensus*) and "a seed of religion" (*semen religionis*) in all human

---

2. This may appear to be a bold claim, but an examination of the writings of other sixteenth-century reformers reveals that none of them appears to have the same admiration for God's revelation in nature as Calvin.

3. *Jesus Christ and Creation in the Theology of John Calvin* (Allison Park, PA: Pickwick Publications, 1996), 91.

4. Lennart Pinomaa, *Faith Victorious. An Introduction to Luther's Theology* (Philadelphia: Fortress, 1963).

5. Luther frequently contrasts a theology of the cross with a theology of glory. The latter is any attempt to know God apart from the crucified Christ.

6. Paul Althaus, *The Theology of Martin Luther* (Philadelphia: Fortress, 1966), 26.

7. Luther and Calvin, however, in their exegesis of Romans 1:18–20 agree that, apart from God's revelation in Jesus Christ, the revelation in creation results in idolatry, which leaves people "without excuse." For Luther, see *Luther: Lectures on Romans*, ed. Wilhelm Pauck, Library of Christian Classics (LCC), vol. 25 (Philadelphia: Westminster Press, 1961), 23. Calvin, however, does not leave the matter there, but adds, "The apostle in Hebrews 11:3 ascribes to faith the light by which a man can gain real knowledge from the work of creation," Comm. Romans 1:20.

8. Comm. Psalm 19:7, translation amended.

beings.[9] Following the Apostle Paul's line of reasoning in Romans 1:18–25, Calvin concludes that although this vague knowledge of God cannot be effaced, it leads to idolatry and leaves them without excuse.[10]

When Calvin comes to God's revelation in creation in chapter 5, the result is much the same. Here too he extols the majesty and beauty of the created order. "Wherever you cast your eyes," he exclaims, "there is no spot in the universe wherein you cannot discern at least some sparks of God's glory." Alluding to Hebrews 11:3, he adds that "this skillful ordering of the universe is for us a sort of mirror in which we can contemplate God, who is otherwise invisible."[11] Even "the most untutored and ignorant persons see more than enough of God's workmanship in his creation to lead them to break forth in admiration of the Artificer [Creator]."[12]

However, despite this "dazzling theater" of God's glory,[13] "scarcely one man in a hundred is a true spectator of it!"[14] Even worse, "Although the Lord represents both himself and his everlasting Kingdom in the mirror of his works with very great clarity, such is our stupidity that we grow increasingly dull toward so clear testimonies and they flow away without profiting us."[15]

This is why we need God's special revelation in Scripture if we are to read the creation aright, not to mention God's revelation in Jesus Christ. Here Calvin uses his famous image of spectacles. For it is only "with the aid of the spectacles" of Scripture that our "confused knowledge of God" is cleared away.[16] The reformer makes the same point in the preface (*Argumentum*) to his Genesis commentary. The world is "a mirror in which we *ought* to behold God," but our eyes are not "sufficiently clear-sighted to discern what the fabric of heaven and earth represents, or that the knowledge to be hence attained is sufficient for salvation." The net effect is that we are rendered inexcusable. But with "Scripture as our guide and teacher, God not only makes plain those things which otherwise escape our notice, but almost compels us to behold them, as if he had assisted our dull sight with spectacles."[17]

Not only that, but in order to understand aright and appreciate God's revelation in the creation, we must begin with Christ as revealed in the Gospels. This

---

9. *Institutes* 1.3.1 and 1.4.1. I am using the LCC translation of the *Institutes* edited by John T. McNeill and translated by Ford Lewis Battles (Philadelphia: Westminster, 1960).
10. Ibid., 1.4.1.
11. Ibid., 1.5.1.
12. Ibid., 1.5.2. Referring later to Psalm 8:2–4 Calvin asserts that we have "a clear mirror of God's works in humankind," *Institutes* 1.5.3.
13. Ibid., 1.5.8. Calvin frequently refers to the creation as a theater of God's glory. Cf. 1.6.2; 1.14.20; 2.6.1; 3.9.2; Comm. Gen. 1:6; Comm. Ps. 138:1; Comm. 1 Cor. 1:21; and Comm. Acts 14:17.
14. Ibid.
15. Ibid., 1.5.11.
16. Ibid., 1.6.1. Calvin uses the image of spectacles also in 1.14.1 and in the "Argument" in his Genesis commentary.
17. "Argument" to the Commentary on Genesis (Grand Rapids: Eerdmans, 1948), 61.

whole matter is summarized eloquently in another passage in the preface to his Genesis commentary. After citing 1 Corinthians 1:21, he writes,

> For the apostle thus intimates that God is sought in vain under the guidance of visible things; and that nothing remains for us but to betake ourselves immediately to Christ; and that we must not therefore begin with the elements of this world but with the Gospel, which sets Christ alone before us with his cross. . . .[18] Nothing shall we find, I say, above or below, which can raise us up to God until Christ shall have instructed us in his own school.[19]

Does this mean that the revelation in creation is of no value except to point to our ingratitude and render us inexcusable? That is only true of the unregenerate and those who are blind in their sin. For the believer who views the created order with the eyes of Scripture, the creation is another source of revelation; for in considering the heavens and the earth—and God's handiwork in the creation of humanity—"we may seek confirmation in the true knowledge of God."[20]

Note in the following passage—again from the Genesis *Argumentum*—how the revelation in Jesus Christ is not antithetical to that in creation but is another aspect of it

> For Christ is that image in which God makes visible to us not only his heart (*pectus*) but also his hands and feet. I call his *heart* that secret love by which he lovingly embraces us in Christ; by his *hands* and *feet* I understand those works of his which are displayed before our eyes.[21]

For in the world "we have a clear image of God."[22] As we read in Hebrews 11:3, "By faith we understand that the worlds were framed by the word of God. . . ," Calvin comments

> In the whole architecture of his world God has given us clear evidence (*luculentum testimonium*) of his eternal wisdom, goodness, and power, and though he is invisible in himself he shows himself to us in some measure [*quodammodo*] in his works. The world is rightly called the mirror of divinity. . . .[23]

As David Steinmetz concludes his essay on "Calvin and the Natural Knowledge of God," for Calvin, "In spite of the human fall into sin the created order continues to function as a theater of God's glory."[24]

Thus, it is quite apparent that God's revelation in creation is a significant second source of revelation. "The majesty of God is in itself incomprehensible to us, but he makes himself known *by his works and by his Word*" (emphasis mine).[25] In and of itself the revelation through God's works does not lead to a

---

18. Calvin, no less than Luther, holds to a *theologia crucis*, not a *theologia gloriae*.
19. "Argument," Genesis Commentary, 63.
20. Ibid., 64.
21. Ibid., 64.
22. Comm. Hebrews 11:3, W. B. Johnston translation (Grand Rapids: Eerdmans, 1963), 160.
23. Ibid., translation amended.
24. David Steinmetz, *Calvin in Context* (New York/Oxford: Oxford University Press, 1995), 32.
25. Comm. Hab. 2:20. Reference from the Old Testament commentaries are from reprints by Eerdmans of the Calvin Translation Society in Edinburgh, 1843–55.

saving knowledge of God in Christ, but it complements that special revelation and adds an element not to be found in the written Word. The beauty of creation should be a constant source of wonder and praise on the part of God's children.[26] But the Word—or one might add, faith—is essential to that praise and wonder. "We must come," Calvin says elsewhere, "to the Word, where God is truly and vividly described to us from his works, while these very works are appraised not by our depraved judgment but by the rule of eternal truth."[27]

II. The Inspiration of Scripture

Calvin's discussion of the inspiration of Scripture does not come until he deals with the church in book 4, chapter 8, of the *Institutes*. The discussion occurs in several places where Calvin is engaged in a polemic against certain errors of the Roman Catholic Church. It is in this context that Calvin comes the closest to a formal doctrine of the inspiration of Scripture.

Calvin, like all the reformers, had a high view of Scripture, and, like them, believed the Scriptures to be inspired by the Holy Spirit.[28] Hence to the Reformation slogan, *sola scriptura*, might well be added *ex spiritu sancto*. The authority of Scripture as well cannot be divorced from its inspiration. In both cases the Holy Spirit plays a crucial role.

Almost every discussion of Calvin's view of the inspiration of Scripture eventually comes to the question as to whether he believed in the verbal inspiration of Scripture. There is considerable evidence that indicates that Calvin does believe in verbal inspiration. For example, he frequently speaks of God having *dictated* his message to the prophets and apostles. Daniel, for example, "did not speak from his own discretion, but whatever he uttered was dictated by the Holy Spirit."[29] Not only the Prophets but also the Psalms and historical accounts in the Old Testament were "composed under the Holy Spirit's dictation."[30]

Concerning the *locus classicus* for the doctrine of the inspiration of Scripture, 2 Timothy 3:16, Calvin acknowledges that the apostle here is speaking of the Old Testament, but he implies that these words apply to all of Scripture.

> This is the principle that distinguishes our religion from all others, that we know that God has spoken to us and are fully convinced that the prophets did not speak of themselves, but as organs of the Holy Spirit uttered only that which they had been commissioned from heaven to declare. All those who wish to profit from the Scriptures must first accept this as a settled

26. This theme is developed and further illustrated in a fine chapter in Randall Zachman's book *Image and Word in the Theology of John Calvin*, chapter 1, "The Universe as the Living Image of God" (Notre Dame, IN: University of Notre Dame Press, 2007).
27. *Institutes* 1.6.3.
28. Here the reformers were one with the ancient church including the medieval theologians. The difference is the Catholic Church's appeal to tradition in validating Scripture and the reformers' appeal to the self-authenticating (*autopistos*) character of Scripture. More about this later . . .
29. Comm. Daniel, preface, 79. In one case Calvin says that "the ancient prophecies were dictated by *Christ*" (Comm. 1 Peter 1:11, emphasis mine).
30. *Institutes* 4.8.6.

principle, that the Law and the prophets are not teachings handed on at the pleasure of men or produced by men's minds as their source, but are dictated by the Holy Spirit.[31]

The apostles were to expound the ancient Scriptures as fulfilled in Christ and not apart from "Christ's Spirit as precursor [*praeeunte*] in a certain measure [*quodammodo*] dictating the words."[32]

Quite apart from the question as to whether the phrase "the Spirit dictates" or "dictated by the Spirit" is to be taken literally or figuratively, there is massive evidence to indicate that for Calvin the Bible contains the oracles of God and that the biblical writers were amanuenses, instruments, and organs of the Holy Spirit. "The apostles were sure and genuine scribes [*amanuenses*] of the Holy Spirit, and their writings are therefore to be considered oracles of God."[33] The prophets were "organs" and "oracles" of the Holy Spirit. "For God wanted his Word to be always received from the mouth of man no less than if he had openly appeared from heaven."[34] Moses "wrote his five books not only under the guidance of the Spirit, but as God himself had suggested them speaking out of his own mouth."[35] Thus we have in Scripture a book whose words "are those of God and not of men."[36] In sum, "God is its author."[37]

This is one side of the issue. But there is another side where Calvin recognizes discrepancies and even errors of a certain sort in Scripture.[38] Calvin explains these discrepancies and errors by pointing out that despite their inspiredness the biblical authors were still human and children of their time. The prophets, for example, "were endowed with a peculiar insight above all others," but "even their preaching is both obscure . . . and embodied in types."

> Besides, however remarkable the knowledge in which they excelled, inasmuch as they had of necessity to submit to the common tutelage [*paedagōgiam*] of the people, they also are to be classed as children. Finally, no one there possessed discernment so clear as to be unaffected by the obscurity of the time.[39]

Calvin scholars have tried to resolve this tension in various ways. However, I believe it is anachronistic to discuss Calvin in terms of "verbal inspiration."

---

31. Comm. 2 Timothy 3:16.
32. *Institutes* 4.8.8.
33. Ibid., 4.8.9.
34. Comm. 1 John 4:1.
35. Comm. Exodus 31:18. Moses, when writing Scripture, acted "not as a man but as an angel speaking under the impulse of the Holy Spirit (*instinctu spiritus sancti*)" . . . , Comm. Gen. 49:5.
36. Comm. Hebrews 3:7.
37. *Institutes* 1.7.4.
38. See, for example, Calvin's comments on Romans 3:4 and his commentary on Hebrews 10:6: The apostles "were not over-scrupulous (*adeo religiosi*) in quoting words providing they did not misuse Scripture for their convenience." Cf. similar explanations in his commentaries on Hebrews 2:7, Romans 10:6, and Acts 7:14–16.
39. *Institutes* 2.11.6.

He never used the term. We should keep in mind that Calvin had no formal doctrine of inspiration as such. Instead we have countless occasional references to inspired writers. They reflected their humanity in various ways as they composed the Scriptures, but at the same time they were organs, instruments, and vessels of the Holy Spirit. The result is a Bible that is thoroughly trustworthy. More than that we need not know.

III. The Authority of Scripture and the *Testimonium*

One of the distinctive and permanent contributions of Calvin to theology is his notion of the internal, secret witness (*testimonium*) of the Spirit to the authority of the Bible. Luther also believed this but he did not teach it with the same force and consistency as Calvin.[40] Nor do we find the precise usage in Martin Bucer.[41]

In the oft-quoted and celebrated section of the *Institutes* (1.7.4–5) Calvin affirms that the authority of Scripture is authenticated by the inner witness of the Holy Spirit. This thesis finds ready acceptance in most quarters, although when investigated carefully, several questions often arise: Is this argument for the authority of Scripture too subjective? Is not the argument ultimately circular? What is the nature and power of Scripture apart from the inner witness of the Spirit? And finally, what weight should be given to the additional "proofs" for the authority of Scripture in the following chapter (8)?

In chapter 8, Calvin indicates that there are several confirmatory evidences of the authority of Scripture. In the words of the title of this chapter, "So Far as Human Reason Goes, Sufficiently Firm Proofs (*probationes*) Are at Hand to Establish the Credibility of Scripture." Note the qualification: "so far as" (*quatenus*). Nevertheless, one must not dismiss these "proofs" as of little value.[42] As Calvin points out, once one has established the certainty concerning Scripture that faith requires (the argument of chapter 7, which I will tend to shortly), "these arguments become very useful aids (*aptissima adminicula*)."[43]

What are these aids and helps? Before listing them, Calvin notes in passing that "our hearts are more firmly grounded when we reflect that we are captivated with admiration for Scripture more by grandeur of subjects than by grace of language . . . for the sublime mysteries of the Kingdom of heaven came to be expressed in mean and lowly words. . . ." If you want eloquent writings, read Demosthenes or Cicero, Plato and Aristotle![44] However, even the greatest

---

40. See the brief account of Luther's view of the authority of Scripture in J. K. S. Reid, *The Authority of Scripture* (London: Methuen, 1957) 62–65.

41. For Bucer see W. P. Stephens, *The Holy Spirit in the Theology of Martin Bucer* (London: Cambridge University Press, 1970), chapter 6.

42. Take, for example, Wilhelm Niesel. He is right in noting that Calvin "did not intend [these arguments] as conclusive proofs." But he is wrong in adding "Hence they are not of great value. . . ," *The Theology of Calvin* (Philadelphia: Westminster, 1956), 37.

43. *Institutes* 1.8.1.

44. Ibid.

orators will not move you as Scripture, for there "the majesty of the Spirit . . . is evident everywhere."[45]

In this connection one should take note of another notion of the reformer, namely, that of accommodation.[46] One of the reasons for the plain language of Scripture is that in order for God to communicate effectively to us, God must address us in language appropriate to our finitude. In an oft-quoted passage Calvin makes this point in an unforgettable manner.

> For who even of slight intelligence does not understand that, as nurses commonly do with infants, God is wont in a measure, to "lisp" in speaking to us? Thus such forms of speaking do not so much express clearly what God is like as accommodate the knowledge of him to our slight capacity. To do this he must descend far beneath his loftiness.[47]

Continuing now with these "aids," which are enumerated in chapter 8, the first is the antiquity of the Scriptures, for they "outstrip all other writings in antiquity."[48] Calvin then points to miracles and fulfilled prophecies, "which so clearly breathe the divine revelation as to convince sane men that it is God who speaks" (in Moses and the prophets).[49] Another indication of the authority of Scripture is the way the law of Moses "was wonderfully preserved by heavenly providence rather than by human effort."[50] The New Testament also is supported by "solid props (*solidis fulturis*)."[51] Finally, there is "the consent of the church" and the testimony of the martyrs who so trusted the Scripture that they sealed its authority by their blood.[52]

Such testimonies to the authority of Scripture are not to be lightly dismissed; nor are they to be overestimated. Calvin concludes this chapter with the telling

---

45. Ibid., 1.8.2.

46. Ford Lewis Battles, who was one of the first to treat extensively Calvin's use of accommodation, provides the historical background for this usage and points out that "Since the time of Tertullian, accommodation has frequently been appealed to in the Latin West." "God Was Accommodating Himself to Human Capacity," in Ford Lewis Battles, *Interpreting John Calvin*, ed. Robert Benedetto (Grand Rapids: Baker, 1996), 123. Cf. Edward A Dowey Jr., *The Knowledge of God in Calvin's Theology*, 3rd edition (1951; repr., Grand Rapids: Eerdmans, 1994), 4–17. Calvin was not unique in his use of accommodation. Zwingli and others before him also believed that God had accommodated Himself to human ways of speaking. Cf. David Wright, "Calvin's Accommodating God," in *Calvinus Sincerioris Religionis Vindex*, ed. Wilhelm H. Neuser and Brian G. Armstrong (Kirksville, MO: Sixteenth Century Journal Publishers, 1997).

47. *Institutes* 1.13.1. The same terminology is used in a sermon on Ephesians 4:20–24. Here he imagines the situation of his auditors and speaks in the first person: "God, having pitied my ignorance, brings himself down as much to my capacity, so that he even lisps (*voire mesmes il begaye*), as you might say, to tell me his secrets in a sweet and loving fashion, as if one wishing to feed a little babe should chew his meat for him, in order that he should have no more to do but to swallow it down; and shall I nevertheless remain a dullard still?" *John Calvin's Sermons on Ephesians*, revised translation of Arthur Golding (Carlisle, PA: Banner of Truth Trust, 1975), 423.

48. *Institutes* 1.8.3.

49. Ibid., 1.8.5–8.

50. Ibid., 1.8.9.

51. Ibid., 1.8.11.

52. Ibid., 1.8.12–13.

comment, "But those who wish to prove to unbelievers that Scripture is the Word of God are acting foolishly, for only by faith can this be known."[53] Calvin argues similarly in his famous reply to Cardinal Sadoleto in 1539:

> Christian faith must not be founded on human testimony, nor propped up by doubtful opinion or human authority, but engraved on our hearts by the finger of the living God, so as not to be obliterated by human error . . . [for] it is God alone who enlightens our minds to perceive his truth, who by his Spirit seals it upon our hearts, and by his sure testimony of it confirms our conscience.[54]

This, in effect, is the line of reasoning Calvin takes in 1.7.4–5. I am discussing these chapters in reverse order because I want to focus on the all-important *testimonium* of the Holy Spirit. As Calvin has suggested above, no apologetic can convince an unbeliever that the Bible is indeed the Word of God. "They who strive to build up firm faith in Scripture through disputation are doing things backwards."[55] Moreover, believers also require a certainty that will "banish all doubt." That kind of certainty, the "certainty which piety requires" comes only from "the secret testimony of the Spirit."[56] For "Scripture will ultimately suffice for a saving knowledge of God only when its certainty is founded upon the inward persuasion of the Holy Spirit."[57]

This appeal to the Holy Spirit, rather than to rational proofs or argumentation, may come as a surprise to those not familiar with Calvin's theology. Calvin, in effect, is appealing to experience, even a type of mystical experience. Nowhere is this clearer than in his classic lines in 1.7.5 of the *Institutes*:

> Let this point therefore stand: that those whom the Holy Spirit has inwardly taught truly rest upon Scripture, and that Scripture indeed is self-authenticated; hence, it is not right to subject it to proof and reasoning. And the certainty it deserves with us, it attains by the testimony of the Spirit. . . . We seek no proofs, no marks of genuineness upon which our judgment may lean; but we subject our judgment and wit to it as to a thing far beyond any guesswork! . . . but we feel that the undoubted power of his divine majesty lives and breathes there [in Scripture].

This passage must not be seen in isolation from what Calvin says about the self-authenticating nature of Scripture, or from the external evidences cited in chapter eight. Nevertheless, this appeal to internal secret witness of the Holy Spirit is crucial to his view of the authority of Scripture.

---

53. Ibid., 1.8.1–3.
54. "Reply to Sadolet," in *Calvin: Theological Treatises*, LCC, vol. 22 (Philadelphia: Westminster, 1954), 244.
55. *Institutes* 1.7.4.
56. Ibid., 1.7.1, 1.7.4. In 1.7.4 Calvin speaks of "the *secret* (*arcano*) testimony of the Spirit. Later, in this same section he refers to "the *inward* (*interiore*) testimony of the Spirit." There is no difference. Both expressions speak to the same reality.
57. Ibid., 1.8.13.

The Circular Argument

As noted above, some orthodox types are uncomfortable with this grounding of the authority of Scripture in what looks like a mystical experience.[58] But also from a liberal perspective, this appeal to the internal witness of the Holy Spirit as the ultimate ground of the authority of Scripture is regarded as the "Achilles' heel of the Protestant system."[59] For admittedly there is no rational "objective" basis for belief in the Bible as the Word of God when one appeals to God himself, although this does not mean that by appealing to the testimony of the Spirit Calvin is thereby taking refuge in an *asylum ignorantiae* (an asylum of ignorance).[60] The argument is obviously circular: Why do we believe the Bible is the Word of God? Because God by His Spirit assures us of this truth. How does God do this? Through the Bible.

The argument is indeed circular but it is a "logical circle."[61] Thereby we are not left to an existential subjectivism or psychological mysticism. The appeal to the Spirit cannot be separated from the Word. As Calvin points out in chapter 9 of the *Institutes*,

> For by a kind of mutual bond the Lord has joined together the certainty of his Word and of his Spirit so that the perfect religion of the Word may abide in our minds where the Spirit, who causes us to contemplate God's face, shines; and that we in turn may embrace the Spirit with no fear of being deceived when we embrace him in his own image, namely, in the Word.[62]

Thus the subjective and objective coalesce. The result is "a conviction that requires no reasons, a knowledge with which the best reason agrees—in which the mind truly reposes more securely and constantly than in any reasons."[63]

This should not be taken to mean that Scripture does not possess an intrinsic authority apart from the witness of the Spirit to the believer. That is, the Spirit does not impart authority to the Scripture but rather confirms in our hearts the authority that it already possesses. For Scripture is *autopistos*, or "trustworthy in and of itself."[64] Calvin uses this term only once in the *Institutes* (1.7.5)[65]

---

58. Several of the following paragraphs are taken from my book, *Calvin's First Catechism: A Commentary* (Louisville, KY: Westminster John Knox, 1997), 58–60.

59. David Friedrich Strauss, cited in Karl Barth, *Church Dogmatics* I/2 (Edinburgh: T. & T. Clark, 1956), 537.

60. The phrase comes from Werner Krusche, *Das Wirken des Heiligen Geistes*, (Göttingen: Vandenhoeck & Ruprecht, 1957), 210.

61. Barth, *Church Dogmatics* I/2:535.

62. *Institutes* 1.9.3.

63. Ibid., 1.7.5.

64. The definition of Richard Muller cited in Henk van den Belt, *The Authority of Scripture in Reformed Theology* (Leiden: Brill, 2008), 122.

65. Van den Belt has found ten other references in various writings of Calvin (see, *Authority of Scripture*, 14). Unfortunately, they are not always recognizable in English translations. However, in the commentary on Acts 26:26–27 it is translated literally as "self-authentic."

but it is significant. "Let this point therefore stand: that those whom the Holy Spirit has inwardly taught truly rest upon Scripture, and that Scripture indeed is self-authenticated (*autopistos*); hence it is not right to subject it to proof and reasoning."[66] This is Calvin's—and the reformers'—answer to Rome, which maintained that the church validated the authority of Scripture. Prior to his discussion of the Spirit's witness to the authority of Scripture Calvin discusses this issue and concludes, "Scripture exhibits fully as clear evidence of its own truth as white and black things do of their color, or sweet and bitter things do of their taste."[67]

The point of Calvin's argument in the *Institutes* is "not only to prepare our hearts to receive it [the authority of Scripture] with reverence but also to remove every doubt."[68] The role of the Spirit in this process is to seal on our hearts the truth of God as revealed in the Scriptures.[69] The Spirit bears witness to what Scripture intrinsically is. The truth of Scripture is objectively there, but it is ineffective without the internal testimony of the Spirit. Hence the cruciality of this important notion of the internal witness of the Spirit as developed by Calvin. At the same time, the witness of the Spirit cannot be separated from the "majesty" of Scripture and its self-authenticating power.

CONCLUSION

It is quite apparent that for Calvin it is never the Word alone but the Word that is the product of the inspiration of the Spirit, the Word that is confirmed as the very Word of God by the inner testimony of the Spirit. Hence for Calvin, at least, it is not sufficient to say simply *sola scriptura*, because for Scripture to be effective and meaningful, it must always be accompanied by the Spirit. The Spirit in turn is not a lone ranger, but almost always works through its chosen instrument, the Word of God.[70] The singular emphasis on the relationship of the Word and the Spirit is one of Calvin's distinctive contributions to theology and only confirms Calvin's reputation of being "the theologian of the Holy Spirit." At the same time, one must keep in mind the reformer's special emphasis on the revelation of God in the created order.

---

66. *Institutes* 1.5.1.
67. Ibid.
68. Ibid., 1.7.1.
69. Comm. 1 John 2:27.
70. I say "almost always" because there are times when Calvin says that the Spirit directs and guides believers apart from any direct connection with the Word. See my essay, "Governed and Guided by the Spirit. A Key Issue in Calvin's Doctrine of the Holy Spirit," in *Das Reformierte Erbe. Festschrift für Gottfried W. Locher zu Seinem* 80. *Geburtstag.* Teil 2 hrsg. von H. Oberman, E. Saxer et al. (Zurich: Theologischer Verlag, 1992).

PART II—THE RECEPTION OF CALVIN'S DOCTRINE OF SCRIPTURE IN THE LATE SIXTEENTH AND SEVENTEENTH CENTURIES

Introduction

As noted in part I, Calvin's view of revelation is not limited to Scripture, for Calvin's treatment of the revelation of God the Creator in book 1 of the *Institutes* contains within it the notion of a two-fold revelation of God: God's revelation in creation and God's revelation in God's Word. This was to have a significant impact on the French (Gallican), Belgic, and Westminster Confessions.

In the seventeenth century, the age of orthodoxy, when a more rationalistic approach began to dominate, one of the issues was to what extent certain key Reformed Orthodox theologians followed Calvin in affirming the revelation in creation and the secret, internal witness of the Spirit to the divinity of Scripture. Another issue was the relative importance of the *autopistos* nature of Scripture regarding the authority of Scripture. Here the work of a leading Reformed theologian will be examined, namely, Francis Turretin (1623–1687), and to some extent other Reformed theologians of this period, particularly Johannes Wollebius. Finally, in the late seventeenth century we will look at two of the Puritan "divines," namely, John Owen (1616–1683), and Thomas Watson (1620–1687).

I. Post-Reformation Reformed Confessions

It is not quite accurate to describe the French (Gallican) Confession of 1559 as "post-Reformation" for Calvin himself had a hand in it. However, it is the first of the Reformed confessions that is not regional. Earlier Reformed confessions such as Zwingli's Sixty-seven Articles of 1523, the Ten Theses of Berne, the First Confession of Basel (1534), and the Geneva Confession of 1536 (probably composed by both Calvin and Farel) did not have national or synodical approval.

Despite persecution, the number of Reformed Protestants in France had grown to about 400,000 by the year 1555. In September 1557, thirty-five members of the Reformed Church in Paris were arrested and seven were executed. The French Reformed Christians appealed to Calvin for help, but he was unable to influence the king of France. Along with their appeal they sent a copy of a brief confession of eighteen articles composed in 1557 addressed to the king. This became the basis of an expanded Genevan version of thirty-five articles written by Calvin, Viret, and Beza.

The Genevan draft had thirty-five articles, but the French Synod revised it, producing the final version of 40 articles. It was adopted by the Paris Synod meeting in secret on May 23, 1559. The moderator of the Synod was François de Morel, Calvin's friend and former pupil. This confession later came to be known as the Confession La Rochelle, since it was confirmed by a synod held in La Rochelle,

France, in 1571. At this point the Barthian scholar Arthur Cochrane detects a disastrous deviation from the original Genevan version. For now article 2 reads,

> As such this God reveals himself to man, firstly in his works, in their creation, as well as their preservation and control. Secondly, and more clearly, in his Word, which was in the beginning revealed through oracles, and which was afterward committed to writing in the books which we call the Holy Scriptures.[71]

What Cochrane finds offensive is the fact that now we have two sources of revelation: the created order and Scripture. This was not in the original Genevan version, so Cochrane suspects that some French ministers who did not really understand Calvin added this second source of revelation. He attributes this to "the influence of the rediscovery of Stoicism in the so-called humanism that was contemporaneous with the Reformation." Thereby "natural theology here first gained an entry into Reformed confessions."[72]

Whether this is "natural theology" in the modern sense of the phrase is questionable. In any case, Cochrane is wrong on two counts. Calvin had a hand in the final 1559 version and approved it; and in his Geneva Catechism (1542/45) and elsewhere he had stated a position like that of the French Confession. For example, consider the response to question 25:

> Why do you add that [God] is the creator of heaven and earth? Answer: Because he has manifested himself to us by his works (Ps. 104; Rom. 1:20) we ought to seek him in them. Our mind cannot comprehend his essence. But the world is for us like a mirror in which we may contemplate him in so far as it is expedient for us to know him.[73]

The Belgic Confession (1561), composed by the martyr Guido de Bres,[74] eventually became the official confession of the Dutch Reformed Church.[75] A revised version was sent to Geneva for its approval, which it received. It is similar in many ways to the French Confession which de Bres apparently used as his model. Here, too, the confession reflects Calvin's influence—and that of the

---

71. This translation is from Philip Schaff's *The Creeds of Christendom*, reprinted in Arthur Cochrane, *Reformed Confessions of the Sixteenth Century* (Louisville, KY: Westminster John Knox, 2003), 144.

72. Cochrane, *Reformed Confessions*, 138.

73. This is a translation from the French version found in Thomas F. Torrance, *The School of Faith* (London: James Clarke, 1959), 8.

74. It is frequently maintained that de Bres was assisted by Adrian Savaria, professor of theology at Leiden, H. Modetus, chaplain to William of Orange, and Godfrey van Wingen. However, Nicolaas H. Gootjes concludes that these men were only "consultants rather than co-authors," *The Belgic Confession. Its History and Sources* (Grand Rapids: Baker, 2007), 36.

75. It did not receive unanimous approval until 1580, although it was adopted by the Synod of Wesel in 1568 and by the Synod of Emden in 1571. This is also the official confession of the Reformed Church in America and the Christian Reformed Church in North America.

French Confession—in its positing of a twofold revelation. However, there are some interesting variations. It reads,

> We know [God] by two means: First, by the creation, preservation and government of the universe; which is before our eyes as a most elegant book, wherein all creatures, great and small, are as so many characters leading us to "see clearly the invisible things of God, even his everlasting power and divinity," as the Apostle Paul says (Rom. 1:20). All which things are sufficient to convince men and leave them without excuse. Second, he makes himself more clearly and fully known to us by his holy and divine Word, that is to say, as far as is necessary for us to know in this life, to his glory and our salvation.[76]

Note that now the phrase is added that this knowledge of God in creation leaves "men without excuse." Also, whereas the French Confession speaks of a double *revelation*, the Belgic Confession speaks of a double *knowledge of God*. "There is thus, corresponding to God's self-revelation *in* God's work and word, a knowledge of God *through* that work and word."[77]

We find nothing of this sort in another Reformed confession of this era, namely, the Scots Confession of 1560, written under the direction of John Knox, Calvin's friend and admirer. And unlike most Reformed Confessions, there is no paragraph on the authority of Scripture, only a passing reference in chapter 18. However, in the later Westminster Confession of Faith the same approach is taken that we find in the French and Belgic Confessions. Chapter 1 begins in the following way:

> Although the light of nature and the works of creation and providence, do so far manifest the goodness, wisdom, and power of God, as to leave man inexcusable; yet they are not sufficient to give that knowledge of God and of his will, which is necessary unto salvation; therefore it pleased the Lord . . . to reveal himself and to declare his will unto his Church. . . .[78]

The only other confession in the Reformed tradition that acknowledges a twofold revelation of God is that of the Waldenses in 1655. According to Philip Schaff, "This Confession belongs to the Calvinistic family and is in part an abridgment of the Gallican Confession of 1559. It is still in force, or at least highly prized

---

76. This is the version of article 2 found in *Ecumenical Creeds and Reformed Confessions* (Grand Rapids: Board of Publications of the Christian Reformed Church, 1988).

77. Jan Rohls, *Reformed Confessions: Theology from Zurich to Barmen* (Louisville, KY: Westminster John Knox, 1998), 31.

78. This text is found in *The Constitution of the Presbyterian Church (U.S.A.)*, Part 1, *Book of Confessions* (Louisville, KY: Office of the General Assembly, Presbyterian Church (U.S.A.), 1999), 6.001. The Westminster Larger Catechism puts the matter a little differently: Q. 2. "How doth it appear that there is a God?" A. "The very light of nature in man, and the works of God, declare plainly that there is a God; but the Word and Spirit only, do sufficiently and effectually reveal him unto men for their salvation," *Book of Confessions*, 7.112.

among the Waldenses in Italy."[79] Article II reads, "That this God has manifested himself to men by his works of Creation and Providence, as also by his Word revealed unto us. . . ."[80] Richard Muller summarizes the issues here very nicely:

> While there is no foundational status given to natural theology in either the Reformed confessions or in the theology of the Reformers generally, both the confessions and the dogmatic systems acknowledge the presence of God in the created order. What is more, this revelation is recognized differently by the regenerate and the unregenerate.[81]

Another distinctive contribution of Calvin's, which is explicitly picked up in both Reformed confessions and to some extent in early seventeenth-century orthodoxy, is his belief that the conviction that the Bible is the Word of God ultimately rests on the secret or inward testimony of the Spirit (*internum testimonium Spiritus*).[82] In the next chapter, as noted above, Calvin lists a number of arguments or aids which help to "establish the credibility of Scripture."[83]

This approach is followed in the French, Belgic, and Westminster Confessions, although in the latter case with a slight—some might say significant—modification. In the case of the French Confession the key phrase ("inward illumination of the Holy Spirit") is used to confirm the canonicity of the Scriptures as accepted by Protestants and no further "proofs" or evidences are given. Article III lists all the canonical books, followed by Article IV with,

> We know these books to be canonical and the sure rule of our faith, not so much by the common accord and consent of the church, as *by the testimony and inward illumination of the Holy Spirit*, which enables us to distinguish them from other ecclesiastical books upon which, however useful, we cannot find any articles of faith (emphasis mine).[84]

The Belgic Confession takes a similar approach. Article V has as its heading, "Whence the Holy Scriptures Derive Their Dignity and Authority" and then reads,

> We receive all these books [the canonical ones which have just been listed], and these only, as holy and canonical, for the regulation, foundation, and confirmation of our faith, . . . not so much because the church receives and approves them as such, but more especially *because the Holy Spirit witnesses in our hearts that they are from God* . . . (emphasis mine).[85]

---

79. *The Creeds of Christendom*, edited by Philip Schaff, revised by David S. Schaff (Grand Rapids: Baker reprint, 2007), 757.

80. Schaff, *Creeds of Christendom*, 758.

81. Richard A. Muller, *Post-Reformation Reformed Dogmatics: Holy Scripture*, vol. 2, 2nd ed. (Grand Rapids: Baker Academic, 2003), 154.

82. *Institutes* 1.7.4.

83. This phrase is taken from the title of chapter 8 of the *Institutes*.

84. In Cochrane, *Reformed Confessions*, 145.

85. In *Ecumenical Creeds and Reformed Confessions*, 81.

Then follows in abbreviated form something like Calvin's secondary evidences of the divinity of Scripture, such as their special content and the fact that "the things foretold in them are being fulfilled."

The Westminster Confession, however, reverses the order in its discussion of the authority of Scripture (I. 5). It does not begin with an appeal to the internal witness of Scripture but rather with several "arguments whereby it doth abundantly evidence itself to be the Word of God" (nine in all).[86] But then it adds, "yet, not withstanding, our full persuasion and assurance of the infallible truth and divine authority thereof, is from *the inward work of the Holy Spirit*, bearing witness by and with the Word in our hearts (emphasis mine).[87] Is this change in order significant, a departure from Calvin and an illustration of a "modified scholasticism"?[88] George S. Hendry, longtime professor of systematic theology at Princeton Seminary, finds no problem here in his interpretation of the confession. He suggests that the various qualities of the Bible "serve a useful purpose in directing us toward the authority of Scripture," but as with Calvin, "the doctrine of 'the inner witness of the Holy Spirit' . . . completes and rounds off the doctrine of inspiration."[89]

It is clear that at least two of Calvin's contributions to the doctrine of revelation and the authority of Scripture have been received almost verbatim in three Reformed confessions. Moreover, the self-authenticating (autopistic) nature of Scripture is also reflected in several Reformed confessions. The Belgic Confession affirms that we believe the Scriptures to be the Word of God "especially because the Holy Spirit witnesses in our hearts that they are from God; and *because they have the evidence of this in themselves*" (Article V, emphasis mine).[90]

The Second Helvetic Confession (1566) says little about the inspiration and authority of Scripture but simply states that both the Old and New Testaments are "the true Word of God and . . . *have sufficient authority of themselves*, not of men" (emphasis mine).[91] The Westminster Confession, as noted earlier, lists many of the same qualities of the Word that Calvin does, after which it adds, "whereby it doth abundantly evidence itself to be the Word of God,"[92] thereby implying the self-authenticating character of Scripture.

---

86. They are similar to Calvin's list: the testimony of the church, the heavenliness of the matter, the majesty of the style, the way of salvation, etc.

87. In *The Book of Confessions*, 6.005. The next section (6.006) adds, "we acknowledge the inward illumination of the Spirit of God to be necessary for the saving understanding of such things are revealed in the Word."

88. The expression "modified scholasticism" is from John Leith, *Assembly at Westminster: Reformed Theology in the Making* (Richmond, VA: John Knox, 1973), 65. For Leith this expression is not derogatory, for he states, "The new task that theology faced after 1560 was inevitable and ought not to be judged good or bad in itself, but as a necessary stage in the development of any community or theology," 65.

89. *The Westminster Confession for Today* (1960; repr., Richmond VA: John Knox, 1962), 31–32.

90. *Ecumenical Creeds & Reformed Confessions*, 65.

91. *The Constitution of the Presbyterian Church (U.S.A.)*, Part 1, *Book of Confessions*. (Louisville, KY: Office of the General Assembly, Presbyterian Church (U.S.A.), 1996), 5.001.

92. Ibid., 6.005.

II. Seventeenth-Century Reformed Theologians

The seventeenth century is generally regarded as the period of Orthodoxy and, depending on one's perspective, an era of increasing scholasticism. However, already in the latter part of the sixteenth century one finds illustrations of this trend of systemization. Calvin's successor Theodore Beza is often cited as an example. Scholars are sharply divided as to whether this development represents a logical and necessary continuation of the theology of the reformers or a precipitous decline into a rationalistic scholastic orthodoxy.[93] The question, in short, is one of continuity or discontinuity between Calvin and the later Orthodox theologians. I do not intend to enter this debate but rather let a representative theologian of this period speak for himself.[94]

My basic criteria for determining the extent to which Calvin's approach to Scripture is reflected in Orthodox Reformed and Puritan theologians will be found in how closely they share Calvin's enthusiasm for the revelation in creation, and the role the Spirit plays in their understanding of the inspiration and authority of Scripture, particularly the *internum testimonium*, as well as how much external signs (*indicia*) are appealed to as "proofs" of the divinity of Scripture as over against the self-authenticating nature of Scripture.

Heinrich Heppe maintains that as far as the authority of Scripture is concerned, "all Reformed dogmaticians are in essential agreement, since all adduce the *testimonium Spiritus sancti* as the real proof, besides which they adduce various other arguments as auxiliary proofs of lesser value."[95]

Francis Turretin might be cited as an exception in this connection, although his conclusions are similar to Calvin's. In his major theological work, *Institutes of Elenctic Theology*, the Second Topic, "The Holy Scriptures" runs to 113 pages.[96] He cites a few church fathers as well as Melanchthon, but there is nary a reference to Calvin in this section.[97] Nor does he mention the *internum testimonium*

93. Taking the former view are people like Paul Helm, Willem J. van Asselt, and above all Richard Muller. Those who take a negative view of this development include Jack Rogers, Holmes Rolston III, Basil Hall, and R. T. Kendall.

94. On this issue see the perceptive essay by Carl Trueman "Calvin and Calvinism," in *The Cambridge Companion to John Calvin*, ed. Donald K. McKim (Cambridge, England: Cambridge University Press, 2004).

95. Heinrich Heppe, *Reformed Dogmatics: Set Out and Illustrated from the Sources*, ed. Ernst Bizer (London: George Allen and Unwin, 1950), 23.

96. Turretin, *Institutes of Elenctic Theology*, vol. 1, trans. George Musgrave Giger, ed. James T. Dennison Jr. (Phillipsburg, NJ: P & R Publishing, 1992). However, in the prolegomena that precedes the discussion of Scripture (the First Topic) the subject is the nature of theology. Here Turretin discusses at some length the question of "whether natural theology may be granted." Similar to Calvin (but with no reference to him) Turretin argues that "the institution of religions in the world most clearly proves natural theology." Scripture itself indicates that "God has given to man both an innate and acquired knowledge of himself" (e.g., in Romans 1:18–20; 2:14–15; Acts 14:15–17, etc.) but this natural knowledge of God is not "sufficient for salvation" (7–9).

97. However, according to Richard Muller, Turretin cites Calvin's works in over sixty places. "It needs also to be noted that citations are not an adequate index to the reception or influence of a given thinker. . . . " Muller, "The 'Calvinists' Respond to Calvin," (unpublished lecture, Geneva, May 25, 2009).

explicitly although the idea is there. In his Sixth Question he asks, "From what source does the divine authority of the Scriptures become known to us?" He answers the question in a scholastic fashion. He concedes that the church is "the instrument and means through which I believe," but the Holy Spirit is the efficient cause from which I am induced to believe. A second reason is found in the marks of the Bible (similar to the so-called secondary "proofs"). However, he concludes, "If it be asked whence or from what I believe, I will answer, from the Holy Spirit who produces that belief in me."[98]

This sounds very much like Calvin. Again, when discussing the perspicuity of Scripture, Turretin reflects Calvin's influence when he writes, "We hold that the Spirit of illumination is necessary to make [the Scriptures] intelligible to believers."[99] The doctrine of perspicuity, therefore, "does not exclude the means necessary for interpretation," but neither does this "exclude the need for the internal light of the Spirit."[100]

However, he goes beyond Calvin in his concern for the inerrancy of Scripture. He has a lengthy discussion of the original texts of Scripture and argues strenuously against those who are not satisfied with the Masoretic Text and who "have recourse to the 'newness' of the [vowel] points! . . . as if the punctuation was only a human invention devised by the Masoretes and therefore founded upon human authority, not upon divine and infallible authority."[101] This led to the famous—or infamous—Helvetic Consensus Formula (1675) which is best known for its contention that the Hebrew vowel points were inspired.[102] J. H. Heidegger was the principal author, but Turretin was also involved and was instrumental in getting four Protestant cantons (Zurich, Basel, Bern, and Schaffhausen) to accept it.

In some ways, Turretin's theology represents the culmination of Reformed Orthodox theology and is not that different from three of his illustrious predecessors who were contemporaries: Johannes Wollebius (1586–1629), Gisbert Voetius (1589–1676), and Herman Witsius (1636–1708). All of them also appeal to the autopistic nature of Scripture and the internal witness of the Spirit to the divinity and authority of Scripture. But again there is not the exuberance of Calvin in regard to the glory of God in creation.

We saw earlier that the post-Calvinian Reformed confessions allude to what Calvin referred to as the self-authenticating (autopistic) nature of Scripture. Seventeenth-century Reformed Orthodox theologians are even more explicit in

98. Turretin, *Elenctic Theology*, 87.
99. Ibid., 143.
100. Ibid., 144. As Turretin continues the discussion, he finds support in Chrysostom, Irenaeus, Augustine, and Cyprian (145), but not in Calvin!
101. Ibid., 115. Here Turretin is critical of the School of Saumur in France and in particular "the celebrated Louis Cappel who . . . undertook most strenuously to defend the newness of the points as a recent invention of the Masoretes" (117).
102. This confession was used in Switzerland for half a century. The full text is found in John H. Leith, ed., *Creeds of the Churches: A Reader in Christian Doctrine from the Bible to the Present*, rev. ed. (Richmond, VA: John Knox, 1973), 309–23.

their use of this term. But "the use of *autopistos* by Calvin differs from the scholastic use of the term in Reformed orthodoxy," for the latter tended to give more weight to the importance of what they called the *principium externum*, the marks that distinguish Scripture.[103]

III. The Puritans

With some of the earlier Puritans there is overlapping with certain Orthodox dogmaticians, particularly Francis Turretin. John Owen (1616–1685)[104] and Thomas Watson (1620–1686) lived during most of the seventeenth century and were thus contemporaries of Voetius and Turretin. Moreover, Owen is also related to the Orthodoxy of that period.

One has the same problem with many of the Puritan divines that we encountered with the Orthodox Reformed dogmaticians: namely, that they rarely refer to Calvin even though most of them regarded themselves as Calvinists. Consequently, when it comes to revelation and Scripture one can only infer links with Calvin. Explicit acknowledgment of indebtedness to Calvin is rare.

I shall limit myself to an examination of two of the most prominent Puritan theologians: Thomas Watson and John Owen.

Thomas Watson

In Thomas Watson's *A Body of Divinity*[105] we find not only a broad continuity with Calvin when it comes to Scripture but also an approach that is akin to Calvin with one important exception. Watson was a prolific author, but his *Body of Divinity* was his magnum opus and was not published until after his death.

Watson begins his *Body of Divinity* with a discussion of "Man's chief end," because he is following the pattern of the Westminster Larger Catechism. He first discusses what it is to glorify God, which consists of four things: (1) appreciation, (2) adoration, (3) affection, (4) subjection.[106] This is followed by why we must glorify God. Watson again lists four reasons, the fourth being "creatures below us and above us." Here he cites Psalm 19:1 and then elaborates with a passage that matches Calvin for eloquence and exuberance:

> The curious workmanship of heaven sets forth the glory of its Maker; the firmament is beautiful and penciled out in blue and azure colors, where the power and wisdom of God may be clearly seen. 'The heavens declare his glory': We may see the glory of God blazing in the sun and twinkling in the stars. Look into the air, the birds, with their chirping music, sing hymns of praise to God. Every beast in its kind glorifies God. Isaiah 43:21.[107]

---

103. van den Belt, *Authority*, 303–5.
104. Carl Trueman argues that calling Owen "a Puritan" is not a very helpful category for understanding his theology. See Trueman's book *John Owen: Reformed Catholic Renaissance Man* (Aldershot, England: Ashgate, 2007).
105. Thomas Watson, *A Body of Divinity* (London: The Banner of Truth Trust, 1965).
106. Ibid., 7.
107. Ibid., 10.

In part 2, "God and his Creation," Watson makes similar comments and then proceeds to the Scriptures. He begins with Question 2 which affirms that the Word of God is "the only rule to direct us how we may glorify and enjoy [God]." Citing 2 Timothy 3:16, he adds that "it is given by divine inspiration" and "is to be highly reverenced and esteemed because we are sure it came from heaven, 2 Peter 1:21."[108]

This is followed by a fairly lengthy discussion of the authority of Scripture. Like the Westminster Larger Catechism he begins with "seven cogent arguments which may evince it to be the Word of God." These are taken from the catechism and are similar to those used by Calvin. However, Watson does not follow this up with the ultimate appeal to the authority of Scripture, the internal witness of the Spirit, as the catechism does, which is surprising in that he was a famously experiential theologian. The closest he comes is in his amplification of the sixth argument: namely, "The mighty power and efficacy that the Word has had upon the souls and consciences of men." For example, "It has changed their hearts." He concludes this discussion in this way: "Now, the Scriptures having such an exhilarating, heart-comforting power in them, shows clearly that they are of God, and it is he who has put the milk of consolation in their breasts."[109]

This is not exactly the internal witness. Watson comes close in one of his closing exhortations. "Bless God that he has not only written his Word, but sealed it upon thy heart and made it effectual."[110] However, Watson is similar to Calvin and to the general Reformation principle of Scripture being the best interpreter of Scripture: He writes, "The Scripture is to be its own interpreter, or rather the Spirit speaking in it." Then he uses an interesting analogy: "Nothing can cut the diamond but the diamond; nothing can interpret Scripture but Scripture.[111] Here again we have a Calvinist who is not altogether a Calvinian, at least not in regard to the approach to Scripture.

John Owen

The same cannot be said of John Owen, "the prince of the English divines," a leader among the Congregationalists, and according to some Puritan scholars, "a genius with learning second only to Calvin's."[112]

In the midst of many activities he managed to write more than eighty works.[113] In 1674 he published *Pneumatologia*, a classic work on the Holy Spirit.

108. Ibid., 26.
109. Ibid., 29.
110. Ibid., 38.
111. Ibid., 31. Also, as over against the Enthusiasts, "The Spirit of God acts regularly, it works in and by the Word," 33.
112. Joel R. Beeke and Randall J. Pederson, *Meet the Puritans: With a Guide to Modern Reprints* (Grand Rapids: Reformation Heritage Books, 2007), 456. I am indebted to this study for much of the following information.
113. Beeke and Pederson refer to a reprint edition of sixteen volumes of the works of John Owen totaling nine thousand pages (Edinburgh: Banner of Truth Trust, 1996). I am using an older edition, John Owen, *The Works of John Owen*, ed. William H. Goold, 24 vols., (Edinburgh and London: Johnston and Hunter, 1850–55).

In volume 4 of his *Works* he continues his discourse on the Holy Spirit beginning with "The Reason of Faith" or "An Answer unto That Inquiry, 'Wherefore We Believe the Scripture to Be the Word of God.'"[114] This discussion goes on for 234 pages. He cites very few writers and for the most part simply supports his arguments with Scripture passages. In the midst of this lengthy discussion he makes several references to the role of the Spirit in confirming the divine origin of Scripture. They are occasional and scattered throughout the first half of this treatise. For example,

> If it be asked how I know this Scripture to be a divine revelation, to be the Word of God, I answer:
>
> 1. I do not know it demonstratively, upon rational, scientific principles, because such a divine revelation is not capable of demonstration, 1 Thess. 2:13.2. But I believe it so to be with faith divine and supernatural, resting on and resolved into the authority and veracity of God himself, evidencing themselves unto my mind, my soul, and conscience by this revelation itself, and not otherwise.[115]

There is no precise reference to the internal witness of the Spirit, but it has similarities to Calvin who eschewed any attempts to prove the authority of Scripture by rational proofs. A little later Owen relates the authority of Scripture to an earlier discussion of how one comes to faith: "We also here suppose the internal effectual work of the Spirit begetting faith in us . . . without which we can believe neither the Scripture nor anything else with faith divine."[116]

Owen later refers to "the infinitely glorious properties" of God's revelation of himself, which offer some assurance to the believer. This is, in effect, the autopistic nature of Scripture. This is stated explicitly in another passage where he says that "Scripture is recognized to be self-authenticating or trustworthy in itself, i.e., *autopistos*."[117] But these external evidences are also effective because of the work of the Holy Spirit. They cannot be separated from the internal work of the Spirit that produces faith. Both are important: "the internal work of the Holy Spirit on the minds of men, enabling them to believe, and the external work of the same Holy Spirit, giving evidence in and by the Spirit unto its own divine original."[118]

Owen does not make as much of the revelation of God in creation, but it is there. In his Greater Catechism, for example, he begins by asking, "What is Christian religion?" Answer: "The only way of knowing God aright and living

114. Owen, *Works*, vol. 4, Prefatory Note 2, dated London: 1677.
115. Ibid., 70.
116. Ibid., 72.
117. Ibid., vol. 16, 309. For a further discussion of Owen in this connection see Muller, *Post-Reformation Reformed Dogmatics*, vol. 1, 265–69.
118. Owen, *Works*, vol. 4, 102. In his "Greater Catechism" Owen says almost the same. In Question 4 it is asked, "How do you know them [the Scriptures] to be the Word of God?" Answer: "By the testimony of God's Spirit, working faith in my heart to close with the heavenly majesty and clear divine truth that shineth in them"—and eight supporting texts are then given. *The Works of John Owen*, vol. 1, ed. William Goold (London and Edinburgh, 1850), 470.

unto him." Question 2: "Whence is it to be learned?" Answer: "From the holy Scripture only."[119] However, later in this catechism (chap. 5, Q. 1), Owen discusses "the works of God," which include creation and providence, but there is no development of this along the lines of Calvin in his Geneva Catechism.

However, in a treatise called *Divine Original*, Owen refers to three ways that God reveals himself, the first being in God's works of creation and providence. Here he emphasizes the self-authenticating nature of these works—"Wherever they are seen and considered, they undeniably evince that they are so"[120]—but he does not follow Calvin's point that they are only edifying if one views them with the spectacles of Scripture.

CONCLUSION

With the exception of the Reformed confessions cited earlier, *direct* dependence on Calvin's understanding of revelation in general and the inspiration and authority of Scripture is minimal. However, the theologians cited here generally appear to take the same approach to these issues that Calvin does. That is, they suggest "arguments" or "aids" to support the credibility of Scripture, but such evidences are always secondary. The ultimate ground for the certainty of the divinity of Scripture is always the inward persuasion of the Holy Spirit, the famous *internum testimonium*. Thus, in the last analysis, it may be more accurate to say that some of these writers reflect Calvin's theology more than they consciously and directly receive it. Particularly in the works of the Orthodox theologians, there is little discussion of the revelation in the creation. Instead, they frequently discuss natural theology as over against revealed theology. The net result is that with both the Orthodox theologians and the Puritans, there is both continuity and discontinuity, although rarely, if ever, is there an outright rejection of Calvin's approach to revelation and the inspiration and authority of Scripture.

119. Ibid., vol. 1, 470.
120. Ibid., vol. 16, 311.

Chapter 2

Calvin on the Revelation of God in Creation and Scripture

Modern Reception
and Contemporary Possibilities

MARK HUSBANDS

> If the present trends in membership decline continue, the only churches
> left in the West by the middle of the next [twenty-first] century will be
> Roman Catholic, Orthodox, and conservative evangelical. Protestantism as
> we know it will have ceased to exist. The end of Reformed theology may
> well coincide with the end of the Reformed churches.[1]

As Bruce McCormack's trenchant observation indicates, the contemporary
state of Reformed church-life and theology portends an uncertain future. Well
aware of the fact that the term "Reformed" is contested and that there are numerous, and sometimes competing, ways of identifying with *the* Reformed tradition,
there is no dispute that John Calvin stands at the headwaters of Reformed theology. Accordingly, those who wish to identify themselves as "Reformed" ought
to be able to demonstrate the ways in which they stand in continuity with a
theological tradition beginning with John Calvin. Put differently, to depart in
crucial ways from Calvin's treatment of the doctrines of revelation and Scripture

---

1. Bruce L. McCormack, "The End of Reformed Theology? The Voice of Karl Barth in the
Doctrinal Chaos of the Present," in *Reformed Theology: Identity and Ecumenicity*, ed. Wallace M.
Alston and Michael Welker (Grand Rapids: Eerdmans, 2003), 53.

might well mean that one is not particularly Reformed after all. While for many, this is of no real concern, for those more familiar with the febrile temperature of debate over the future of Reformed churches, it is a matter of grave significance. At the very least, critical observation of the neglect or even loss of key facets of Calvin's theology represents a harbinger to those who still hope for the long-term viability of Reformed theology.

An initial understanding of the general shape of Calvin's treatment of revelation and Scripture can be acquired by placing his work in a larger cultural and historical frame. For instance, Calvin recognizes two complementary sources of knowledge: the "book of Scripture" and the "book of nature." Despite the fact that Calvin employs the classical Stoic notion that all persons possess an innate *sensus divinitatis*, or awareness of divinity,[2] nowhere does he assert that natural revelation either (1) leads to a saving knowledge of God or (2) ratifies God's self-revelation in Scripture. In addressing the authority of Scripture, Calvin insists that "credibility of doctrine is not established until we are persuaded beyond doubt that God is its Author," adding, "thus, the highest proof of Scripture derives in general from the fact that God in person speaks in it."[3]

Refusing to separate heart and mind—*fides quae creditur* (the content of faith as revealed by God) and the *fides qua creditur* (the faith by which the believer receives and holds the revelation of God)—Calvin maintains that a "firm and certain knowledge of God's benevolence" is founded upon the promise of Christ revealed to us through the work of the Spirit. Not only does he conceive of revelation in terms of God's grace and the movement of the Spirit, but he also maintains that God mercifully illumines our minds and strengthens our trust in the Word of God.[4] Only in Holy Scripture, Calvin argues, do "we learn that God is for us the sole and eternal source of all life, righteousness, wisdom, power, goodness, and mercy."[5] In fact, the pride of place accorded to Scripture is a defining mark of Calvin's theology. At the same time, this poses something of a challenge to those who seek to identify with the Reformed tradition while assimilating the truth of Christianity to something other than the biblical witness.

The contested nature of modern Reformed theology calls for renewed attention to historiography. Here the work of Richard Muller is patently helpful, for he has ably demonstrated that the Reformers and their orthodox and scholastic successors are united in believing that Scripture is the Word of God. Similarly, there is common agreement among Calvin and subsequent "Calvinists" that Scripture is to be regarded as the *principium cognoscendi* (principle of knowing) or final norm for theology. In Muller's own words:

    2. John Calvin, *Institutes of the Christian Religion*, ed. John T. McNeill, trans. Ford Lewis Battles, Library of Christian Classics (Philadelphia: Westminster Press, 1960), 1.3.1.
    3. Ibid., 1.7.4.
    4. Ibid., 3.2.7.
    5. I. John Hesselink and John Calvin, *Calvin's First Catechism: A Commentary Featuring Ford Lewis Battles' Translation of the 1538 Catechism*, (Louisville, KY: Westminster John Knox, 1997), 8.

> We can certainly speak of a development of the Reformed doctrine of
> Scripture from the Reformation into the era of orthodoxy . . . but it is quite
> incorrect to assert that the Reformers understood Scripture as anything
> other than the infallible, inspired Word of God and the sole foundation for
> Christian teaching.[6]

By the eighteenth and nineteenth centuries, much of what Calvin had sought
to establish vis-à-vis the authority of Scripture had been cast aside with the rise
of so-called historical consciousness. The rise of historicism had considerable
negative consequences for classical doctrines of revelation and Scripture. As
Brian Gerrish notes,

> From a strictly historical point of view, there can be no reason to grant
> privileged status to Christian claims or Christian literature, even though
> we may have a special interest in them simply because they are part of
> our history. On the contrary, the task will be to bring any religious claims
> whatever under the scrutiny of commonly accepted standards of inquiry.[7]

Commonly accepted standards of inquiry in the modern period turned to be
inimical to basic Christian claims regarding revelation and the authority of
Scripture. The upshot of this development was that it became increasingly difficult for the church to garner widespread academic and public acceptance of its
faith in the God of the gospel.

This chapter considers the reception history of Calvin's doctrines of revelation and Scripture in the work of three modern theologians: Friedrich D. E.
Schleiermacher (1768–1834), Herman Bavinck (1854–1921), and Karl Barth
(1886–1968). The rise of historical consciousness makes for an intriguing back-
drop for our consideration of the development of modern Reformed theology.
Moreover, an examination of each of these figures reveals significant details
about the challenge and promise of retrieving Calvin's doctrines of revelation
and Scripture in the modern world.

I. HIGHLIGHTS IN THE HISTORY OF RECEPTION
FROM THE EIGHTEENTH TO THE TWENTIETH CENTURY

Friedrich D. E. Schleiermacher (1768–1834)

In the intervening years between the death of Calvin (1564) and the birth of
Schleiermacher (1768), Western culture came to regard the human subject as
the principle source of meaning, resulting in a considerable redefinition of the
meaning of "religion." Following a shift toward immediacy and interiority,

6. Richard A. Muller, *After Calvin: Studies in the Development of a Theological Tradition*, (New
York: Oxford University Press, 2003), 11.
7. B. A. Gerrish, "Errors and Insights in the Understanding of Revelation: A Provisional
Response," *The Journal of Religion* 78, no. 1 (1998): 69.

religion gradually comes to occupy a thoroughly private, rather than public, role in the West.[8] This dramatic shift bore telling consequences for religious commitment and doctrine. This is painfully displayed in a letter written by Friedrich Schleiermacher to his father on January 21, 1787:

> Faith is the regalia of the Godhead, you say. Alas! dearest father, if you believe that without faith no one can attain to salvation in the next world, nor to tranquility in this—and such, I know, is your belief—oh! then pray to God to grant it to me, for to me it is now lost. I cannot believe that he who called himself the Son of Man was the true, eternal God; I cannot believe that his death was a vicarious atonement.[9]

This confession was heartbreaking for Friedrich's father who, weighing the consequences of disowning Friedrich and hoping to elicit from his son genuine repentance and a return to faith, responds:

> You no longer worship the God of your father, no longer kneel at the same altar with him. . . . I can add no more except the assurance that with sorrowing and heavy heart, I remain your deeply compassionate and loving father.[10]

Surprisingly, Brian Gerrish maintains that Schleiermacher did not, in fact, lose faith in Christ, but only lost his "first understanding of it."[11] Perhaps this is so, but what is certain is Schleiermacher's commitment to thoroughly modern assumptions about the nature of Scripture, hermeneutics, history, and theological anthropology led him to set aside a number of classical doctrinal commitments upheld by Calvin. With this in mind, let us consider in greater detail the way in which Schleiermacher did or did not successfully receive Calvin's doctrines of revelation and Scripture.

First, keep in mind the fact that Schleiermacher's thought was highly nuanced and complex, which leads him to construct a leading "subjective correlate" for every Christian concept. Accordingly, "revelation" for Schleiermacher is neither bound to, nor normed by any strictly objective reality. Instead, revelation is understood and posited within the context of individual self-consciousness (*Selbstbewußtsein*). Scripture, therefore, plays no determinate role in revelation beyond that of providing testimony to the highest representation of human feeling or immediate experience of absolute dependence: namely, Jesus Christ. This, of course, calls for a particular way of ordering the relation of self and Scripture as is evident in §128 of *The Christian Faith*, which begins with the thesis: "The authority of Holy Scripture cannot be the foundation of faith in Christ; rather

---

8. William T. Cavanaugh, *Theopolitical Imagination* (London and New York: T. & T. Clark, 2002), 20–22.
9. Cited in B. A. Gerrish, *A Prince of the Church: Schleiermacher and the Beginnings of Modern Theology* (Philadelphia: Fortress, 1984), 25.
10. Ibid., 25–26.
11. Ibid., 26.

must the latter be presupposed before a peculiar authority can be granted to Holy Scripture."[12] Given that faith arises out of the subjective experience of absolute dependence, it is not surprising to find that Schleiermacher contends that the imagination, rather than the external Word of God, constitutes the "highest and most original element in us, and that everything besides it is merely reflection upon it" to which he adds, "you will know that it is our imagination that creates the world for you, and that you have no God without the world."[13] Setting aside the question of whether or not Schleiermacher can successfully defend himself against the inevitable charge of panentheism, the most important thing for our purposes is the question of whether or not Schleiermacher is able to coordinate his doctrines of revelation and Scripture with Calvin's.

Second, arguably, Schleiermacher stands in closest proximity to Calvin on the question of the relationship of revelation and piety. Breathing new life into the discussion of religion, Schleiermacher substantially renews attention to religious experience. Not surprisingly, he famously argues that true piety is neither a question of knowing or doing but is rather an issue of feeling or experience. The common element in all genuine expressions of piety, he argues, is the awareness of being absolutely dependent upon, or in relation to, God. According to Schleiermacher, "God signifies for us simply that which is the co-determinant in this feeling and that to which we trace our being in such a state; and any further content of the idea must be evolved out of this fundamental import assigned to it."[14] Notably, he writes, "to feel oneself absolutely dependent and to be conscious of being in relation with God are one and the same thing."[15] Although there appears to be a significant parallel here between Schleiermacher's treatment of the feeling of absolute dependence and Calvin's affirmation that "Men of sound judgment will always be sure that a sense of divinity which can never be effaced is engraved upon men's minds,"[16] the family resemblance is more apparent than real. The crucial difference between these two positions is this: Calvin resists appealing to the innate *sensus divinitatis* as a foundation upon which one might reasonably construct a dogmatic project. In addition, his insistence that there is a "seed of religion" given to everyone does not serve nearly as positive a role as does Schleiermacher's feeling of absolute dependence. Instead, Calvin underscores the innate *sensus divinitatis* in order to lay bare the force of Paul's argument in Romans 1:20 that no one is ἀναπολογή τους, "without excuse." Calvin writes, "Indeed, the perversity of the impious, who though they struggle furiously are unable to extricate themselves from the fear of God, is abundant testimony that this conviction, namely, that there is

12. Friedrich Schleiermacher, *The Christian Faith*, ed. H. R. Mackintosh and James Stuart Stewart (Edinburgh: T. & T. Clark, 1928), 591.
13. Schleiermacher, *On Religion*, 53.
14. Friedrich Schleiermacher, *The Christian Faith*, ed. H. R. Mackintosh and James Stuart Stewart (Edinburgh: T. & T. Clark, 1928), 17.
15. Ibid., 17.
16. *Institutes* 1.3.3.

some God, is naturally inborn in all, and is fixed deep within, as it were in the very marrow."[17]

Whereas Calvin regards Scripture as the *principium cognoscendi* of dogmatic work, insisting upon humility and obedience to "the things which we know have come from God,"[18] Schleiermacher takes a quite opposite view of the matter, protesting, as we have seen, that "the authority of Holy Scripture cannot be the foundation of faith in Christ."[19] Dissolving the necessary link between Holy Scripture and faith not only represents a profound break with Calvin, but it also leads to a number of entirely regrettable errors, not the least of which is Christian supersessionism (of which Schleiermacher appears to have been guilty). Schleiermacher's evaluation of Jewish Scripture leads him to accord value only to the prophetic books and the Psalms, leading him to declare that "the real meaning of the facts would be clearer if the Old Testament followed the New as an appendix."[20] As Christine Helmer argues, "Discontinuity is achieved by the historical appearance of Christ, which, for Schleiermacher, eliminates the need to base Christian faith and theology on the Old Testament (CF, § 27.3, 132.3)."[21]

One final observation about Schleiermacher's view of Scripture illustrates the considerable chasm separating Schleiermacher and Calvin. In the course of providing an exposition of the sacrifice, death, and resurrection of Christ, Calvin insists that when Jesus was on the cross crying out the words of Psalm 22:1, "My God, my God, why have you forsaken me?" his suffering and sacrificial death constitutes a genuine victory over sin and the devil. Calvin writes, "By his wrestling hand to hand with the devil's power, with the dread of death, with the pains of hell, he was victorious and triumphed over them, that in death we may not now fear those things which our Prince has swallowed. . . ."[22] By way of contrast, Schleiermacher denies the truth of the biblical witness by calling into question the Scriptural claim that Jesus' death is truly salvific. He regards the doctrine of Christ's vicarious satisfaction as nothing more than a "magical caricature" of the truly "redemptive" work of Christ. Not surprisingly, the term "redemptive" means something quite different for Schleiermacher than it did for Calvin. For Schleiermacher, the only way to make sense of the reconciling and redemptive work of Christ is to see all of it as an expression of Jesus' compassion for humanity. In the absence of a robust biblical account of atonement, the redemptive work of Christ is reduced to this: "The climax of His suffering, we hold then, was sympathy with misery."[23] Claiming that faith in the resurrection is a "doctrine of

17. Ibid.

18. John Calvin, *Sermons on the Epistle to the Ephesians*, revised version of translation by Arthur Golding (London, 1577; Edinburgh: Banner of Truth Trust, 1973), 233.

19. Schleiermacher, *The Christian Faith*, 591.

20. Ibid., 611.

21. Christine Helmer, "Schleiermacher's Exegetical Theology and the New Testament," in *The Cambridge Companion to Friedrich Schleiermacher*, ed. Jacqueline Mariña (New York: Cambridge University Press, 2005), 236.

22. *Institutes* 2.16.11.

23. Schleiermacher, *The Christian Faith*, 436–37.

[the] Scripture" and not "the doctrine of the Person of Christ," Schleiermacher claims that the only historically reliable accounts of Jesus as those events following his baptism up to his arrest. Commenting on the challenge of preaching and the problem of history, Dawn DeVries concedes that "on rare occasions when historical questions are raised [by Schleiermacher], it is to highlight their inconsequentiality for faith." The consequence of Schleiermacher's perspective is that "the Gospel stories are taken as examples, allegories, symbols, expressions of consciousness, poetic expressions of doctrine"[24] but not, we might add, true narratives of God's saving work in and through the history of Jesus. By contrast, for Calvin, incarnation, baptism, atonement, and resurrection were all of central importance, without which one could not hope for salvation.

In sum, our examination of Schleiermacher's work shows that he thoroughly departed from Calvin with respect to the fundamental and authoritative sources of knowledge of God. Instead of connecting revelation to Scripture in a manner that would attest to the authority of biblical revelation, "revelation" is itself transposed into the phenomenological realm of the experience of God-consciousness. As a result, his reconstruction of the doctrine of God (in which a discussion of the Trinity is no more than an appendix to *The Christian Faith*) and Christology (to name just two of a number of crucial dogmatic loci) no longer bears a family resemblance to the classical Reformed tradition represented in the theology of Calvin. Even if one grants that Calvin and Schleiermacher proclaimed the same God, they did so on entirely different claims regarding revelation and Scripture.

Herman Bavinck (1854–1921)

Published just over a century ago, Herman Bavinck's four-volume *Gereformeerde Dogmatiek* is the standard bearer of classic Dutch Reformed theology. In many ways, Bavinck's dogmatics constitutes a remarkable witness to the abiding significance of Calvin's theology. Like Calvin, he believes that all revelation, general and special, is fundamentally eschatological in orientation. For both figures, Christ constitutes the center and telos of revelation. In a passage as beautiful as it is concise, Bavinck writes, "The aim of revelation, after all, is to re-create humanity after the image of God, to establish the kingdom of God on earth, to redeem the world from the power of sin, and, in and through all of this, to glorify the name of the Lord in all his creatures."[25] The affinity between Bavinck's own account of revelation and Calvin's is clearly evident in his allusion to Calvin's depiction of the relationship between divine revelation and creation as the theater of God's glory.[26]

24. Dawn DeVries, *Jesus Christ in the Preaching of Calvin and Schleiermacher*, 1st ed. (Louisville, KY: Westminster John Knox, 1996), 89.
25. Herman Bavinck, *Reformed Dogmatics: Prolegomena*, vol. 1, ed. John Bolt and John Vriend (Grand Rapids: Baker Academic, 2003), 347.
26. *Institutes* 1.6.2.

Well aware of the tragic pedigree of nineteenth-century mediating and rationalist theologies (cf. Schleiermacher, among many others), Bavinck maintains that the term "revelation" is not an empty vessel waiting to be filled by us. Rather, "revelation" is the activity of a personal God who, in the course of enacting saving fellowship, draws close to us in Word and Spirit.[27] Refusing to look upon "nature" as a realm devoid of the knowledge and revelation of God, Bavinck makes genuine progress toward dismantling an ancient dualism between nature and supernature. While in many ways, this is a positive extension of the opening chapter of Paul's letter to the Romans, he substantially qualifies Calvin's treatment of the *sensus divinitatis* (1.3.1) alongside the external witness of creation. "Even the common folk and the most untutored," Calvin writes, "cannot be unaware of the excellence of divine art, for it reveals itself in this innumerable and yet distinct and well-ordered variety of the heavenly host."[28] Bavinck further claims that all revelation is supernatural for "the heavens are telling the glory of God; and the firmament proclaims his handiwork." Thereby establishing the basis for the caution that, "those who wish to banish the supernatural from religion, hence from their prayers, from their communion with God, are killing religion itself."[29]

The difference between Bavinck and Calvin follows from the recognition that Deist and rationalist confidence in the eighteenth century raised challenges that Calvin did not have to face. In opposition to this misplaced confidence in general revelation, Bavinck supports Calvin's appeal to the *sensus divinitatis* (1.3.1–3; 1.4.1; 2.2.18) while sharply distinguishing general revelation from natural theology. Two substantial points follow from this.

First, by resisting the notion that "nature" constitutes a discrete, autonomous field of human inquiry, Bavinck both affirms the value of natural knowledge of the world and forestalls regarding such knowledge as a starting point for the knowledge of God. Well within the classical Christian tradition, Bavinck writes,

> The carnal person does not understand God's speech in nature and history. He or she searches the entire universe without finding God. But Christians, equipped with the spectacles of Scripture, see God in everything and everything in God. For that reason we find in Scripture a kind of nature poetry and view of history such as is found nowhere else. With their Christian confession, accordingly, Christians find themselves at home also in the world. They are not strangers there and see the God who rules creation as none other than the one they address as Father in Christ.[30]

Second, revealing his debt to Calvin, Bavinck maintains that left to ourselves, we are unable to accurately see and comprehend God's work: "God's revelation in Scripture and in Christ provides the spectacles of faith that enable us

---

27. Bavinck, *Reformed Dogmatics*, 295.
28. *Institutes* 1.5.2.
29. Bavinck, *Reformed Dogmatics*, 308.
30. Ibid., 321.

to understand general revelation better, as well as a basis for encounters with non-Christians."[31] Reference to the "spectacles of faith" underscores Bavinck's allegiance to Calvin, insisting that general revelation is an insufficient basis for saving fellowship with God. Bavinck argues that general revelation furnishes no more than "knowledge of God's existence and some of his attributes such as goodness and justice, but it leaves us absolutely unfamiliar with the person of Christ, who alone is the way to the Father (Matt. 11:27; John 14:6; 17:3; Acts 4:12)."[32] Similarly, he insists that failing to grant access to knowledge of God's gracious reconciliation of humanity in Christ, general revelation does nothing more than to "instill fear but not trust and love."[33] Given the limits of general revelation, and Bavinck's reliance upon Calvin's doctrine of revelation, let us consider his treatment of Scripture as the place where God reveals the promise of redemption and human flourishing in Christ.

Bavinck accords pride of place to Scripture, insisting that "there is no knowledge of Christ apart from Scripture, no fellowship with him except by fellowship in the word of the apostles."[34] In like manner, he maintains that "Scripture everywhere asserts that God can and actually does reveal himself to human beings, not only by nature and history, by the heart and conscience, but also directly and in the way of extraordinary means," adding, "God reveals himself not only *in* human beings but also—by special words and deeds—*to* human beings."[35] The extraordinary affection that Bavinck has for biblical revelation issues is one of his most important contributions to the doctrine of Scripture: namely, his treatment of an "organic theory of inspiration"[36] under the aegis of his account of the "servant form" of the Word of God.

Refusing to countenance the view that revelation constitutes an order of reality beyond nature, Bavinck rejects a wide range of views commonly associated with a so-called mechanical view of inspiration. Far from emphasizing the supernatural at the expense of the historical existence of the prophets and apostles, he maintains that an organic view of inspiration casts light upon a rich understanding of the relationship between divine and human action.

According to Bavinck, a doctrine of revelation worthy of the name is one that correctly orders the relationship of God and human authors.[37] Not surprisingly, his own account of the "servant form" of the Word allows for such a coordination by offering an "organic account of inspiration." The term "organic" here effectively denotes the fully *human* character of Scripture without thereby denying its divine origin and purpose. By giving serious attention to the divine gift of freedom, Bavinck holds out a view of inspiration that resists the suggestion that God's action eclipses the humanity of the biblical authors. Instead, God's

31. Ibid., 302. Cf. Calvin, *Institutes* 1.6.1.
32. Ibid., 313.
33. Ibid.
34. Ibid., 472.
35. Ibid., 430.
36. Ibid., 435–48.
37. Ibid., 428.

relation to human authors is one that secures the full expression of their distinctive character, various prose styles, and intellect: "God never coerces anyone" Bavinck writes, adding that "He treats human beings, not as blocks of wood, but as intelligent and moral beings."[38] Evidently, an organic view of inspiration seeks to do justice to both the divine origin and human authorship of Scripture while at the same time deals honestly with critical challenges to the trustworthiness of Scripture.

It is certainly worth asking about the relative success of one of Bavinck's central decisions: namely, to secure confidence in the trustworthiness of the human authors on the basis of an analogy between Christ and the Bible. While certainly correct in affirming that God did not "spurn anything human to serve as an organ of the divine," the appeal to the incarnation of the Son of God does not fully account for the critical difference between the incarnation of the Word and the inspiration of human authors.[39]

Bavinck's commitment to Scripture as the "servant form" stems from the recognition that inspiration alone would not make a collection of writings the "word of God." Attention to the unity of the form and content of Scripture leads him to insist that Scripture is the word of God because "it has the Word-made-flesh as its matter and content."[40] Once this connection between the divine Word and written words is established, Bavinck extends the christological affirmation of the kenosis of the divine logos in Philippians 2:7 to the creaturely or organic form of Scripture, declaring that just as the Word became flesh—thereby becoming "a servant, without form or comeliness"—so too did the revelation of God enter "the world of creatureliness, the life and history of humanity, in all the human forms . . . right down into that which is humanly weak and despised and ignoble."[41]

The appeal to the incarnation in order to secure confidence in both the full humanity of the biblical authors and Scripture's divine authority is less than entirely successful for a number of reasons. If this analogy is to be finally helpful, it must be able to resolve the problem of how one might properly extend the unique hypostatic union of Christ's two natures to the inspiration of Scripture without raising undue conceptual, if not doctrinal, confusion. For God *as* human is the Subject of our redemption, to which no other reality may lay claim, including Holy Scripture.

Scripture is a thoroughly creaturely entity. While having its origin in the intention and work of the triune God, we should avoid thinking of the biblical text in terms commonly associated with the christological heresy of adoptionism. Just as sanctification is not strictly a divinely appointed means whereby we come to share in the divine nature, the conceptual integrity of biblical inspiration does not require that we posit a divine ontology to the written word. An

38. Ibid., 432.
39. Ibid., 434.
40. Ibid., 435.
41. Ibid., 434.

appeal to the analogy of the two natures of Christ confuses matters at precisely this point. Without acknowledging important differences between the incarnate Word and the dual authorship of Scripture, Bavinck imperfectly maintains that this analogy secures the belief that "Scripture is totally the product of the Spirit of God, who speaks through the prophets and apostles, and at the same time totally the product of the activity of the authors."[42] At its best, an organic theory of inspiration offers us a fitting affirmation of the way in which the Spirit of God sanctifies creaturely things, thereby making them holy and fitting for divine service. It is true that "the organic view of revelation and inspiration brings with it the notion that the ordinary human life and natural life, so far from being excluded, is also made serviceable to the thoughts of God."[43] But Bavinck could have said all of this without making such an unguarded appeal to the analogy of two-nature Christology.

More positively, Bavinck's own account of the inspiration of Scripture bears a striking family resemblance to Calvin's. In point of fact, his account of the servant form of the Word would be lost without his own substantial treatment of the Spirit's work. Anticipating a move made a century later by John Webster (in *Holy Scripture*), Bavinck captures the way in which the individual literary styles, handling of sources, memory, reflection, and experiences are all sanctified by the Spirit and made fitting for their divinely appointed tasks. The human, Bavinck writes, retains its own creaturely skill and experience, while becoming "an instrument of the divine" such that the "personality of the authors is not erased but maintained and sanctified."[44]

In sum, by offering an organic notion of inspiration Bavinck offers a cogent doctrine of revelation and Scripture that, in important ways, echoes Calvin's conviction that "the highest proof of Scripture derives in general from the fact that God in person speaks in it." However, a significant difference between Bavinck and Calvin is, as noted, the absence of an appeal by Calvin to the analogy of two-nature Christology. Rather than taking up the question of the ontology of Scripture, Calvin directs our attention to the work of the Spirit: "For as God alone is a fit witness of himself in his Word, so also the Word will not find acceptance in men's hearts before it is sealed by the inward testimony of the Spirit."[45]

Turning our attention to the theology of Karl Barth we find another modern theologian whose reception of Calvin's doctrines of revelation and Scripture occurred at a crucial point in his own theological development.

42. Ibid., 435. B. B. Warfield who in seeking to protect the claim that Scripture can be truly human, yet without error, exhibits greater care than does Bavinck saying, "the analogy holds good a certain distance. . . . But the analogy with Our Lord's Divine-human personality may easily be pressed beyond reason. . . . Between such diverse things there can exist only a remote analogy; and, in point of fact, the analogy in the present instance amounts to no more than that in both cases Divine and human factors are involved, though very differently." Benjamin Breckinridge Warfield, *The Inspiration and Authority of the Bible* (Philadelphia: Presbyterian and Reformed Pub. Co., 1948), 162.
43. Bavinck, *Reformed Dogmatics*, 435.
44. Ibid., 443.
45. *Institutes* 1.7.4.

Karl Barth (1886—1968)

Francis Watson begins his treatment of Barth's understanding of the Bible with the prudent judgment that "from beginning to end, Barth's *Church Dogmatics* is nothing other than a sustained meditation on the texts of Holy Scripture."[46] Drawing a similar conclusion, Richard Burnett states that "no theologian since John Calvin has been more committed to biblical exegesis," adding that "there are over fifteen thousand biblical references throughout the *Church Dogmatics* and more than two thousand examples of detailed exegesis of specific biblical passages."[47] However naive Barth's extended theological exegesis and confidence in Scripture may appear to some, the significant number and popularity of his courses in biblical exegesis at Göttingen and Münster display his keen interest in the vital reception of Scripture for the academy and the church. On the question of apparent naiveté, Watson writes:

> Of all modern theologians, Barth is the least inhibited by the fear of appearing to be naive, and it is precisely his willingness to speak naively about the Bible—with a directness and a clarity that are both the bestowal of the biblical subject-matter and the hard-won product of unceasing intellectual self-discipline—that gives life and warmth to his theological writing.[48]

One of Barth's oldest friends and colleagues, Eduard Thurneysen, offers a similar assessment of Barth's approach to Scripture and Christian theology in an essay titled "Karl Barths Theologie der Frühzeit," declaring, "Barth is no abstract thinker . . . and 'abstract' here would mean: liberated from Scripture. . . . he is and remains a student and teacher of Holy Scripture. Whoever would seek to understand him otherwise, will not understand him at all."[49]

The following argument shows that Barth's genuine affection for Scripture follows, in part, from his study of Calvin's theology and exegetical practice. With this in view, let us consider the broad outlines of Barth's reception of Calvin's doctrines of revelation and Scripture. Barth's 1922 lectures on Calvin show significant lines of agreement between these two figures. Five brief points of analysis may help us to better comprehend Barth's reception of Calvin's doctrine of Scripture. Following these analyses are brief comments on the relationship between Calvin's and Barth's respective doctrines of revelation.

First, Calvin's appeal to the "Scripture principle" captures Barth's attention. Barth sees Calvin's appeal to the authority of Scripture as a search for a "norm by which to regulate the relations, the question for a rule of faith and life, of knowledge

46. Francis Watson, "The Bible," in *The Cambridge Companion to Karl Barth*, ed. J. B. Webster (New York: Cambridge University Press, 2000), 57.

47. Richard E. Burnett, *Karl Barth's Theological Exegesis: The Hermeneutical Principles of the* Römerbrief *Period* (Grand Rapids: Eerdmans, 2004), 9.

48. Watson, "The Bible," in *The Cambridge Companion to Karl Barth*, 57–58.

49. Eduard Thurneysen, "Karl Barth's Theology Der Frühzeit," in *Antwort. Karl Barth Zum Siebzigsten Geburtstag Am 10. Mai 1956* (Zurich: Zollikon-Zürich, 1956), 832; translation from Karl Barth and Eduard Thurneysen, *Revolutionary Theology in the Making; Barth-Thurneysen Correspondence, 1914–1925* (Richmond: John Knox Press, 1964), 12.

and action."[50] Barth maintains that Calvin has indeed found a critical norm with which to judge the pretense of forms and orders that purported to be a "bringing down of the eternal to the temporal."[51] For Barth, the Scripture principle provided the Reformers with a critical norm by which to glorify God while undermining the putative authority of temporal powers that had falsely set themselves up as legitimate expressions of the fulfillment of the form and order of God's rule.

Barth is rightly impressed by the fact that immediately after arriving in Geneva, Calvin began to lecture on the Epistle to the Romans. Drawing out the significance of this practice while, at the same time, revealing his own affection for Paul's letter, Barth writes,

> Wherever, as with the Reformed, it is a matter of acting *with* God and *for* God, knowledge *of* God has to come first. And wherever it is a matter of knowledge of God, what else calls for consideration but the Bible, the Epistle to the Romans?[52]

Along similar lines, he commends the way in which Calvin holds together the ethical concern for glorifying God with the insistence upon allowing Scripture to constitute the proper norm or authority for knowledge of God. He writes,

> The ethical norm did not imply any abandonment of this gospel but was meant to lead back the more forcefully to it. Knowledge of God engenders a desire to act. A desire to act engenders a new seeking of God. The new question for God engenders new knowledge of God. That is the way that Reformed thinking goes.[53]

Second, in the course of evaluating Calvin's exegetical practice, Barth arrives at a deep appreciation for his extraordinary objectivity in reading Scripture.[54] Not to be confused with a modern, scientific understanding of the term, "objectivity" here pertains most of all to divine action and speech. Put differently, "objectivity" follows directly from the conviction expressed in book 1.7 of the *Institutes*, namely, that Scripture is self-authenticating in as much as God actively bears witness to himself in and through Scripture. Like Calvin, Barth is utterly convinced that no genuine hearing of God's Word can occur apart from biblical exegesis. Scripture, therefore, occupies a unique place in the relationship between God and his church. He speaks of this relationship in terms of a vital or living encounter between God and the hearers of Scripture: "The spring does not flow of itself. It has to be tapped. Its waters have to be drawn. The answer is not already there, we have to ask what it is" to which he adds, "The Bible calls for objective study."[55] Barth further describes Calvin's attention to the objectivity of Scripture in the following manner:

50. Karl Barth, *The Theology of John Calvin* (Grand Rapids: Eerdmans, 1995), 387.
51. Ibid.
52. Ibid., 388.
53. Ibid.
54. Ibid., 389.
55. Ibid., 388.

We can learn from Calvin what it means to stay close to the text, to focus with tense attention on what is actually there. . . . Calvin once wrote of Luther's exegesis that he was not too much concerned about the literal wording or the historical circumstances of the text but was content to derive fruitful doctrine from it (*Briefe*, 217). We see gentle criticism here. Calvin wanted to derive fruitful doctrine *from* the actual wording and historical circumstances, not by ignoring them. This is a feature of the way he goes about his task. Thus he engaged in textual criticism insofar as he was able with the tools available and without having the philological skills of an Erasmus. Nor did he shrink from higher criticism, seriously questioning the authenticity of 2 Peter and Jude, and definitely contesting Paul's authorship of Hebrews.[56]

Third, Barth discerns that the authority of Scripture, for Calvin, follows from divine action: "Hence the Scriptures obtain full authority among believers" Calvin writes, "only when men regard them as having sprung from heaven, as if there the living words of God were heard."[57] Barth follows Calvin very closely here by regarding Scripture as the *principium cognoscendi* (foundation or principle of knowledge) of revelation. Barth captures this in the disarmingly terse locution: "God's Word means that God speaks."[58] Dismissing any and all efforts to reduce revelation to an idea or thing, Barth insists that "God's Word is not just the formal possibility of divine speech," for "what God speaks is never known or true anywhere in abstraction from God Himself. It is known and true in and through the fact that He Himself says it, that He is present in person in and with what is said by Him."[59] Accordingly, he insists that Scripture is the textual locus of divine speech. Moreover, Barth shows his debt to Calvin by exhorting us to believe that the "Word of God" is preeminently spiritual, personal, and directed toward purposive ends.

Barth is entirely correct to draw the connection between (1) the claim that Scripture is *autopistos* (self-authenticating), requiring no supplement or creaturely support, and (2) the formative work of the Spirit. When we look only to our consciences, Calvin writes, we are "perpetually beset by the instability of doubt or vacillation." For this reason, we ought to "seek our conviction in a higher place than human reasons, judgments, or conjectures, that is, in the secret testimony of the Spirit."[60] Although this appeal to the "inner testimony of the Spirit" is often employed in the service of *epistemic* arguments, it is evident that Calvin is much more concerned with the theological question of divine reconciliation than he is preoccupied with trying to find a compelling response to the question of how we can be certain that this is of God. As is so often the case with Calvin, his attention is fastened upon the redemptive significance of all of Christian doctrine, including the doctrines of revelation and Scripture. In

56. Ibid., 389.
57. *Institutes* 1.7.1.
58. Karl Barth, *Church Dogmatics,* I/1, ed. Geoffrey William Bromiley and Thomas F. Torrance, (Edinburgh: T. & T. Clark, 2004), 136. (Hereafter cited as *CD.*)
59. *CD* I/1, 137.
60. *Institutes* 1.7.4.

the proposition that "the highest proof of Scripture derives in general from the fact that God in person speaks in it" we learn:

> The prophets and apostles do not boast either of their keenness or of any-thing that obtains credit for them as they speak; nor do they dwell upon rational proofs. Rather, they bring forward God's holy name, that by it the whole world may be brought into obedience to him.[61]

Here, attention to God's speech, despair of one's own intelligence, and the priority of God's name are all drawn together in the service of a single purpose: namely, that "the whole world may be brought into obedience in him." In much the same way, Barth counsels vigilance in calling upon the Holy Spirit. Arguing that "the Spirit which enlightens the community is not its own spirit but the Holy Spirit," he claims that any genuine hope that our ministry and witness may be truly of service to God and the world demands that we never cease to call upon God with the prayer, *Veni, Creator Spiritus*, come Holy Spirit![62] Calvin and Barth share a common conviction that God's self-revelation in Scripture has, as its proper goal, the calling and nurture of the Christian church in order that the gospel is proclaimed in the world.

Moving beyond Barth's 1922 lectures on Calvin we arrive at a fourth obser-vation. In the preface to the second edition of *The Epistle to the Romans*, Barth defends his own exegetical practice in the face of critics such as Adolf Jülicher and Hans Lietzmann. Accused of being an opponent of historical criticism Barth responds by insisting that "the critical historian needs to be more critical."[63] As if this provocation was not enough to unsettle Barth's opponents, he insists that critical interpretation requires that "the Word ought to be expressed in the words . . . till I have almost forgotten that I am not its author; till I know the author so well that I allow him to speak in my name and am even able to speak in his name myself."[64] Even if we were to regard these comments as an instance of rhetorical excess—depicting a goal that enables the reader to privilege the text rather than a historical reconstruction of the world in which a given author may or may not have lived—we might still ask what could possibly have led Barth to arrive at *this* understanding of the critical interpretation of Scripture?

Just prior to his remarks on the nature of "criticism" Barth clearly indicates that Calvin's exegesis stands as a model for the development of his own account of reading Scripture. Following Calvin's insistence that "God alone is a fit wit-ness of himself in his Word,"[65] Barth writes:

> By genuine understanding and interpretation I mean that creative energy . . . which underlies the systematic interpretation of Calvin. . . . For example, place the work of Jülicher side by side with Calvin: how energetically Calvin, having first established what stands in the text, sets

61. Ibid.
62. *CD* 3/2, 832.
63. Karl Barth, *The Epistle to the Romans* (New York: Oxford University Press, 1968), 8.
64. Ibid.
65. *Institutes* 1.7.4.

himself to re-think the whole material and to wrestle with it, till the walls which separate the sixteenth century from the first become transparent! Paul speaks, and the man of the sixteenth century hears. The conversation between the original record and the reader moves round the subject matter, until a distinction between yesterday and to-day becomes impossible. If a man persuades himself that Calvin's method can be dismissed with the old-fashioned motto, 'The Compulsion of Inspiration,' he betrays himself as one who has never worked upon the interpretation of Scripture.[66]

Calvin's tireless effort to understand "what stands in the text" led him to move round "the subject matter" until "a distinction between yesterday and to-day becomes impossible." What most impressed Barth about Calvin's approach to reading Scripture was his determined attention to the subject-matter (*Sache*) of the text. This was something that Barth would never forget. The distance between Barth and a great deal of modern biblical and theological scholarship follows from his enduring commitment to the real *Sache*, or true subject matter of the biblical text. For Calvin and Barth alike, the true subject matter of Scripture is the triune God.

If the task at hand was simply one of providing an account of Barth's reception of Calvin's doctrine of Scripture this would all be well and good, but what about the doctrine of revelation? Sadly, the question of Barth's account of revelation is often shrouded by the controversy surrounding his polemical attack on Emil Brunner in the 1934 essay, "Nein!"[67] If we were to step back a bit from the immediate question of Barth's uncompromising rejection of natural theology we might more clearly discern points at which Calvin and Barth share common cause.

First of all, Calvin's doctrine of natural revelation presents a number of challenges. For instance, while he maintains a high regard for the beauty and wonder of the created order—arguing that a general knowledge of God the Creator is available to everyone independent of Scripture—this knowledge only reveals that God is Creator.[68] For others, God reveals Godself to be the Redeemer, leaving us with the impression that two groups of individuals have a very different understanding of the triune God. In principle, this results in a twofold knowledge of God where for some God is known as Creator and for others God is known as both Creator and Redeemer. Along these lines, Calvin claims, following his interpretation of Hebrews 11:3, that we ought properly to regard the world as the "mirror of divinity" on the grounds that "there is sufficient clearness for man to gain a full knowledge of God, by looking at the world" and he insists that they "to whom he has given eyes, see sparks of his glory, as it were, glittering in every created thing"; the faithful gladly confess that the "world was no doubt made, that it might be the theatre of the divine glory."[69]

---

66. Barth, *The Epistle to the Romans*, 7.
67. Karl Barth, "Nein! Antwort an Emil Brunner," *Theologische Existenz heute!* 14 (München, 1934). ET: *Natural Theology* (London: Centenary Press, 1946).
68. *Institutes* 1.2.1.
69. John Calvin, *Calvin's New Testament Commentaries,* vol. 12, *Hebrews and 1 & 2 Peter*, ed. David W. Torrance and Thomas F. Torrance (Grand Rapids: Eerdmans, 1994), cf. Hebrews 11:3.

For Calvin, the *semen religionis*, or seed of religion, remains in human persons even after the fall. However, the noetic effects of the fall are so profound as to render problematic any general knowledge of God apart from the corrective lenses or spectacles of Scripture illumined by the Holy Spirit. As Calvin writes, "Yet that seed remains which can in no wise be uprooted: that there is some sort of divinity; but this seed is so corrupted that by itself it produces only the worst fruits."[70] If the fall of humanity is so profound as to render us nothing more than "a perpetual factory of idols,"[71] then it becomes rather difficult to champion the existence of natural revelation with any real enthusiasm. Returning to Barth's work we can find a number of concrete historical and dogmatic settings in which to observe the contrast between Calvin's view of revelation and his own.

In 1923, Barth entered into a public dispute with one of his former teachers, Adolf Harnack. In the course of this dispute, we find a statement that sheds considerable light on why Calvin and Barth took such different paths when it comes to the doctrine of revelation. In his response to Harnack, Barth insists that the Reformers did not actually need something akin to historical criticism because they "still had the courage not to avoid the offense of revelation."[72] We have seen how much Barth appreciated Calvin's theology and yet, the intellectual and cultural crisis of the Enlightenment has given Barth an abiding sense that methodological and moral challenges facing Christian theologians in the modern world were, in many ways, very different from those which beset Calvin. This allows for the claim that the difference between Barth and Calvin here is not principally a matter of their basic dogmatic convictions, but rather, an indication of quite different responses to the given intellectual contexts in which they lived.

So what did Barth mean by claiming that the Reformers "still had the courage not to avoid the offense of revelation"? Simply put, it is still possible to speak of the world as the "theatre of God's glory" when one possesses a living awareness that the true subject matter of the New Testament is Jesus—a living Subject who not only speaks but does so in such a fashion as to take hold of us. Under these circumstances one still has the courage to face the likelihood that at any moment a chasm might open up between creaturely judgments concerning God and the divine self-revelation in the Word made flesh.[73] Refusing to countenance the widely held view that modernity has established an inescapable set of criteria with which to judge all theological claims, Barth sought to retrieve a way of reading Scripture and doing theology that would effectively displace

---

70. *Institutes* 1.4.4.

71. Ibid., 1.11.8.

72. Karl Barth, "An Answer to Professor Von Harnack's Open Letter," in *The Beginnings of Dialectic Theology*, ed. James M. Robinson (Richmond: John Knox Press, 1968), 178. Harnack's objection to Barth's theology was sufficiently strong as to occasion the following response to Barth: "I sincerely regret that your answers to my questions only show the size of the chasm that separates us, but what is important is neither my theology nor yours, only that the gospel is taught aright. But if your method should gain the ascendency, it will not be taught any more at all, but exclusively handed over to revival preachers, who freely create their understanding of the Bible and set up their dominance." *Beginnings of Dialectic Theology*, 174.

73. *CD* II/2, 441; IV/1, 124.

the reigning tradition of historical criticism from the nineteenth century on. In doing so, he was able to recover an understanding of revelation and Scripture that betrays a strong family resemblance to Calvin.

When asked about Harnack and historical criticism in an interview in 1934, Barth offered the following illuminating response: "Modernism taught us to study the text of the Bible more closely. This close study is indispensable."[74] Had Barth stopped here, Harnack would have possessed a sense of accomplishment. However, Barth went on from this point to say, "I always tell my students to look through and beyond that method and listen in the Scriptures for the voice of God himself." Standing in substantial opposition to the critical historical enterprise of figures such as Harnack, it is instructive to see that Barth's exhortation to listen "in the Scriptures for the voice of God himself" is a matter of considerable urgency. Though separated by approximately four hundred years, it is evident that Calvin and Barth substantially agree with each other at this point.

Barth maintains that in the exercise of his prophetic office, Jesus Christ alone speaks words of life: "He alone according to John 10:3f is the Shepherd whose voice His sheep hear, who calls and leads them out by name, and whom they follow when they hear His voice," adding to this the words of Acts 4:12, "for there is no other name under heaven given among men, whereby we must be saved."[75] Attesting to the biblical witness of Christ being the light of the world (John 8:12), Barth develops an astoundingly, if unexpected, positive view of the revelation of Christ outside of the church.

Barth's affirmation of the existence of *extra muros ecclesiae*, (commonly spoken of as "secular parables" or "lesser lights") represents the fact that together, he and Calvin affirm, though on entirely different foundations, the existence of God's revelation in the natural world. In this secular sphere, Barth argues, we must not only be prepared to encounter such words, but we have a Christian obligation to listen to them with great care in order to properly discern the witness of Christ: a witness that, according to Barth, may occur even outside of the church:

> In the narrow corner in which we have our place and task we cannot but eavesdrop in the world at large. We have ears to hear the voice of the Good Shepherd even there too, distinguishing it from the voice of other clamant voices, and therefore, as we hear it, not moving out of the circle and ministry of His Word, but placing ourselves the more definitely and deeply within it.[76]

Provided we remember that Christ is the light of the world, we ought to regard these "secular parables" as true witnesses to the one Word of God, Jesus Christ. According to Barth, beyond the words of the Bible and the witness of the church, Jesus Christ raises up "extraordinary witnesses to speak true words of this very different order." In view of Barth's conviction that "theology will not

---

74. Donald Grey Barnhouse, "An Interview with Karl Barth," *Eternity* 35, April (1994): 20.
75. *CD* IV/3, 95.
76. *CD* IV/3, 117.

try to illuminate the heavens with a searchlight mounted on earth, but will try to see and understand earth in the light of heaven,"[77] we ought to recognize that true words even *extra muros ecclesiae* (spoken beyond the walls of the Church) do no more than reflect Christ's witness. As such, their truths may not be taken as having independent authority: "They are true words only as they refer back to their origin in the one Word, i.e., as the one true Word, Jesus Christ Himself, declares Himself in them."[78]

While there are a number of differences between Calvin and Barth, the preceding analysis shows the existence of substantial points of agreement. With this in place, let us turn our attention to a brief examination of the contemporary promise and challenges of retrieving Calvin's doctrines of revelation and Scripture.

II. CONTEMPORARY PROMISE AND CHALLENGES

A careful reader will no doubt have already drawn together a number of the disparate lines of this argument and have anticipated much of what is stated here in brief. Nonetheless, two important observations can be made regarding the promise of Calvin's work for the contemporary period.

First, there are few theologians in the history of the church who have succeeded as well as Calvin in drawing together the objective and subjective dimensions of faith. Calvin's determined efforts to elucidate the work of the Spirit in aiding our understanding of Scripture underscores not only the intimate relationship of Word and Spirit, but also points toward the disruptive and gracious reality of the God of the gospel. In and through the mighty works of God we come to see that God is, in Christ, *pro nobis* (for us). Accordingly, contemporary Christians would benefit from extended and careful reflection upon Calvin's elegant and spiritually moving depiction of the coextensive work of Word and Spirit:

> The Holy Spirit so inheres in His truth, which He expresses in Scripture, that only when its proper reverence and dignity are given to the Word does the Holy Spirit show forth His power. And what has lately been said—that the Word itself is not quite certain for us unless it be confirmed by the testimony of the Spirit—is not out of accord with these things. For by a kind of mutual bond the Lord has joined together the certainty of his Word and of his Spirit so that the perfect religion of the Word may abide in our minds when the Spirit, who causes us to contemplate God's face, shines; and that we in turn may embrace the Spirit with no fear of being deceived when we recognize him in his own image, namely, in the Word. So indeed it is. God did not bring forth his Word among men for the sake of a momentary display, intending at the coming of his Spirit to abolish it.

77. Karl Barth, "The First Commandment as an Axiom of Theology," in *The Way of Theology in Karl Barth: Essays and Comments,* ed. Martin Rumscheidt (Allison Park, PA: Pickwick Publications, 1986), 74.
78. *CD* IV/3,123.

Rather, he sent down the same Spirit by whose power he had dispensed the Word, to complete his work by the efficacious confirmation of the Word.[79]

Far from trusting in our exegetical mastery or philological skill, Calvin is rightly convinced that confidence in Scripture (which would, of course, require diligent study of its meaning and historical setting, etc.,) can only truly arise out of the work of the Spirit. Not only this, but the Spirit proceeds from the Father in order that God's Word "may abide in our minds" so that we in turn may embrace God. As stated earlier, Calvin insists that a "firm and certain knowledge of God's benevolence" is founded upon the promise of Christ revealed to us through the work of the Spirit.

Second, Calvin's attention to Holy Scripture as the definitive source for knowledge of God has broader implications for how one might order, or arrange, divine and human action. Earlier we noted that Calvin began the *Institutes* with the affirmation that "Nearly all the wisdom we possess, that is to say, true and sound wisdom, consists of two parts: the knowledge of God and of ourselves." Only Calvin does not simply stop there. He *orders* these two "sources" of knowledge, asserting that "without knowledge of God there is no knowledge of self." To this, he adds, "it is certain that man never achieves a clear knowledge of himself unless he has first looked upon God's face, and then descends from contemplating him to scrutinize himself."[80] Much of contemporary theology departs from Calvin at this point, seeing no encouragement for their own decidedly voluntarist account of human freedom. Breaking with his late-modern contemporaries, Christof Schwöbel rightly discerns the deeply faithful way in which the Reformers conceived of the relationship between God and humanity:

> According to the Reformers, God's action and human action have to be strictly distinguished in order to perceive their proper relationship. God's action in creation, revelation and inspiration establishes the relationship between the creator and his creatures, in which God is the creative ground for their existence and where he discloses the truth about his relationship to humanity and enables human beings to accept the truth of revelation as the certainty of faith.[81]

While contemporary theologians may well seek to hold onto the dogmatic claim that God mercifully grants saving fellowship to human creatures, a refusal to follow Calvin in maintaining the proper order between the *opus Dei* (the work of God) as the creative ground and the *opus hominum* (the work of human beings) would signal a marked departure from classical Christianity.

Perhaps not surprisingly, one of the distinctive features of the modern period is a transposition of revelation from a major key—enabling the church to sing the praises of God's glory in response to divine *self*-disclosure—to a minor key

79. *Institutes* 1.9.3.
80. Ibid., 1.1.2.
81. Christof Schwöbel, "The Creature of the Word: Recovering the Ecclesiology of the Reformers," in *On Being the Church: Essays on the Christian Community*, ed. Colin E. Gunton and Daniel W. Hardy (Edinburgh: T. & T. Clark, 1989), 119.

depicting pathos and loss. In this latter context, considerable pressure can be felt to dispense with the notion that "revelation" is first of all a subset of the personal address and action of a gracious God. In Calvin's day, to speak of "revelation" was to attend to the creative and redemptive work of the triune God. In effect, divine revelation not only had to do with the personal communication of the God of the gospel, but also entailed the view that God's speech authoritatively discloses particular events, revealing the fulcrum of history in the birth of young Jewish boy on the outskirts of the Roman Empire.

Calvin's insistence upon the priority of divine action allows for the corresponding creaturely attestation or witness to the presence and action of God. God's speech unveils (1 Sam. 9:15), proclaims (Exod. 25:22), and reports (Gen. 32:29; 41:25), setting forth God's overarching purposes for creation and history. However, when belief and knowledge are detached from one another, as surely happened under the crisis of the Enlightenment, authority previously granted to divine revelation is displaced by reason or experience. Listen to John Locke's classic formulation of the way in which reason functions in the Enlightenment period as a faculty of knowledge over and above God's gracious self-communication:

> Reason must be our last judge and guide in everything. I do not mean that we must consult reason, and examine whether a proposition revealed from God can be made out by natural principles, and if it cannot, that then we must reject it; but consult it we must, and by it examine whether it be a revelation from God or no; and if reason finds it to be revealed from God, reason then declares for it, as much as for any other truth, and makes it one of her dictates.[82]

Had Locke followed Calvin by appealing to the Holy Spirit as the cause of certainty, he might have been able to mitigate the otherwise rationalist tenor of his argument while drawing his account of revelation much closer to that of Reformed theology. This path, however, was not taken. Very few Enlightenment figures, it turns out, chose to follow Calvin and as a result, the essential connection between belief and knowledge was severed, leaving the nineteenth-century with the task of having to choose between the "religion of Christ" or the "Christian religion." A retrieval of Calvin's theology in general, and a positive grasp of his theology of revelation and Scripture, might well enable us to recover our bearings and thus possess genuine hope of finding our way through the thicket and brambles of late-modernity.

CONCLUSION

We began this chapter with the claim that simply identifying oneself with the Reformed tradition is no guarantee that one shares common cause with the theology of John Calvin. As our exposition of the reception of Calvin's doctrines of

---

82. John Locke, *An Essay Concerning Human Understanding*, ed. John W. Yolton (London: Everyman, 1993), 4.19.14.

revelation and Scripture in the theological work of Schleiermacher, Bavinck, and Barth has shown, while there are many ways to be "Reformed," not all of them stand in genuine continuity with Calvin. If the goal of Christian theology is to know God and to glorify God with our entire being, then we would do well to pay particularly acute attention to Calvin, for he has an almost singularly determined grasp on the Pauline conviction that we are not our own, for having been liberated out of the bondage of wickedness, we are to glorify God (1 Cor. 6:19).

Christian theology, for Calvin, was never a preoccupation with the task of constructing a formal system of doctrine. Rather, it is principally a matter of providing direction in the service of nurturing true affection for God. Brian Gerrish rightly argues that the root of piety for Calvin is faith: "But faith is more than intellectual belief or assent. It is a matter of the heart rather than the brain—a matter, that is, of the whole person."[83] It is wrong, however, to set mind and heart against each other in the fashion indicated by Gerrish, for Calvin himself refuses to do so:

> Therefore our mind must be otherwise illumined and our heart strengthened, that the Word of God may obtain full faith among us. Now we shall possess a right definition of faith if we call it a firm and certain knowledge of God's benevolence toward us, founded upon the truth of the freely given promise in Christ, both revealed to our minds and sealed upon our hearts through the Holy Spirit.[84]

In the midst of our blindness and ingratitude, a gracious and loving Lord grants us a "firm and certain knowledge of God's benevolence." As Calvin expresses it, Scripture is "the basis whereby faith is supported and sustained; if it turns away from the Word, it falls."[85]

The promise of Calvin's theology for future generations lies in his remarkable and compelling exposition of the Christian life. Christian faith, for Calvin, is an integrated whole, in which just as "knowledge of God engenders a desire to act," a desire to act "engenders a new seeking of God."[86] In a remarkable and enduring fashion, Calvin's theology informs a mature account of the Christian life called into being by the living voice of the Good Shepherd, born, sustained, and marked by the perfecting work of the Spirit, so that we might carry out a concrete life of heartfelt devotion and obedience to the triune God of the gospel.

83. Brian Gerrish, preface, in *John Calvin: Writings on Pastoral Piety*, ed. Elsie Anne McKee (New York: Paulist Press, 2001), xv.
84. *Institutes* 3.2.7.
85. Ibid., 3.2.6.
86. Barth, *The Theology of John Calvin*, 388.

SECTION 2
CALVIN'S THEOLOGY
OF UNION WITH CHRIST
AND ITS RECEPTION

Chapter 3

Union with Christ
and the Double Grace

Calvin's Theology and Its Early Reception

J. TODD BILLINGS

Union with Christ is a wide-ranging motif in John Calvin's thought. [1] As a theme particularly significant for his doctrine of salvation, Calvin speaks about the gifts of justification and sanctification as "the sum of the gospel," received in union with Christ by the Spirit.[2] This essay examines the development and key features of Calvin's theology of union with Christ and what he calls the "double grace" of justification and sanctification[3] and then continues with a sketch of the early history of reception of this theme. I give a brief account of how and why the language of union with Christ and the double grace appears in Calvin and trace some of the ways in which Calvin's teaching is received in the confessional period of early modern Christian history.

---

1. I am grateful to the *International Journal of Systematic Theology* for giving permission for certain parts of the following article to be reprinted in sections of this essay: J. Todd Billings, "John Calvin's Soteriology: Key Issues in Interpretation and Retrieval," *International Journal of Systematic Theology* 11:4 (October 2009): 428–47.
2. Calvin, *Institutes of the Christian Religion*, ed. John T. McNeill; trans. Ford Lewis Battles (Philadelphia: Westminster, 1960), 3.3.1.
3. See Ibid., 3.11.1.

CALVIN'S THEOLOGY OF UNION WITH CHRIST

Scope of Topic

The nature and scope of our topic need to be sharpened so as to avoid the projections of modern categories onto Calvin's thought.

There is a sense in which Calvin does not have a sharply defined "theology" of "union with Christ," in the same way that he has a "theology" of baptism, or even a "theology" of justification by faith. The phrase "union with Christ" is best seen as a shorthand for a broad range of themes and images that occur repeatedly through a wide range of doctrinal topics (*loci*). These images are often clustered together—like participation in Christ, ingrafting in Christ, union with Christ, adoption, and participation in God.

Moreover, this pattern of images does not present a Christ-and-the-individual mysticism. Instead, Calvin gives a distinctly communal accent to these images for salvation (incorporated into Christ means being incorporated into Christ's communal body), functioning within a Trinitarian framework with a strong emphasis on the Spirit's role in uniting believers to Christ. Calvin uses these images in relation to a very wide range of doctrinal loci, as I explore below.

In this way, Calvin does not treat union with Christ as a single, discrete locus that simply stands on its own. To speak about Calvin's theology of union with Christ is to speak about a cluster of related thoughts and images in his thought related to participation, union, engrafting, and adoption. To some extent, this cluster of images fills a different function in different doctrinal and polemical contexts. This essay is not a comprehensive overview of his union with Christ language, but it has a soteriological focus: the meaning of union with Christ as it relates to justification and sanctification, which Calvin calls the "double grace" that believers receive in union with Christ.

Union with Christ in Calvin's Context and in Calvin's Early Work

In Calvin's early writing, he makes significant use of union with Christ imagery in his account of justification. Calvin speaks of believers being adopted as children of the Father, engrafted into Christ, and experiencing such "participation in him [Christ] that, although we are still foolish in ourselves, he is our wisdom before God; while we are sinners, he is our righteousness; while we are unclean, he is our purity."[4] Adoption, engrafting, and participation in Christ are all images used in expositing justification—and the way in which believers are declared righteous before God is based upon the righteousness of Jesus Christ.

To set the proper context for understanding Calvin's doctrines of justification, we should examine the doctrine that Calvin inherits as a second generation member of the evangelical (Protestant) movement. Justification by grace

---

4. *Institutes of the Christian Religion*, from the 1536 edition, trans. Ford Lewis Battles (Grand Rapids: Eerdmans, 1986), 37.

through faith alone was a key exegetical and doctrinal insight of Martin Luther, developed by Philipp Melanchthon, and incorporated into the Reformed tradition by Calvin, Vermigli, Bucer, and others. Although the Reformation was in many ways a revival of Augustinianism on the point of justification, Scripture was seen as providing a corrective to Augustine and the quite diverse Augustinian tradition of scriptural interpretation. Luther shares with Augustine a strong theology of sin: sin holds the human will in bondage, unable to perform any meritorious work on its own. They also share a robust theology of grace, in which the Spirit effects the regeneration that God initiates rather than making the process dependent on a synergy of divine and human wills.

Yet Luther departed from the received interpretation of Augustine on the meaning and significance of the biblical term "justification." According to these interpretations of Augustine, "justification" refers to the process of internal renewal by the Spirit in the believer.[5] Augustine's view is not Pelagian, because the Spirit is the effectual cause of this renewal. Yet, in this schema, God declares believers righteous because they are being made righteous through the holiness imparted and infused by the Spirit. In contrast to this, Luther makes two moves—one with great clarity and the second with more subtlety. Both are apparent by 1520 in his work *The Freedom of the Christian*.[6] First, Luther argues that the righteousness that justifies believers is alien and external—contained in Jesus Christ himself—and thus received by faith as a fully sufficient gift. As such, "justification" refers not to the gradual process of transformation by the Spirit but to the change in God's decision or judgment toward believers—believers who have accessed the alien righteousness of Jesus Christ by faith. Luther's second departure from Augustine is that the process of growth and renewal in Christ becomes notionally distinct from that of "justification" such that "justification" is not an internal transformation of the believer but rather a change in status before God because of the alien righteousness of Christ. Therefore, believers are at once holy "saints" and "sinners," still in need of redemption. Melanchthon, who shared much with Luther's theology on this point,[7] was particularly clear in highlighting the notional distinction between justification and sanctification. Melanchthon strongly emphasized the distinction: justification

---

5. Calvin largely concedes that Augustine does not properly distinguish justification from regeneration. See *Institutes* 3.11.15.

6. For an exposition of Luther's doctrine of justification in 1520 with its notional distinction from sanctification, see Carl Trueman, "*Simul peccator et justus*: Martin Luther and Justification," in *Justification in Perspective*, ed. Bruce L. McCormack (Grand Rapids: Baker Academic, 2006), 75–92. Luther's notional distinction between justification and sanctification becomes particularly pronounced by the time of his 1535 commentary on Galatians.

7. The degree to which Melanchthon has continuity with Luther on justification is a point of significant scholarly dispute. For a brief statement of the case for strong continuity, see Trueman, "Martin Luther and Justification," 88–92; for an overview of key historiographic issues on this dispute, see J. Todd Billings, "The Contemporary Reception of Luther and Calvin's Doctrine of Union with Christ," in *Calvin and Luther: The Unfinished Conversation* (Göttingen: Vandenhoeck & Ruprecht), forthcoming.

justification is a legal declaration of righteousness, as in a courtroom, and sanctification or regeneration is the internal work of the Spirit in believers.

Maintaining clarity about this distinction was seen as crucial in an early Lutheran doctrine of justification by faith. This doctrine operated within a theology of union with Christ—but justification itself became the focus because the Augustinian approaches that Luther and Melanchthon opposed also worked within a theology of union with Christ, but with a different theology of justification. Thus, for a second-generation theologian like Calvin, the question is not whether to have a broadly Augustinian theology of "union with Christ" but what *kind* of theology of union with Christ. On this question as it pertains to justification, Calvin sides with the basic convictions of Luther and Melanchthon,[8] who approach justification as God's decision to justify a sinner on the basis of Christ's external righteousness, making the internal process of renewal notionally distinct from justification.

Inherent in this early Reformational (Lutheran and Reformed) account of justification was an opposition to Rome—but there were also attempts toward compromise. Calvin participated in the Regensburg Colloquy of 1541 with Melanchthon, Martin Bucer, and others, which explored mediating possibilities on justification with Rome. Calvin left the colloquy early, apparently with some skepticism about the possibility of compromise.[9]

Of course, agreement with Rome would have required compromise on two sides. In 1547, the Council of Trent spelled out the Roman Catholic position in a way that also rejected compromise on justification. Trent's pronouncement reaffirms the view, long connected with Augustine, that justification refers to the internal process of renewal by the Spirit, the ground upon which the outward status of being called "righteous" is based. Thus, believers are not justified by an alien (external) righteousness, but the process of regeneration. As a part of this, Trent denies that justification is simply the change in God's judgment toward the sinner involving the forgiveness of sins. Instead, justification "is not only a remission of sins but also the sanctification and renewal of the inner person through the voluntary reception of the grace and gifts by which an unrighteous person becomes a righteous person."[10] Indeed, Trent condemns those for whom justification is "either by the sole imputation of the righteousness of Christ or by the sole remission of sins, to the exclusion of grace and charity . . . or that the grace by which we are justified is only the goodwill of God."[11]

---

8. While this claim is developed in the portrait below of Calvin's view of justification, Calvin's overall affirmation of Lutheran soteriology is also indicated by his subscription to Melanchthon's revised version of the Augsburg Confession in 1540 without reservation, including its doctrine of justification therein.

9. Alexandre Ganoczy, "Calvin's Life," trans. David L. Foxgrover and James Schmitt, *Cambridge Companion to John Calvin* (Cambridge: Cambridge University Press, 2004), 15.

10. Council of Trent, Sixth Session, chapter 7, Translation from Alister McGrath, *Historical Theology* (Malden, MA: Blackwell, 1998), 192.

11. Ibid.

In light of Trent's prohibition, it is striking to consider Calvin's definition of justification in 1543 retained without revision through the final 1559 edition of the *Institutes*. "Therefore, we explain justification simply as the acceptance with which God receives us into his favor as righteous men. And we say that it consists in the remission of sins and the imputation of Christ's righteousness."[12] Calvin articulates, in quite precise terms, the definition of justification that would be prohibited by Trent—and he retains this definition after Trent. While in Calvin's "Antidote to Trent" he insists that justification is inseparable from sanctification,[13] he continues to insist upon describing justification as "the gratuitous acceptance of God" grounded wholly in the imputation of Christ's righteousness.[14] In terms of the doctrine of justification, it is clear that Calvin seeks to be "orthodox" by an early Reformational standard, affirming that justification involves God's free pardon of sin because of the external righteousness of Jesus Christ imputed onto the believer.

This conviction about justification endures throughout Calvin's work. Its importance does not fade (in the 1539 *Institutes* he writes that justification by faith is "the main hinge on which religion turns," keeping this through the final edition).[15] But as he enters into his "program" of writing commentaries and revising the *Institutes*—as well as various doctrinal disputes—this doctrine of justification becomes increasingly incorporated into a larger theological fabric in which the cluster of images related to union with Christ is key.

Expansion of Theme Through Calvin's "Program" of Biblical Exegesis

Calvin's exegesis of the book of Romans is key for the expansion and development of Calvin's theology of union with Christ and the double grace. Calvin was working on his Romans commentary at the same time as his 1539 *Institutes*, the edition of the *Institutes* that moves it from a catechism to a theological system. In the prefaces to these two works, he outlines his "program" that he would follow for the next two decades. The commentaries would strive for "lucid brevity" in unfolding "the mind of the writer" in Scripture.[16] The *Institutes* include a "sum of religion" to prepare readers to profit from Scripture, organized into a series of exegetically derived "commonplaces." The ordering of the loci in the *Institutes* appears to emerge largely from Calvin's reading of the book of

---

12. *Institutes* 3.11.2.

13. "It is not to be denied, however, that the two things, Justification and Sanctification, are constantly conjoined and cohere; but from this it is erroneously inferred that they are one and the same." "Antidote to Trent," ed. Henry Beveridge (Edinburgh: Calvin Translation Society, 1851) from *Tracts and Treatises in Defense of the Reformed Faith,* vol. 3, Thomas F. Torrance (Grand Rapids: Eerdmans, 1958), 115–16.

14. Ibid., 116.

15. *Institutes* 3.11.1.

16. *Calvin's New Testament Commentaries: Romans and Thessalonians,* trans. Ross MacKenzie (Grand Rapids: Eerdmans, 1960), 1. Hereafter cited CNTC.

Romans.[17] Indeed, Calvin is open about the exegetical centrality of Romans for his program. "If we have gained a true understanding of this Epistle, we have an open door to all the most profound treasures of scripture."[18]

In light of this, it is not surprising that in the 1539 and 1543 *Institutes*, the cluster of images related to union with Christ expands greatly—not only in his section on justification but also in sections on the sacraments, the *imago Dei*, the Trinity, Christ, and the Spirit. Because of the centrality of Romans, the images of union, participation, and engrafting are spread throughout the *Institutes*. Moreover, as Calvin continues his program in the writing of biblical commentaries in the 1540s and the 1550s, these images form a "cluster" that appear in numerous commentaries as complementary images, even where there is no warrant from the immediate biblical context for this clustering.[19] The book of Romans is used by Calvin as an exegetical key to the rest of Scripture as well as a doctrinal key for the *Institutes*.

In light of this, it is worth examining how, exactly, Calvin expounds justification, sanctification, and union with Christ in *Romans*. According to Calvin's analysis, the first five chapters of Romans focus on "the main subject of the whole Epistle," namely, "that we are justified by faith."[20] In Calvin's exposition of these chapters, there is particular emphasis on the inadequacy of human works to make us righteous before God—we are in need of "the righteousness of faith," which is, in fact, "the righteousness of Christ."[21] Yet, faith is not a work meriting God's pardon, but the instrument for receiving God's mercy offered to sinners in Jesus Christ. "When, therefore, we are justified, the efficient cause is the mercy of God, Christ is the substance (*materia*) of our justification, and the Word, with faith, the instrument. Faith is therefore said to justify, because it is the instrument by which we receive Christ, in whom righteousness is communicated to us."[22] Thus, faith is the mode to apprehend Christ, who alone possesses the righteousness by which sinners are justified. In these chapters, Calvin argues that it is imperative to understand that justification takes place by grace through faith, because "men's consciences will never be at peace until they rest on the mercy of God alone."[23]

It is in the exposition of chapters 6 and 8 that sanctification and talk of the double grace enters prominently into Calvin's commentary. In Calvin's reading of Romans, the earlier chapters on justification provide the indispensable context for these chapters.

17. See Richard Muller, *The Unaccommodated Calvin* (Oxford: Oxford University Press, 2000), 119–30.

18. CNTC: Romans, 5.

19. See J. Todd Billings, *Calvin, Participation, and the Gift: The Activity of Believers in Union with Christ* (Oxford: Oxford University Press, 2007), 93–94.

20. CNTC: Romans, 5.

21. Ibid., 73.

22. Ibid.

23. Ibid., 71.

In the image of being united with Christ in chapter 6 (glossed by Calvin as an "engrafting" into Christ),[24] we see how "no one can put on the righteousness of Christ" in justification "without regeneration, Paul uses this as the basis of exhortation to purity and holiness of life."[25] Thus, although believers are not declared righteous on the basis of their good works, the Spiritual renewal and works of regeneration always accompany God's free pardon in justification. "The truth is that believers are never reconciled to God without the gift of regeneration. Indeed, we are justified for this very purpose, that we may afterwards worship God in purity of life."[26] In the *Institutes*, passages from Romans 6 are later incorporated into a section that explains how the doctrine of justification does not dampen zeal for good works, but frees persons to actually serve God with their works rather than perform works as acts of merit.[27] This fits into Calvin's view of Christian obedience in which the conscience is allowed to rest from the "perpetual dread" of fulfilling God's law (because of justification), so that the Christian is empowered by the Spirit to obey God "cheerfully and in great eagerness"—performing good works in gratitude, not because it is required for justification.[28] While Calvin emphasizes that justification and sanctification are inseparable in his reflections on Romans 6, he also suggests a logical (but not temporal) ordering of being "justified" for the purpose that "afterwards" the life of holiness lived would not be focused on acquiring righteousness before God, but serving God in eager gratitude.[29]

In Romans 8, many of the earlier themes related to justification and sanctification continue, but several key features are added that characterize Calvin's theology of union with Christ. First, the Spirit is portrayed as the agent of union with Christ—apart from the Spirit's work in believers, Christ is like a "dead image or a corpse."[30] The Spirit dwells in believers and mediates Christ to believers. Second, union with Christ is set in the Trinitarian context of adoption. Calvin accents the Trinitarian dimensions of the Spirit enabling believers to call out to God as "Abba, Father" as adopted children of God (who are one with Christ). Third, this section includes emphatic statements about the inseparability of justification and sanctification. "We must always bear in mind the counsel of the apostle, that free remission of sins cannot be separated from the Spirit of regeneration. This would be, as it were, to rend Christ asunder."[31] "Let believers, therefore, learn to embrace Him [Christ], not only for justification, but also for sanctification, as He has been given to us for both of these purposes, that they may not rend Him asunder by their own mutilated

---

24. Ibid., 124.
25. Ibid., 8.
26. Ibid., 122.
27. *Institutes* 3.16.2.
28. Ibid., 3.19.4–5.
29. For more exploration of the question of the logical ordering of justification and sanctification in recent reception, see Horton, 88–92.
30. CNTC: Romans, 164.
31. Ibid.

faith."[32] In light of this final point, Calvin draws the following inferences in the 1539 edition of the *Institutes*:

> But, since the question concerns only righteousness and sanctification, let us dwell upon these. Although we may distinguish them, Christ contains both of them inseparably in himself. Do you wish, then, to attain righteousness in Christ? You must first possess Christ; but you cannot possess him without being made partaker in his sanctification, because he cannot be divided into pieces [1 Corinthians 1:13]. Since, therefore, it is solely by expending himself that the Lord gives us these benefits to enjoy, he bestows both of them at the same time, the one never without the other. Thus it is clear how true it is that we are justified not without works yet not through works, since in our sharing in Christ, which justifies us, sanctification is just as much included as righteousness.[33]

Thus, not unlike the two natures of Christ as defined by Chalcedon that are "without confusion" or mixture, and yet "without division" and "without separation," Calvin argues for the inseparability (yet distinction) of the double grace based on the oneness of Jesus Christ himself. Thus, also in 1539, Calvin writes,

> By partaking of him [Christ], we principally receive a double grace: namely, that being reconciled to God through Christ's blamelessness, we may have in heaven instead of a Judge a gracious Father; and secondly, that sanctified by Christ's spirit we may cultivate blamelessness and purity of life.[34]

In this short passage, we see how the inseparability of justification and sanctification is found in the person of Christ. By participation in Christ through faith, believers enter into a Trinitarian drama of encountering a gracious Father who pardons our sin because of Christ's blamelessness (justification) and a powerful Spirit who sanctifies believers for new life (sanctification). Both of these aspects are accessed through participation in Christ; but both aspects would be damaged if the two sides of the double grace were mixed or collapsed into one another.

Many of the continued extensions and expansions of this theme of union with Christ continue along the lines outlined above, particularly following the themes from the book of Romans. Some start to be developed with particular clarity in occasional works, such as Calvin's sacramental theology and his disputes with Lutherans such as Heshusius and Westphal. In other places, the cluster of images and themes related to union with Christ is extended to even more loci—including, by 1559, in his discussions of the incarnation, the atonement, and the resurrection, along with the earlier topics of justification, baptism, the Lord's Supper, the *imago Dei*, predestination, and the Christian life.[35]

32. Ibid., 167. The image of rending Christ asunder is also used in Calvin's commentary on Romans 6:1.
33. Cf. the editorial strata indicated in *Institutes* 3.16.1.
34. Cf. the editorial strata indicated in *Institutes* 3.11.1.
35. See Billings, *Calvin, Participation, and the Gift*, 101 and 108–16 on prayer and the Christian life. On predestination, see *Institutes* 3.24.1.

For the purposes of our focus on the double grace in union with Christ, there are three developments that are particularly significant: Calvin's use of the church fathers on union with Christ, the double grace in writings on the Christian life, and Calvin's polemic against Osiander in the 1559 *Institutes*.

Calvin's Use of the Church Fathers on Union with Christ

The topic of Calvin's use of the church fathers is a broad and complex one, and space does not allow a complete overview of Calvin's use of the patristic writings. Yet it is worth noting that Calvin does make use of patristic material on the theme of union with Christ and the double grace, incorporating patristic language (and at times patristic distinctions) into his account.

Like other sixteenth-century interpreters of the church fathers, Calvin does not approach them in a "disinterested" way. On the one hand, he is interested in finding commonality between his own theology and patristic writings as much as possible—thus vindicating his claim (contra Rome) that the Reformation is not a "new" movement, of "recent birth."[36] On the other hand, Calvin seeks to be clear about Scripture as the final authority, so he is quite willing to point out "errors" in the patristic writings when he judges them as inconsistent with Scripture.

On the topic of union with Christ, the key authors that Calvin engages are Irenaeus, Augustine, Cyril of Alexandria, and Bernard of Clairvaux. Drawing upon Irenaeus, in *Bondage and Liberation of the Will*, Calvin seeks to clarify that finding one's life in Christ rather than oneself is not an annihilation of the created human nature, but a restoration of it.[37] In a greater way than Irenaeus, Augustine is a major figure of engagement for Calvin. Calvin, like Luther, is deeply indebted to Augustine's overall theology of sin and grace. In addition, on the double grace Calvin draws upon particular passages about faith and Jesus Christ as the righteousness of believers.[38] Yet Calvin openly parts from Augustine on the issue of justification (in a similar way to Luther, above).[39] With Cyril of Alexandria's writings, Calvin makes selective use of his union with Christ theme on the Lord's Supper, repeatedly drawing upon Cyril's image of the body and blood of Christ as life-giving for the receiver.[40] Finally, Calvin makes a selective use of the work of Bernard of Clairvaux for Calvin's overall theme of union with Christ, in his critique of a Roman Catholic theology of merit, and for the justifying qualities of faith.[41] In all of these cases, Calvin draws upon

---

36. See the *Epistle Dedicatory to Francis, King of the French*, in *Institutes*, 1536 edition, 5–6.

37. See *The Bondage and Liberation of the Will: A Defence of the Orthodox Doctrine of Human Choice Against Pighius*, trans. Graham I. Davies, ed. A. N. S. Lane (Grand Rapids: Baker Books, 1996), 71–72.

38. For example, see *Institutes* 3.12.3, 3.12.8, and 3.14.4.

39. *Institutes* 3.11.15.

40. For an account of this, see Billings, *Calvin, Participation, and the Gift*, 49–50.

41. For example, see *Institutes* 3.12.3, 3.12.8, 3.13.4, 3.15.2. See Dennis Tamburello, *Union with Christ: John Calvin and the Mysticism of St. Bernard* (Louisville, KY: Westminster John Knox, 1994).

patristic writings with the learned sensitivity of a humanist scholar yet also for the doctrinal and polemical purposes that suit his needs. Yet the fact that Calvin incorporates their language into his positive position, and draws additional distinctions for his position while engaging their thought, indicates that his engagement with patristic writings did influence his thought.

The Double Grace and the Christian Life

Through the development of Calvin's "program," the soteriological movement within the double grace appears increasingly in Calvin's writings on the Christian life, prayer, and his theology of the "sacrifice of praise" in the Lord's Supper. For the most part, these sections do not seek to give precise doctrinal schemas as much as pastoral instruction. Nevertheless, it is important to see how Calvin is arguing for a consistent piety in these different areas, grounded in the double grace, accessed through union with Christ by the Spirit.

For example, consider Calvin's chapter on prayer, which undergoes significant expansion in the course of his theological program. His 1559 additions are particularly revealing. With reference to Romans 8, Calvin writes in the final edition that "to pray rightly is a rare gift"—properly done in and through the power of the Spirit, for "our natural powers would scarcely suffice." Yet, believers must also be watchful in prayer—expending great effort— for saying that the Spirit empowers prayer ought not to lead us to "vegetate in that carelessness to which we are all too prone."[42] Stated differently, prayer is a Spirit-enabled human activity—one in which the Spirit activates human beings to pray to God as Father by the Spirit's power. But the indispensable context for this action is that our confidence to approach God in prayer is provided by justification. While Calvin admonishes his readers to include a confession of sin in prayer, it must be done in the confidence that characterizes prayer overall—confidence derived "solely from God's mercy." "For if anyone should question his own conscience, he would be so far from daring intimately to lay aside his cares before God that, unless he relied upon mercy and pardon, he would tremble at every approach."[43] Why should we have this confidence? Because we pray as ones who belong to the Mediator, Jesus Christ, who offered a sufficient blood sacrifice on our behalf. For God was "appeased by Christ's intercession, so that he received the petitions of the godly."[44] In light of this, Calvin frequently warns against the sin of ingratitude in prayer,[45] and readers are admonished to offer prayers as a "sacrifice of praise and thanksgiving."[46] Prayer is an act of Spirit-empowered gratitude, an act in which the conscience is calmed, because prayer is an act aware of the

---

42. *Institutes* 3.20.5.
43. Ibid., 3.20.9.
44. Ibid., 3.20.18.
45. Ibid., 3.20.14, 19, 28, 41.
46. Ibid., 3.20.28.

fully sufficient Priestly sacrifice and intersession of Jesus Christ, a sacrifice for forgiveness received in justification.

A very similar logic is followed in Calvin's polemic against the Mass in *Institutes* 4:18 when Calvin sharply distinguishes between the once for all sacrifice of the cross, to "wash sins and cleanse them that the sinner . . . may return into favor with God," and the "sacrifice of praise" performed in grateful thanksgiving to God.[47] The sacrifice of praise, which includes the whole life of sanctification and "all the duties of love," has "nothing to do with appeasing God's wrath, with obtaining forgiveness of sins, or with meriting righteousness."[48] For Calvin, the Mass reprehensibly confuses the two forms of sacrifice, offering the Mass as a sacrifice acquiring merit. In doing so, the Mass mixes the two sides of the double grace—failing to see that our righteousness before God is found in Jesus Christ alone and his once for all sacrificial work and that the Christian life as a "sacrifice of praise" is a life of gratitude in response to Christ's sacrifice. These reflections flesh out the pastoral implications of the double grace for the Lord's Supper.

While many other passages could be cited reflecting the influence of the double grace of union with Christ on Calvin's view of the Christian life, it is worth noting that these sections seem to have a greater emphasis upon pastoral instruction than precise, doctrinal clarity. In the section on prayer above, it does not begin with a precise statement of the double grace, but interweaves themes amidst giving practical "rules for prayer" and an exposition of the Lord's Prayer. In a similar way, when Calvin includes material about the mortification and vivification of the believer in the final edition of the *Institutes* (as part of regeneration, 3:3–10), he includes it before his discrete chapter on justification. This ordering has puzzled some commentators, since as we see from the material surveyed above, the grace of regeneration takes on its character as Spirit-empowered gratitude in light of justification.[49]

Nevertheless, in this section, Calvin still defines justification very clearly as the "free imputation of righteousness" in contrast to regeneration.[50] Calvin gives sufficient clarity in these sections to counter a view of the Christian life based upon the calculus of works righteousness, but in this context he does not broach the more technical disputes about the nature of justification and sanctification. His focus is to give pastoral instruction about the Christian life, being clear that while faith alone justifies, faith necessarily leads to an active life of pursuing holiness by the Spirit's power.[51] The logic of this pastoral instruction fits with what he states in his chapter on justification: that sanctification is the "second of these gifts" of the double grace, for until one understands "the nature of his [God's]

---

47. Ibid., 4.18.13.

48. Ibid., 4.18.16.

49. For an account of recent debates about the logical priority of justification, see Horton on the modern reception history, especially 90–91.

50. *Institutes* 3.3.1.

51. This section's particular focus on pastoral instruction for the Christian life is indicated, as well, by chapter 3:6–10 being popularly published separately from the *Institutes* as *The Golden Book of the True Christian Life.*

judgment concerning you, you have neither a foundation on which to establish your salvation nor one on which to build piety toward God."[52]

Osiander Controversy

Calvin expands and develops his theology of the double grace as part of a polemic against Andreas Osiander in the 1559 edition of the *Institutes*. Osiander himself died in 1552, thus the timing may appear strange for a heated dispute. However, during the 1550s, Calvin was accused by his Lutheran opponents of being Osiandrian in theology, and thus his polemic against Osiander. Osiander was a Catholic priest who had converted to Lutheranism, and then was disowned by his fellow Lutherans for denying a forensic doctrine of justification by faith.[53] Osiander argued that the righteousness of Jesus Christ is infused in believers by faith such that they "participate in the divine nature" (2 Pet. 1:4) through union with Christ. As such, Jesus Christ is the righteousness of salvation, but his righteousness is *infused* and not forensically imputed. With the loss of forensic imputation, a key Reformational feature of the doctrine of justification by faith was lost, and there was no longer ground to clearly distinguish between justification and sanctification: they were both part of a process of the infusion of Christ's righteousness, received in union with Christ.

Calvin is determined to prove the "Osiandrian" accusation false—and reaffirm his Reformational Orthodoxy on the issue of justification by faith alone. Yet, there is no doubt that he has some commonalities with Osiander. Together with Osiander, Calvin uses emphatic language about the oneness of believers with Christ, and the indwelling of Christ by the Spirit. Indeed, for Calvin, the double grace is not a set of abstract benefits acquired in themselves. This double grace is acquired as part of an intimate union with Christ. "He [Osiander] says that we are one with Christ. We agree."[54] In fact, in his 1559 polemic against Osiander, Calvin goes on to write one of his most emphatic statements about affirming the reality of this union with Christ:

> Therefore, that joining together of Head and members, that indwelling of Christ in our hearts—in short, that mystical union—are accorded by us the highest degree of importance, so that Christ, having been made ours, makes us sharers with him in the gifts with which he has been endowed. We do not, therefore, contemplate him outside ourselves from afar in order that his righteousness may be imputed to us but because we put on Christ and are engrafted into his body—in short, because he deigns to make us one with him.[55]

attributes

Thus, for Calvin, affirming the imputation of Christ's righteousness (justification) should not just be seen as a dry, abstract legal decree. Justification

---

52. *Institutes* 3.11.1.
53. See David Steinmetz, *Reformers in the Wings* (Philadelphia: Fortress, 1971), 91.
54. *Institutes* 3.11.5.
55. Ibid., 3.11.10.

is irreducibly forensic, but it is accessed as part of the double grace of union with Christ—a "mystical union" of intimacy with the believer, Christ dwelling within the believer.

But for Calvin, an intimate union with Christ should not lead one to downplay the forensic character of justification as the imputation of Christ's righteousness. Indeed, Calvin claims that Osiander makes serious exegetical and doctrinal errors in his proposal that rejects the forensic character of justification. First, in Osiander's conception of union by the infusion of Christ's divine nature, "he [Osiander] does not observe the bond of this unity," namely, "to be united with Christ by the secret power of his Spirit."[56] For Calvin, union with Christ is always the work of the Holy Spirit. Second, Osiander's infusion of Christ's divine nature results in a "confusion of the two kinds of grace" in union with Christ, namely, justification and sanctification[57]—a distinction Calvin goes on to defend against Osiander on scriptural grounds.[58]

Third, and perhaps most decisively, Calvin complains that Osiander grounds the justifying work in Christ's divine nature, to the exclusion of his human nature. This moves deeply against the logic of Jesus Christ as the Mediator in his divine-human state.[59] But even more significant for Calvin is that this diminishes a crucial scriptural and doctrinal connection: the cross of Christ and the forgiveness of sins. Here, Calvin argues that "we are justified in Christ, in so far as he was made an atoning sacrifice for us."[60] Yet, this act of atonement is not performed simply in the divine nature. "For even though Christ if he had not been true God could not cleanse our souls by his blood, nor appease his Father by his sacrifice, nor absolve us from guilt . . . yet it is certain that he carried out all these acts according to the human nature."[61] This final point is significant for Calvin because it shows that he maintains a strong link between the cross of Christ and justification. By the instrument of faith, believers are justified in union with Christ. But they are not simply united to a "divine nature" that is righteous because it is divine or even united to a second Adam who lived a righteous life and hypothetically could have died a natural death. Rather, the righteousness of Jesus Christ is the righteousness of the cross—the mystery of the cross connected to the "wondrous exchange" language which is so closely related to imputation—in which the sin of sinners is imputed upon Christ, and the righteousness of Christ is imputed to sinners. As Calvin writes elsewhere, "that, receiving our poverty unto himself, he [Christ] has transferred his wealth to us; that, taking the weight of our iniquity upon himself (which oppressed us), he has clothed us with his righteousness."[62]

---

56. Ibid., 3.11.5.
57. Ibid., 3.11.6. In this section, Calvin gives a response to Osiander's reading of Romans 4:4–5 and 8:33 in support of his interpretation.
58. Ibid., 3.11.12.
59. Ibid., 3.11.8.
60. Ibid., 3.11.9.
61. Ibid.
62. Ibid., 4.17.2.

EARLY RECEPTION OF CALVIN'S THEOLOGY OF UNION
WITH CHRIST AND THE DOUBLE GRACE

The Reformed tradition is not a tradition inspired just by Calvin, or Calvin with other Reformers in Geneva. It pulls together strands from Geneva, Zurich (Zwingli, Bullinger), Strasbourg (Bucer), and, because of its rapid expansion, a widening list of international authors and national communions. Moreover, since Scripture is the final authority—rather than Calvin—for the Reformed tradition, there is no strict obligation to cite or argue for compatibility with Calvin in formulating a Reformed teaching. Nevertheless, Calvin's writings were widely translated and distributed in Reformed communities. And the influence of his writings was significantly wider than the number of times he was cited or quoted.

If one conceives of Calvin's "influence" in terms of the question of whether there is broad continuity between Calvin and those who claim a Reformed heritage in the following two centuries, one faces the "Calvin versus the Calvinist" historiographical issue. As this issue is thematized in the twentieth century, the following essay by Horton discusses it in relation to union with Christ in some depth. However, at this point it is worth noting that some see a radical discontinuity between Calvin and the "Calvinists" precisely on the topic of union with Christ. After discussing the late sixteenth- and seventeenth-century covenant theology, which was incorporated into the Westminster standards in 1646–47, Charles Partee writes, "to put the point briefly and sharply, Calvin is not a Calvinist because union with Christ is at the heart of his theology—and not theirs."[63]

Without doubt, in the generations after Calvin, Reformed theology undergoes a certain amount of development. In particular, already in the sixteenth century, we see the beginnings of a "federal" theology of the covenant: a theology in which Adam is the "federal" head of a covenant of works (or a covenant with creation), and Christ is the federal head of the covenant of grace. Along with this came a number of other developments, including further covenantal distinctions, distinctions and debates about the doctrine of election, and an increasing attempt to think in a Trinitarian way in covenantal categories.

While we examine the developments that relate to union with Christ and the double grace below, several issues should be kept in mind. First, although it is possible for a modern scholar to develop a doctrine of union with Christ from Calvin that *could be* incompatible with these later developments, it does not follow that these developments are necessarily incompatible with a theology of union with Christ that has very significant continuity with Calvin. In fact, the discussion below suggests that a serious attempt was made to incorporate a

---

63. Charles Partee, *The Theology of John Calvin* (Louisville, KY: Westminster John Knox, 2008), 27.

theology of union with Christ and the double grace that bears the marks of Calvin into early federal and later Puritan forms of covenantal theology.[64]

Moreover, for this theological topic in particular, historians need to carefully consider the variety of theological methods used by both Calvin and later Reformed thinkers on a topic such as union with Christ. Historical theologians arguing for discontinuity often compare the pastoral parts of Calvin's *Institutes* to scholastic or polemical sides of later Reformed Orthodoxy.[65]

Yet, on their own, these observations mean little unless they are willing to assess the pastoral dimensions of later teaching in Reformed Orthodoxy as well as the scholastic dimensions of Calvin's thought. As we will see below, pastoral teaching about union with Christ does not cease but thrives among the same authors who enter into polemics about justification and adopt an ad hoc use of Aristotle for theological purposes. But, in a similar manner, Calvin's work on union with Christ is not exhausted by pastoral works like the chapters of the *Institutes* gathered into the *Golden Book on the True Christian Life*. Rather, Calvin's work on union with Christ includes both highly technical and polemical material at some points (with a constructive use of Aristotle at points),[66] doctrinal instruction at others, and pastoral advice about the Christian life at other points. Calvin enters into different modes of discourse on union with Christ to accomplish different goals, much as later Reformed thinkers do as they face new circumstances that require different types of defenses, expositions, and pastoral instructions.

The survey below briefly examines two areas of reception and influence: first, union with Christ and the double grace in the Reformed confessions and, second, the assimilation of these themes in Calvin into the doctrinal and pastoral works of later Reformed theologians. I examine key examples below to illustrate particular instances of reception, assessing continuity and development from Calvin's theology of union with Christ and the double grace.

Confessions

Already in the sixteenth century, Reformed Christianity was an international movement, and a large number of confessional documents were being produced in the sixteenth and seventeenth centuries. This brief account will give a few examples of confessions where an influence of Calvin on this point is discernable, as well as a brief consideration of the Westminster Standards, given their considerable influence in the English-speaking world.

64. Stated differently, while Partee can argue that there are systematic theological reasons for Calvin's theology of union with Christ being incompatible with "the Calvinists," historically one still needs to consider the Calvinists on their own terms when they seek to incorporate this theme into their theology.

65. For example, see Joseph McLelland, "Sailing to Byzantium: Orthodox: Reformed Dialogue: A Personal Perspective," in *The New Man: An Orthodox and Reformed Dialogue*, ed. John Meyendorff and Joseph McLelland (New Brunswick, NJ: Agora Books, 1973), 16–17.

66. See Billings, *Calvin, Participation, and the Gift*, 46–49.

The Belgic Confession, written in the Netherlands in 1561 and receiving the endorsement of Calvin by letter, becomes the main general confession of faith for the Dutch Reformed tradition. Written by Guido de Bres with the French Confession of faith (which Calvin had a hand in writing) as a key source,[67] the confession shows the distinct marks of Calvin's thought in many ways. On the topics related to union with Christ and the double grace, the confession has three articles: the first (article 22) introducing the role of faith and union with Christ and then an article on justification (article 23) and sanctification following (article 24). Read as a unit, there is considerable continuity with the portrait of Calvin's account above. It is "the Holy Spirit" who "kindles in our hearts a true faith that embraces Jesus Christ, with all his merits, and makes him its own, and no longer looks for anything apart from him."[68] Christ is the object of faith, and through faith by the Spirit's power believers "embrace" Christ—his merits (righteousness) and his person. It is not faith that saves, but "faith is the instrument that keeps us in communion with him [Christ] and with all his benefits." In article 23, justification is "the forgiveness of sins because of Jesus Christ" based not on "ourselves or our own merits" but "on the sole obedience of Christ crucified, which is ours when we believe in him." This pardon results in "freeing the conscience from the fear, dread, and terror of God's approach." Article 24 continues with a discussion of sanctification and good works. Like Calvin, the Belgic Confession insists that sanctification is inseparable from justification, yet it must be distinguished. Faith produces not only justification but also the new life of the Spirit; indeed, "it is impossible for this holy faith to be unfruitful in a human being." Thus works proceed from "the good root of faith," even though they "do not count toward our justification — for by faith in Christ we are justified, even before we do good works."

In contrast to the Belgic confession, most Reformed confessions are not able to trace their theological origins directly to the influence of Calvin and Geneva. Yet there are many examples that display material continuity. The Heidelberg Catechism, for instance, displays a rich theology of union with Christ at many points, but the sources for the Heidelberg are quite varied and include Philippist Lutheran influences and strong influences from Zurich (with Bullinger), which have their own theologies of union with Christ. Therefore, the theology of union with Christ is not necessarily an indication of Calvin's influence.[69] Nevertheless, whether emerging from a reception of Calvin or a combination of influences, the Heidelberg Catechism does have striking statements about union

---

67. For more on Calvin and the French Confession, see Wulfert de Greef, *The Writings of John Calvin: An Introductory Guide,* trans. Lyle D. Bierma (Louisville, KY: Westminster John Knox 128–29.

68. Quotations from the Belgic Confession and the Heidelberg Catechism are taken from the Christian Reformed Church in North America's translation of 1988, available in *Ecumenical Creeds and Reformed Confessions* (Grand Rapids: Faith Alive, 1988).

69. As Lyle Bierma argues, the theological focus of the Heidelberg Catechism "is nearly always on common theological ground between the followers of Melanchthon, Calvin, and Bullinger." Bierma, *An Introduction to the Heidelberg Catechism* (Grand Rapids: Baker Academic, 2005), 102.

with Christ. Even the first question and answer can be read as an exposition of the double grace of union with Christ:

> Q. *What is your only comfort in life and in death?*
> A. That I am not my own, but belong—body and soul, in life and in death—to my faithful Savior Jesus Christ.
> He has fully paid for all my sins with his precious blood, and has set me free from the tyranny of the devil. He also watches over me in such a way that not a hair can fall from my head without the will of my Father in heaven: in fact, all things must work together for my salvation.
> Because I belong to him, Christ, by his Holy Spirit, assures me of eternal life and makes me wholeheartedly willing and ready from now on to live for him.

In the question and first sentence of the response, union with Christ language is emphatic: that I "belong—body and soul, in life and in death—to my faithful Savior Jesus Christ." The second sentence in the answer speaks of the reception of the forgiveness of sins through the payment and victory of the cross (justification), followed with a note of comfort related to God's providence. Then, the final line returns to union with Christ and describes the grace of sanctification by the Holy Spirit giving assurance and then empowering the believer to be "willing and ready from now on to live for him [Christ]." While the structure of the double grace of union with Christ is implicit rather than explicit, it does reflect a logic and ordering similar to what one sees in Calvin's theology of union with Christ in the Christian life described above.

Indeed, more so than many confessions (like the Belgic) with a primarily doctrinal interest, significant portions of the Heidelberg Catechism have parallels with Calvin's doctrine of the Christian life. Question 86 speaks about having been "delivered" from our state of sin and misery by God's grace alone through Christ and asks "why then must we still do good?" After crediting Christ's redeeming work, the catechism answers that "we do good because Christ by his Spirit is also renewing us to be like himself, so that in all our living we may show that we are thankful to God for all he has done for us, and so that he may be praised through us." Thus, sanctification is a Spirit-empowered act of thanksgiving and praise to God, in which the Spirit is renewing believers to be like Christ. The next question clarifies that sanctification is not an optional "extra" to salvation but a necessary part of it; the following questions and answers define this "genuine repentance" or "conversion" in terms of dying to the old self and coming to life in the new self. These and other sections of the catechism contain material parallels with Calvin's work on the Christian life discussed above, even as the Heidelberg Catechism has its own approach and modes of expression. Nevertheless, while the Heidelberg reflects broad continuity with Calvin, it is not necessarily reflecting the "influence" of Calvin. The Catechism's terms are sufficiently broad that they could reflect the influence of one or all of the chief theological sources in Melanchthon, Calvin, and Bullinger.

Finally, moving forward nearly a century from the Belgic and Heidelberg in the 1560s, the Westminster Standards present a major Reformed confession and catechism incorporating the federal theology of Reformed Orthodoxy.[70] What has happened to the theology of union with Christ and the double grace, as we have seen in earlier confessional documents?

On the one hand, in the Standards, and the Larger Catechism most explicitly, we find strong language about the believer's union with Christ, including the mystical union. After noting that we are made "partakers of the benefits of Christ" through the Holy Spirit (Q & A 58), the catechism addresses that notion of the union with Christ.

> Q. 66 What is that union which the elect have with Christ?
> A. The union which the elect have with Christ is the work of God's grace, whereby they are spiritually and mystically, yet really and inseparably, joined to Christ as their head and husband; which is done in their effectual calling.[71]

It is hard to see how this could reflect the "absence" of a theology of union with Christ, because union with Christ is a "real" and "inseparable" bond with Christ by the Spirit. The language is more technical, but certainly as emphatic on this point as Calvin's common ways of speaking about the union, as well as that which was seen in the Belgic and Heidelberg. Yet, without doubt, this material continuity is incorporated into a quite specific doctrinal context. At this point in the catechism it is particularly significant that it is "the elect" who have union with Christ. God's election was exposited earlier in the catechism and has just been exposited specifically with regard to the invisible church, whose members "enjoy union and communion with him [Christ] in grace and glory."[72]

On justification, there is strong continuity between all three Westminster Standards and Calvin's account. The Shorter Catechism defines justification as "an act of God's free grace, wherein He pardoneth all our sins, and accepteth us as righteous in His sight, only for the righteousness of Christ imputed to us, and received by faith alone."[73] The continuity in this brief definition with Calvin's definition discussed above in *Institutes* 3:11:1 is considerable, if not exact. The Standards also articulate that justification is inseparable from sanctification, but both are received by faith that "receives" and "rests on" Christ and his righteousness. "Faith, thus receiving and resting on Christ and His righteousness, is the alone instrument of justification: yet it is not alone in the person justified, but is ever accompanied with all other saving graces, and is no dead faith, but worketh by love."[74] The relation between the two is further clarified in Question & Answer 77 of the Larger Catechism: "Although sanctification be inseparably joined with justification, yet they differ, in that God in justification imputeth the righteousness of Christ; in

---

70. For a brief account of the historical background of the Westminster Standards, see 114.

71. Westminster Larger Catechism, in *Book of Confessions* (Louisville, KY: General Assembly, Presbyterian Church (U.S.A.), 2004), 203–4.

72. Ibid.

73. Westminster Shorter Catechism, Question and Answer 23, in Ibid., 178.

74. Ibid., 135.

sanctification His Spirit infuseth grace, and enableth to the exercise thereof."[75] Once again, the basic contrast shared with Calvin of imputation for justification and the infusion of the Spirit for sanctification is reflected here.

However, once again, the setting for many of these statements reflects a doctrinal context that has undergone development since Calvin. First, in addition to justification and sanctification, a third benefit of partaking of Christ is listed: adoption. In Calvin, this was not considered a third benefit, but it was a prominent biblical and theological image used to speak about the double grace of union with Christ. In addition, one continues to see a pronounced emphasis on election as the context for justification. In the article on justification, for example, the Westminster Confession says, "God did, from all eternity, decree to justify all the elect, and Christ did, in the fullness of time, die for their sins, and rise again for their justification: nevertheless, they are not justified, until the Holy Spirit doth, in due time, actually apply Christ unto them."[76] While Calvin had a robust theology of election, the confession shows a particular concern here for showing how eternal decrees are applied in time with justification and also reflects the doctrinal decision of the Synod of Dort (1618–19) in clearly articulating that God's decree of justification—applying Christ's atoning work—is effectual only for "the elect." Overall, what both of these differences indicate is an increasing concern with the *ordo salutis*: the order of salvation through which God's eternal decisions are accomplished. Although the Westminster Standards do not posit a temporal gap between the double grace, there is greater concern for an "ordering" grounded in God's election, moving to effectual calling, justification by faith, adoption, sanctification, repentance, and good works, followed by an exposition of the law. While such an ordering could be reconstructed in Calvin—particularly in the overall movement from justification to sanctification and the third use of the law—the systematization in the form of the Westminster Standards certainly differs from Calvin's approach as well. With significant material continuity on justification, sanctification, and the mystical union, these doctrines are fit within a larger framework—particularly the context of Christ's active obedience as fulfilling the covenant of works in justification.

Assimilation in Works on Doctrine and the Christian Life

In considering the development of Reformed teaching, it is helpful to see how the doctrine of union with Christ and the double grace is incorporated into early developments related to the theology of the Covenant and election as well as how the trajectory of using this motif is extended in discourse about the Christian life. Our account will use the work of Heidelberg theologian Caspar Olevian (1536–1587) and English theologian John Owen (1616–1683). Olevian is a significant mediating figure between the covenantal theology of the

75. Ibid., 205.
76. Ibid., 136.

Reformers and the federal theology of later Reformed Orthodoxy. As a third generation theologian of the Reformation, Olevian connects a strong doctrine of union with Christ and the double grace, or "the double benefit" of Christ, with the doctrine of predestination and an increasingly differentiated doctrine of the covenant. John Owen, in contrast, inherits and works within a quite developed tradition of federal theology (similar to that seen in the Westminster Standards). Within this framework, Owen gives a nuanced account of justification and sanctification in union with Christ. Both figures write about this topic not only for doctrinal or polemical purposes, but also with a rich pastoral vision for the Christian life. In this sense, they are continuing the precedent in Calvin's work of considering union with Christ to be a rich theme on doctrinal and pastoral levels, the clarity of which merits polemic defense, if necessary. Arguably, doctrinal developments such as the covenant of works actually enhance the pastoral and experiential sense of the doctrine rather than diminish it.

Caspar Olevian

Having studied with Calvin, Olevian lectured through Calvin's *Institutes* and published a *Epitome* of the *Institutes* in 1586.[77] But Olevian, developing the work of his colleague Ursinus, was also an important mediating figure in what would be used in developing federal theology with the federal headship of Adam, a covenant of works before the fall, a clear emphasis upon the divine efficacy in predestination, and the combination of conditional with unilateral emphases in the covenant of grace.[78] Amidst these developments, Olevian shows profound concern for the doctrine of the union with Christ and the double grace, which he calls the "double benefit" of justification and sanctification, constituting the "substance of the covenant."[79]

Olevian saw himself as continuing a Reformational tradition beginning with Luther and continuing with Calvin.[80] Thus, in approaching the double benefit of union with Christ, Olevian reflects the concern of both Reformers, seeking to safeguard the forensic character of justification and the sense of sanctification as a life of gratitude; yet he also wants to keep sanctification inseparable from justification. One way in which Olevian holds these concerns together is through setting union with Christ firmly within a covenantal context. On the one hand, the first use of the covenantal law shows that sinners cannot keep God's law; thus the external righteousness of Christ is necessary to be imputed to believers (in justification) for salvation. In this, Olevian works with a Gospel-law distinction similar

---

77. See R. Scott Clark, *Caspar Olevian and the Substance of the Covenant* (Grand Rapids: Reformed Heritage Books, 2008), 84.

78. It was Ursinus who "introduced into Reformed theology the idea of a covenant of nature initiated at creation—the forerunner of the covenant of works." Bierma, *German Calvinism in a Confessional Age* (Grand Rapids: Baker, 1997), 62. While Olevian further develops this notion from Ursinus, his view should not be identified with that of later federal theologians like Cocceius. See Bierma, *German Calvinism*, 117, 139–40.

79. Clark, *Caspar Olevian*, xviiii.

80. Ibid., 38.

to Luther's.[81] In addition, the covenantal context made it possible to incorporate the doctrine of election such that God chooses freely to declare the elect righteous by the righteousness of Christ not based on future works of any sort. On the other hand, like Calvin, having clearly grounded justification in this forensic declaration, Olevian insists that sanctification is inseparable from justification. [82] As part of this account, Olevian weaves in a doctrine of the mystical union of believers with Christ as the key way to hold together different dimensions of living in covenant with God. In union with Christ by the Spirit, the covenant promises are put into effect. Thus, the reception of the gifts of justification and sanctification are not conditional upon works but are nevertheless reflected through works, as a citizen of the covenantal kingdom serves Christ as the king.[83] In this way, there is also a mutual dimension to the covenant as well, requiring bilateral commitments, even though God alone is the source of salvation and the double benefit of the covenant. This mutual, covenantal dimension of serving Christ as the king is empowered by the Spirit and unfolds gradually in obedience in the life of the believer: "what Olevian has done is bring even the essence of the covenant into the realm of the personal experience of the believer."[84] In this context—rich with the language of the calming of the conscience and assurance of forgiveness through God's covenant promise—Olevian offers an emphatic and pastoral theology of sanctification that gives important roles for the means of grace and obedience empowered by the Spirit, which all takes place within the visible assembly of the church and is rooted in a mystical union with Christ.[85] His emphasis on Word and sacrament as the means of grace is enhanced by his covenantal emphasis, for Word and sacrament are the covenantal "means and instrument" through which "God works salvation," testifying to the "substance of the covenant of grace."[86] Olevian's developments in connecting union with Christ and the double grace more deeply with covenant and election keep a strong pastoral dimension to the doctrine and preserve the basic content of the double grace from Calvin, while setting it in a modified doctrinal context.

John Owen

Like Olevian, John Owen sees himself in the heritage not only of Calvin but of a range of early Reformed thinkers (as well as early church fathers). But unlike Olevian, Owen inherits and works within a well-developed federal theology of the covenant, in which Adam is the federal head of the covenant of works, and Christ is the head of the covenant of grace. Yet this framework does not mute a theology of union with Christ and the double grace that has substantial commonality with Calvin, and developments which, like Calvin, see the doctrine

81. Ibid., 149.
82. Ibid., 187.
83. As Bierma points out, Olevian makes a very strong connection between the covenant and the notion of the kingdom of God. See Bierma, *German Calvinism*, 70–71.
84. Ibid., 160.
85. Clark, *Caspar Olevian*, 188–89.
86. Olevian quoted and translated in ibid., 191.

of union with Christ and the double grace as a doctrine that needs doctrinal precision and defense as well as development for pastoral purposes in the church. On the polemical side, Owen faced challenges in his day to the forensic doctrine of justification. In particular, in his 1677 book on justification, Owen draws upon the Reformational notion that faith is an instrument for apprehending Christ: thus justification is not grounded on any human act, not even the act of faith. The language of instrumentality had become controversial among Protestants at the time.[87] Yet Owen asserts with the Reformational tradition that "we are justified by faith alone, but not by faith which is alone."[88] Faith leads to works of love. In *Of Communion with God the Father, Son, and Holy Ghost*, Owen shows how this fits together through three graces received in "communion with Christ:" first, the "acceptance with God" through justification, including the cleansing of sins and imputation of Christ's righteousness; second, the grace of "sanctification" by God makes the saints "acceptable" and "lovely" to God through giving the Holy Spirit to indwell and give new life to believers, giving them "light" in understanding, "obedience" in the will, "love" in the affections, and "faith" in all;[89] third, adoption functions as a summative category for speaking about the "privileges" that come for those in communion with Christ.[90] While Owen is careful to see the first two graces as distinguishable yet inseparable, the biblical image of adoption is one that shows how the legal and relational images of union with Christ hold together. Owen emphasizes the importance of the legal transition from "*the family of the world and Satan into the family of God*" but also the relational benefits that come from having the "*privileges and advantages*" of God's family.[91] The legal declaration that one belongs to God's family frees the saint to serve God in voluntary obedience: "the children of God do freely, willingly, genuinely—without fear, terror, bondage, and constraint, go forth unto all holy obedience in Christ."[92] While adding adoption as a third grace (like the Westminster Standards) differs from Calvin, his construal of adoption displays remarkable continuity with Calvin's own account emerging from his theology of union with Christ[93] and his emphasis on voluntary Christian freedom in the *Institutes* 3:19. For both figures, adoption is a favored category when giving pastoral instruction on the Christian life.

John Owen had a highly developed theology of the mystical union of believers with Christ.[94] Union with Christ, set in the context of the covenant of grace, is tied to the incarnation as well as the indwelling of the Spirit. As such, in speak-

87. See Kelly Kapic, *Communion with God: The Divine and the Human in the Theology of John Owen* (Grand Rapids: Baker Academic, 2007), 123.
88. John Owen, *The Works of John Owen*, ed. William H. Goold, 24 vols. (Edinburgh and London: Johnston & Hunter, 1850–55), 5:104.
89. Owen, *Works*, 2:172.
90. Ibid., 2:172–73.
91. Ibid., 2:207; italics in original.
92. Ibid., 2:213.
93. See Billings, *Calvin, Participation, and the Gift*, 108–16.
94. See Randall C. Gleason, *John Calvin and John Owen on Mortification* (New York: Peter Lang, 1995), 90–95.

ing about the benefits of salvation brought about by the Spirit, Owen says that "they are all communicated to us by virtue of our union with Christ. Hence is our adoption, our justification, our fruitfulness, our perseverance, our resurrection, our glory."[95] As part of this theology of union with Christ, Owen shares with other Puritans (and theologians of the Dutch "further Reformation") a keen interest in the "spiritual marriage" imagery of the church as the bride of Christ.[96] This allegorical rendering of the Song of Songs was particularly prominent in preaching and in devotional works focusing on the Lord's Supper where the imagery of union with Christ was very strong.[97] On this point, Owen and the Puritan tradition certainly go beyond Calvin in their interest in the spiritual marriage metaphor, but their act of doing so testifies to the vitality of the theology of union with Christ (and its popular transmission to preaching and devotional works) in this seventeenth-century context.

In sum, although I am not claiming through these selected cases that all of the later Reformed tradition follows the paths of Olevian and Owen, they do present illustrative examples of widespread trends in which the doctrine of union with Christ and the double grace both flourished and further developed in the late sixteenth and seventeenth centuries. In general, they retain Calvin's emphasis on justification as a forensic declaration of God, which is distinct yet inseparable from sanctification. Preserving this framework, the doctrine is eventually developed in the larger context of an increasingly differentiated doctrine of the covenant and a clarified doctrine of election. Eventually, it also sees the development of a rich "adoption" motif to speak about the double grace as well as a "spiritual marriage" motif, developed much more explicitly than in Calvin. Through all of these developments, the doctrine of union with Christ and the double grace continued to be a doctrine that required clarity from alternatives (and thus polemical defense, at times), but also spoke quite directly to the realm of Christian experience. Like Calvin's *Golden Book of the True Christian Life*, Olevian, Owen, and many others could articulate union with Christ and the double grace in a deeply pastoral and devotional way.

---

95. Owen, *Works*, 21:140.
96. See Kapic, *Communion with God*, 152–54; Arie de Reuver, *Sweet Communion: Trajectories of Spirituality from the Middle Ages through the Further Reformation*, trans. James A. De Jong (Grand Rapids: Baker Academic, 2007), esp. chapter 5.
97. See Leigh Eric Schmidt, *Holy Fairs*, 2nd ed. (Grand Rapids: Eerdmans, 2001), 158–68.

Chapter 4

Calvin's Theology of Union with Christ and the Double Grace

Modern Reception and Contemporary Possibilities

MICHAEL S. HORTON

Among the many retrievals of Calvin's teaching in recent years (especially in the quincentenary celebration of his birth) is his emphasis on the motif of union with Christ. Although his body of work cannot be called a "system" in the modern sense, especially if one assumes a "central dogma" from which all doctrines are deduced, it is undeniable that "mystical union" is an important motif that plays a formative role in his explication of the application of redemption as well as the nature of the church and the sacraments. In this brief compass, I restrict myself to recent reception history on Calvin's understanding of union and justification (nineteenth century to the present) and then offer some suggestions concerning the relevance of Calvin's view for contemporary faith and practice.

RECEPTION HISTORY: NINETEENTH CENTURY TO THE PRESENT

Nineteenth-century historical theology was especially drawn to the "Great Idea" approach: locating a central dogma from which everything else in the system could be deduced, explained, and contrasted with rival systems. Of course, Calvin defended an Augustinian doctrine of God's sovereignty and predestination when exegetical and polemical occasion required. However, this emphasis can hardly be considered a central dogma from which the whole system is deduced, especially when it is not even mentioned in his summary of the Christian faith (the Geneva Catechism). (Nor indeed does it assume this role in later confessions.) Nevertheless, God's sovereignty and predestination became a way of explaining or criticizing Calvin and Reformed theology, by friend and foe alike. By contrast, the entire Lutheran system allegedly is deduced from the doctrine of the justification of the ungodly.

Among others such as Max Goebel, Matthias Schneckenburger was particularly successful in defining Reformed Christianity as the champion of union with Christ over against Lutheran forensicism.[1] Alexander Schweitzer, practical theologian at the University of Zurich and pastor of the Grossmünster, pressed the central thesis argument as a way of contrasting Lutheran and Reformed systems. Even the more judicious Philip Schaff spoke of contrasting *personalities* between Lutherans and Reformed churches.[2]

There has been dissent from the central dogma thesis in general and, more specifically, the idea that predestination or God's sovereignty functions as this organizing center of Reformed theology in contrast to Lutheranism. One example is a terrific 1908 essay by B. B. Warfield.[3]

1. Schneckenburger, *Vergleichende Darstellung des lutherischen und reformirten Lehrbegriffs* (Stuttgart, 1855). Matthias Schneckenburger (1804–48), *Vergleichende Darstellung des lutherischen und reformirten Lehrbegriffs*, ed. Eduard Güder, 2 vols. (Stuttgart: J. B. Metzler, 1855).
2. Philip Schaff, *Creeds of Christendom, with a History and Critical Notes*, 3 vols., 6th ed., vol. 1, *The History of the Creeds* (New York: Harper & Brothers, 1877), § 39. In his *Theological Propaedeutic* (New York: C. Scribner's Sons, 1916), 120, he refers to Schneckenburger's above-cited work as "remarkably acute and discriminating."
3. This essay originally appeared as "Calvinism" in *The New Schaff-Herzog Encyclopedia of Religious Knowledge*, ed. Samuel Macauley Jackson, DD, LLD. (Funk and Wagnalls Company, New York, 1908), 359–364. I am quoting from the essay as it appears reprinted in volume 5 of *The Works of Benjamin B. Warfield* (Grand Rapids: Baker Book House, 1991), 353–66. "It is unfortunate that a great body of the scientific discussion" throughout the nineteenth century "has been carried on somewhat vigorously with a view to determining the fundamental principle of Calvinism, has sought particularly to bring out its contrast with some other theological tendency, commonly with the sister Protestant tendency of Lutheranism" (*The Works of Benjamin B. Warfield*, 355). Of course, there are differences—some even significant. "But it is misleading to find the formative principle of either type of Protestantism in its difference from the other; they have infinitely more in common than in distinction. And certainly nothing could be more misleading than to represent them (as is often done) as owing their differences to their more pure embodiment respectively of the principle of predestination and that of justification by faith." Warfield added, "The doctrine of predestination is not the formative principle of Calvinism, the root from which it springs. It is one of its logical consequences, one of the branches which it has inevitably thrown out." If one is looking for a "central truth," Warfield explains, it is for Reformed theology's "complete dependence upon the free mercy of a saving God," and it is in defending this truth that predestination has its proper place. Nor is belief in predestination a Reformed peculiarity but is simply "Augustinianism" (356). "Just as little can the doctrine of justification by faith be represented as specifically Lutheran," Warfield remarks. It is as dearly loved and clearly taught by the Reformed. While emphasizing the glory of God as the goal of salvation, "Calvinism asks with Lutheranism, indeed, that most poignant of all questions, What shall I do to be saved? and answers it as Lutheranism answers it" (ibid.). Others (e.g., B. G.

The pertinence of these decisions vis-à-vis the proximity of Lutheranism and Reformed theology is especially important with respect to the history of reception regarding Calvin and union. A typical trajectory among many Roman Catholic interpreters conceives of Calvin's theology as a series of contrasts, with a radical diastasis between God and humanity, transcendence and immanence, reality and signs.[4] Even as careful a Calvin scholar as Alexandre Ganoczy approaches Calvin with similar presuppositions.[5] More heavy-handed is the interpretation offered more recently by John Milbank and his colleagues in the working circle of Radical Orthodoxy.[6] Obviously, this interpretation gives little attention to Calvin's considerable emphasis on union with God in Christ. This thesis is pressed in spite of Calvin's explicit and sometimes stern criticisms of nominalism and an emphasis on divine-human communion (indeed participation) that appears already in the opening paragraph of the *Institutes*.[7]

At the opposite end of the spectrum are those who interpret Calvin's emphasis on union with Christ as somehow a substitute for, or at least a way of downplaying, the significance of forensic justification. Ironically, this position seems to share the assumption of Calvin's critics that an exclusively forensic doctrine of justification is inimical to a thoroughgoing concept of mystical union.

Armstrong, Basil Hall, J. B. Torrance, and R. T. Kendall) have sought to locate a sharp discontinuity between Calvin and Reformed Orthodoxy. However, this thesis has been challenged with considerable effect in recent scholarship (e.g., Richard Muller, Willem van Asselt, Irena Backus, Lyle Bierma, Paul Helm, Carl Trueman, and R. Scott Clark). See, for example, Richard Muller, *After Calvin* (New York: Oxford University Press, 2004).

4. Kilian McDonnell, *John Calvin, the Church, and the Eucharist* (Princeton, NJ: Princeton University Press, 1967), sees Calvin as a nominalist with a diastasis between God and humanity (25). A superb analysis of Calvin's Chalcedonian Christology, which makes such a diastasis impossible, may be found in E. David Willis, *Calvin's Catholic Christology: The Function of the So-Called Extra Calvinisticum in Calvin's Theology*, Studies in Medieval and Reformation Thought, ed. Heiko A. Oberman et al., vol. 2. (Leiden: E. J. Brill, 1966). In my view, the most sympathetic and sound interpretation of Calvin's theology of union and justification from a Roman Catholic interpreter is offered by Dennis E. Tamburello, *Union with Christ: John Calvin and the Mysticism of St. Bernard* (Louisville, KY: Westminster John Knox, 1994).

5. Alexandre Ganoczy, *The Young Calvin*, trans. David Foxgrover and Wade Provo (Louisville, KY: Westminster/John Knox, 1987), 185–87.

6. John Milbank, Catherine Pickstock, Graham Ward, *Radical Orthodoxy* (London and New York: Routledge, 1999); John Milbank, *Being Reconciled: Ontology and Pardon* (London and New York: Routledge, 2003); "Can a Gift Be Given? Prolegomena to a Future Trinitarian Metaphysic," *Modern Theology*, 11, no. 1 (1995), 119–61; "Alternative Protestantism" in *Creation, Covenant and Participation: Radical Orthodoxy and the Reformed Tradition*, ed. James K. A. Smith and James H. Olthuis (Grand Rapids: Baker Academic, 2005), 25–41.

7. The opening paragraph reads, "Nearly all the wisdom we possess, that is to say, true and sound wisdom, consists of two parts: the knowledge of God and of ourselves. But, while joined by many bonds, which one precedes and brings forth the other is not easy to discern. In the first place, no one can look upon himself without immediately turning his thoughts to the contemplation of God, in whom he 'lives and moves' (Acts 17:28). . . . indeed, our very being is nothing but subsistence in the one God . . . [Yet] we cannot seriously aspire to [God] before we begin to become displeased with ourselves." John Calvin, *Institutes of the Christian Religion*, ed. John T. McNeill, trans. Ford Lewis Battles, Library of Christian Classics (Philadelphia: Westminster Press, 1960), 1.1.1.

Forensic Justification *versus* Union

In 1910, Émile Doumergue, following Schneckenburger, defended this inter-pretation.[8] It should be noted that a similar trend in Luther studies contrasts Luther with Lutheran Orthodoxy, interpreting Luther as closer to East-ern Orthodox (indeed, "Osiandrian") conceptions of *theosis* than to forensic justification.[9]

In recent years, some evangelical scholars have suggested that union ren-ders imputation redundant.[10] Sometimes a contrast is drawn between a "cov-enantal framework" and a "bookkeeping framework" (as in Robert Gundry) or between a "covenantal" concept of justification and a "Lutheran" doctrine (as in Norman Shepherd).[11] If Christ's righteousness becomes ours by our incor-poration into him through baptism, then why do we even need the category of imputation?[12] These are not new theses drawn simply from fresh primary research, but belong to a history of reception, at least resembling the sweeping contrasts of nineteenth-century Lutheran and Reformed historiography if not directly dependent on them.[13] In these proposals, I suggest, we learn more about the scholar's theology than Calvin's.

Like the "Luther versus Lutheranism" thesis (which is broader than the Hel-sinki circle), the "Calvin versus Calvinism" thesis dominated much of Calvin

8. Émile Doumergue, *Jean Calvin, les hommes et les choses de son temps*, vol 4, *La pensée religieuse de Calvin* (Lausanne: Georges Bridel et Cie, 1910), 275.

9. Known as the New Finnish Interpretation of Luther, a group of Helsinki-based theologians (led by Tuomo Mannermaa) argues that Luther's doctrine of justification is basically the East's doctrine of *theosis*. This thesis was introduced to a wider American audience by Carl E. Braaten and Robert W. Jenson, *Union with Christ: The New Finnish Interpretation of Luther* (Grand Rapids: Eerdmans, 1998). For a response, see Carl R. Trueman: "Is the Finnish Line a New Beginning," *Westminster Theological Journal* 65 (2003), 231–44 and Robert W. Jenson, "Response to Seifrid, Trueman, and Metzger on Finnish Luther Research," ibid., 245–50. If we are to follow this inter-pretation, it was Andreas Osiander (sharply criticized by Flacius and Calvin) rather than Lutheran Orthodoxy that properly understood the genius of Luther's own mystical theology. For my own interaction and comparison of Calvin with this line of interpretation, see Michael S. Horton, *Cov-enant and Salvation: Union with Christ* (Louisville, KY: Westminster John Knox, 2007), 129–215.

10. Paul Louis Metzger, "Mystical Union with Christ: An Alternative to Blood Transfusions and Legal Fictions," in *Westminster Theological Journal* 65 (2003), 201–14; Mark Seifrid, "Paul, Luther, and Justification in Gal 2:15–21," *Westminster Theological Journal* 65 (2003), 215–30; Seifrid, *Christ, Our Righteousness: Paul's Theology of Justification* (Downers Grove, IL: InterVarsity, 2000), 175; Robert Gundry, "The Nonimputation of Christ's Righteousness," in *Justification: What's at Stake in the Current Debates*, ed. Mark Husbands and Daniel J. Treier (Downers Grove, IL: Inter-Varsity, 2004), 18–39; Don Garlington, "Imputation or Union with Christ? A Response to John Piper," *Reformation and Revival Journal* 12 (2003): 45–113.

11. This argument is made throughout Norman Shepherd's *The Call of Grace: How the Cov-enant Illuminates Salvation and Evangelism* (Phillipsburg, NJ: P&R, 2000).

12. See, for example, Michael F. Bird, "Incorporated Righteousness: A Response to Recent Evangelical Discussion Concerning the Imputation of Christ's Righteousness in Justification," *Jour-nal of the Evangelical Theological Society* 47 (2004): 253–75; Bird, *The Saving Righteousness of God: Studies on Paul, Justification and the New Perspective* (Eugene, OR: Wipf & Stock, 2007).

13. Schneckenburger, *Vergleichende Darstellung des lutherischen und reformirten Lehrsbegriffs*. Some of the Reformed debates are well documented by William Borden Evans, *Imputation and Impartation: The Problem of Union with Christ in Nineteenth-Century American Reformed Theology* (Ann Arbor, MI: U.M.I., 1996).

research especially through the remarkable energies of Thomas F. Torrance and James B. Torrance. Also seeking to harmonize Calvin with the East, these scholars contrasted Calvin with Reformed Orthodoxy in terms of a realistic-ontological-participationist scheme over against "the Latin heresy" of merely legal relations.[14] A similar position is argued more recently (and carefully) by Julie Canlis.[15]

More recently still, Charles Partee has argued the case for mystical union not only as Calvin's central dogma but as a way of rejecting the exclusively forensic character of justification.[16] Partee avers to belonging to no school of Calvin interpretation, but he is clearly in the "Calvin versus Calvinism" camp. The "two-covenant theology" of the Westminster Confession "has produced centuries of disastrous theological consequences."[17] "To put the point briefly and sharply, Calvin is not a Calvinist because union with Christ is at the heart of his theology—and not theirs."[18] Turning directly to the theme of union, Partee states up front that the goal for Calvin is "participation in [Christ], not divinization."[19] At the same time, Partee sees union with Christ as rendering forensic imputation redundant—or worse, a "legal fiction": "In imputation God declares a believer forgiven, but this is a judicial fiction since the person does not become essentially or substantially holy." He adds,

> Calvin continues to use the language of imputation, but the categories of both subjective impartation and objective imputation should be rejected in favor of Calvin's own emphasis on Christ for us (Book II) and Christ in us (Book III). By insisting that assurance of forgiveness is found in Christ alone, Calvin comes near to moving this discussion beyond the categories of imputation and impartation to union with Christ. Sinful natures and sinful actions are forgiven in the new life made possible by his resurrection victory.[20]

In Partee's view, therefore, Calvin sees union with Christ as a way of circumventing forensic justification (imputation).[21]

14. James B. Torrance, "The Vicarious Humanity and Priesthood of Christ in the Theology of John Calvin," in *Calvinus Ecclesiae Doctor*, ed. W. H. Neuser (Kampen: Uitgeversmaatschappij J. H. Kok B. V., 1978), 69–84; "The Concept of Federal Theology—Was Calvin a Federal Theologian" in *Calvinus Sacrae Scripturae Professor*, ed. W. H. Neuser (Grand Rapids: Eerdmans, 1994), 15–40.

15. Julie Canlis, "Calvin, Osiander, and Participation in God," *International Journal of Systematic Theology* 6, no 2 (April 2004): 172.

16. Charles Partee, "Calvin's Central Dogma Again," in *The Sixteenth Century Journal* 18.2 (Summer 1987), 191–99. Also in *The Theology of John Calvin* (Louisville, KY: Westminster John Knox, 2008). In the latter, he offers a qualification: "To be precise, 'union with Christ' is not presented as the central dogma based on the older philosophical view of 'essence,' but as a central doctrine around which other doctrines in fact cluster based on the newer (Wittgensteinian) conceptualization of 'family resemblances'" (xvi n. 8).

17. Partee, *The Theology of John Calvin*, 17.

18. Ibid., 27.

19. Ibid., 167.

20. Ibid., 181.

21. Partee follows Alister McGrath's debatable analysis of Calvin's alleged differences with Luther on justification (Partee, *Theology of John Calvin*, 224; see McGrath, *Iustitia Dei*, 3rd ed. [Cambridge: Cambridge University Press, 2005], 224–25).

Partee appeals to Barth's verdict that union with Christ is central in Calvin's theology.[22] He also follows Schneckenburger's suggestion that "for Lutheran theology, union with Christ is the result of the process of justification while for Reformed theology union with Christ is the condition for the process of justification."[23] Compounding the strangeness of Schneckenburger's reference to justification as a *process* for both traditions (without criticism), Partee affirms this contrast in spite of his own citations of Calvin that prove the contrary: "Justification is God's acceptance on the basis of remission of sins and the imputation of Christ's righteousness (III.11.2)" (224), a righteousness that "is communicated to us 'by imputation' (III.11.23)" (227), "by imputation" (Com. Rom. 3:31) (228); "'The gift of righteousness is not an endowment but an imputation' (Com. Rom. 5:17)" (228). Many interpreters (like Billings) argue that forensic imputation and union with Christ are strongly emphasized in Calvin with thorough consistency, but Partee judges that this leaves the issue "bridged by assertion rather than explanation."[24]

Union *with* Forensic Justification

Lying between the extreme positions I have summarized is a broad consensus that interprets Calvin as teaching a forensic doctrine of justification within the broader context of union with Christ. Conservative Reformed and Presbyterian theologians have typically followed this line, from the sixteenth century to the present day. They recognized the similarities between the neo-Hegelian "mediating school" and Andreas Osiander's attempt to substitute a Neoplatonist ontology of mystical union for forensic justification.[25] Like Osiander, these theologians transform the genuine humanity of Christ into a "spiritualized" and cosmic Christ who replaces the Holy Spirit. "The Christ within (as some of the Friends [Quakers] also teach), is, according to this system, all the Christ we have. Ebrard, therefore, in one view, identifies regeneration and justification": we are pronounced just on the basis of this new life infused.[26] All crucial distinctions between God and humanity, the Son and the Spirit, and justification and regeneration are dissolved.

Needed was a fresh era of historical research that would seek to interpret Calvin without such heavily freighted dogmatic agendas. Leading the way in the twentieth century in this regard was the work by W. Kolfhaus, *Christusgemeinschaft*

22. "The centrality of this doctrine [of union] is emphasized by Karl Barth. Union with Christ 'has a comprehensive and basic significance for Calvin. Indeed, we might almost call it his conception of the essence of Christianity'" (195, quoting Barth, *CD* IV/3, 2, 550–51).

23. Partee, *Theology of John Calvin*, quoting Tjarko Stadtlund, *Rechtfertigung und Heiligung bei Calvin* (Neukirchen-Vluyn: Neukirchener Verlag, 1972), 118.

24. Partee, *Theology of John Calvin*, 229.

25. See the superb summary in Charles Hodge, *Systematic Theology*, 3 vols. (New York: Charles Scribner's Sons, 1872), 3:21–25.

26. Hodge, *Systematic Theology*, 24. It is worth noting that this identification of justification and regeneration is also maintained by N. T. Wright in *What Saint Paul Really Said: Was Paul of Tarsus the Real Founder of Christianity?* (Grand Rapids: Eerdmans, 1997), 113–29.

bei Johannes Calvin (Neukirchen: Buchhandlung des Erziehungsvereins, 1939). The consistency of union and forensic justification was assumed also by Ronald S. Wallace and François Wendel.[27] Wilhelm Niesel also represents this interpretation, nicely distinguishing Calvin's view of mystical union from medieval theories.[28] Besides providing a definitive bibliography of Calvin research on this topic, Cornelis Venema analyzed Calvin's concept of the "twofold grace" in Calvin's theology in careful detail.[29]

Union with Christ has also gained increasing prominence in systematic theology, especially through the work of Westminster Seminary professors John Murray, Richard B. Gaffin Jr., and Peter Lillback—and, most recently, Mark A. Garcia.[30] In the 1970s, Westminster was embroiled in controversy over the views of systematician Norman Shepherd, whose criticism of the "Lutheran" color of traditional Reformed views in favor of a *unio* emphasis led to his departure from the school. However, Gaffin, Lillback, and Garcia affirm both the centrality of union with Christ and the irreducibly forensic character of justification as basic and explicit features of Calvin's soteriology. At the same time, unlike Murray, these interpreters emphasize the distinctiveness of Calvin's soteriology over against Luther's.[31] They also interpret Calvin's view of union as central, wary of any dependence of sanctification on justification.

Among this circle of scholars, Mark Garcia has offered the most comprehensive historical-theological account to date.[32] Methodologically, Garcia states that differences between Lutheran and Reformed accounts should be taken into

27. Ronald S. Wallace, *Calvin's Doctrine of the Christian Life* (Edinburgh: Oliver and Boyd, 1959), 17–27. François Wendel, *Calvin: The Origins and Development of His Religious Thought*, trans. Philip Mairet (New York: Harper & Row, 1963), 256–62.

28. Wilhelm Niesel, *Theology of Calvin*, trans. Harold Knight (Philadelphia: Westminster Press, 1956), 127–30. Elsewhere he wrote, "This *unio mystica* must be clearly distinguished from the mystical union with the Divine, described by the mystics. . . . The relationship here is not between created being and Divine being but between the sinner and the Redeemer. It is not a doctrine of being (ontology) but a doctrine of salvation (soteriology)." In *Reformed Symbolics*, trans. D. Lewis (Edinburgh/London: Oliver and Boyd, 1962), 184–85.

29. Cornelis Paul Venema, "The Twofold Nature of the Gospel in Calvin's Theology: The '*Duplex Gratia Dei*' and the Interpretation of Calvin's Theology" (PhD diss., Princeton Theological Seminary, 1985).

30. See Richard B. Gaffin Jr., *Resurrection and Redemption: A Study in Paul's Soteriology* (Phillipsburg, NJ: P&R, 1978), which highlighted the redemptive-historical significance of the resurrection as a forensic event. It is this event that is central in Paul's thinking, more than any particular element of the *ordo salutis* (including justification). For a more recent (and, in my view, more balanced) summary of his interpretations on Calvin and union, see Richard B. Gaffin Jr., "Justification and Union," in *A Theological Guide to Calvin's Institutes*, ed. David W. Hall and Peter Lillback (Phillipsburg, NJ: P&R, 2008), 248–69.

31. Peter Lillback, *The Binding of God: Calvin's Role in the Development of Covenant Theology* (Grand Rapids: Baker, 2001). See esp. 183–93 on contrast with Luther—which Garcia affirms (29–30).

32. Mark A. Garcia, *Life in Christ: Union with Christ and Twofold Grace in Calvin's Theology* (Milton Keynes/Colorado Springs: Paternoster, 2008). This impressive work is far from being obsessed with the Lutheran-Reformed contrast and union as eliminating any dependence of sanctification on justification. However, both feature prominently in his interpretations of Calvin.

greater account, though they should not be exaggerated.[33] Reflecting the growing acceptance of Muller's criticisms regarding the "central dogma thesis," Garcia nevertheless argues that union with Christ is "a singularly determinative idea
in Calvin's *soteriology.*"[34]

Garcia offers more nuance than some of his colleagues in comparing Luther
and Calvin: "At least this much is clear: Luther's revolutionary theology of justification by faith alone included, as an indispensable element, the recasting of
traditional teaching on union with Christ in terms of its indissoluble connection
to justification."[35] Nevertheless, the emphasis is clearly on discontinuity.

Similar to Kolfhaus's treatment, a volume by Roman Catholic scholar Dennis Tamburello sees union and forensic justification as compatible elements in
Calvin's theology.[36] In addition, Calvin's concept of union is treated in relation
to Bernard of Clairvaux, on whom Calvin drew explicitly and repeatedly. One
benefit of such contextualization is that it challenges our tendency to treat our
favored teachers—in this case, Calvin—as geniuses who rose Phoenix-like from
the ashes of their environment. Furthermore, given the influence of Bernard on
Luther, it challenges exaggerated assumptions about the distance between the
reformers on this point.

Recently, J. Todd Billings has written an outstanding monograph notable for
its balance, brevity, and careful avoidance of heavily freighted agendas imposed
on Calvin.[37] At the same time, he takes seriously the criticism of recent scholars
who assume that Calvin's emphasis on the sovereignty of God and his gift of
grace in Christ (especially extrinsic imputation) eliminates genuine reciprocity.[38] Billings observes,

> Contemporary critics of Calvin usually have a hidden ledger in mind: 'par-
> ticipation' is rightly articulated by Thomas; or 'deification' is definitively
> stated in late Byzantine theologies; or 'reciprocity' is properly understood
> by Marcel Mauss or by other Gift theorists. In general, there is imposition
> of external criteria upon Calvin's theology, and Calvin is found to fall short
> of the standard at hand.[39]

As with any other figure, it is appropriate to interpret Calvin first of all on his
own terms and only then to compare and contrast him with one's own favored
dogmas.

33. Ibid., 7.
34. Ibid., 18.
35. Ibid., 68.
36. Tamburello, *Union with Christ.* Tamburello follows Kolfhaus in suggesting that "'engrafting
into Christ' provides the 'inner indissoluble cohesion' of Calvin's conception of the salvific work of
God" (84–85).
37. J. Todd Billings, *Calvin, Participation, and the Gift: The Activity of Believers in Union with
Christ* (Oxford/New York: Oxford University Press, 2007).
38. Ibid., 11.
39. Ibid., 14–15.

Calvin's approach to participation is distinct; it cannot be subsumed under any general ontology:

> He sees participation in Christ as constituted by the *duplex gratia*, the graces of justification and sanctification, which are inseparable but distinguishable. Against Catholic and Orthodox theologies of impartation, Calvin believes that justification is accomplished by God's free pardon in imputation. While there is a sense in which imputation is a forensic act—as in Melanchthon—Calvin's account of imputation is inextricably tied to union with Christ: believers come to 'possess' Christ and his righteousness.[40]

There is no central dogma in Calvin's theology, Billings observes, although union with Christ is clearly important.[41] Billings takes a *via media* between what he calls the "Anti-Legal School" (Julie Canlis, James Torrance) on one hand, and, on the other hand, those who downplay union in favor of justification by itself (Edward A. Dowey, A. N. S. Lane, T. H. L. Parker).[42]

Drawing on the careful scholarship of Heiko Oberman, Richard Muller, and others, Billings decisively refutes both the historical claim that Calvin was trained in nominalism by John Major and the caricature of Calvin's allegedly nominalist theology of union in salvation and the sacraments. Billings demonstrates that Calvin had no theological affinity with a nominalist rejection of analogical participation in God.[43]

With ample citations, Billings concludes that for Calvin sanctification is given with justification in this union. "Yet the first grace of free pardon provides the indispensable context for the second."[44] With Luther, Calvin affirms the "marvelous exchange" (*mirifica commutation*, 4.17.2), in which the forensic provides the ground for the transformative, and this carries over into his eucharistic views. There is indeed a sacrifice of thanksgiving in the Eucharist, but on the basis of the completed sacrifice of atonement offered by Christ. "In an exact parallel to the relationship of the *duplex gratia*, the second sacrifice 'depends' upon the first."[45] As Calvin says, the second sacrifice "has nothing to do with appeasing God's wrath, with obtaining forgiveness of sins, or with meriting righteousness; but is concerned solely with magnifying and exalting God."[46]

A final interpreter to be mentioned is Bruce McCormack, who affirms union with Christ but challenges the assumptions of a participationist ontology. He eschews the "central dogma" thesis as well as any contrast between Lutheran and Reformed doctrines of justification.[47] "Lutheran and Reformed theologians

---

40. Ibid., 15.
41. Ibid., 19.
42. Ibid., 23.
43. Ibid., 28–62.
44. Ibid., 107.
45. Ibid., 132.
46. *Institutes* 4.18.16.
47. Bruce McCormack, "What's at Stake in Current Debates over Justification?" in *Justification: What's at Stake in the Current Debates,* ed. Mark Husbands and Daniel J. Treier (Downers Grove, IL: InterVarsity, 2004), 81.

disagreed on a number of things, but the one thing on which there was no disagreement was the central importance of justification by grace through faith. . . . At the heart of the Reformation understanding of justification lay the notion of a positive imputation of Christ's righteousness."[48]

McCormack refers to T. F. Torrance's insistence that Calvin's realistic language of union in treating the Supper (book 4) should be read prior to reading his heavily forensic interpretation of Christ's atoning work (book 2) and justification (book 3). Understandably, McCormack finds this not only heavy-handed but hermeneutically odd. Nevertheless, part of the blame for antiforensic readings like Torrance's must be laid at the feet of the reformers themselves, McCormack argues.[49] Because they did not challenge the underlying ontology, the reformers "continued to subscribe to ontological assumptions which could, logically, only fund a Catholic ordering of regeneration and justification (to the detriment of their own definition of justification)."[50] For Aquinas, God's work *within* us is the source of justification.[51] Regeneration is the basis for the nonimputation of sin.[52] However, Luther still saw faith as logically prior to imputation, which "would seem clearly to require a certain logical priority of regeneration (a work of God 'in us') over justification." Thus, the break with medieval ontology was incomplete.[53]

Calvin was clear—even clearer than Luther—that justification is nothing other than "the remission of sins and the imputation of Christ's righteousness." He rejects Osiander's subversion of imputation in favor of an infusion of Christ's divine essence. For Osiander, God "justifies not only by pardon but by regenerating." There is no justification without renewal, but "to be justified means something different from being made new creatures."[54] "In making this distinction between 'essential righteousness' and 'acquired righteousness,'" writes McCormack, "Calvin made a significant contribution not only to the Reformed understanding of justification but also to Protestantism in general."[55]

From a traditional Reformed perspective, McCormack's controversial move, however, is to suggest that for Calvin justification is even logically prior to regeneration.[56] Nevertheless, McCormack argues, Calvin was not consistent on this point. "At several points in the *Institutes*, Calvin appears to make 'union with Christ' to be logically, if not chronologically, prior to both justification and

48. McCormack, "What's at Stake?" 82–83.
49. Ibid., 84
50. Ibid.
51. Ibid., 90.
52. Ibid., 92.
53. Ibid., 94.
54. *Institutes* 3.2.2, 5, 6.
55. McCormack, "What's at Stake?" 100.
56. Ibid. "In saying, 'Whomever, therefore, God receives into grace, on them he at the same time bestows the spirit of adoption [Rom 8:15], by whose power he remakes them to his own image,' Calvin makes justification to be logically prior to—and the foundation of—that bestowal of the Spirit of adoption by means of which the believer is regenerated. On this view, regeneration would have to be seen as the logical consequence of the divine verdict registered in justification."

regeneration."[57] Some of McCormack's objections to Calvin's way of stating the nature of this union (especially when Cyril's accent is discernable) raise the question as to whether McCormack himself regards union as a metaphor more than an actual state of affairs.[58] He argues that the problem is that this "union" is indistinguishable from regeneration. "Only the strict emphasis upon imputation is capable of closing the door with finality upon the Medieval Catholic view."[59] McCormack believes that the real confusion comes with Calvin's "more nearly patristic understanding" of the Supper, which contradicts "the forensicism of his doctrine of atonement and justification. . . ."[60] At this point, Calvin was simply naive about the ontological presuppositions of Cyril of Alexandria.[61]

Today, McCormack laments, it is Protestants from whom we hear that a forensic doctrine of justification is a "legal fiction." Calvin's answer—namely, to see justification and sanctification as gifts simultaneously given—no longer impresses. "Today's Protestants give every indication of wanting to understand justification as being itself transformative."[62] Instead of trying to fit justification into a Platonic ontology of participation in pure being, McCormack encourages us to recognize the distinctively forensic ontology that justification itself generates.[63] Human judges hope to describe a state of affairs accurately; their judgment is not effective.

> God's verdict differs in that it creates the reality it declares. God's declaration, in other words, is itself constitutive of that which is declared. God's word is always effective. . . . So a judicial act for God is never merely judicial; it is itself transformative. To put it this way is to suggest that the faith that receives the divine verdict is itself produced by that verdict.[64]

This is better than reverting to union in order to counter the charge of a "legal fiction."[65]

Thus, "the horticultural image" of engrafting (union) "is subordinated to the legal" in Paul's thinking (Rom 9–11).[66] McCormack properly observes that the New Testament concept of "union with Christ" need not—and must not—be interpreted within a Greek metaphysical scheme (i.e., as ontological participation). Though hardly without ontological implications, Paul's concept of union is eschatological and ethical.[67] It presupposes a "covenantal ontology."[68] "To put it this way is to tease out the ontology embedded in my earlier contention that union with Christ takes its rise through a unity of wills, not through a

57. Ibid., 101.
58. Ibid., 102.
59. Ibid.
60. Ibid., 104.
61. Ibid.
62. Ibid., 105.
63. Ibid., 106.
64. Ibid., 107.
65. Ibid., 110.
66. Ibid., 112.
67. Ibid., 112–13.
68. Ibid., 113.

unity of substances."[69] We have to stop thinking in terms of a contrast between ontological and forensic. Rather, we need to find the *right* ontology. Justification establishes a forensic ontology in which God's verdict effects the world of which it speaks.[70]

Evaluating the Research

In the light of the evidence, the only plausible interpretation is that Calvin taught a "union with forensic justification" position. However, there remains a spectrum of tenable interpretations within this perspective. I would divide the relevant questions into one historiographical and two theological ones: (1) In terms of historical presuppositions, is it appropriate to formulate our interpretation of Calvin's concept of union principally in distinction from Luther/Lutheranism? (2) In terms of theological argument, granted that justification and sanctification are gifts of union with Christ, is there any relationship between these gifts within that union? In other words, does the common basis of justification and sanctification in the believer's union with Christ eliminate any causal relationship between these distinct gifts?

Reformed versus Lutheran?

Implausibly, Lutheran theologian Thomas Coates suggested that Calvin had "little room" for the concept of union with Christ, stressing instead the exclusively forensic character of justification. When Calvin approaches nearest that idea on occasion, "Nowhere, perhaps, does Calvin's dependence on Luther appear more clearly, and perhaps by the same token, nowhere does Calvin's theology come so close to genuine warmth."[71] However, it is just as implausible to treat Calvin's view of union as a distinctive contribution with little connection to Luther.

First, it is common to contrast Lutheran and Reformed soteriologies in terms of a "law-gospel" contrast and a "covenantal" paradigm, respectively. In other words, while Lutherans focus on justification apart from works, Reformed theologians emphasize the continuity of one covenant of grace. However, the distinction between law and gospel (and the priority of the former) was not only given clear expression in Reformed theology, it was also given systematic expression in the covenant of works and the covenant of grace.[72] Of course, these refinements cannot be found ready-made in Calvin, but the substance is there. With respect to our reconciliation and justification, the covenant of law and the covenant of promise indicate for Calvin "the contradictory nature of the two schemes."[73]

69. Ibid., 115.

70. Ibid.

71. Thomas Coates, "Calvin's Doctrine of Justification," *Concordia Theological Monthly* 34, no. 6 (June 1963): 325–34, quoted in Charles Partee, *The Theology of John Calvin*, 223.

72. See Michael Horton, "Law, Gospel, and Covenant," *Westminster Theological Journal* 64, no. 2 (2002): 279–88.

73. John Calvin, *Commentary on Galatians,* trans. John King (repr., Grand Rapids: Baker, 1996), on Gal. 3:10–12.

Calvin referred to law and gospel in two different senses, which we may identify in terms of (1) a redemptive-historical unity from promise to fulfillment (Old and New Testaments) and (2) a contrast between covenantal principles in obtaining justification.[74] When emphasizing the first (especially against the Anabaptists), Calvin does indeed see the gospel throughout the law (Old Testament), but whenever the second sense comes into view, he is simply "Lutheran."[75] Like Paul (Rom. 3:21–22), Calvin could include both senses even in the same sentence.

Calvin's nuance is lost in Partee, just as it is in Barth and the Torrances. Partee writes, "The main and specific point that Calvin makes in this section of the *Institutes* [book 2] is that grace takes precedence over law."[76] Calvin sees the law as preparation for the gospel, says Partee[77]—which, of course, he does, but in the redemptive-historical sense (basic continuity, with growing clarity) and then later especially in the principial-covenantal sense (basic antithesis with respect to acceptance before God). Collapsing these distinctions, however, Partee suggests that for Calvin "the gracious law is God's promise of salvation and the gracious gospel is the fulfillment of that promise. In his earlier writings Calvin followed Luther's emphasis on and order of 'law before gospel,' but later, Calvin teaches that grace precedes law."[78] Partee does not offer a footnote for this "later" view. Lacking such evidence, it seems more appropriate to accept that the diversity that Partee recognizes in Calvin on this point is due to the subtlety with which he uses the categories of law and gospel.[79]

It is clear enough that Partee's main objection is to the developing Reformed tradition's correlation of law and gospel with the covenant of works and the covenant of grace, respectively. "The role of the law in the covenant of works is a post-Calvin topic."[80] Again, this obscures more than it explains. Calvin certainly held that humanity "in Adam" is obligated to fulfill the law as a covenant of life and that Christ fulfilled this Adamic commission, meriting life for his posterity.

74. See Michael Horton, "Calvin and the Law-Gospel Hermeneutic," *Pro ecclesia* 6 (1977): 27–42.

75. In spite of his excessive rhetoric at times, Luther too displayed a similar nuance (see "How Christians Should Regard Moses," in *Luther's Works: Word and Sacrament I*, ed. E. Theodore Bachmann [Philadelphia: Muhlenberg, 1960], 35:161–74; hereafter *LW*). See also Timothy Wengert, *Law and Gospel: Philip Melanchthon's Debate with John Agricola of Eisleben over Poenitentia* (Grand Rapids: Baker, 1997). It was even Melanchthon who introduced the category of the "third use of the law" (to guide believers). The developing nuance, evident in Melanchthon, is discerned in Calvin's treatment of continuities and discontinuities (*Institutes* 3.17).

76. Partee, *The Theology of John Calvin*, 136.

77. Ibid., 137.

78. Ibid.

79. Partee later states, "Calvin declares that 'the word 'gospel,' taken in the broad sense, includes those testimonies of his mercy and fatherly favor which God gave to the patriarchs of old (II.9.2)" (Ibid., 142). This is an accurate description. However, Calvin most certainly did not see the severe and conditional threats of the Sinai covenant themselves as "testimonies of [God's] mercy and fatherly favor" any more than he saw Jesus' warnings about eternal judgment as such.

80. Ibid., 137.

In fact, the substance of the "covenant of law" is found in Irenaeus and Augustine.[81] Ironically, given his strong statements of discontinuity above, Partee says, "Turning from the law's purpose to its effects, Calvin suggests that the moral law would produce eternal salvation if it could be completely observed (II.7.3). In this line Calvin veers closest to the Westminster Confession's concept of a once-valid-but-now-rejected covenant of works."[82]

Garcia refers to Luther's "puzzling exhortation to believers" to ignore "the whole of active righteousness and the law," turning one's whole attention away from the law to grace.[83] However, precisely the same exhortation may be found in Calvin.[84] In both cases, the question is how trembling believers may find peace. Garcia follows Lillback in contrasting Calvin's "covenantal" and Luther's "law-gospel" approach. However, once again this is comparing apples and oranges. No less than Luther does Calvin recognize a clear contrast between law and gospel with respect to justification. For those who believe that subsequent Reformed theology simply refined the reformer's thinking in terms of a covenant of law and a covenant of promise, these two hermeneutics are entirely consistent.

Quoting Calvin regarding God's acceptance of the believer's works as good for the sake of Christ,[85] Garcia judges, "Consequently, whereas Luther warned believers to avoid the law, Calvin pointed his readers to the biblical imperatives of covenantal obedience."[86] This facile contrast (especially given Luther's exposition of the Ten Commandments in the Small Catechism and fierce opposition to the antinomians) verges on caricature. "In short," Garcia adds, "'Luther's understanding of justification by faith alone had no room for inherent righteousness, while Calvin's view required it as an inseparable but subordinate righteousness.'"[87] This conclusion is all the more remarkable when Garcia himself quotes Calvin's defense of Luther against Pighius in 1543:

> When Luther spoke in this way about good works, he was not seeking to deprive them of their praise and their reward before God. Nor did he ever say that God does not accept them or that he will not reward them; but he

---

81. Irenaeus, *Against Heresies*, 4.25, from *The Ante-Nicene Fathers*, ed. Alexander Roberts and James Donaldson (repr., Grand Rapids: Eerdmans, 1989), 5.16.3, 554; 4:13.1, 24; 4.15.1 and 4.16.3, 25–26; Augustine, *City of God* 16.28, trans. Henry Bettenson, ed. David Knowles (New York: Penguin, 1972), 688–89.
82. Partee, *The Theology of John Calvin*, 138–39. Obviously, "once-valid-but-now-rejected covenant of works" is Partee's judgment rather than a general consensus, at least among confessional Reformed/Presbyterian churches.
83. Garcia, *Life in Christ*, 75–76.
84. For example, see John Calvin, *Institutes* 3.19.2: When discussing justification, Calvin cautions emphatically that "the question is not how we may become righteous but how, being unrighteous and unworthy, we may be reckoned righteous. If consciences wish to attain any certainty in this matter, they ought to give no place to the law."
85. *Institutes* 3.17.5.
86. Garcia, *Life in Christ*, 76.
87. Ibid., 77, quoting Lillback, *The Binding of God*, 192.

wanted to show only what they are worth if they are considered by themselves apart from God's fatherly generosity.[88]

Garcia helpfully suggests that Lillback's sharp contrast between Luther and Calvin might have been more nuanced if he had compared Melanchthon and Calvin.[89] Furthermore, he notes similarities with Luther's view.[90] However, the question is whether Garcia's concern to stress the distinctiveness of Calvin's soteriology (over against Lutheranism) encourages him to miss some of the unmistakably "Lutheran" aspects of Calvin's thinking.

Second, while there is room for recognizing different nuances, attempts to identify Calvin's view in contrast with Luther is too heavily freighted. According to Garcia, Luther—and especially Melanchthon and subsequent Lutheranism—can only speak of sanctification as a necessary consequence of justification, while Calvin can talk about faith and works flowing from union with Christ.[91] This ignores a wealth of material in Luther, of which only a few examples can be mentioned here. In his "Against the Antinomians," Luther asserted, "This doctrine is not mine, but St. Bernard's. What am I saying? St. Bernard's? It is the message of all of Christendom, of all the prophets and apostles."[92] Calvin's well-attested appreciation for Bernard, particularly with respect to mystical union (the marital metaphor), follows in Luther's steps.

Luther's advance turned upon his recognition that this marriage is first judicial—the imputation of our sin to Christ and his righteousness to sinners, and then (as a consequence) a growing relationship of trust, love, and good works in which the union is realized subjectively more and more.[93] Far from rejecting the believer's actual righteousness (sanctification), Luther says that Christ's imputed righteousness "is the basis, the cause, the source of all our own actual righteousness."[94] In *The Freedom of a Christian*, he writes,

> We conclude, therefore, that a Christian lives not in himself, but in Christ and his neighbor. Otherwise he is not a Christian. He lives in Christ through faith, in his neighbor through love. By faith he is caught up beyond himself into God. By love he descends beneath himself into his neighbor. Yet he always remains in God and in his love.[95]

88. Garcia, *Life in Christ*, 78. Quoted from *The Bondage and Liberation of the Will: A Defence of the Orthodox Doctrine of Human Choice against Pighius*, ed. A. N. S. Lane, trans. G. I. Davies (Grand Rapids: Baker, 1996), 26.

89. Garcia, *Life in Christ*, 78n97.

90. Ibid., 117.

91. Ibid., 111–12.

92. Martin Luther, "Against the Antinomians" in *Luther's Works: The Christian in Society IV*, American Edition, ed. Franklin Sherman (Philadelphia: Fortress, 1971), 47:110.

93. The prominence of the union motif in Luther is evident, for example, in his treatise, "The Freedom of a Christian" (*LW* 31:351).

94. Martin Luther, "Two Kinds of Righteousness," *LW* 1, ed. Harold J. Grimm (Philadelphia: Fortress, 1957; reprint, 1971), 31:298.

95. *LW* 31:371; cf. Cornelius P. Venema, "Heinrich Bullinger's Correspondence on Calvin's Doctrine of Predestination," *Sixteenth Century Journal* 17 (1986), 435–50.

Faith suffices not only for justification, but is the constant source of the believer's renewal and service toward others.

Faith not only justifies; it "unites the soul with Christ as a bride is united with her bridegroom," says Luther. "At this point a contest of happy exchanges takes place. . . . Is that not a happy household, when Christ, the rich, noble, and good bridegroom, takes the poor, despised, wicked little harlot in marriage, sets her free from all evil, and decks her with all good things?"[96] Throughout this treatise (as elsewhere), Luther uses "faith" as shorthand for union with Christ. Faith is sufficient not only for justification, but for sanctification, since it grasps Christ and therefore both gifts. The entire treatise explores the logic of engrafting/union as a way of connecting forensic justification and new obedience. In fact, the mystical union of Christ and the believer was so prominent in Luther's thinking that he could sometimes tend to blur the distinction between Christ and the believer. It was such occasionally extreme statements that Osiander transformed into a formal theory.

I am not suggesting that there are no discontinuities between Luther and Calvin on certain aspects of this topic, but they lie more in emphases. Calvin emphasizes more than Luther the reality of the new life that is given in union with Christ. While Calvin strongly affirms the *simul iustus et peccator*, he just as strongly affirms the "more and more" of progressive sanctification. According to Lutheran theologian Jane E. Stohl, Luther had more of an "eschatological reserve." "For Calvin the transformation of the believer is measurably advanced and manifest, whereas for Luther the reality of redemption remains deeply hidden until the Last Day."[97] As becomes especially evident in their differences over the Eucharist, Calvin's distinctive contribution is found not as much in denials of Luther's views as much as a fuller exposition of features that are underdeveloped in the German reformer. As Philip Walker Butin observes, Calvin complements Luther's emphasis on God's gracious descent in Christ with God's equally gracious raising of believers together with Christ through the work of the Spirit. "Calvin's approach at this point thus complements and completes the 'downward' Lutheran emphasis on incarnation with an equal 'upward' emphasis on resurrection and ascension."[98]

Calvin certainly formulates the connection between justification and sanctification, not to mention his sacramental theology, with greater appeal to and emphasis on union with Christ. In fact, this emphasis is no doubt crucial to his pneumatological stress that is much more pronounced in Calvin (especially on the Supper) than in Luther. Nevertheless, I think it is an exaggeration of the evidence to suggest that Calvin introduced an entirely new paradigm. Furthermore,

---

96. Martin Luther, "The Freedom of a Christian," *LW* 31:351.

97. Jane E. Stohl, "God's Self-Revelation in the Sacrament of the Altar," in *By Faith Alone: Essays on Justification in Honor of Gerhard O. Forde*, ed. Joseph A. Burgess and Mark Kolden (Grand Rapids: Eerdmans, 2004), 107.

98. Philip Walker Butin, *Revelation, Redemption, and Response: Calvin's Trinitarian Understanding of the Divine-Human Relationship* (New York: Oxford University Press, 1995), 118.

Reformed theology's refinements (esp. the two-covenant scheme) drew the law-gospel contrast with respect to justification into a more historically sensitive horizon, not by forgetting the *unio* motif but by articulating it more clearly within the contrasting headships of Adam and Christ.

Union and the Logical Priority of Justification

Calvin's undeniable interest in union with Christ buttresses rather than undermines his exclusively forensic understanding of justification. Union with Christ is certainly the broader category in Calvin's thinking that encompasses justification and sanctification (as well as election and glorification). However, the breadth of this motif in no way makes justification a secondary doctrine in Calvin's soteriology. Calvin regarded justification as "the primary article of the Christian religion," "the main hinge on which religion turns," "the principal article of the whole doctrine of salvation and the foundation of all religion."[99] In his response to Cardinal Sadoleto, Calvin wrote that justification is "the first and keenest subject of controversy between us."[100] Like apostle Paul, Calvin began treating the theme of union with Christ not in explaining justification but in addressing the relationship between justification and renewal.

Early in his career, Calvin's familiarity with patristic sources was largely secondhand—namely, through reading Luther's citations. Later on, however, he became a patristics scholar in his own right, perhaps even surpassing Luther himself.[101] Irenaeus and the Cappadocians, Cyril of Alexandria, Augustine, Hillary of Poitiers—and Bernard—figure prominently. He refers to Bernard frequently (at least twenty-one times in the *Institutes* alone), especially when discussing the "marvelous exchange" in union with Christ.[102]

In spite of its obvious importance in his thinking, Calvin never introduces union with Christ as a central dogma or even as an integrating theme for soteriology generally. Rather, it is an always ready-to-hand way of explaining the relationship of justification to sanctification, the communion of saints, and the sacraments. The Spirit grants sinners the gift of faith through the gospel, and this same faith receives Christ for both justification and sanctification. As noted in the companion essay by Billings, Calvin does not begin his *Commentary on Romans* with the union motif; in fact, he asserts in his introduction that justification is the main subject of the epistle. However, like Paul, he introduces union with Christ as a way of relating sanctification to justification. Calvin insists that

99. *Institutes* 3.2.1, 3.11.1, and Sermon on Luke 1:5–10 in *Corpus Reformatorum* (*CR*), 46.23.

100. "Calvin's Letter to Cardinal Sadoleto," in *Calvin's Tracts and Treatises*, trans. Henry Beveridge (Grand Rapids: Eerdmans, 1958), 1.41.

101. See A. N. S. Lane, *John Calvin: Student of the Church Fathers* (Edinburgh: T. & T. Clark, 1999).

102. *Institutes* 3.20.1. On the number of references to Bernard, see François Wendel, *Calvin: Origins and Development of His Religious Thought*, trans. Philip Mairet (New York and London: Harper & Row, 1963), 127n43. For a thorough study of the influence of Bernard on Calvin, see Tamburello, *Union with Christ*.

Christ's work *for* us must be distinguished but never separated from his union *with* us and work *within* us, both of which are accomplished by the Spirit.[103] The grace that justifies and renews is not a principle that is infused by the sacraments. Rather, it is nothing less than *Christ himself,* delivered to us *by the Spirit* who unites us to Christ *through faith.*

Even more than other reformers, though, Calvin emphasized union with Christ as the link between justification and sanctification. In so doing, his soteriology focuses not only on the cross but also on the resurrection (and ascension), charging with an eschatological and pneumatological energy that defies any caricature of an impersonal transaction. Gaffin, Garcia, Billings, and others have explored that point with great skill. Thus, even his law-gospel contrast becomes located in a redemptive-historical narrative rather than in any abstract principle of inherent antithesis. Where medieval scholasticism concentrated on the infusion of supernatural habits (something done within the believer but at a distance), and some Protestants like Andreas Osiander simply collapsed faith into regeneration (as sanctification), the believer into Christ, Christ's humanity into his deity, and everything into God, Calvin focuses on the role of the Holy Spirit as the bond of our union with Christ. That we are in Christ *and* that Christ is in us are both due to the mediation of the Spirit. "But faith is the principal work of the Holy Spirit."[104]

Drawing, like Luther, on the wide range of biblical analogies for this union, Calvin's judicial emphasis with respect to *justification* is complemented by the organic imagery of union and engrafting in relation to the *inner renewal* and communion with Christ, including his holiness. Thus, commenting on John 17, Calvin explains, ". . . having been engrafted into the body of Christ, we are made partakers of the Divine adoption, and heirs of heaven."[105] "This is the purpose of the gospel," he says, "that Christ should become ours, and that we should be engrafted into his body."[106] Though justified by an alien righteousness imputed, we cannot grasp Christ without receiving all of his benefits.[107] All of those who are justified are united to Christ and become fruit-bearing branches. Calvin says that we are "in Christ (*in Christo*) because we are out of ourselves (*extra nos*)," finding our sanctification as well as our justification not by looking within but by clinging to Christ.[108]

Garcia lays some stress on Melanchthon's treatment of renewal as a necessary consequence of imputation. Sanctification necessarily follows justification (the "necessity principle").[109] However, Calvin grounds both in union. "Unlike

---

103. *Institutes* 3.1.1.

104. Ibid., 3.1.4.

105. John Calvin, *Commentary on the Gospel according to John,* trans. William Pringle, Calvin's Commentaries (repr., Grand Rapids: Baker, 1996), 166; commenting on John 17:3.

106. John Calvin, *Commentary on the Gospel according to John,* 166.

107. A forerunner in the new exploration of Calvin's concept of the *duplex beneficium* is Cornelis P. Venema, "The Twofold Nature of the Gospel in Calvin's Theology."

108. Quoted in Garcia, *Life in Christ,* 116.

109. Ibid., 123.

Melanchthon, therefore, Calvin thus immediately and vigorously locates the relation of Romans 5 to 6, and of justification to sanctification, in the doctrine of union with Christ."[110] Garcia labors the point that for Calvin sanctification

> does not flow from the imputation of Christ's righteousness but from Christ himself with whom the Spirit has united believers. In other words, for Calvin, sanctification does not flow from justification. . . . Rather, together they are "effects," or, better, aspects of union with Christ.[111]

This seems to me to present a false dilemma. Calvin does maintain that Spirit-given faith unites us to Christ for justification and sanctification, but he also sees justification as the basis for sanctification. Aside from whether Melanchthon offered similar exegesis of the relevant passages, Garcia quotes Calvin as saying, "for since we are clothed with the righteousness of the Son, we are reconciled to God, and renewed by the power of the Spirit to holiness."[112] Doesn't "since" imply some dependence?[113] Why must the double grace via union cancel the logical dependence of sanctification on justification within that union? Calvin teaches that justification and sanctification are found "in Christ" through faith *and* that the forensic declaration is the basis for the transformative effects of this union.[114]

McCormack's analysis is insightful at many points, highlighting both the significance of forensic justification in Calvin and the unfinished task of challenging certain aspects of medieval ontology. Nevertheless, alleged tensions between this view and Calvin's strong participationist language employed in his eucharistic discussions do not seem as evident to Calvin—or to me—as McCormack suggests. For Calvin, union with Christ is a wider horizon than justification, without displacing the importance of this "main hinge" in soteriology. Calvin's pneumatological emphasis, which we meet again in his formulation of the way in which Christ is communicated to us in the Supper, is already apparent in his treatment of the mystical union.

The question of the *ordo salutis* (i.e., the logical sequence from election to glorification) is important because it clarifies the relationship between God's work for us and God's work within us. However, McCormack interprets Calvin (and Luther) as having given logical priority to justification over union (including regeneration), while Gaffin and Garcia defend the reverse priority. In my view, both views fail to recognize that for Calvin union with Christ is not a "moment" in the *ordo salutis* like election, effectual calling, justification, sanctification, and glorification but is a more general way of speaking about all of our spiritual blessings being found in Christ rather than in ourselves. In fact, Question and Answer 66 of the Westminster Shorter Catechisms states that we are united to Christ in effectual calling—which, of course precedes both

110. Ibid., 125.
111. Ibid., 146.
112. Quoted in ibid., 127.
113. See also chap. 3, p. 55, above.
114. See Gleason, *John Calvin and John Owen on Mortification*, 59.

justification and sanctification. In my view, this is more consistent with Calvin's view than either Gaffin's or McCormack's interpretations, since they both seem to assume that union is a definite "link" in the golden chain of the *ordo salutis* rather than a way of speaking about the whole of our salvation.

John Murray was certainly able to affirm the importance of the two-fold grace in our union with Christ while emphasizing that sanctification always rests upon justification:

> We are not to suppose, however, that this transition means that sanctification can be divorced either in fact or in the development of its meaning from the justification *on which it rests* and with which it is inseparably connected . . . If the mediation of Christ is always in the forefront in justification, it is likewise in sanctification.[115]

With Gaffin, we can still affirm that in Calvin's view all of our spiritual blessings are found in union with Christ, but with McCormack we can agree that justification is the forensic basis for this union, without having to make justification logically prior to effectual calling (and therefore, prior to faith). In effectual calling, the Spirit grants the faith to receive Christ for justification and for sanctification, but, analogous to God's performative utterance in creation, it is the forensic verdict ("Let there be!") that evokes the inner renewal that yields the fruit of the Spirit ("Let the earth bring forth . . ."). Furthermore, Calvin's "more nearly patristic" emphasis in his eucharistic teaching does not in any way compete with the forensic aspect. Rather, it richly highlights the point that while justification makes us legal beneficiaries of adoption, sanctification, and glorification, these additional gifts constitute an organic and mystical participation of believers in Christ.

Taking root in the forensic soil of justification, from which it derives its effective power as well as its legal basis, union with Christ produces the life of Christ within believers. It is not simply *like* Christ's life (*imitatio Christi*); it *is* Christ's life into which we are baptized. Repeatedly in Calvin's treatment of a variety of subjects (the persons of the Trinity, the hypostatic union, the relationship between justification and sanctification, and the sacraments), we find the formula "without confusion or division." Justified once and for all through faith by a righteousness that is external (alien) to us, we are nevertheless united to Christ by an inseparable communion so that, in spite of our weaknesses, we will always seek our salvation in him.[116]

So when we consider ourselves, there is nothing but despair; when we consider ourselves *in Christ*, there is faith, which brings hope and love in its train. In the gospel, God calls forth a new world of which Christ is the sun and we are drawn into his orbit. Where medieval theology, codified at Trent, developed its *ordo salutis* by appealing to various infusions of a gracious substance into the soul, enabling meritorious cooperation on our part, Calvin insists that all of our

---

115. John Murray, *The Epistle to the Romans* in The New International Commentary on the New Testament series (Grand Rapids: Eerdmans, 1959, 1965), 212; emphasis added.
116. *Institutes* 3.2.24.

blessings—justification and sanctification—are found only in Christ, through the Spirit.[117]

CONCLUSION: CONTEMPORARY POSSIBILITIES

Calvin's treatment of union with Christ offers enormous potential in contemporary faith and practice. Eastern Orthodox, Roman Catholic, and Protestant synergism treat mystical union as an alternative to forensic justification, while Calvin's view comprehends both. Only by restricting a robust notion of participation to a Neoplatonic ontology can one judge that Calvin lacks a theology of union. The dilemma between a unilateral relationship of divine power exercised upon passive subjects and a synergistic scheme of spiritual and moral ascent may exist for modern theologians, but it is not Calvin's problem.

His treatment reveals strong affinities with Luther, yet his emphasis on the resurrection, ascension, and Pentecost offers a more richly pneumatological perspective that is more affirming of the reality of the new creation's powers at work in this present age. With Luther, he affirms God's descent to us (a theology of the cross) and the justification of the ungodly, but he also stresses the resurrection and the Spirit's work in raising us up with Christ in newness of life as an experienced reality. In Calvin's approach, God's unilateral gift of grace in election, redemption, effectual calling, and justification is the source of a living, active, and transformative relationship of covenantal reciprocity. No less realistic than a Neoplatonic definition, Calvin's understanding of participation is nevertheless shaped by distinctly biblical notions of covenantal koinonia rather than the more metaphysically freighted language of participation in essence (*methexis*). It is the atmosphere of head and members, firstfruit and harvest, vine and branches, husband and wife. The problem with which Calvin wrestles is not that of nature and grace, but of sin and grace. It is not because they are human (and God acts only unilaterally and extrinsically) that persons cannot cooperate in their own regeneration and justification, but because they are bound by sin and helpless to respond to God positively apart from radical grace. There is no fusion of essences or infusions of supernatural substances, but a sharing of an inheritance that has been won by our elder brother.

Only God's sovereign gift can create not only a new status before God, but a new life of love and grateful obedience. Thus synergistic accounts not only deny a crucial aspect of union with Christ but also eliminate the objective basis for the active life of faith in good works. Passive recipients of God's gracious gift, we nevertheless become active gift-givers to our neighbors as a result: hence, the repeated call to obedience, fruit-bearing, and love in Scripture. It is synergism that settles for false alternatives. In Calvin's expression, "Surely those

117. Ibid., 3.16.1.

things which are connected do not destroy one another!"[118] Forensic justification through faith alone is the fountain of union with Christ in all of its renewing aspects.[119] Therefore, justifying faith is not itself the same as participation in Christ but is the means by which we do so.[120]

Although Calvin's conception of union with Christ avoids false antitheses between God's sovereign grace (a unilateral gift of life and forensic justification) and a relational and transformative participation in God, justification remains the judicial basis of mystical union and its transforming effects. As Geerhardus Vos expressed it,

> In our opinion Paul consciously and consistently subordinated the mystical aspect of the relation to Christ to the forensic one. Paul's mind was to such an extent forensically oriented that he regarded the entire complex of subjective spiritual changes that take place in the believer and of subjective spiritual blessings enjoyed by the believer as the direct outcome of the forensic work of Christ applied in justification. The mystical is based on the forensic, not the forensic on the mystical.[121]

Therefore, we are not looking away from justification when we consider union with Christ, sanctification, and glorification, but we are surveying in wonder the vast benefits that are ours on the basis of this judicial verdict. This does not mean that every gift of this union is forensic, but rather that the entire line of the *ordo salutis* is forensically charged.

God's speech creates *ex nihilo* and also generates transforming effects within creation itself. A unilateral act of grace activates specific creatures to yield the fruit that they were "worded" to bear. And because God is the Trinity, this powerful speech comes from the Father, in the Son, and brings about its effect in us by the Spirit. God's gracious gift establishes the unconditional basis for a genuinely reciprocal and covenantal relationship.

Therefore, Calvin's concept of union with Christ has enormous ecumenical significance. Unlike its synergistic rivals, this account provides ample space for an exclusively forensic justification *and* transformative renewal—even a form of deification. It would be most appropriate to conclude with a marvelous summary from Calvin:

---

118. Ibid., 3.2.25.

119. For more on this topic (especially in relation to Calvin's debate with Osiander), see Horton, *Covenant and Salvation*, 143–44.

120. John Calvin, *Commentaries on the Epistles of Paul to the Galatians and Ephesians*, trans. William Pringle, Calvin's Commentaries (repr., Grand Rapids: Baker, 1996), commenting on Ephesians 3:17 (CO 51:186–87).

121. Geerhardus Vos, "The Alleged Legalism in Paul's Doctrine of Justification," in *Redemptive History and Biblical Interpretation*, ed. Richard B. Gaffin Jr. (Phillipsburg, NJ: P&R, 1980), 384. The same point is made by Louis Berkhof, *Systematic Theology*, 452, against those who would make the imputation of Christ's righteousness to depend on mystical union rather than vice versa. See also John V. Fesko, *Justification: Understanding the Classic Reformed Doctrine* (Phillipsburg, NJ: P&R, 2008), chapter 10.

We see that our whole salvation and all its parts are comprehended in Christ. We should therefore take care not to derive the least portion of it anywhere else. If we seek salvation, we are taught by the very name of Jesus that it is "of him." If we seek any other gifts of the Spirit, they will be found in his anointing. If we seek strength, it lies in his dominion; if purity, in his conception; if gentleness, it appears in his birth. For by his birth he was made like us in all respects that he might learn to feel our pain. If we seek redemption, it lies in his passion; if acquittal, in his condemnation; if remission of the curse, in his cross; if satisfaction, in his sacrifice; if purification, in his blood; if reconciliation, in his descent into hell; if mortification of the flesh, in his tomb; if newness of life, in his resurrection; . . . if inheritance of the Heavenly Kingdom, in his entrance into heaven; if protection, if security, if abundant supply of all blessings, in his Kingdom; if untroubled expectation of judgment, in the power given him to judge. In short, since rich store of every kind of good abounds in him, let us drink our fill from this fountain, and from no other.[122]

122. *Institutes* 2.16.19.

SECTION 3
CALVIN'S THEOLOGY
OF ELECTION
AND ITS RECEPTION

Chapter 5

Election

Calvin's Theology and Its Early Reception

CARL R. TRUEMAN

INTRODUCTION

In addressing the issue of the nature and reception of Calvin's theology of election, the historian of doctrine is faced with an immediate methodological problem: the topic apparently presupposes that Calvin's theology was, in terms of its content, somehow unique or distinct; and thus its reception will be relatively straightforward to trace. Neither is in fact the case; and, indeed, Calvin would have regarded any hint of originality or uniqueness on his part as something highly troubling and to be carefully avoided. The unfortunate application of the term "Calvinism" to what is more properly considered to be Reformed Orthodoxy is misleading here, as it divorces Reformed theology from past Christian tradition and unnecessarily isolates Calvin as a source of doctrinal formulation.[1]

---

1. Standard treatments of Calvin's theology include Wilhelm Niesel, *The Theology of John Calvin*, trans. Harold Knight (London: Lutterworth Press, 1956); François Wendel, *Calvin: The Origins and Development of His Religious Thought*, trans. Philip Mairét (New York: Harper & Row, 1963). Both contain discussions of predestination, though Niesel accords the doctrine a principal structural importance in Calvin's thought that has been refuted by more recent scholarship.

Given this, it is far better to work on the basis that Calvin was, perhaps at best, first among equals, both in his own day and then in subsequent Reformed discussion of the doctrines of election and predestination. Indeed, he was not so much a source of doctrine as part of the larger reception of Augustinian anti-Pelagianism in the early modern period.[2]

This also points to one further problem which the term "Calvinism" has bequeathed to posterity: the temptation to demand that Calvin answer questions which were never posed—or at least not posed in particularly loaded forms—in his own day. The classic example of this is limited atonement, one of the so-called Five Points of Calvinism. Did Calvin, or did he not, believe in limited atonement? The problem here is that the question to which "limited atonement" is the answer itself arose out of a reaction to particular strands of the reception of Calvin's thought; and to demand that he, a sixteenth-century theologian, answer the question by the criteria of seventeenth-century theology is historically implausible and, even at the level of systematic theology (a discipline that often operates with a certain level of historical detachment), is fraught with all kinds of difficulties and temptations to distortion.[3]

SOURCES

While much theological scholarship has tended to focus on the 1559 *Institutes* as a normative source for Calvin's doctrine on a whole variety of different topics, it is increasingly apparent that this privileging of this one book over Calvin's life and other writings is insufficiently sensitive to the context of his life and work.[4] After all, Calvin himself intended the *Institutes* in large part as a theological handbook to the exegetical work contained in his commentaries; and much of Calvin's theology was also worked out in the heat of controversies that were only alluded to within the pages of his magnum opus. Further, recent research has highlighted the rhetorical strategies at work in the shaping of the *Institutes*, particularly with reference to the ordering of doctrinal topics, so the reader needs to be careful as to what conclusions can and should be drawn solely on the basis of this one book.[5] Thus, in addition to the *Institutes*, sources for Calvin's under-

---

2. On the methodological problems of interpreting the development of Reformed theology on the basis of a normative Calvin and a subsequent tradition of Calvinism, see Richard A. Muller, *After Calvin: Studies in the Development of a Theological Tradition* (New York: Oxford University Press, 2003).

3. On this issue, contrast the approaches of James B. Torrance, "The Incarnation and 'Limited Atonement,'" *Evangelical Quarterly* 55 (1983), 83–94; and Richard A. Muller, *Christ and the Decree: Christology and Predestination in Reformed Theology from Calvin to Perkins* (Grand Rapids: Baker, 1988).

4. For a good example of an almost exclusive focus on the *Institutes* as the basis for assessing Calvin's theology, see Alister E. McGrath, *A Life of John Calvin: A Study of the Shaping of Western Culture* (Oxford: Blackwell, 1990).

5. The definitive study of Calvin and rhetoric, and its impact upon the shaping of his thought, is Olivier Millet, *Calvin et la Dynamique de la Parole: Étude de rhétorique réformée* (Geneva: Slatkine, 1992).

standing of election include his commentaries, particularly perhaps the 1539 commentary on Romans; his engagement with Catholic polemicist, Pighius, over the nature of election, providence, and the human will; and his clash with Jerome Bolsec over reprobation.[6]

Too much ink has been spilled over the precise significance of the placement of predestination in the 1559 *Institutes*, separate from providence and subsequent to Christology. It is always a great temptation for theologians to read theological motivation behind every action; but it has been argued quite plausibly by Richard Muller that the ordering of topics in the *Institutes* is not driven by any inherent shape or structure that Calvin saw in the very essence of Christian doctrine itself, but rather by the identification of the order of topics in Paul's Letter to the Romans, as articulated by Philipp Melanchthon. Thus, the notion that the placement of election in a position separate from providence and subsequent to Christology and discussion of the Christian life does not necessarily represent a more christological or somehow less harsh or deterministic view of the doctrine than that offered by others. Put simply, the position of the topic in the *Institutes* does not appear to be theologically motivated at that level; at least, a theological motive is not a necessary hypothesis for its position.[7]

CALVIN ON ELECTION AND PREDESTINATION

Like Luther, Calvin regards election and predestination as an important conceptual foundation for his understanding of justification by grace through faith. Thus, in his 1539 *Reply to Cardinal Sadoleto*, he argues that justification must be gratuitous because it is based on election, which is itself gracious. This is, of course, part and parcel of the common understanding of the Reformers, that the struggle in which they were engaged with Rome was analogous to the struggle in which Augustine had engaged with the Pelagians.[8]

This basic concern for election as the basis for the gracious nature of salvation is clear from the manner in which Calvin introduces election in the 1559 *Institutes*. In 3.21.1 he points to the fact that the gospel is preached unequally to all, that some respond to the word while others do not:

6. Calvin's attack on Pighius is available in English as *The Bondage and Liberation of the Will: A Defence of the Orthodox Doctrine of Human Choice against Pighius*, trans. A. N. S. Lane (Grand Rapids: Baker, 1996); the Genevan Consensus (against Bolsec on eternal predestination) is in James T. Dennison, ed., *Reformed Confessions of the 16th and 17th Centuries in English Translation: 1523–1552*, vol. 1 (Grand Rapids: Reformation Heritage Books, 2008). This latter text is also found, along with John Calvin's *A Defence of the Secret Providence of God*, in *Calvin's Calvinism*, trans. Henry Cole (Grand Rapids: Reformed Free Printing Association, n.d.).

7. See Muller, "Establishing the *ordo docendi*: The Organization of Calvin's *Institutes*," in idem, *The Unaccommodated Calvin: Studies in the Foundation of a Theological Tradition* (New York: Oxford University Press, 2000).

8. John Calvin, *Tracts and Letters*, trans. Henry Beveridge (Edinburgh: Calvin Translation Society, 1844), vol. 1, 44.

> In actual fact, the covenant of life is not preached equally among all men, and among those to whom it is preached, it does not gain the same acceptance either constantly or in equal degree. In this diversity the wonderful depth of God's judgment is made known. For there is no doubt that this variety also serves the decision of God's eternal election.[9]

The discriminating factor is thus not intrinsic to the people who respond or do not respond, but rather finds its cause in the secret will of God.

This question of why some respond and others do not parallels a similar question raised by Augustine, who reflected on the question of why some infants arrive safely at the baptismal font while others do not, again in the context of pointing to God's extrinsic decision as the basis for salvation.[10] Calvin stresses that positive response to God's Word is a sign of God's mercy and, indeed, God's mercy cannot be truly understood until the truth of election is properly grasped. Thus, election is part and parcel of the Protestant polemic against any notion of merit in the Christian life. Indeed, in the same chapter, he goes as far as to say that we can never come to know the unconditional mercy of God until such time as we come to know his eternal election. This primary concern—the rejection of the notion of merit as any basis for election—continues as a theme throughout the treatment of the subject in the *Institutes*.

Calvin's understanding of election operates within well-established lines of anti-Pelagian discourse. He regards the doctrine as connecting both to God's sovereignty, by which all things are determined, and to human depravity, by which responding positively to the gospel is out of the power of fallen human beings. For the former, Calvin is so clear on this point that he rejects explanations of evil that see evil actions and events as the result of a merely permissive will of God, a position which he regards as fundamentally unscriptural, even going so far as to criticize some of Augustine's statements on this matter as unfortunately worded. How God connects to evil is a mystery, but that all things are willed by him is scriptural teaching; nothing occurs with him merely as a passive observer.[11] Even the fall of Adam was the result of divine predestination, though this was done with justice and does not involve God in any moral sin or culpability for evil.[12] In light of this, it is worth reiterating that the separate positioning of providence, in *Institutes* 1, and election, in *Institutes* 3, is rhetorically significant but does not have any major theological impact: there is not chance with God; all actions and events are foreknown and predetermined by him (e.g., *Inst.* 1.16.2); and salvation is no special exception

9. John Calvin, *Institutes of the Christian Religion*, trans. Ford Lewis Battles, ed. John T. McNeill (Philadelphia: The Westminster Press, 1960), 3.21.1.

10. Augustine, "Letter 217, 19," in *Letters 211–270*, trans. Roland Teske, *The Works of Saint Augustine* II/4 (New York: New City Press, 2005), 61. I am grateful to the Rev. Dr. Peter Sanlon for drawing my attention to this passage.

11. *Calvin's Calvinism*, 244; cf. *Institutes* 1.18.1; also his comments on Rom. 9, *Commentaries on the Epistle of Paul the Apostle to the Romans*, trans. John Owen (Edinburgh: Calvin Translation Society, 1849), 362.

12. *Institutes* 3.23.7–11

to this rule. In light of this, the fall is a moral watershed but not an onto-logical one: it decisively impacts human moral ability; but even before the fall human beings were utterly dependent upon the predestination and providence of God.

Calvin does, however, nuance his position by distinguishing between causes. The ultimate cause of all things is God's will; but, since this has no rule higher than God himself and is unfathomable to mere creatures, it should not be a subject for speculation or held to account to mere human, creaturely standards of justice or rationality. Thus, when we look at, for example, reprobation, we should not attempt to understand it in terms of this ultimate cause but rather in terms of proximate causes: people are condemned by God because of their actual wickedness. This distinction in causes, common in the Middle Ages, will appear frequently in subsequent Reformed writing as a means of precluding speculation about God's hidden will.[13]

In this context, Calvin is clear that God's eternal decrees are always infallibly executed in time. Thus, in *Institutes* 1.17.14, he uses a discussion of the sparing of Nineveh after the preaching of Jonah, to argue that the prophecy was implic-itly conditional, that the preaching was the means God had determined to use to bring about the city's repentance, and that therefore this is no evidence for God's knowledge of the future to be uncertain or merely conjectural. He closes the section by quoting Isaiah 14:27, "The Lord of Hosts has purposed, and who will annul it? His hand is stretched out, and who will turn it back?'"

For Calvin, the existence of sin is both a problem and a factor that needs to be taken into account in discussion of predestination. Consistent with his com-mitment to both God's sovereignty and the fact that God cannot be made mor-ally responsible for human sin, he argues that Adam fell voluntarily into sin and that all human beings are now bound by the moral determination of that fallen nature inherited from him. In arguing this, he sees himself as standing firmly in line with both Augustine and Luther.[14] As a result of the fall, without grace human beings necessarily sin and act in an evil way; they can in no sense merit God's grace by their own strength.[15]

Given the fact that Calvin connects predestination both to God's relation-ship to the world as Creator to creature (an ontological connection) and to the impact of sin on human beings as rendering them incapable of turning to God in their own power or of meriting grace in any way, he finds the conceptual foundation of salvation in his notion of the double decree. For Calvin, the decree of predestination is double: to election and to reprobation. God is who he is and will do what he will do. It is absurd, according to Calvin, to have election without reprobation, because both originate in the will of God; and both are to be judged ultimately not by any human criteria of justice or equity but rather by

13. Ibid., 3.23.8–9.
14. *The Bondage and Liberation of the Will*, 40; *Institutes* 1.15.8.
15. *The Bondage and Liberation of the Will*, 149–50.

God's own glorious purposes.[16] God's righteousness has priority over all crea-turely notions of the same and is a rule unto itself, to be assessed solely by itself.[17]

In controversial contexts, the assertion of the double decree is important in Calvin's 1551–52 clash with Jerome Bolsec, who was expelled from Geneva by the magistrates after a trial by the civil magistrates. Interestingly enough, while Geneva did seek advice from other Swiss cities, support for Calvin from thence was at best lukewarm, which is not surprising, given that Heinrich Bullinger, Reformation leader in Zurich, was essentially committed to a single predestinarian scheme.[18]

The response of Bullinger is an indication that the Reformation did not involve an absolute consensus on all aspects of the doctrine of predestination. Thus, Bullinger disliked talk about reprobation and instead focused on predesti-nation as God's will to save the elect while passing over the nonelect. Yet, earlier in the Reformation, Luther had clashed with Catholic humanist, Erasmus, and argued that, because nothing happens without God first willing it to happen, therefore all things were determined by God's will; the clear inference of this is that both election and reprobation are caused by God's will. Melanchthon, Luther's lieutenant, however, was, in contrast to his mentor, even more cau-tious than Bullinger, moving in the late 1520s to a position remarkably close to that of Luther's nemesis, Erasmus, which gave the human will a decisive role in salvation; and he coupled this with a desire to see the doctrine of predestination avoided by preachers. Calvin's double predestinarian view separates him some-what from Bullinger, though not to the extent of setting them in fundamental disagreement over the anti-Pelagian nature of salvation; and his disagreement on the matter with Melanchthon seems not to have affected either their mutual friendship or admiration.

Despite all the noise that has surrounded this doctrine, in asserting dou-ble predestination, Calvin is hardly innovating: Gottschalk, Bradwardine, and Wyclif are but three medieval precedents one could mention who held to a similar position. But on this point Calvin is more precise and consistent than Augustine, who generally tended to conceive of predestination as single, to life, although he did make occasional references that point in the direction of a sharper, double predestinarian position in his later works.[19] Calvin, however, took the opportunity of the Bolsec controversy to make his double predestinar-ian position normative for Genevan pastors through the publication and adop-tion of the Genevan Consensus.

The point where Calvin's doctrine breaks with the medieval anti-Pelagian tradition is the connection he draws between election and assurance. For

---

16. *Institutes* 1.23.1.

17. Ibid., 1.23.2; cf. *Romans*, 361, commenting on Rom. 9:18.

18. See Cornelis P. Venema, *Heinrich Bullinger and the Doctrine of Predestination* (Grand Rap-ids: Baker, 2002).

19. Cf. Augustine's single predestinarian teaching in *Enchiridion* 27, where election is clearly defined as drawing people out of the fallen mass of humanity, while leaving others in their sin, with comments in the *Tractates on John* 48.4, where, commenting on John. 10:26, he speaks of God predestining to damnation, a point most naturally read as referring to reprobation.

medievals, the whole notion of assurance as normal or typical of the Christian life was somewhat alien, undermining as it did the ethical imperatives of the Christian life. Calvin, however, in line with the trajectory of Protestant thought from Luther, regarded assurance as, if not of the essence of saving faith, certainly as an expected concomitant of normal Christian experience. The connection between election and assurance was forged in dramatic terms by Luther in his 1525 treatises, *On the Bondage of the Will*, where predestination was seen as the only sure basis for anchoring the promises of the Christian life and thus guaranteeing that the believer could be assured of God's favor. Calvin continues in this trajectory as part of his polemic against merit: human beings can only be assured of salvation if merit is completely ruled out; merit is completely ruled out by the doctrine of God's election; thus a knowledge of God's election is central to assurance.[20] In the same chapter, to those who argue that predestination leads to pride and complacency, Calvin argues that, on the contrary, when believers know they merit nothing, they are truly humbled.

In addressing predestination, Calvin objects to Melanchthon's somewhat Erasmian notion that predestination should not be preached,[21] arguing instead that it is the preacher's task to declare the whole counsel of God, as revealed in his word, not to discriminate between what is useful and what is not. This is consistent with Calvin's basic idea that predestination is not simply an abstract theological truth, but has profound practical implications as well. It is part and parcel of that twofold knowledge, with reference to which the *Institutes* begins, that is of the essence of Christian piety.

One final point in reference to Calvin's teaching on election is his reference to Christ as "the mirror" of election. Calvin's fondness for images drawn from the world of optical science is well-known, though this image appears to have been drawn from Augustine. Christ is the mirror of election because he did not earn the right to be Son of God but was so freely; and was afterward given the honor to share his gifts with others. Christ is thus himself an example of God's election. This is an important part of Calvin's understanding of predestination, with clear polemical and pastoral implications. Polemically, it is part of his rejection of the notion that merit plays any part in God's decision to elect. The elect person is chosen not because of any intrinsic merit or righteousness but purely as a free gift of God. Of course, Christ was righteous; but Calvin's point is that it was not his righteousness that made him Son of God and Head of the Church; rather it was a free, gracious decision of God himself that did so, and, as such, he is paradigm of the election of the church as a whole. The pastoral corollary to this is the fact that the believer does not engage in introspection to find the reason for election but looks outwardly to Christ, to see there God's grace most clearly revealed. In a famous passage in *Institutes* 3.22.1, he says,

20. See *Institutes* 3.21.1.
21. See ibid., 3.21.3.

If they [those proposing election on the basis of foreknown merits] shift the argument to individual persons where they find the inequality more objectionable, they ought at least so to tremble at the example of Christ as not to prate irresponsibly about this lofty mystery. He is conceived a mortal man of the seed of David. By what virtues will they say that he deserved in the womb itself to be made head of the angels, only-begotten Son of God, image and glory of the Father, light, righteousness, and salvation of the world? Augustine wisely notes this: namely, that we have in the very Head of the church the clearest mirror of free election that we who are among the members may not be troubled about it; and that he was not made Son of God by righteous living but was freely given such honor so that he might afterward share his gifts with others.

The reference to Augustine shows a further point of continuity with Augustine on the matter of predestination since he also argued that Christ was the object of predestination as he was to be made incarnate.[22] It is also a point of significance for later Reformed Orthodoxy as it will be picked up and developed in significant dogmatic ways: it points clearly toward the standard Reformed position that Jesus Christ was mediator according to his person (and thus according to both natures); and also stands in positive relation to the seventeenth-century Reformed development of the notion of the covenant of redemption between the Father and the Son.

PRELIMINARY NOTE ON CALVIN AND THEOLOGICAL AND PEDAGOGICAL DEVELOPMENTS

In a short essay such as this, there is not time to address the many issues that arose after Calvin relative to the doctrine of election, and so much of what follows will focus less on individual thinkers and more on the broad confessional statements produced by the Reformed churches during the sixteenth and seventeenth centuries, statements that were generally not concerned to deal with many of the intramural debates that arose, such as that between infralapsarians and supralapsarians.

The form of expression did change as Reformed Protestantism reintroduced the language of medieval theology into its discourse, a point which has been seen by some as involving a reversion to a more deterministic view of the world built on Aristotelian causality, something sometimes laid almost single-handedly at the feet of men like Calvin's successor, Theodore Beza, and others such as Jerome Zanchi.[23] To put the point succinctly: there had been much discussion

22. *De praedestinatione sanctorum*, 31.

23. See, for example, Ernst Bizer, *Frühorthodoxie und Rationalismus* (Zurich: EVZ, 1963); Joseph Daninte, "Les Tabelles sur la Doctrine de la Prédestination par Theodore de Bèze," *Revue de Théologie et de Philosophie* 16 (1966), 365–77. For thoroughgoing critiques of such arguments, see Muller, *After Calvin*; also Paul Helm, "Calvin (and Zwingli) on Divine Providence," *Calvin Theological Journal* 29 (1994), 388–405.

of the nature of grace, necessity, and contingency in the Middle Ages, large parts of which were extremely useful to Protestants when it came to nuancing their understanding of election, reprobation, and the concomitant problems and questions that these doctrines tended to raise. Given that the most deterministic treatise written in the Reformation was arguably Luther's *De Servo Arbitrio*, it was definitely to the advantage of Protestants in general that they familiarize themselves with the medieval material in order to present more satisfying accounts of divine foreknowledge and the human will.

In this context, Calvin's disdain (and apparent lack of detailed knowledge of) medieval distinctions stands in marked contrast to later generations of the Reformed, but there is no need to assume that this change in form is indicative of fundamental changes in content or purpose.[24] The continuities can be seen in the basic concerns being safeguarded (the sovereignty and unilateral nature of God's grace) and the doctrinal points being elaborated (double predestination, etc.). Yet the language used does not reflect that of Calvin for the simple reason that Calvin did not need to make the fine distinctions that later polemics and pedagogy demanded of Protestant theologians. When faced with a Bellarmine or Arminius, the need for a theologically precise vocabulary was intensified, and just such was already at hand from medieval forebears.

The apparent resurgence of interest in Aristotle and deployment of Aristotelian causal language do not in themselves indicate the development of a hardening determinism with Reformed theology. We have already noted that Calvin, like Luther, saw all things, even the fall itself, as predetermined by God; and Aristotelian language was not eliminated by the Reformation, only to reappear again; it never left university discourse, and, as Protestantism established itself within the universities in the later sixteenth century, it simply came to adopt many of the relevant forms. In fact, Aristotle's corpus continued to shape the basic foundations of Western thought until the Enlightenment (in terms of general metaphysics) and the late nineteenth century (in terms of logic), and the Reformation did not alter the fundamental trajectories of this, which had actually been set in the twelfth and thirteenth centuries.[25]

Further, even Calvin himself occasionally used Aristotelian causality in the context of issues relating to election and predestination. Thus, in his reply to Pighius, he points out that, according to Aristotelian causality, if human nature is wicked and depraved, then all of its actions, though voluntary and spontaneous with reference to the individual's will, must yet be wicked and depraved. Aristotelian causality binds nature and actions together.[26]

24. One example of Calvin's disdain for, and ignorance of, medieval theological conceptual vocabulary, is his rejection of the distinction between God's absolute power and ordained power in *Institutes* 3.23.2. In fact, he rejects the term but teaches the concept, as shown by David C. Steinmetz, *Calvin in Context* (New York: Oxford University Press, 1995), 40–52.

25. See Carl R. Trueman, *The Claims of Truth: John Owen's Trinitarian Theology* (Carlisle: Paternoster, 1998), 34–44.

26. *The Bondage and Liberation of the Will*, 49–50.

In this regard, it is also worth noting the problems associated with the question of so-called limited atonement: while the question has been asked by numerous scholars as to whether Calvin held to the later position, it is actually somewhat anachronistic to pose the matter in this way. The later position developed in the context of reactions to Arminianism and Socinianism, of which Calvin was blissfully unaware. Certainly his theology helped to create the context where such questions needed to be asked; and it is arguable that the concerns of later "limited atonement" advocates stand in continuity with those of Calvin himself; but to demand of a sixteenth-century theologian that he conform to, or even answer questions based on, the standards of seventeenth-century Reformed Orthodoxy, is not an appropriate one for the careful historian. The same applies to an extent to later debates about supra- and infralapsarianism: precise and finely tooled theological taxonomy developed after the death of Calvin to which it is inappropriate to hold his own views.

REFORMED CONFESSIONS
IN THE SIXTEENTH CENTURY

Reformed theology was, of course, an ecclesiastical movement and thus not formally dependent on the views of any private individual or minister for its doctrinal positions; rather, it expressed its commitments through confessional documents. The sixteenth century was rich in such production, particularly in the era subsequent to the Council of Trent, when Catholicism had formally declared itself on many contested heads of doctrine, and both ecclesiastical and geographical politics made it necessary for Protestants to do the same.

Among the major confessional statements of the mid- to late sixteenth century are the Scots Confession (1560), the Belgic Confession (1561), the Heidelberg Catechism (1563), the Hungarian Confession (1562), the Second Helvetic Confession (1566), and the Thirty-nine Articles (1563/71).

The Scots Confession

The guiding hand behind the Scots Confession was that of the reformer, former resident of Geneva, and friend of Calvin, John Knox. While Knox himself wrote a massive treatise on predestination to refute an Anabaptist (possibly in an attempt to ingratiate himself with Calvin after the diplomatic disasters caused by his *First Blast of the Trumpet against the Monstrous Regiment of Women*) the confession contains only one article (no. 8) on election, in which the focus is on election *in Christ*, with the argument of the article being devoted to a statement of Christology and the benefits that the believer possesses through this union. As such, it arguably emphasizes more the Augustine-Calvin trajectory on Christ as the mirror of election than Calvin's development of the notion of double predestination.[27]

The Belgic Confession

Scholars generally agree that the Belgic Confession was the work of Huguenot pastor and martyr, Guillaume de Brès. Article 16 deals with election, stating simply that God manifested his mercy by electing some out of mere goodness to salvation and his justice by leaving the rest to perish.[28] The Article is followed by discussion of Christology.[29] As such, the confessional statement does not go as far as Calvin in making explicit a notion of double predestination, though this is perhaps to be expected in a document that was designed to represent a Reformed consensus.

The Heidelberg Catechism

The Heidelberg Catechism, produced by Zacharias Ursinus for the Elector Palatine, Frederick III, contains no article on predestination, even though Ursinus was an Orthodox Reformed theologian. The reason for this would appear to be related to the political situation in the Palatinate, where Frederick III had moved from Lutheranism to the Reformed faith. In the years after the death of Luther in 1546, Lutheranism was significantly divided on the issue of predestination, with the so-called Gnesio-Lutherans pursuing a path that attempted to remain consistent with the Luther of 1525, while the so-called Philippists, or followers of Melanchthon, opted for a more moderate, if not quasi-Erasmian approach. With Frederick III's move to the Reformed faith, he desired to try to forge an ecumenical consensus in the Palatinate between the Philippists and the Reformed, and the Heidelberg Catechism was part of this overall agenda. Thus, predestination was kept out of sight.[30]

The Hungarian Confession

The Hungarian Confession is structured in a Trinitarian manner, dealing with the various topics of theology in terms of Father, Son, and Holy Spirit. In the section on the Son, the confession argues (article 3.16) that God has made

27. Philip Schaff, *The Creeds of Christendom,* 6th ed., vol. 3 (Grand Rapids: Baker reprint of 1931 ed., 2007), 444–45.

28. Ibid., 401.

29. On the Belgic Confession, see Nicolaas H. Gootjes, *The Belgic Confession: Its History and Sources* (Grand Rapids: Baker, 2007).

30. For the text of the Catechism, see Schaff, *Creeds,* 3:307–55. On the history and context of its composition, see Lyle D. Bierma, ed., *An Introduction to the Heidelberg Catechism: Sources, History, and Theology* (Grand Rapids: Baker, 2005); Willem van't Spijker, ed., *The Church's Book of Comfort* (Grand Rapids: Reformation Heritage Books, 2009).

human sin the opportunity for revealing his glory by electing some to eternal life, demonstrating his love and grace, and by preparing other vessels for destruction, thus revealing his power, wrath, and justice.[31] Significantly, in an earlier article (3.2), the confession states that Jesus Christ was appointed as mediator between God and the elect in eternity, again reflecting Calvin's own emphasis on Christ as elect and as the mirror of election.[32]

The Second Helvetic Confession

The Second Helvetic Confession was the handiwork of Heinrich Bullinger, the successor of Luther's old nemesis, Huldrych Zwingli. While friendly to Calvin, Bullinger did not agree with Calvin's position on double predestination. It is thus not surprising to find that chapter 10 of the confession, following on from discussion of free will in chapter 9, uses predestination and election as synonyms and focuses on the single predestination of the elect to life.[33] This is followed, in chapter 11, by a statement concerning the predestination and election of Christ as mediator, and this as providing the eternal basis for the historical incarnation.[34]

The Thirty-Nine Articles

The Thirty-nine Articles of the Church of England were a slight revision of the earlier Forty-two Articles (1553), made by convocation in 1563, though the final version was not approved until 1571, due in part to wrangling over article 29 ("Of the Wicked which eat not the Body of Christ") caused by diplomatic negotiations with the German Lutheran princes. In their final form, article 17, "Of predestination and election," offered a simple statement of single predestination, along with a basic *ordo salutis*: election, calling, justification, adoption, increasing conformity to Christ, and eternal life.[35] This no doubt reflects the need for the articles to foster a broad consensus, as it is clear that Calvin's double predestinarianism had caused some tension in the reign of Edward VI when Bartholomew Traheron, returning from exile in Geneva, clashed with the more Melanchthonian John Hopper on precisely this issue.[36] The lack of elaboration meant that the article would soon become vulnerable to interpretations that subverted the original anti-Pelagian intent.

In short, even a brief survey of Reformed confessional material from the mid-sixteenth century indicates that there was a basic and broad anti-Pelagianism

---

31. E. F. K. Müller, *Die Bekenntnisschriften der reformierten Kirche* (Leipzig: Böhme, 1903), 381.
32. Ibid., 378.
33. Schaff, *Creeds*, 3:252–54.
34. Ibid., 3:254–58.
35. Ibid., 3:497.
36. See Carl R. Trueman, *Luther's Legacy: Salvation and English Reformers, 1525–1556* (Oxford: Clarendon Press, 1994), 215–35.

consensus on the matter of predestination and, while Calvin's more strict double predestinarian views did not enjoy widespread confessional status, this position was certainly not excluded; indeed, it seems likely that the confessions were framed as they were in order to embrace the anti-Pelagian diversity of the early Reformation. Further, Calvin's development of election in relation to Christ, and thus his rooting of Christology in the eternal and inner workings of the Godhead, was not a theme unique to him but one that was both confessional and that would bear fruit in the coming years.

REACTION IN THE LATER SIXTEENTH CENTURY

It was not long, however, before cracks in the anti-Pelagian edifice of Reformed theology began to show. In England, the lectures by Peter Baro in his (in)famous sermons on the book of Jonah, *In Jonam prophetam praelectiones 39* (London, 1579), brought him under suspicion for his views on free will and predestination in Cambridge in the 1570s, and, indeed, into conflict with the authorities. Baro's apparently deviant teaching had to be addressed directly by the church, and so Archbishop of Canterbury, John Whitgift, ultimately responded with the so-called Lambeth Articles. What the Baro controversy made clear was the fact that the simple teaching of article 17 of the Thirty-nine Articles was simply too ambiguous in the developing polemical situation to safeguard the anti-Pelagian consensus of the earlier generation of Calvin, Bullinger, Cranmer, and company. Indeed, by the late sixteenth century, previous assumptions about how the articles would be read no longer applied.

The nine articles of the Lambeth Articles arguably represent a position on predestination that is more in accord with the details of Calvin's own approach than the Thirty-nine Articles, though, again, the generic nature of Calvin's own thinking in this area is sufficient to prevent any claims that he represented a unique influence on their formulation. Article 1 of the Lambeth Articles clearly states a double predestinarian position, with election and reprobation enjoying a parallel status; article 2 denies that election is based on foreseen merit; article 3 asserts, in typical Augustinian fashion, that the number of the elect is fixed; article 4 asserts that those not predestined are condemned on account of their actual sins; and the final six articles cumulatively point to the fact that effectual, saving grace, is particular, not general. On each of these points, the articles are arguably more precisely in conformity with the theological tradition of Calvin than the Thirty-nine articles; and the clarity on predestination indicates a clear sympathy for a Genevan rather than a Bullinger/Zurich position.[37]

37. Schaff, *Creeds*, 3:523–25.

The fact that the Anglican Church found it necessary to draw up such supplementary articles at the end of the sixteenth century indicates the strain then being placed on the original Thirty-nine Articles by the apparent breakdown of the anti-Pelagian consensus within Anglicanism. While approved by both Archbishops Whitgift and Hutton, they yet failed to enjoy the approbation of Queen Elizabeth, ostensibly on the ground that the Lambeth Synod, which approved them, had met without her permission. Still, they were to enjoy more formal status when the Irish Articles were composed in 1615.

Perhaps the single most influential development, after the death of Calvin, was pioneered by a one-time student at the Genevan Academy and pupil of Theodore Beza, Calvin's successor, named Jacob Arminius. Arminius came from the Netherlands and, while initially enamored with the Geneva articulation of election, later came to reject it and replace it with a modified predestinarianism that effectively overturned Calvin's approach at key points.[38] Drawing on theological and philosophical models provided by Jesuit theologians such as Luis Molina and Francisco Suárez, Arminius proposed a species of divine knowledge between the typical medieval distinction of God's knowledge of simple intelligence (God's knowledge of everything of which he is capable) and his knowledge of vision (God's knowledge of that which he has determined to do). Middle knowledge, or *scientia media,* was God's knowledge of all possible worlds and all the possible outcomes contained therein. This knowledge is a conditioned and consequent knowledge of future contingents. Soteriologically, this was useful in apparently solving the problem of divine sovereignty and human freedom: humans freely chose to believe in Christ; and God actualized that world that contained the outcomes he so desired, even as these outcomes were the result of human free choice.[39]

The unacceptable theological implications of this for the Reformed Orthodox were twofold: first, it allowed for a free contingency that denied that God was the logically prior specifying cause of actions and events; and, second, the notion of human depravity was dramatically attenuated, given the fact that, for Luther, Calvin, and company, sinful human beings could never, under their own power, turn to Christ unless specifically predestined and moved to do so by God. Thus, middle knowledge represented a rejection of anti-Pelagianism in terms of both its ontology and its soteriology: ontologically, it allowed for a radical contingency that gave human action a logical priority over God's foreknowledge; and, soteriologically, it allowed the human decision to turn to Christ a truly decisive role in salvation.[40]

---

38. Arminius's works are available in translation: *The Works of James Arminius,* trans. James Nichols and William Nichols, 3 vols. (Grand Rapids: Baker, 1986).

39. On Arminius theology, and its connection to Jesuit thought, see Richard A. Muller, *God, Creation, and Providence in the Thought of Jacob Arminius* (Grand Rapids: Baker, 1991); Eef Dekker, "Was Arminius a Molinist?" *Sixteenth Century Journal* 27 (1996), 337–52.

40. The definitive Reformed response came from William Twisse, first prolocutor of the Westminster Assembly: *Dissertatio de Scientia Media* (Arnhme, 1639).

THE REMONSTRANCE OF 1610
AND THE SYNOD OF DORDRECHT, 1618–19

As Arminianism gained ground in the Netherlands, it became the focus for a political struggle, dividing the Dutch regents and precipitating a theological battle between the Remonstrants (Arminian churchmen), so called because of their publication of a Remonstrance in 1610, and the Reformed Orthodox, or Counter-Remonstrants. The Remonstrance proposed five basic doctrinal points relative to salvation, the cumulative effect of which is the repudiation of the kind of anti-Pelagian theology articulated by Calvin and the Reformed. Article 1 makes predestination the result of God's foreknowledge of who will have faith and persevere to the end. Article 2 argues for a hypothetically universal atonement that only has saving value for those who trust in Christ. Article 3 stresses the need for individuals to be born again through the gracious activity of God, an article which, in itself, does not appear on the surface to challenge standard anti-Pelagian theology. Article 4, however, elaborates on the issue and makes it clear that grace is not irresistible; by implication, therefore, conversion is a cooperative exercise in which the human will has a decisive role. Finally, article 5 offers a highly equivocal view of the perseverance of the saints.[41]

The Remonstrance precipitated an intellectual, theological, and political struggle in the Netherlands that came to a head in 1618–19 when, at the Synod of Dordrecht, the Reformed Orthodox, or Counter-Remonstrants, routed their theological and political opponents in front of delegates from various European states, including England. The resulting doctrinal statement, the Canons of Dort, offered four points covering five heads of doctrine in response. Article 1.7 is perhaps the key one with regard to predestination:

> Election is the unchangeable purpose of God, whereby, before the foundation of the world, he hath, out of his mere grace, according to the sovereign good pleasure of his own will, chosen, from the whole human race, which had fallen through their own fault, from their primitive state of rectitude, into sin and destruction, a certain number of persons to redemption in Christ, whom he from eternity appointed the Mediator and head of the elect, and the foundation of salvation.[42]

There are several important points in this article. First, the object of election in this passage is clearly human beings considered in their fallen state. This is technically known as infralapsarianism, as opposed to supralapsarianism, the idea that the object of election is human beings considered in their unfallen, pristine state. This does not mean that all who were at Dort were infralapsarians: as is typical of the way such documents functioned at the time, this infralapsarian

41. Schaff, *Creeds*, 545–49.
42. Ibid., 582.

bent did not prevent supralapsarians from endorsing the document.[43] It also gave the document a somewhat more moderate tendency than the double pedestinarian position of Calvin: although the supra/infra distinction is not identical to that between double and single predestinarians, it does allow the divines at Dort to use language in article 1.15 that defines reprobation as God leaving the reprobate in their unbelief, a point that seems less strident than the position advocated by Calvin.[44] Second, the article also references the appointment of Christ as Mediator; this would seem to stand in line with Calvin's earlier reference to Christ as the mirror of election and also to represent a concept that some thirty years later will receive terminological expression in the language of covenant of redemption, or *pactum salutis*.

This points also to the second head of doctrine on the death of Christ. Articles 2.3 and 2.4 make it clear that Christ's death is of infinite value, based on the hypostatic union of perfect humanity and the second person of the Trinity and on the wrath of God that was visited upon Christ. This infinite sufficiency, however, is qualified by the finite efficiency of the atonement, as expressed in 2.8, whereby it is made clear that the divine intention of Christ's appointment as Mediator and Sacrifice was the redemption of the elect. Thus, we see clearly a nexus between election and Christology, consistent with Calvin's earlier conceptualizations, which adopts the standard sufficiency/efficiency distinction codified by Peter Lombard in his *Four Books of Sentences*.[45]

BRITISH CONFESSIONAL CODIFICATION IN THE SEVENTEENTH CENTURY

The establishment of Reformed Protestantism, both politically and institutionally, in the latter part of the sixteenth century, in places such as England, Scotland, and the Low Countries, had an influential impact on the way in which the theology of the Reformed tradition was developed, taught, and expressed. In this regard, the most significant creedal expressions of the Reformed faith were the Irish Articles (1615) and the Westminster Standards (1640s).

The Irish Articles

The Irish Articles were the production of the Episcopal Church of Ireland and in many ways represent the kinds of developments taking place in the Reformed faith in the seventeenth century, the rising independence of the Irish Church

---

43. On the issue of infra- and supralapsarianism, note that the categories are logical, not chronological. In other words, infralapsarians believed that the decree was from eternity and that it was not introduced as an emergency measure after the fall. Rather, the point is that, for infralapsarians, God, in eternity, first decreed creation, then fall, then election; and all this prior to the actual execution of any part of the plan in time.

44. Schaff, *Creeds*, 555.

45. *IV Libri Sententiarum* 3.20.3.

relative to its Anglican parent, and the ongoing concerns with closing confessional loopholes witnessed to by the earlier Lambeth Articles in 1595, which were themselves incorporated into Irish Articles.

On the confessional front, the articles have provoked some disagreement among commentators. An early critic, Peter Heylyn, regarded them as a surreptitious attempt by the more radically Reformed to impose views more strictly in line with Calvin upon the Church of Ireland, in large part because of their positive appropriation of the Lambeth Articles, but also for other distinctives at the time, such as the identification of the pope as the antichrist.[46] On the other side, R. B. Knox simply regarded the Irish Articles as substantially little more than an elaboration of the doctrine of the Thirty-nine Articles.[47]

Whatever the truth of the relationship between the Irish Articles and the Thirty-nine Articles, it is clear that the former involve a massive elaboration of the latter, whereby the matter of predestination, dealt with in a single article (17) in the Thirty-nine Articles, is expanded to seven (11 through 17) in the Irish Articles. In article 11, God's sovereignty is established, and, consistent with the way in which the conceptual language of Reformed Orthodoxy was developing in sophistication, the point is made that this does not remove but rather establishes the liberty and contingency of second causes. Additionally, in article 16, the typical Calvinian emphasis on election and predestination as the foundation of assurance is also made. Most significantly, in article 12, drawn from the Lambeth Articles, a clear statement is made concerning double predestination, which includes the fixed number of the elect: "By the same counsel God hath predestinated some unto life, and reprobated some unto death: of both which there is a certain number, known only to God, which can neither be increased nor diminished."[48] The placement of the doctrine directly subsequent to, and as a subset of, providence and divine sovereignty, is not that which one finds in Calvin's *Institutes*; but, as noted above, there are reasons beside the dogmatic that can explain Calvin's topical ordering, which are, in themselves, quite adequate to account for this; and the Irish Articles are a confessional document, not part of an exegetical handbook; and thus topical ordering would inevitably be shaped by different concerns and criteria. No explicit connection is made to election and the atonement in articles 29 and 30, which state simply that Christ "came as a lamb without spot to take away the sins of the world."

Ultimately, the Irish Articles' significance lies in the fact that they represented the formal enshrining of the Calvinist consensus in the early seventeenth century. While the principal author, James Ussher, saw them as doing little more than elaborating and explicating theology already implicit in the Thirty-nine Articles, they actually defined the Irish Church in a way that marked it off from

---

46. *Aerius redivivus* (Oxford, 1670), 394.

47. Cited by Alan Ford, *James Ussher: Theology, History, and Politics in Early-Modern Ireland and England* (Oxford: Oxford University Press, 2007), 89.

48. Schaff, *Creeds*, 3: 528.

mainland Anglicanism. The latter was to become, under the tutelage of William Laud in the 1620s and 1630s, implacably opposed to the theology that the Irish Articles represented. That theology was arguably (and ironically) of the Anglican Church's founding fathers who would have had little issue with the main points of Calvin's theology of election.[49]

The Westminster Assembly

The Westminster Assembly, authorized by Parliament, sat between 1643 and 1653, although its main work was completed by 1649. It was originally convened in order to revise the doctrine and liturgy of the Church of England, but parliamentary desire to recruit the Scottish Presbyterians for the conflict against King Charles I led to the signing of the Solemn League and Covenant in late 1643, which paved the way for the addition of Scottish commissioners and the broadening of the Assembly's brief to a more wholesale reformation of the church along Reformed and Presbyterian lines.

The key documents produced by the Assembly were The Directory of Public Worship (1645), the Larger and Shorter Catechisms (1648), and the Westminster Confession of Faith (1647). Like the Canons of Dort, these documents were the production of an assembly, with no individual having a dominant hand in composition; nevertheless, we know from the recently edited minutes of the Assembly that Calvin was frequently cited as an authority; and thus the Standards were intended to be part of the ongoing tradition of Reformed Orthodoxy which sought self-consciously to stand in continuity with the work of an earlier generation of Reformers.[50]

The language that the Westminster divines used with reference to predestination is careful and cautious. In chapter 3 of the confession, "Of God's Eternal Decree," there is a general statement about God's foreordination of everything that comes to pass, yet in a manner that involves no sin on his part or violence to creaturely freedom or secondary causes (3.1); a rejection of any notion of conditional foreknowledge (3.2); then four paragraphs (3.3–3.6) dealing with election; and finally, a paragraph on reprobation (3.7) and a caution (3.8) about an over-speculative approach to the doctrine of predestination as a whole.[51] Significantly, the Assembly used studiedly different language to speak about election and reprobation: the elect are predestinated and foreordained (3.3); the reprobate are passed by and ordained to their fate. The linguistic difference is perhaps small; but it is still noteworthy that it makes a subtle distinction, thus preventing any precise parallelism between the two and hinting, albeit cautiously, at a more infralapsarian construction of the decree.

---

49. Ford, *James Ussher*, 102.
50. See Chad Van Dixhoorn, "Reforming the Reformation: Theological Debate at the Westminster Assembly 1642–1652," PhD diss. (University of Cambridge, 2004).
51. *Westminster Confession of Faith* (Glasgow: Free Presbyterian Publications, 1976), 28–31.

The Westminster Standards also articulate a fairly well-developed covenant theology. The language of "covenant of works" is not yet rigidly fixed as the term for the pre-fall arrangement with Adam, so, while the standard term is used in the Confession (Westminster Confession of Faith, WCF 7.2), the Catechisms prefer "covenant of life" (Larger Catechism 20; Shorter Catechism 12). In Reformed Orthodoxy, the pre-fall arrangement sets one of the basic structures for understanding Christology, particularly in terms of Paul's arguments from Adam to Christ in Romans 5 and 1 Corinthians 15, and so this also provides a nexus for Christology and predestination in the economy of salvation.

Chapter 8 of the confession picks up on the earlier Reformed emphasis on Christ as himself elect, and in 8.1 speaks explicitly of his eternal appointment as Mediator for the elect. This is then the foundation for his incarnation and his earthly ministry (empowered by the Holy Spirit, 8.3), and also for his death and intercession on behalf of "all those whom the Father hath given unto Him" (WCF 8.5). This is a robust statement of particular redemption, of a kind that is not found explicitly in Calvin, but which is arguably built upon elements clearly present in Calvin's theology: predestination and the election of Christ as Mediator. In this context, it is of little more than chronological significance that the language of the covenant of redemption is absent from the Standards: while the term had surface in David Dickson's 1638 address to the General Assembly of the Church of Scotland, references to the appointment of Christ as Mediator by the Father in terms of covenant language did not really start to appear with any frequency in Reformed theology until the latter half of the 1640s, effectively too late to have had significant impact on the Assembly.[52]

POSTCONFESSIONAL DEVELOPMENTS

The mid- to late seventeenth century witnessed not only the development of Reformed theology into its most elaborate forms, with figures such as Francis Turretin, John Owen, Edward Leigh and Petrus van Mastricht producing voluminous works articulating and defending the Reformed faith,[53] it also saw the development of yet more theological sub-traditions within the Reformed world. The most significant of these was undoubtedly Amyraldianism, the name given to a particular stream of theology that found its origin in the work of theologians at the School of Saumur in France, particularly a Scotsman, John Cameron, and a Frenchman, Moïse Amyraut.

52. See Alexander Peterkin, ed., *Records of the Kirk of Scotland, Containing the Acts and Proceedings of the General Assemblies from the Year 1638 Downwards* (Edinburgh: Peter Brown, 1843), 159; Carol A. Williams, "'The Decree of Redemption Is in Effect a Covenant': David Dickson and the Covenant of Redemption," PhD diss. (Calvin Theological Seminary, 2005); Carl R. Trueman, *John Owen: Reformed Catholic, Renaissance Man* (Aldershot: Ashgate, 2007), 80–99.

53. Francis Turretin, *Institutio theologiae elencticae*, 3 vols. (Geneva, 1679–85); Edward Leigh, *A Systeme or Body of Divinity* (London, 1662); Petrus van Mastricht, *Theoretico-practica theologia* (Amsterdam, 1682–87).

The Catholic French context was culturally fertile soil for a form of Reformed theology that was perhaps a little less rigid on key points than one might find elsewhere, where Reformed thinkers were essentially in control; and this is what Amyraldianism provided. What Amyraldianism did was offer a form of hypothetical universalism that softened some of the stricter positions, particularly on atonement, while yet maintaining the basics of the Reformed faith: the sovereignty of God; the universal fall of humanity in Adam and its subsequent depravity; and the sovereign, particular election of some to salvation.

While Amyraldianism, like all theological movements, contained a certain amount of diversity, its basic distinctive was the way in which it reordered the divine decrees in order to establish an objective basis for God's universal love toward humanity. In standard Reformed Orthodoxy, of the Dort or Westminster variety, the divine decree to appoint Christ as Mediator was logically subsequent to the decree to elect. In other words, God first decides to elect a subset of the human race and then decides to appoint Christ as Mediator to be a sacrifice and an interceder on their behalf. Thus, the meaning of Christ's mediation is decisively shaped—one might even say "delimited"—by the decree of election.

In Amyraldian theology, however, the logical ordering of the decrees is changed, placing the decree to appoint Christ as Mediator in a position logically prior to the decree to elect some to salvation. This has significant impact on the understanding of Christ's mediation. First, it generates a universalism whereby statements such as "Christ died for all" are in a sense true. Thus, those passages in Scripture that speak of a universality to God's love, and, indeed, a universality to the scope of Christ's death, can be read in a straightforward way that requires no theological nuancing or even equivocation. [54]

Second, it requires either a distinction in scope between Christ's death and his intercession (the former for all, the latter only for the elect) or an equivocal understanding of "all" or "world" whereby Christ does die for the whole world, but not equally for the whole world. The impact of predestination is still important theologically and poses obvious homiletic and pastoral challenges. For example, while the Amyraldian scheme would enable a pastor to tell a troubled congregant that Christ had indeed died for him or her, it is arguable that the key question for assurance in such circumstances would not be "Did Christ die for me?" but rather "Is Christ interceding for me?" Thus, the *particularism* of election is still operative; the Amyraladian scheme has not defused the problems of particularity; rather, it has shifted them from the cross of Calvary to the right hand of the Father in heaven. [55]

---

54. Amyraut's major exposition of predestination and redemption is found in his *Brief traitté de la predestination et de ses principales dependances* (Saumur, 1634).

55. These are the points made (positively and approvingly) by two modern writers on the subject: R. T. Kendall, *Calvin and English Calvinism to 1649* (Oxford: Oxford University Press, 1979); Alan C. Clifford, *Atonement and Justification* (Oxford: Oxford University Press, 1990). For a response to Kendall, see Paul Helm, "Calvin and the Logic of Doctrinal Development," *Scottish Journal of Theology* 34 (1981), 179–85; idem, *Calvin and the Calvinists* (Edinburgh: Banner of Truth, 1982).

Despite the title of Brian Armstrong's influential book on the subject—*Calvinism and the Amyraut Heresy*—Amyraldiansim was not considered a heresy by the Reformed Orthodox but rather an error. There is a clear qualitative difference between the terms used for, say, Arminians and Socinians, and those applied to the adherents of the School of Saumur. Thus, while theologians such as Francis Turretin and John Owen were vigorously critical of certain aspects of Amyraldian thought, they considered the debates to be largely intramural, between learned brethren, and not between antithetical theological camps. It is in this broader context that we need to read the narrower polemical intent of, say, Turretin's authoring of the Helvetic Formula Consensus, which addressed both Amyraldian universalism and certain issues of biblical text criticism, specifically the debates surrounding the antiquity of the Masoretic vowel points.[56]

John Owen is even more interesting from this perspective. He is happy to refer to John Cameron as a very learned theologian and to list him among his close allies on the issue of divine justice, yet he was also the finest exponent of particular redemption, the nexus point of predestination and Christology, in the seventeenth century.[57] Responding to claims that Christ's death only made salvation a hypothetical possibility, and was not in itself effectual, Owen penned his *The Death of Death in the Death of Christ* in 1647. In this work, he assumed the basic predestinarian scheme of Reformed Orthodoxy, and the unity of Christ's mediatorial office, in terms of the identical scope of both his death and consequent intercession. He also argued that because Christ's death could only be a sacrifice for those on whose behalf he was appointed Mediator, all talk of Christ's death having infinite value on the grounds of the hypostatic union of the divine and the human was specious. This was because both the hypostatic union and the sacrifice were determined by the logically prior covenant of redemption between Father, Son, and Holy Spirit. In this work, we therefore see the final development of the kind of ideas we first saw in Calvin, where Christ is himself the prime example of God's election.[58]

THE COLLAPSE OF REFORMED ORTHODOXY

The late seventeenth century and the eighteenth century saw a major collapse, both on the continent and in Britain, of the tradition of Reformed Orthodoxy stemming from Calvin. On the continent, the impact of Cartesianism in universities led to an erosion of the metaphysical context in which traditional orthodoxy had flourished. Nowhere was this seen more dramatically than in the

56. For the text of the Helvetic Formula Consensus, see Müller, *Bekenntnisschriften*, 861–70.

57. For Owen's approval of Cameron, see *The Works of John Owen*, 23 vols. (London: Johnstone and Hunter, 1850–53), vol. 10, 488. He will also link him with Voetius as "those two thunderbolts of theological war" and considers his arguments of divine justice to be far superior to those of Samuel Rutherford (*Works*, vol. 10, 507).

58. The text is in *Works* 10:139–428. For an analysis of Owen on Christ as Mediator, as it connects to his doctrines of God and predestination, see Trueman, *The Claims of Truth*.

Academy at Geneva, where Francis Turretin's own son, Jean Alphonse, symbolized in many ways the rejection of the kind of finely tooled theological system that his father had so ably articulated and which had underpinned documents such as the Helvetic Formula Consensus. For Jean Alphonse Turretin, such precise theology was the cause of division, and thus part of the problem he wished to overcome, not part of its solution.

In England, the Clarendon Code of the early 1660s drove the Puritans, the primary advocates of Reformed Orthodoxy, not only out of the established church but also out of the establishment in general: no longer were the universities, with their libraries and traditions of academic discourse, to be available to the Reformed. The result was catastrophic for orthodoxy: within a generation or two, English Presbyterianism had degenerated into Unitarianism and moralism.[59] Even so, there were a few who defended traditional predestinarian theology. The strict Baptist, John Gill, as a man born somewhat out of time, produced a major system of theology that argued for a clear supralapsarian and double predestinarian position, within the framework of traditional covenant theology, as modified by his sacramental theology. Gill was a polymath: his DD was awarded for his Hebraic studies (and that by the University of Aberdeen, since, as a non-Anglican, he was barred from receiving a degree from Oxford or Cambridge) and was also the author of a major commentary on the entire Bible as well as many controversial pamphlets defending a Reformed understanding of the doctrines of grace.[60]

Gill's close friend, the hymn writer, Augustus Montague Toplady, was the most sophisticated defender of such anti-Pelagianism within the Anglican fold, even penning a history of theology, with specific reference to the Anglican Church, *The Historic Proof of the Doctrinal Calvinism of the Church of England* (London, 1774) the polemical purpose of which was to establish the point that the thought of Calvin and the Reformed Orthodox was the position of the original Anglican Articles and Canons. This work also contained what is possibly the first reference to Calvinism as being defined by the five basic points of Dort. Thus, with Toplady, we see that the battles over the very nature of Anglican theological identity in general and connections to the early Reformed in particular, which the broad and concessive nature of the Thirty-nine Articles had helped to facilitate in the sixteenth century, continued into the eighteenth, though now more as a sideshow than a central part of the narrative. Toplady died young, aged only thirty-seven; the fact that his funeral was taken by his nonconformist friend, Gill, perhaps symbolizes the marginal nature of Toplady's theology to mainstream Anglicanism at this point. Perhaps the clash of the revivalist preachers, George Whitefield and John Wesley, was the last hurrah

---

59. Interestingly enough, the leading eighteenth-century Unitarian, Joseph Priestley, was still an admirer of latter day colonial Puritan and orthodox theologian, Jonathan Edwards, on the issue of determinism. See Robert E. Schofield, *The Enlightened Joseph Priestley* (Philadelphia: Penn State Press, 2004), 78.

60. John Gill, *A Complete Body of Doctrinal and Practical Divinity* (London, 1839).

for the traditional debate in eighteenth-century Anglicanism; but even here the arguments of Wesley were probably not derived from any extensive reading of the original literature arising from the debates between Calvin and his contemporaries or even Remonstrants and Reformed.[61]

CONCLUSION

The reception of Calvin's doctrine of election from the sixteenth to the early eighteenth century is problematic on the grounds that he did not have a particularly distinctive contribution that he made in this area. While his articulation of the double decree was a sharper formulation than that with which contemporaries such as Heinrich Bullinger were comfortable, it was scarcely unique in the history of Western theology, enjoying some precedent in Augustine, and clearly being consistent with the position articulated by numerous medieval theologians. Nevertheless, it is worth noting this difference even among the early Reformers in order to understand that there was (with the exception of the later Melanchthon) consensus on the broad contours of anti-Pelagian theology in the Reformation but not precise agreement on every point. Bullinger's failure to give wholehearted support to Calvin's attacks on Bolsec is a clear witness to this fact. Even allowing for this diversity, however, the key area where Calvin and his contemporaries made a significant contribution was not so much in the content of the doctrine as the connection they made between predestination and the issue of Christian assurance.

In the decades following Calvin, there appeared a Reformed Protestantism that was defining itself confessionally over against Catholicism and Lutheranism. While certain new debates emerged, most notably those between infra- and supralapsarians, these were intramural affairs; Reformed confessions typically adopted infralapsarian positions, but this did not exclude those of supralapsarian convictions from endorsing them.

At the end of the sixteenth century, however, the Reformed predestinarian consensus was breaking down. Peter Baro in England and Jacob Arminius on the continent not only questioned Reformed positions but offered alternative readings of Scripture and the doctrine of God that effectively overturned previous positions. This led to a further round of confessionalization in documents such as the Lambeth Articles, the Canons of Dort, and the Westminster Standards, which repristinated the old orthodoxy and further elaborated it. Later developments, such as Amyraldianism and the covenant of redemption, were only tangentially relevant to this latest phase of confession writing.

Finally, as the Enlightenment started to make significant inroads into the intellectual foundations of university curricula in the late seventeenth century,

---

61. See John Wesley, *Predestination Calmly Considered* (London, 1752). Interestingly enough, John Gill weighed in on the battle with Wesley: *The Doctrine of Predestination Stated, and Set in the Scripture Light* (London, 1752).

the old anti-Pelagian Augustinianism, of which Reformed Orthodoxy was a part, effectively collapsed. The eighteenth century saw a few influential advocates of the older positions, most notably Gill and Toplady. Yet the shift to Enlightenment epistemologies served to undermine confidence in the Bible, while Enlightenment ethics made the whole notion of predestination and federal theology somewhat distasteful and implausible. The stage was set for a fundamental reconstruction of large parts of Christian doctrine, not least those of predestination and election.

Chapter 6

Calvin's Theology of Election

Modern Reception
and Contemporary Possibilities

SUZANNE MCDONALD

HIGHLIGHTS IN THE HISTORY OF RECEPTION FROM THE EIGHTEENTH TO THE TWENTIETH CENTURY

In turning to the modern reception of Calvin's theology of election, it is inevitable that at times we are not dealing simply, directly, and exclusively with "Calvin's doctrine of election." We are also dealing with the way in which this has been received and reexpressed in the light of ongoing Reformed reflection on the subject as this is found, for example, in the Canons of Dort and the Westminster Standards. While the focus here will be on responses to Calvin himself, we will also be encountering reactions to accounts of election in which the basic ingredients remain those of Calvin, but in which there are also added flavors that reflect the methods and concerns of Calvin's successors.[1]

---

1. Like Carl Trueman in the preceding essay, I do not accept that a significant wedge can be driven between Calvin's account of election and that of his seventeenth-century Reformed successors. For a fine summary and analysis of the "Calvin versus the Calvinists" debate see Stephen R. Holmes, "Calvin against the Calvinists?" in *Listening to the Past: the Place of Tradition in Theology* (Grand Rapids: Baker Academic, 2002), 68–85.

This is seen particularly in two historical illustrations that indicate the extent to which the doctrine of election remains a storm center of theological controversy. Disputes over election play a part in defining a movement (Methodism) and fracturing a church (the Church of Scotland). Almost from the outset, the eighteenth-century Methodist revival movement in England and Wales reflects a split between the "Arminian" position of the Wesley brothers and the "Calvinist" position of George Whitefield and Howell Harris. Many of the issues at stake mirror the debates outlined in the previous chapter on the extent of the atonement, the source of faith, and the relationship between faith and election that culminate in the Synod of Dort.[2] In the nineteenth century, two prominent Scottish theologians (Thomas Erskine and John McLeod Campbell) questioned the scriptural and theological validity of "limited atonement," with McLeod Campbell being deposed from his ministry by the Church of Scotland on conviction of heresy for violating the Westminster Standards.[3]

In order to focus specifically on how aspects of Calvin's doctrine of election are received in this period, however, we will turn to a brief exploration of the two most significant reexpressions of the doctrine from within the Reformed tradition. Both Friedrich Schleiermacher and Karl Barth adopt some fundamental premises from Calvin while rejecting others, with each building his own particular doctrinal edifice upon a selective appropriation of Calvin's thought. The issues raised by the ways in which Schleiermacher and Barth respond to Calvin will lead to the second section of the chapter: some reflections on how contemporary theology might continue fruitfully to engage with Calvin's account of election.

Friedrich D. E. Schleiermacher (1768–1834)

At first glance, Friedrich Schleiermacher might seem an unlikely champion of Calvin's approach to the doctrine of election, but he is clear and forthright in his support of what he considers to be the nonnegotiable fundamentals of Calvin's account. He comes strongly to Calvin's defense in the midst of

2. Although, as Carl Trueman notes in the previous chapter, it is unlikely that John Wesley was particularly well-versed in the details of the earlier debates.

3. This in turn echoes aspects of the eighteenth-century "Marrowmen" controversy within the Church of Scotland, in which the church's General Assembly condemned the seventeenth-century treatise *The Marrow of Divinity* as incompatible with the Westminster Standards on several matters, including the extent of the atonement. *The Marrow* clearly and strongly upholds that Christ died only for the elect; the Assembly considered this to be incompatible with the equally clear and strong upholding of the universal offer of the gospel. For a brief orientation to the Marrow controversy and the thought and context of Erskine and McLeod Campbell, see the relevant articles in Nigel M. de S. Cameron, ed., *Dictionary of Scottish Church History and Theology* (Downers Grove: InterVarsity, 1993). For a recent account of Erskine's theology see Don Horrocks, *Laws of the Spiritual Order: Innovation and Reconstruction in the Soteriology of Thomas Erskine of Linlathen* (Wipf & Stock, 2007). For an overview of McLeod Campbell's thought see J. B. Torrance's introduction to the reprint of McLeod Campbell's *The Nature of the Atonement* (Grand Rapids: Eerdmans, 1996). For an exhaustive account of the Marrow controversy, see David C. Lachman, *The Marrow Controversy 1718–1723: An Historical and Theological Analysis* (Edinburgh: Rutherford House Press, 1988).

Reformed-Lutheran debate on the subject in his 1819 essay, *On the Doctrine of Election, Particularly in the Light of Herr Dr. Bretschneider's* Aphorisms.[4] The affirmation of these fundamentals and also the objections he raises to Calvin's doctrine in this essay are reiterated and developed when Schleiermacher turns to the subject of election in *The Christian Faith*.[5] A sketch of some key aspects of his account of election in *The Christian Faith* will highlight both the positive and negative aspects of his reception of Calvin and illustrate how he develops his highly distinctive position by building on elements of Calvin's thought in the light of his own theological priorities.

Turning first to those aspects of his approach that most clearly reflect Calvin's, Schleiermacher strongly insists on the absolute unconditionality of God's electing decree. All human beings are equally caught up in a common state of sinfulness, such that it is purely by the gracious electing will of God that some are called into fellowship with Christ, at the time of God's choosing by the effectual work of the Holy Spirit. Election is not based upon any merit in those chosen, and there is no capacity for turning to God in faith apart from that which God gives. We are in effect spiritually dead until we become a new creation in Christ by the Spirit.[6] God is therefore entirely sovereign over our response to him: faith is the pure gift of God, and Schleiermacher is clear that it is equally the will and determination of God to withhold that gift. In accord with Calvin, he therefore rejects the notion that while election is the active will and determination of God, "rejection" is a mere passing over aside from God's active willing.[7] Rejection, too, is the outcome of the will and foreordination of God, who determines human rejection of (or lack of exposure to) the gospel as well as its acceptance.

Election is therefore the basis of faith, rather than faith being in any way the condition of election. Schleiermacher explicitly rejects the notion that God's electing decree could rest upon foreseen faith and perseverance, since neither of these is possible apart from the will and determination of God. Election is

---

4. For an excellent English translation, see Friedrich Schleiermacher *On the Doctrine of Election, with Special Reference to the* Aphorisms *of Dr. Bretschneider,* Columbia Series in Reformed Theology, translated with an introduction and notes by Iain G. Nicol and Allen G. Jorgenson (Louisville, KY: Westminster John Knox, 2012).

5. I will be drawing mainly on the most readily accessible presentation of Schleiermacher's account of the doctrine (*The Christian Faith,* eds. H. R. Macintosh and J. S. Stewart (Edinburgh: T. & T. Clark, 1928), §§ 116–120), but the earlier essay mentioned here is of considerable interest and importance. For a summary and brief analysis, see Matthias Gockel, "New Perspectives on an Old Debate: Friedrich Schleiermacher's Essay on Election," *International Journal of Systematic Theology* 6 (2004): 301–18. See also his *Barth and Schleiermacher on the Doctrine of Election,* (Oxford: Oxford University Press, 2006). In the 1819 essay, Schleiermacher makes clear that he prefers to engage with Calvin himself rather than the views encapsulated in the Canons of Dort, which he considers to be an unduly harsh development of Calvin's position.

6. See Schleiermacher, *Christian Faith,* 534–35, 539–41.

7. Schleiermacher, *Christian Faith,* 550–51. Schleiermacher affirms the use of the term "passing over" in the context of his own distinctive position on the doctrine (548), but as an indication that this is a temporal rather than an eternal reality, without implying any distinction between God's determination of the elect and the rest of humanity.

dependent upon nothing but the decree of God and there can be no human response that falls outside of it.[8] In election, as in every aspect of the divine government of the world, everything takes place according to God's foreordination. This also means that to the question as to why some are brought into fellowship with Christ rather than others, and why at one particular time and not another, the only acceptable answer is that this is the good pleasure of God.[9]

Although not included in his account of election in *The Christian Faith*, in his essay *On the Doctrine of Election*, he further echoes aspects of Calvin's presentation of the doctrine by flatly rejecting any suggestion that this overall approach undermines human freedom and moral responsibility, or that it leads either to pride or despair, and also in urging that we seek assurance of our election firstly in Christ, and then in the sanctifying work of the Holy Spirit within us.[10]

Schleiermacher's understanding of election therefore upholds and reemphasizes several key themes that are central to Calvin's approach. He considers that Calvin's position is the best reflection of the scriptural witness to the basic human predicament, the priority of God's grace, and the nature of God's redeeming work in Christ. To Schleiermacher, it also best expresses the reality of true self-consciousness, and therefore true God-consciousness, by demonstrating our absolute dependence on God's will and determination for the gift of salvation. Although there is no space here to give an account of Schleiermacher's wider theological priorities, this is an illustration of how his thinking on election reflects a fundamental theme of his theology as a whole.

Nevertheless, while Schleiermacher seeks to place himself firmly within the overall framework set by Calvin, like many before and after him he resists the pull toward predestination to damnation, and its correlate of confining the saving work of Christ to a limited number of those predestined to salvation. Three interwoven themes are particularly important in demonstrating both his debt to Calvin and his radical departure from Calvin's conclusions: the role of history in the unfolding of election, Schleiermacher's insistence on the single will of God in election, and the universalist trajectory of his account of the doctrine.

History, as a category for understanding election, is important with regard both to individuals and to nations.[11] He agrees with Calvin that turning to God in faith in response to God's effectual call is the sign of our election and our personal appropriation of it. He also agrees with Calvin that we can make no assumptions about the reprobation of those who have not yet come to faith, since God alone knows the time in their personal life history when he will effectually call his elect. Schleiermacher pursues this trajectory to offer a thoroughgoing

---

8. Schleiermacher, *Christian Faith*, 557. For the impossibility of any disparity between divine foreknowledge and divine foreordination, see also 550–51.

9. Ibid., 552. The concept of God's good pleasure in election is a major theme of § 120.

10. See Gockel, "New Perspectives," 306.

11. This paragraph summarizes some of the key points of §117, which is specifically devoted to the topic, but the theme permeates his entire account.

historical account of the nature and unfolding of election. His central point is that it is a condition of createdness that things unfold in time, including the spread of the gospel. It is quite simply impossible for all individuals—and all nations—existing at any one time to encounter the gospel and come to believe. Under the conditions of time and history, then, it is inevitable that many will die either never having heard or never having responded positively to the gospel. That some hear and some do not hear, and that some accept it and some do not, is all under the sovereign control of God, within his overall governance of the world of which the electing decree is a part.

While Schleiermacher develops the concept of the historical unfolding of election at more length than Calvin, there is nothing in what has been said so far with which Calvin would disagree. Where Schleiermacher and Calvin part company is in Schleiermacher's preference for confining the language of rejection to the lack of response to the gospel within history. For Schleiermacher, that some should not hear or respond is the outcome of the preaching of the gospel under the conditions of created time and history but is not necessarily the final word in relation to eternal destiny.[12] He considers that since God has created a world in which the gradual unfolding of things in time means that it is impossible for all people alive at any given time to hear and accept the gospel, if salvation were to be entirely dependent upon receiving the gift of faith in this life, then this would set the pattern of God's government of the world at odds with God's saving will.[13]

Calvin, of course, would not accept any such incompatibility. For him, the temporal receiving of the gospel (or not) is precisely the *expression* of God's saving (and reprobating) will in his governing of the world. As such, those people to whom God has determined that the light of the gospel does not come, or by whom it is not accepted, are the rejected whom God has eternally foreordained to damnation. That Schleiermacher thinks otherwise reflects a very different understanding of the nature and content of God's electing decree. It is here that we turn to the second of the three themes: Schleiermacher's desire to speak unequivocally of the single will of God in election.

Schleiermacher recognizes that Calvin seeks to maintain the one will of God in election by asserting, as noted above, that God equally wills to reject as well as to elect, rather than seeing election as the will of God and allowing reprobation to fall outside God's active willing. Schleiermacher also acknowledges that Calvin and the earlier Reformed tradition speak of the one electing will of God as having twin facets, embracing both the demonstration of God's mercy and God's judgment in the elect and reprobate respectively.[14] Nevertheless, Schleiermacher contends that double predestination—God's active predestining of each

12. Schleiermacher, *Christian Faith,* 547–48. The problems raised by the possibility of ultimate exclusion from fellowship with Christ dominate §§ 118–120.

13. Ibid., 539, 549.

14. Ibid., 543–44.

individual either to salvation or to damnation—cannot help but compromise any claim to a single will of God in election.[15]

Schleiermacher's alternative construction of the doctrine completely discards the notion that the electing decree of God is focused on the determination of the salvation or damnation of every single human being. Instead, the electing decree of God is a foreordination to blessedness for the entire human race, based on the understanding that in Christ we see the beginning of the restoration of humanity as a whole.[16] Schleiermacher's carefully worded summary is that there is "a single divine foreordination, according to which the totality of the new creation is called into being out of the general mass of the human race."[17] As he explains, this statement allows for more than one possible outcome when we consider the eternal destinies of particular individuals. On the one hand, for example, there might be the annihilation of those not ultimately part of the new creation in Christ. On the other, there is the possibility that, ultimately, none will be excluded from the new creation.[18]

This leads to the third of our themes: the universalist trajectory of Schleiermacher's doctrine of election. As we have seen, on his understanding of the historical unfolding of election, while it is inevitable that there will always be some who have not yet received the gospel, this does not necessarily imply that any will be eternally lost. By rejecting an individually focused double decree and replacing it with a universal predestination to salvation through Christ in whom the restoration of the whole human race has begun, Schleiermacher refuses to countenance a division in the human race between the elect and the damned, or any notion that Christ's saving work is intended for only one part of humanity.[19] Schleiermacher therefore posits that "all belonging to the human race are eventually taken up into living fellowship with Christ," and that if this is not fulfilled in someone's lifetime, it will be brought about by the continuing saving work of God after that person's death.[20] Schleiermacher recognizes that given the sovereignty of God over our response to him, if there is in fact no continuing saving work of God after death, then Calvin is correct: the electing decree must be one of double predestination.[21] While double predestination is a *logical* possibility on the basis of Reformed theological priorities, however, he rejects it as *theologically* unacceptable.[22] A continuing saving work of God after death is, for him, the only way to reconcile the divine government of the world (which did not allow a person to come to regeneration in life) and the divine plan of salvation (which will not allow this to prevent

---

15. See Ibid., 558.
16. For the single divine ordination to blessedness see ibid., 548–51; for this understanding of the incarnation in the context of election see pp. 535, 540–41.
17. Ibid., 550.
18. Ibid., 550–51.
19. Ibid., 540.
20. Ibid., 549.
21. Ibid., 549–50.
22. Ibid., 543, 551.

the attainment of fellowship with Christ) without God seeming to be arbitrary and capricious.[23]

The all-pervasive rationale for Schleiermacher's rejection of eternal separation from God is in fact the guiding principle of his theology as a whole: that all doctrines must be consonant with and derived from God's primary self-revelation to us, which is our awareness of our absolute dependence on God as the transcendent Other to whom we owe our being.[24] This self-consciousness (which, because it consists of our awareness of our absolute dependence on God, is also God-consciousness) is not purely individual. It is also relational and universal: it is a race-consciousness (by which Schleiermacher means that it embraces the entire human race). This means that for our self- and God-consciousness to be perfect, it must include the corporate solidarity of race-consciousness. Since each individual is part of the whole, if some individuals were excluded from salvation, then the blessedness of those who are saved would be impaired. Perfect acquiescence to the divine good pleasure in election would be all but impossible, he suggests, should any be excluded from fullness of fellowship with Christ, because this would impinge on racial and personal consciousness, and the sorrow caused would "prevent an unalloyed communication of the blessedness of Christ."[25] For this reason, Schleiermacher insists that while we can make a distinction between those who enjoy fellowship with Christ in this life and those who do not, this distinction cannot be of ultimate significance. In his words, it must be a "vanishing antithesis."[26] For Schleiermacher, *all* must be saved if *any* are to enjoy that which constitutes the blessedness of salvation. Returning to his summary of God's electing as "a single divine foreordination, according to which the totality of the new creation is called into being out of the general mass of the human race," Schleiermacher is clear that we should expect the totality of the new creation to be coterminous with the whole of humanity.[27]

In Schleiermacher, then, we see the appropriation of some aspects of Calvin's doctrine of election (most notably its unconditionality and the sovereignty of God over our response to him) and the rejection of others (in particular the idea that the electing decree entails the predestination of individuals to damnation as well as to salvation). We also see the modification of the direction of Calvin's thought on the basis of a very different approach to the overall task of theology.

We now turn to a theologian whose fundamental premises for the practice of theology are entirely different from Schleiermacher's but who shares similar

23. Ibid., 549. See p. 543 for Schleiermacher's assertion that double predestination "has its ground in such divine arbitrariness that we might rightly describe the ordinance as sheer caprice."

24. For a brief outline of Schleiermacher's account of self- and God-consciousness and the "feeling of absolute dependence," see ibid., §§ 3–4.

25. Ibid., 558. Indeed, Schleiermacher goes on to make the effectiveness of Christ's high-priestly mediation dependent upon universal salvation (p. 560).

26. Ibid., 540; see also 543. These themes are pervasive in § 118 in particular but found throughout §§ 118–120.

27. This position is summed up in his postscript to the doctrine, pp. 558–60.

priorities and misgivings when it comes to those aspects of Calvin's doctrine of election that he chooses to affirm and to challenge.

Karl Barth (1886–1968)

Karl Barth's doctrine of election in volume II/2 of his *Church Dogmatics* is worked out in intensive engagement with Scripture, and with Calvin and Reformed Orthodoxy.[28] With this we turn not only to perhaps the most influential Reformed restatement of the doctrine but also to an account that has had a significant and controversial impact on the study of Calvin and his Reformed successors on the subject.

Even though the specific content of his doctrine of election will differ radically from Calvin's, Barth is clear about the first principles that he shares with Calvin. In particular, Barth considers that the sovereign freedom, mystery, and righteousness of God's eternal electing decision must be central to any account of the doctrine and calls directly upon Calvin as a strong ally for each of these themes.[29] With regard to the sovereignty of God, God's electing is entirely of free grace, unconditional, and unconditioned. God's predestination conditions and includes our response to God, rather than our response to God being the condition of God's electing. Since Barth is clear that we are incapable, unaided, of turning to God, God is both sovereign in his electing decision and sovereign over our response to him through the gift or withholding of the efficacious work of the Spirit. With regard to the mystery of God in election, we cannot require God to give an account of his electing. There is no going behind the decision of God to ask why God should have chosen to elect in the way of his choosing, and we have no right to question the nature and content of his electing decree. Indeed, we will bow before it, in recognition that it is no mere arbitrary caprice, but the expression of God's righteousness and wisdom. Barth is also clear that Calvin and the earlier Reformed tradition were correct to conceive of God's eternal electing as double—as involving both election and rejection.

Nevertheless, Barth radically reinterprets and reorients all of these shared themes on the basis of his fundamental critique of Calvin and of Calvin's Reformed successors: that the earlier Reformed approach to election has been insufficiently shaped by and focused on the person of Jesus Christ.[30] Barth considers that it is for lack of a sufficiently Christ-centered approach that Calvin

---

28. When Karl Barth's "doctrine of election" is mentioned, it is almost invariably taken to mean his monumental reworking of the doctrine in volume II/2 of his *Church Dogmatics*, and this will be the focus here. Nevertheless, in his earlier *Göttingen Dogmatics*, Barth presents an account of election which, by his own admission, departs from the Canons of Dort only in a different approach to the relationship between God's eternity and our time, resulting in a moment-by-moment, "actualist" understanding of election. See my "Barth's 'Other' Doctrine of Election in the *Church Dogmatics*," *International Journal of Systematic Theology* 9 (2007): 134–47. See also Gockel, *Barth and Schleiermacher*, for summaries of Barth's earlier and mature engagements with the doctrine.

29. Karl Barth, *Church Dogmatics*, II/2, ed. G. W. Bromiley and T. F. Torrance (Edinburgh: T. & T. Clark, 1957), 19–24. Hereafter *CD* II/2.

30. *CD* II/2, 60–76.

allows the true premises noted above to issue in a false conclusion: the assertion that the electing decree of God consists in his determining of the eternal destiny of every single human either for salvation or damnation. To Barth, this false conclusion is brought about in large part by an undue focus on the fact that some come to faith and some do not (and so, since God is sovereign over our response to him, the deduction from this is that the electing will of God must be the double decree of election and reprobation).[31] In Barth's view, this is to build a doctrine of election by working backwards from the evidence of human response, rather than by starting out with what he considers to be properly christological first principles.

To Barth, we can only have a properly christological foundation for the doctrine of election when we realize that the eternal, sovereign, mysterious, righteous electing decree of God quite simply *is* Jesus Christ.[32] Rather than seeing the eternal electing decree of God as the decision for or against every human being, as Calvin does, Barth interprets it as God's own *self-election* to be God-for-us in Jesus Christ, such that Christ himself "is the decree of God behind and above which there can be no earlier or higher decree and beside which there can be no other."[33] This reorientation of the doctrine is the reason that Karl Barth places his discussion of it within the doctrine of God.[34] Election concerns first and foremost the triune God's own self-determination: the Father elects to send the Son, the Son elects to be the one sent, and the Spirit elects to bring about the incarnation such that the triune relations are not sundered.[35]

It is because Jesus Christ is himself the election of God in this way that Barth maintains that God's electing decree cannot be a "mixed message of joy and terror, salvation and damnation,"—as he considers Calvin's doctrine is—but rather is "the sum of the Gospel . . . the Gospel in a nutshell . . . the very essence of all good news."[36] The will of God in election is not a hidden and fearful

---

31. Ibid., 38–44.

32. Barth sketches this theme in his opening section (§ 32—"The Problem of a Correct Doctrine of the Election of Grace") and develops it in his second (§ 33—"The Election of Jesus Christ").

33. *CD* II/2, 94.

34. See ibid., § 32, 3—"The Place of the Doctrine in Dogmatics."

35. *CD* II/2, 101, 105–6. There is a vigorous debate within Barth studies concerning whether or not Barth in fact makes the election of God the basis of God's triunity and the wider theological implications of such a position. The catalyst for the debate is Bruce L. McCormack's interpretation of the direction of Barth's thought, in "Grace and Being: The Role of God's Gracious Election in Karl Barth's Theological Ontology," in *The Cambridge Companion to Karl Barth,* ed. John Webster (Cambridge: Cambridge University Press, 2000), 92–110; and Paul D. Molnar's questioning of it in his *Divine Freedom and the Doctrine of the Immanent Trinity* (London: T. & T. Clark, 2002), 61–64. See also Kevin Hector, "God's Triunity and Self-Determination: A Conversation with Karl Barth, Bruce McCormack and Paul Molnar," *International Journal of Systematic Theology* 7 (2005): 246–61; Paul D. Molnar, "The Trinity, Election and God's Ontological Freedom: A Response to Kevin W. Hector," *International Journal of Systematic Theology* 8 (2006): 294–306; Edwin Chr. van Driel, "Karl Barth on the Eternal Existence of Jesus Christ," *Scottish Journal of Theology* 60 (2007): 45–61 and McCormack's "Seek God Where He May Be Found: A Response to Edwin Chr. van Driel," *Scottish Journal of Theology* 60 (2007): 62–79.

36. *CD* II/2, 13–14.

mystery involving the salvation of some and the damnation of others, but the open revelation and accomplishment of God's saving purpose.[37]

Given that the eternal election of God is that the Son will assume flesh in the person of Jesus Christ, Barth insists that we speak of Jesus Christ himself as the *subject* of election, and so as "electing God." Jesus Christ is the foundation of election, as both the coauthor of the decree with the Father and the Spirit and also the content of the decree. Barth acknowledges Calvin's stress on our need to look to Christ as the mirror of our election, and that election is only "in Christ," and that it is entirely on the basis of what Christ has done. Nevertheless, he considers that Calvin and the later Reformed tradition cannot help but make the foundation of election something other than Jesus Christ, because he is convinced that neither Calvin nor his successors understood Christ to be the author of the decree, but only the instrument through which the prior decision to save some and not others is accomplished.[38] Whether or not Barth has rightly interpreted Calvin and the tradition on the relationship between Christ and the electing decree of God is strongly contested and has been a prominent issue in the debates concerning the influence that Barth and his followers have had on the interpretation of Calvin's doctrine of election and that of Reformed Orthodoxy.[39] This is a matter that will be taken up again in relation to contemporary currents in the reception of Calvin's doctrine of election.

Just as Barth maintains that Jesus Christ is the subject of election, with the Father and the Spirit, he also insists that Jesus Christ is also the sole *object* of election, the one elect human being. In Barth's terms Jesus Christ is the "elect man" as well as "electing God." Christ's election is "the original and all-inclusive election" which is absolutely unique, and in which the election of all others is comprehended.[40] The *decretum absolutum* of the earlier tradition, which focused on God's electing and rejecting of every single person, has been replaced by the person of Jesus Christ himself.

Not only is Christ the one elect human being for Barth, he is also the only truly rejected human being.[41] Barth shares with Calvin the insistence that God's electing decree is "double"—it includes both election and rejection—but for Barth, both sides of election are concentrated in the person of Jesus Christ.[42] Barth's contention is that God has elected for himself the negative side of the divine predestination, so that rejection "cannot again become the portion or affair of man . . . faith in the divine predestination . . . means faith in

---

37. For the contrast between what Barth considers to be the "hidden" mystery of the inscrutable double decree in Calvin and the "disclosed" mystery that election is God's self-election in Jesus Christ, see especially ibid., 156–61.

38. Extended discussion of Barth's position and his view of Calvin and Reformed Orthodoxy in relation to Christology and election can be found in ibid., 60–76, 110–15.

39. The seminal work in this regard is Richard A. Muller's *Christ and the Decree: Christology and Predestination in Reformed Theology from Calvin to Perkins* (Durham, NC: The Labyrinth Press, 1986).

40. *CD* II/2, 117.

41. See ibid., 319.

42. For a brief account of this, see ibid., 122–25, and more extensively, pp. 161–75.

the non-rejection of man . . . In God's eternal purpose it is God Himself who is rejected in His Son . . . in order that we might not be rejected.[43] Jesus Christ is elect to bear the rejection of the rejected in order that God's saving purpose in election may prevail.

In exploring the implications of this concentration of election in the person of Christ for the rest of humanity, Barth turns first to the election of the community (§ 34). In order to recognize the magnitude of the contrast between Barth and Calvin, we need a reminder that for Calvin, Israel is the elect people of God prior to the coming of Christ, although not every member of the covenant people is of the elect, and so saved. God's double predestination allows for distinctions within the membership of the covenant community. After the coming of Christ, the church is the new people of God, among whom the elect are those who from eternity are chosen to receive the gifts of true faith and perseverance. As was the case with Israel, not all those within the visible community are necessarily of the eternally elect to salvation. For Barth, the *one* elect community consists of *both* Israel *and* the church. This is because the two sides of the one elect community each represent one side of the double predestination of Christ, who is elect to bear the consequences of humanity's rejection of God. Israel represents the judgment from which Christ has rescued humanity and the rejection that Christ has borne away. As those who do not accept the reality of what God in Christ has done, they resist their election, but are not "rejected," because in Christ we see "God's election in which He has determined Himself to take upon Himself the rejection."[44] The church represents the recognition of, and summons to witness to, the divine mercy that is the content and purpose of election. As the community that has received in faith that which Christ has done in his election to bear rejection, it holds out to the rest of humanity the communion and fellowship with God, which is the promise and goal for all.

In turning to the election of the individual (§ 35), Barth laments the fact that this—in the form of predestining individuals either to salvation or damnation—is the primary focus of the doctrine for Calvin and his successors.[45] Instead, Barth maintains that the election of the individual can only find its proper place as dependent upon and included within God's self-election in Jesus Christ. We see the same fundamental pattern here as we find in his account of the two sides of the one elect community. Each individual is included in the one election of Jesus Christ, as someone who reflects one or the other aspect of Christ's double-sided election. The "elect" are those who by the gift of the Spirit, through faith, are drawn into the community of the church, recognizing and living in accordance with the reality of their inclusion in Christ's election. Those who have not (yet) received the gift of the Spirit in this way reject their election, but are not themselves the "rejected." They are only "apparently rejected," failing to live in a way that reflects the fundamental truth of their being: that in Christ they cannot

43. Ibid., 167, see also pp. 166–67.
44. Ibid., 200.
45. Ibid., 306–8.

be rejected. Their choice to reject the reality of their election in Christ is in fact void, because their rejection has been borne and cancelled by Jesus Christ. The church's vocation is to bear witness that all participate in Christ's election, and that "In Jesus Christ . . . thou art not rejected but elected," with the summons to live accordingly.[46]

This means that Barth refuses to allow the response of faith or unbelief to delineate anything ultimate about the reality of our election. Barth rightly points out that Calvin and his successors eschewed simple deductions concerning an individual's final election or rejection on the basis of apparent faith or lack of it. All must be regarded as potentially of the elect, and therefore as those who may come to faith at God's chosen time.[47] Even so, for Calvin, whether or not one comes to and perseveres in faith through the effectual call of the Spirit will finally be the seal of God's eternal predestination either for election or rejection. Through Barth's concentration of the whole of election in the person of Christ, Barth claims that all are objectively included in Christ's election *whether or not* their personal response is faith or unbelief. The division in humanity is not between those determined for salvation and damnation, but between those who are brought to live in the light of the transformation that God has wrought in the whole human situation in Christ and those who continue to live in ignorance or defiance of it.

Criticizing Calvin and his successors, Barth therefore maintains that no one can be uncertain as to whether or not that which Christ has accomplished applies to him or her. For Barth there cannot be a distinction in this regard between the "elect" for whom Christ's work is intended and will avail and the "rejected" for whom it is not and will not. The concentration of the whole of election in Christ means that he is the one who has borne away the rejection of the rejected.[48] In the light of this, while Barth strongly upholds Calvin's (and the Canons of Dort's) affirmation of the preservation of the elect—that God's "Yes" to his elect is irreversible—he rejects the idea that this is an indicator that some have been predestined to salvation and others to damnation. Instead, the "Yes" of God is the affirmation of God's gracious will toward all in the election of Jesus Christ.[49]

As many have pointed out (and puzzled over), Barth's account of election seems to lead straight to *apokatastasis*—the affirmation that all will be saved—and yet Barth himself explicitly rejects this.[50] While universal salvation is that for which we may hope, Barth considers that any assertion that all must of necessity be saved infringes on the sovereign freedom of God, and also on the freedom of the individual to continue to reject God. This leaves us with what he terms the "impossible possibility"—that some, after all, might be lost. The logical (and theological) objections to Barth's reasoning on this point are many, but since the

---

46. Ibid., 322.
47. Ibid., 327–28.
48. Ibid., 325–26.
49. Ibid., 329–33.
50. E.g., ibid., 417–18.

focus here is on how Barth both takes up and turns aside from Calvin's approach to the doctrine, this is not the place to explore them.[51] Perhaps the best way to summarize the difference between Barth's stated position on the ultimate unfolding of election and Calvin's is that for Calvin, the deep mystery of predestination is that God chooses to save any at all: we bow in awe before the mercy and grace of God, that when all deserve only his condemnation, in Christ he has chosen to save some. For Barth, the deep mystery of predestination is how any could ultimately be rejected, and we bow in awe before the mercy and grace of God's self-election to bear our rejection in Christ.

Summary

Reflecting on these key reappropriations and reworkings of Calvin's doctrine of election, it is clear that certain of his insights remain absolutely essential to any articulation of the doctrine from a Reformed perspective—and, of course, completely incompatible with an Arminian approach. As the split in Methodism indicates, and as both Schleiermacher and Barth demonstrate in their own very distinctive ways, there can be no convergence between these views. In particular, for Calvin, Schleiermacher, and Barth, God's eternal election is entirely unconditional, we are wholly incapable of a response of faith to God that is not the gift of God, and the grace of God is irresistible. By the Spirit we are set free by God for God.

It is equally clear that the same conclusions, drawn out by Calvin and his successors, cause anxiety. So, Thomas Erskine and John McLeod Campbell, mentioned at the outset, and both Schleiermacher and Barth, refuse to accept that the only outcome of those Reformed priorities is the idea of individual double predestination and that Christ's death is intended for only a small proportion of the human race. As we will see, the same affirmations and the same questions continue to haunt contemporary theology's appropriation of Calvin's doctrine.

CONTEMPORARY PROMISE AND CHALLENGES

Where might we go from here? In the light of the ways in which aspects of his account of election have been received, reworked, or rejected, what directions might the contemporary exploration of Calvin's doctrine of election take? Although the separation is artificial in many ways, I will offer some suggestions with regard to historical theology in the first instance and then indicate some

51. For a reiteration that Barth's denial of universalism is incoherent, see Oliver Crisp, "On Barth's Denial of Universalism," *Themelios* 29 (2003): 18–29. See also my "Evangelical Questioning of Election in Barth: A Pneumatological Perspective from the Reformed Heritage," in Clifford Anderson and Bruce McCormack, eds., *Karl Barth and American Evangelicalism: Friends or Foes?* (Grand Rapids: Eerdmans, 2011); and *Re-Imaging Election: Divine Election as Representing God to Others and Others to God* (Grand Rapids: Eerdmans, 2010). See also Tom Greggs, "Jesus Is Victor: Passing the Impasse of Barth on Universalism," *Scottish Journal of Theology* 60 (2007): 196–212.

trajectories with regard to contemporary constructive or systematic theology. As with the preceding descriptions, it is only possible to sketch a few options out of many. The intention here is to point to some of the conversations currently taking place and to indicate fruitful possibilities for further development.

Historical Theology

One of the most surprising gaps in all of Calvin studies is the relative lack of recent secondary literature in English on his doctrine of election. Famous (or notorious) as it undoubtedly is—for many, it is the one doctrine associated with Calvin's name—there are relatively few resources to turn to for a detailed exposition and investigation of it. While in no way wishing to revive the mistaken notion that the doctrine of election is the center of Calvin's thought, it is ironic that this, of all doctrines, has been somewhat neglected.[52] A fully orbed account of Calvin's approach would require engagement with his exegesis of key texts in his commentaries, an investigation of his sermons, and contextually alert reflection on his polemical treatises, in addition to drawing on the *Institutes*. Further detailed studies of Calvin's doctrine of election will give historical theology more tools as it continues to reflect on the relationship between Calvin and his Reformed contemporaries and successors, and it will provide contemporary theology with the impetus to engage with the full range of Calvin's thought on the subject.

One area in particular that has been neglected but which is ripe for further investigation is a need to reflect on the method and results of Calvin's exegesis, because no account of his doctrine of election should ignore his exegetical work, but also because, as with any other doctrine, we need to take account of the way in which Calvin understood the nature of his theological enterprise as a whole. In particular, we cannot assume that the *Institutes* provides us with a full account of Calvin's thought on any given subject. As is now widely acknowledged, Calvin intends the *Institutes* to be both an aid to reading Scripture and as a theological companion to his commentaries.[53] As an example of recent significant work in this area, David Gibson explores Calvin's interpretation of a range of central election texts and then compares the ways in which Calvin and Barth exegete Romans 9–11 as a test case for exploring their respective exegetical and

52. For an account of the genre of the *Institutes,* and why neither election nor any other doctrine can be considered the center of Calvin's thought, see Richard A. Muller, *The Unaccommodated Calvin: Studies in the Foundation of a Theological Tradition* (Oxford: Oxford University Press, 2000), especially chaps. 6–8, and in summary, pp. 177–81.

53. A foundational resource is Elsie Anne McKee, "Exegesis, Theology, and Development in Calvin's *Institutio*: A Methodological Suggestion," in Elsie Anne McKee and Brian G. Armstrong, eds., *Probing the Reformed Tradition: Historical Studies in Honor of Edward A. Dowey, Jr.* (Louisville, KY: Westminster/John Knox, 1989), 154–74; see also Muller, *Unaccommodated Calvin* and Stephen Edmondson, "The Biblical Historical Structure of Calvin's *Institutes*," *Scottish Journal of Theology* 59.1 (2006): 1–13.

hermeneutical methods, particularly in relation to christological issues.[54] Gibson's explorations indicate that close attention to Calvin's exegesis in relation to his doctrine of election is likely to continue to prove highly illuminating for historical and systematic studies.

This example of the fruitfulness of exploring Calvin's commentaries for a contemporary reengagement with his doctrine of election also leads to another important field in which further work is needed: continued, careful exposition of specific aspects of Calvin's doctrine in relation to the issues raised by Barth. One of the most important features of Barth's reworking of the doctrine of election is not simply his constructive proposal, but the way in which his approach and his interpretation of the earlier Reformed tradition have become a lens through which to analyze the work of Calvin and his successors. Given the significance of Barth's account, it is inevitable and important that Calvin studies should continue to test the extent to which the claims made by Barth (and those who follow his trajectory) stand up to detailed scrutiny.

One example that remains a source of debate is how we speak of Christology in election in the aftermath of Barth's account. Is Barth unique (as he certainly considers himself to be) in making Jesus Christ the "subject" of election and speaking of him as the electing God rather than merely the instrument of a decree determined apart from him? As we noted above, this is one of the major criticisms that Barth makes of Calvin and the earlier tradition. Careful historical study seems to indicate that Calvin and his successors do indeed have their own way of speaking of Jesus Christ as "electing God," although the electing decree of which he is coauthor is understood very differently (for Calvin, the eternal election of individuals either to salvation or damnation; for Barth God's eternal self-election to be God-for-us in Jesus Christ).[55] In return, however, the question is posed as to whether, in the earlier tradition, the identity of the eternal Son is fully determined by the fact that he is to become incarnate or whether the Son who elects with the Father is still able to be understood apart from what has been made known in Christ. This, for Barth and those who agree with his interpretation of Calvin and the earlier tradition, creates a hidden, unknown God behind Jesus Christ and so undermines the trustworthiness of God's self-revelation in Christ. Whether this is indeed an accurate portrayal of the way in which Calvin and the earlier Reformed tradition understand the Son, who is electing God and eternally *incarnandus*,

---

54. David Gibson, *Reading the Decree: Exegesis, Election and Christology in Calvin and Barth* (London and New York: T. &T. Clark, 2009); and his "A Mirror for God and for Us: Christology and Exegesis in Calvin's Doctrine of Election," *International Journal of Systematic Theology* 11:4 (2009): 448–65.

55. See Muller, *Christ and the Decree*, passim; Bruce McCormack, "Christ and the Decree: An Unsettled Question for the Reformed Churches Today," in L. Quigley, ed., *Reformed Theology in Contemporary Perspective* (Edinburgh: Rutherford House, 2006), 124–42, and Gibson, "A Mirror for God and for Us."

is strongly disputed. The debate continues, and as even this short sketch indicates, the theological as well as historical stakes are high.[56]

For the integrity of both Calvin studies and Barth studies on the doctrine of election, it is therefore important to continue the work of clarifying real rather than supposed differences and the actual rather than assumed implications of these. In particular, careful exploration and exposition of Calvin will allow his work to be heard on its own terms as a true partner in this particular theological dialogue—avoiding the danger of allowing the study of Calvin (and his successors) to become a foil, whether intentionally or not, to the work of Barth. The systematic issues raised in this process are also highly significant, and it is to possibilities for dialogue and further development in this area that we now turn.

Systematic Theology

The doctrine of election remains a lively topic of theological discussion. At the more popular level, there is continued reflection on the doctrine from the perspective of Reformed and Arminian debates in addition to the very popular format of presenting a variety of views on election and cognate issues such as universalism and the freedom of the will.[57] In a more academic context, important issues include the relationship between eternal election and God's triunity, whether or not an Augustinian/Reformed approach to election requires double predestination, and the interest shown in the doctrine from perhaps one of the least likely quarters: process theology.[58] This testifies to a wide-ranging and thought-provoking discussion of election that looks likely to continue for some time to come.

Continued reflection on Calvin's approach has a contribution to make to all of these conversations. Whether or not theologians will wish to reappropriate or

56. See in particular McCormack, "Grace and Being," 94–95; and his "Christ and the Decree" for the concern that Calvin leaves us with a hidden God "behind" what has been revealed in Christ and, by way of comparison, P. Helm, "John Calvin and the Hiddenness of God," in B. McCormack, ed., *Engaging the Doctrine of God: Contemporary Protestant Perspectives* (Grand Rapids: Baker, 2008), 67–82. The issues here are also at the heart of the debate concerning the relationship between election and God's Triunity in Barth (see note 35 above). For a fine overview of this debate in the context of interpreting of Calvin's election Christology, see David Gibson, *Reading the Decree*, chap. 1. See also his "A Mirror for God and for Us," 448–65.

57. There is a plethora of volumes that set various views on such issues side-by-side, such as Chad Owen Brand, ed., *Perspectives on Election: Five Views* (Nashville: Broadman & Holman Publishers, 2006); and the earlier, *Predestination and Free Will: Four Views*, David Basinger and Randall Basinger, eds., (Downers Grove, IL: InterVarsity, 1986); and Robin A. Parry and Christopher H. Partridge, eds., *Universal Salvation? The Current Debate* (Grand Rapids: Eerdmans, 2004).

58. See note 35 above for an indication of the election/Trinity debate; for reflection on alternatives to double predestination within a fundamentally Augustinian/Reformed framework, see Oliver D. Crisp, "Augustinian Universalism," *International Journal for Philosophy of Religion* 53 (2003): 127–45; Bruce L. McCormack, "So That He May Be Merciful to All: Karl Barth and the Problem of Universalism," in Clifford Anderson and Bruce L. McCormack, eds., *Karl Barth and American Evangelicalism: Friends or Foes?* and my *Re-Imaging Election*. For a process doctrine of election, see Donna Bowman, *The Divine Decision: A Process Doctrine of Election* (Louisville, KY: Westminster John Knox, 2002).

otherwise engage sympathetically with Calvin's account of election, however, will obviously depend largely upon first-principle issues highlighted throughout this chapter, such as the affirmation or rejection of the unconditionality of election and the affirmation or rejection of the sovereignty of God over our response to him. For those outside the Reformed tradition, dialogue will continue to consist largely of debating the scriptural and theological validity of such first principles on the basis of irreconcilably different ones. Since this debate has changed relatively little in its fundamentals since the sixteenth and seventeenth centuries, my focus here will be on those within the Reformed theological spectrum for whom these first principles are the scriptural and theological nonnegotiables on which any doctrine of election must be built. With this in mind, I will highlight some aspects of Calvin's thought and method that can fruitfully be explored and also some aspects of the doctrine that are relatively neglected in Calvin, but to which a contemporary Reformed account of election could give further attention.

As was noted above, Calvin's exegetical work is one highly promising area for further study. A more general way in which Calvin's legacy on the doctrine of election can be taken up by contemporary theology is by following his self-conscious attempt to derive his account of election from Scripture. While the extent to which Calvin is successful in his aim might be disputed, continuing constructive work on the doctrine of election can seek to follow his example by attempting to articulate the doctrine in a way that is scripturally focused and exegetically aware. Although this might seem a very obvious comment to make, there is a distinct lack of scriptural reflection and exegesis in Schleiermacher's account of the doctrine, for example, reflecting a very different understanding of the method and sources of theology.[59] This stands in marked contrast with Barth, for whom it is the case, as with Calvin, that the principles and content of his exegesis might be debated, but what cannot be denied is the sustained scriptural engagement that marks his treatment of the subject.

The increased specialization of biblical and theological disciplines means that few contemporary systematic theologians will dare to author commentaries themselves. Nevertheless, a recent example of seeking to follow both Calvin and Barth in endeavoring to allow the contours of Scripture to shape the doctrine is Bruce McCormack, who explores and extends the trajectory offered by Barth and presents a programmatic sketch of a Pauline case for the possibility of Reformed universalism. He considers that scripturally speaking, the only two options are either double predestination as Calvin presents it or universal salvation and that theology should not move too hastily to resolve what Scripture seems to leave open. McCormack therefore does not uphold dogmatic universalism—the assertion that all infallibly will be saved. Rather, he maintains that since Paul leaves open the possibility and hope for universal salvation, theology

---

59. Much the same can be said in relation to Bowman's doctrine of election, which allows process philosophy and theology to be the governing framework within which exploration of the doctrine is set.

should do likewise.[60] His work highlights the ongoing creative tension faced by Reformed theologians who accept the scriptural validity of Calvin's basic theological premises, but remain unconvinced that his conclusions are a full reflection of the scriptural witness.

More broadly, in seeking to follow Calvin's scripturally rooted approach, contemporary systematic theology will find much food for thought in the implications of some recent biblical scholarship. There has been a rich stream of thinking on the nature and purpose of election in relation to Israel, Christ, and the church from the perspectives of Hebrew Bible studies, New Testament studies, and canonical approaches to Scripture.[61] Some themes emerging from these fields of scholarship have considerable potential to enrich doctrinal reflection, and can certainly be seen as complementing as well as supplementing an approach to election that is in sympathy with Calvin's. Among these we find a renewed stress on the corporate as well as individual aspects of election and a focus on election as God's chosen means to further his wider purpose of blessing in the face of human sin.[62] Of particular interest is the binding together of this understanding of election's purpose with the theme that part of the calling of the elect, as individuals and as a community, is to bear "rejection." Election to bear rejection for the sake of furthering God's purpose of blessing might be a summary of the pattern that emerges from several strands of contemporary biblical reflection on the nature and purpose of election in Scripture.[63]

Further exploration of the corporate nature of election provides a welcome opportunity to revisit Calvin's thought in this regard, especially in his Romans commentary. All too often Calvin has been accused of presenting *only* an individualist account of the doctrine. Obviously there is a significant sense in which the focus of the decree is individualized for Calvin, but it is simplistic and inaccurate to make the assumption that because the content of the electing decree is the destiny of each individual human being, the whole of his doctrine is

60. McCormack, "So That He May Be Merciful to All." For an attempt to assert dogmatic universalism, set in the context of the Augustinian/Reformed insistence on the absolute unconditionality of election and the sovereignty of God over our response to him, see Thomas B. Talbott's contributions to Brand, ed., *Perspectives on Election,* and Parry and Partridge, eds., *Universal Salvation? The Current Debate.*

61. Representative works include Jon D. Levenson, *The Death and Resurrection of the Beloved Son: The Transformation of Child Sacrifice in Judaism and Christianity* (New Haven: Yale University Press, 1993); Joel S. Kaminsky, *Yet I Loved Jacob: Reclaiming the Biblical Concept of Election* (Nashville: Abingdon, 2007); Christopher R. Seitz, "The Old Testament, Mission, and Christian Scripture," in *Figured Out: Typology and Providence in Christian Scripture* (Louisville, KY: Westminster John Knox, 2001), 145–57; N. T. Wright, "Christ, the Law and the People of God: The Problem of Romans 9–11," in *The Climax of the Covenant: Christ and the Law in Pauline Theology* (Edinburgh: T. & T. Clark, 1991), 231–57; "Reworking God's People," in *Paul in Fresh Perspective* (Minneapolis: Fortress, 2005), 108–29; Richard Bauckham, *The Bible and Mission: Christian Witness in a Postmodern World* (Carlisle: Paternoster, 2003).

62. This is a major theme of Seitz, "The Old Testament, Mission, and Christian Scripture"; Bauckham, *The Bible and Mission*; and Wright, *Climax of the Covenant.*

63. These themes are notable in Levenson, *The Death and Resurrection of the Beloved Son*; Kaminsky, *Yet I Loved Jacob*; and Wright, *Climax of the Covenant.*

"individualistic." Calvin also offers a rich vein of corporate (and covenantal) thinking, although this must be explored with sensitivity to his sixteenth-century context.

On the other hand, contemporary biblical scholarship's invitation to reflect on election as God's chosen means to further his wider purposes of blessing in the face of human sin is not a major theme in Calvin's approach, beyond the concept of the calling out of the eternally elect. There is plenty of scope for contemporary Reformed articulations of the doctrine of election to explore how themes from recent biblical scholarship might further illuminate our understanding of election.[64]

Finally, while again not wishing to encourage the myth that election is the center of Calvin's theology, we do need to recognize its importance for Calvin's thinking on other topics. So, for example, in addition to issues of soteriology, Calvin's understanding of election is reflected in his account of how we receive the revelation of God, his approach to the image of God, his ecclesiology, and his understanding of the sacraments. In contemporary theology, while some have a lively interest in exploring election and its implications for other doctrines, it is relatively rare for theologians who are exploring *other* doctrines to speak much, if at all, of election. However it is construed, the concept of election is a significant scriptural theme, and it should therefore have a significant place in the broader theological conversation. Theology would be the richer if consideration of election were more regularly integrated into the discussion of a wider range of themes. Given the fraught history (and ongoing polemics) associated with the various approaches to the doctrine, the likelihood of this might be slim, but in this way, too, contemporary theology might learn from Calvin, even where it might not choose to follow his conclusions.

---

64. These are some of the themes that I explore in *Re-Imaging Election*.

SECTION 4
CALVIN'S THEOLOGY
OF THE LORD'S SUPPER
AND ITS RECEPTION

Chapter 7

Doctrine of the Lord's Supper
Calvin's Theology and Its Early Reception

SUE A. ROZEBOOM

To acquaint oneself with Calvin's doctrine of the Lord's Supper, one might well begin with a reading of its treatment in the final edition of his *Institutes*, published in 1559. This, however, is not his last word on the topic, or even, arguably, his consummate word. Calvin is not a man of just one book, so his doctrine of the Lord's Supper as a whole is best received when themes and expressions from various treatments are balanced with one another and finally coalesced. This is so because the aim of each of his works is unique, as the primary audience and occasioning circumstance of each differs; and because Calvin's doctrine itself "develops" over the thirty-some years of his career.[1]

In the essay that follows, we shall explore Calvin's doctrine of the Lord's Supper with the breadth of his expositions at hand, including his various editions of

---

1. Noting the vicissitudes of Calvin's context, Wim Janse suggests Calvin himself "did not envisage phrasing his eucharistic doctrine in a permanent timeless form" ("Calvin's Eucharistic Theology: Three Dogma-Historical Observations," in *Calvinus Sacrarum Literarum Interpres*, ed. Herman J. Selderhuis (Göttingen: Vandenhoeck & Ruprecht, 2008), 40. See also Thomas J. Davis, *The Clearest Promises of God: The Development of Calvin's Eucharistic Teaching* (New York: AMS Press, 1995); Randall C. Zachman, *Image and Word in the Theology of John Calvin* (Notre Dame, IN: University of Notre Dame Press, 2007), 330–42.

the *Institutes*,[2] his catechisms, his pastoral and polemical treatises, and a few of his letters and commentaries. We shall draw out a few themes from his doctrine, teasing strands of his richly plaited thought, mindful from the outset that when we tug at just one strand, several others will ravel right along with it. We begin, however, by situating Calvin and his doctrine of the Lord's Supper within the mid-sixteenth-century movement of reform, and we conclude, ultimately, with a brief foray into his doctrine's early reception.

SITUATING CALVIN

In 1517 Martin Luther (1483–1546) posted ninety-five theses to initiate academic debate about a "side-alley of medieval soteriology—indulgences."[3] Unwittingly, he enflamed a movement of reform that would eventually divide the Catholic Church of the West. At the time, "Jean Cauvin" (1509–1564) of Noyon, France, was eight, maturing in a devout Christian (i.e., Roman Catholic) home. In 1520, Luther was condemned a heretic for having vitiated, among other of the church's practices and teachings, the Mass and its associated doctrines of transubstantiation and sacrifice.[4] Calvin was eleven. His father had just obtained for him a benefice to finance his preparation for priesthood. In August 1523, an Augustinian monk was burned alive in Paris for having read and commented approvingly on the writings of Luther. Luther's works had been circulating widely in Paris for some time, well-received by some, fiercely opposed by others. In August 1523, Calvin was fourteen and had just arrived in Paris to further his education there.[5]

By the mid-1520s, those who pressed for the reform of the church had published numerous, copious writings on the sacraments, including specifically the Lord's Supper. A sampling of works published from 1524 to 1526 is indication enough of this proliferation: In those years, Luther published three treatments of the Lord's Supper, including his *Against the Heavenly Prophets*, a diatribe against the views of "radical" reformer Andreas Bodenstein von Karlstadt (c. 1480–1541), who had published no fewer than five treatises on the Lord's Supper in the previous year. In 1524, Martin Bucer (1491–1551), a Dominican persuaded by Luther's teachings in 1519 and engaged in the reform of south Germany, published *Grund und Ursach*, his biblical and theological *Ground and Principle*,

---

2. In this essay, I am intentionally dealing with the various editions of Calvin's *Institutes*, in part to emphasize how highly developed and richly expressed Calvin's doctrine of the Lord's Supper is already in the 1536, 1539, and 1543 editions of the *Institutes*. For convenience, every quotation of the *Institutes* in this essay is taken from Ford Lewis Battles' translation of the 1559 edition; in the citations, the phrase "from 15__" indicates the previous edition in which the referent word, phrase, or passage first appeared.

3. Diarmaid MacCulloch, *The Reformation* (New York: Penguin Books, 2003), 126.

4. Especially in *The Babylonian Captivity of the Church* (1520).

5. Alexandre Ganoczy, *The Young Calvin*, trans. David Foxgrover and Wade Provo (Philadelphia: Westminster Press, 1987), 49.

for the reform of sacramental practice. In 1525, Ulrich Zwingli (1484–1531), who initiated reform in Zurich, published his *Commentary on True and False Religion*, a liturgy titled *Action or Use of the Lord's Supper*, and, in a year, another treatise, *On the Lord's Supper*. Also in 1525, Johannes Oecolampadius (1482–1531), a learned advocate of reform in Basel, published a volume similar to Bucer's *Grund und Ursach*, two sermons, and a treatise on the sacrament: *Concerning the Natural Exposition of the Words of the Lord, "This Is My Body," according to the Most Ancient Authors*.[6] Finally, Philipp Melanchthon, a protégé of Luther, published *On the Mass* in 1525 even as he was revising and expanding his 1521 *Loci Communes*, or *Common Topics* of theology (which include the sacraments) for republication in 1526. From among these works, diverse views of the sacrament of the Lord's Supper emerged, views which may be (roughly) aligned with either of two principal figures, Luther and Zwingli. In 1526, diversity incited dispute, giving rise to "the first eucharistic controversy" of the Reformation. In 1526, Calvin was seventeen, nearing the completion of his preparatory degree and about to shift his academic focus (at his father's behest) from theology to law.[7]

In 1529, the "first eucharistic controversy" climaxed. For political reasons, Philip of Hesse summoned to Marburg Luther and Melanchthon from Wittenberg, and some of those whom Luther had vilified as "fanatics" and "sacramentarians" in the late 1520s[8]—namely, Zwingli and Oecolampadius from Switzerland and Bucer and Wolfgang Capito from Strasbourg—that they might resolve their theological differences. Mutually agreeable statements were formulated on fourteen topics, but not on the Supper: rebuffing Zwingli, Luther vehemently defended his view marked by his interpretation of Christ's words "This is my body," namely, that the body of Christ is given and received "bodily" "in and under" the elements of bread and wine; Zwingli, too, was resolute in his view marked by his understanding of Christ's corporeal presence in heaven and his interpretation of Christ's words "This is my body" and "The flesh profits nothing" (John 6:63), namely, that the bread and wine are signs symbolizing the body and blood of Christ, which are bestowed spiritually, not in the sacraments. In 1530, another opportunity for conciliation arose but failed in the midst of the Diet of Augsburg.[9] There it became apparent that the Catholic Church of the West had irreparably fractured; there it became apparent, too, that the "Protestant" side of that division was fracturing further, precisely over disagreement about the sacrament of unity, the sacrament of the Lord's Supper.

---

6. *De genuina verborumdomini, hoc est corpus meum, iuxta vetustissimos authores, expositione liber.*

7. Ganoczy, *Young Calvin*, 60 and 174.

8. In a series of treatises, to which Zwingli replied.

9. Charles V summoned the diet, first (it seemed to Luther and Melanchthon) to conciliate Roman Catholic and Protestant strongholds of the empire. Melanchthon (on behalf of the exiled Luther) and his colleagues, however, quickly found themselves on the defensive; he thus composed and presented the Augsburg Confession. Not fully satisfied with this statement of faith, especially its article on the Lord's Supper, Bucer and his south German colleagues composed and submitted the Tetrapolitan Confession. Zwingli also submitted his *Fidei Ratio*.

In 1529–1530, Calvin was in Bourges, completing his degree in law and anticipating further study among Christian humanists in Paris.

Despite the incendiary exchange between Luther and Zwingli, in the early 1530s, Melanchthon and Bucer—more conciliatory in nature—developed greater mutual understanding and even verbal agreement in their respective doctrines of the Lord's Supper.[10] In 1536, they signed a formula of agreement, *The Wittenberg Concord*, in the good hope that building on it, they might repair the breach between Zwingli's followers in Switzerland (both Zwingli and Oecolampadius had died in 1531) and Luther. Bucer's conciliation with the Lutherans on the Lord's Supper infuriated the Swiss—they never again trusted him, nor anyone associated with him. In 1535–1536 Calvin first formulated his thoughts on the Lord's Supper for publication. They appeared in the first edition of his *Institutes*, printed in Basel, the intellectual haven to which Calvin had fled given the increasing persecution of reform-minded humanists in France.

The point of the foregoing chronology—intentionally laden with names, dates, titles and events—is this: To see that by the time Calvin issued his first word on the Lord's Supper in 1536, reformers had already issued countless words on the topic, in publications, disputations, correspondence, sermons, and even informal conversations. His words on the Lord's Supper follow on all their words. *His doctrine is derivative.* He is a second-generation reformer. With respect to the sacraments, Luther's *Babylonian Captivity of the Church* (1520) and Zwingli's *An Attack of the Canon of the Mass* (1523) are vanguard expressions of the Reformation movement. Contextually considered, Calvin's expositions clearly are not. To say this is not to diminish Calvin's doctrine—not at all; it is simply to dispel any notion that Calvin's doctrine of the Lord's Supper is somehow *fundamentally* novel.[11] His doctrine is, to say it again, "derivative"— generated from his earnest reflection on Scripture, the tradition of the church, and the thought of his contemporaries, each source informing the other. Furthermore, his doctrine comes to expression in that period of Reformation history when Protestants were allying their doctrine with or distinguishing it from that of other Protestants as much as from that of the Roman Catholic Church. We do well to bear this in mind as we take up Calvin's works to explore his understanding of the sacrament.

CALVIN'S DOCTRINE OF THE LORD'S SUPPER

As suggested above, Calvin's doctrine can be looked at by way of themes, though the themes themselves can never be wholly isolated from one another. Even in

10. Likely Bucer was adopting Melanchthon's expressions more than Melanchthon was adopting Bucer's, though this is not to suggest Bucer's appropriation was theologically unprincipled.

11. Neither Calvin nor any of his contemporaries, Roman Catholic or Protestant, were interested in being doctrinally novel. They saw themselves—even if they did not always see each other— as bearers of the church's tradition.

one of Calvin's own, single accounts of his teaching, themes emerge and merge, reemerge and remerge, even as they will in our account below. To explore select themes, we shall rely heavily on Calvin's words, sometimes quoting them at length, so that he might speak for himself for our reflection.

Union with Christ

For the 1543 *Institutes,* Calvin drafted a fresh, pastorally rich opening to his discussion of the Lord's Supper, an opening he retained and expanded in each edition of his *Institutes* after. Coming straight off his discussion of baptism he begins with baptism, and with the image of God as a good parent, Calvin writes,

> God has received us, once for all, into his family, to hold us . . . as [children]. Thereafter, to fulfill the duties of a most excellent Father concerned for his offspring, he undertakes also to nourish us through the course of our life. And not content with this alone, he has willed, by giving his pledge, to assure us of this continuing liberality. To this end, therefore, he has, through the hand of his only-begotten Son, given to his church another sacrament, that is, a spiritual banquet, wherein Christ attests himself to be the life-giving bread, upon which our souls feed unto true and blessed immortality (John 6:51). . . . the signs are bread and wine, which represent for us the invisible food that we receive from the flesh and blood of Christ. For as in baptism, God, regenerating us, engrafts us into the society of his church and makes us his own by adoption, so we have said, that he discharges the function of a provident householder in continually supplying to us the food to sustain and preserve us in that life into which he has begotten us by his Word. Now Christ is the only food of our soul, and therefore our Heavenly Father invites us to Christ, that, refreshed by partaking of him, we may repeatedly gather strength until we shall have reached heavenly immortality.[12]

To begin his discussion of the Lord's Supper, Calvin speaks of a profound spiritual reality that is always obtained for us. As in other of his writings on the Lord's Supper, Calvin sets the soteriological stage (if you will) for his exposition of the sacrament itself. While Calvin refers to the sacrament of the Lord's Supper in these stage-setting discussions, his primary interest is a profound, perpetual, spiritual reality: the "mystery of Christ's secret union with the devout,"[13] a union that avails their souls of Christ's flesh and blood for continual nourishment. Once "the devout" are "begotten" by the Word, "regenerated" into new life in Christ, they are *always* in union with Christ; they are *continually*

12. John Calvin, *Institutes of the Christian Religion,* ed. John T. McNeill, trans. Ford Lewis Battles, Library of Christian Classics (Philadelphia: Westminster Press, 1960), 4.17.1, from 1543. Calvin's approach is the same in the *Short Treatise on the Lord's Supper* (1541), in *Tracts and Treatises of John Calvin,* trans. Henry Beveridge, vol. 2 (Eugene, Oregon: Wipf and Stock, 2002; previously published by Edinburgh Printing Company, 1844); hereafter, *Tracts.*
13. *Institutes* 4.17.1.

nourished by his flesh and blood. This is the promise Christ proclaimed in saying "unless you eat the flesh of the Son of Man and drink his blood, you have no life in you. . . . for my flesh is true food and my blood is true drink; those who eat my flesh and drink my blood abide in me, and I in them."[14] In this sermon, says Calvin, Christ "does not refer to the Lord's Supper, but to the continual communication [of his flesh and blood] which we have apart from the reception of the Lord's Supper."[15] Given our union with Christ, by faith, our "souls feed on His flesh and blood in precisely the same way that the body is sustained by eating and drinking."[16]

The "bond" of this union, and therefore the "channel" by whom the devout receive this nourishment is the Holy Spirit. Again speaking of "continual communication" in the context of the Lord's Supper in particular, Calvin writes:

> We do not doubt that Christ's body is limited by the general characteristics common to all human bodies, and is contained in heaven (where it was once for all received) until Christ return in judgment, so we deem it utterly unlawful to draw it back under these corruptible elements or to imagine it to be present everywhere. And there is no need of this for us to enjoy a participation in it, since the Lord bestows this benefit upon us through his Spirit so that we may be made one in body, spirit, and soul with him. The bond of this connection is therefore the Spirit of Christ, with whom we are joined in unity, and is like a channel through which all that Christ himself is and has is conveyed to us. For if we see that the sun, shedding its beams upon the earth, casts its substance in some measure upon it in order to beget, nourish, and give growth to its offspring—why should the radiance of Christ's Spirit be less in order to impart to us the communion of his flesh and blood?[17]

Christ's Spirit imparts to us the communion of Christ's flesh and blood. Christ's Spirit unites us to Christ and, in the bond of that union, continually nourishes us with his body and blood. This is the reality to which the sacrament of the Lord's Supper itself points.

14. John 6:53, 55 NRSV.

15. John Calvin, *The Gospel according to St. John 1–10*, trans. T. H. L. Parker, ed. David W. Torrance and Thomas F. Torrance, (Grand Rapids: Eerdmans, 1995; trans. copyright 1961: Oliver and Boyd), 169–70. In his exegesis of John 6, Calvin does turn to the sacrament, to explain the relation between the sermon and the Lord's Supper: "It is certain that He is now treating of the perpetual eating of faith. At the same time, I confess that there is nothing said here that is not figured and actually presented to believers in the Lord's Supper. Indeed, we might say that Christ intended the holy Supper to be a seal of this discourse" (170).

16. Calvin, *Gospel according to St. John 1–10*, 169–170.

17. *Institutes* 4.17.12, from 1539. The first sentence reflects Calvin's appropriation of the teaching of Zwingli and other Swiss reformers about Christ's ascension, and his rejection of Roman Catholic and Lutheran teachings about transubstantiation and ubiquity respectively. At "the bond of this connection," a marginal note cites a sermon of Chrysostom. History has proven the sermon to be spurious, but this is nothing against Calvin's aim to give patristic warrant for his view. For Calvin's principal discussion of "union with Christ," see *Institutes* 3.1.

The Sacrament Is a Meal

Given our union with Christ, our souls receive a continual communication of Christ's body and blood as spiritual food for the spiritual journey. As just noted, this is the perpetual reality to which the sacrament of the Lord's Supper points. God adopts us in Christ as children, and then, as any good parent would, sustains us—continually.[18]

For Calvin, the Lord's Supper—as a meal—is an image of this promise. Our minds are too dull to comprehend our union with Christ and the communication of his body and blood to our souls.[19] Our faith is too weak to grasp that Christ's body and blood were once offered on the cross in order that they might be offered to us now, as the spiritual life and food of our soul.[20] So God "tempers himself to our capacity" and "attests" to these things with an image.[21] The sacrament is a testimony or proof of God's good will toward us:

> We now understand the purpose of this mystical blessing, namely, to confirm for us the fact that the Lord's body was once for all so sacrificed for us that we may now feed upon it, and by feeding feel in ourselves the working of that unique sacrifice; and that his blood was once so shed for us in order to be our perpetual drink.[22]

As an image, the sacrament shows us what it means for our souls that they are nourished by Christ's body and blood, namely, they are fortified and delighted by these gifts, even as our bodies are fortified and delighted by bread and wine:

> From physical things set forth in the Sacrament, we are led by a sort of analogy to spiritual things. Thus, when bread is given as a symbol of Christ's body, we must at once grasp this comparison: as bread nourishes, sustains, and keeps the life of our body, so Christ's body is the only food to invigorate and enliven our soul. When we see wine set forth as a symbol of blood, we must reflect on the benefits which wine imparts to the body, and so realize that the same are spiritually imparted to us by Christ's blood. These benefits are to nourish, refresh, strengthen, and gladden.[23]

This way of speaking of the sacrament as an image and figure is especially prominent in Calvin's earliest exposition of the sacrament, the 1536 *Institutes*. Calvin's contemporaries readily speak this way, too, including Zwingli, Heinrich Bullinger, and even Melanchthon.[24] Passages in which Calvin speaks this

---

18. *Institutes* 4.17.1, also 4.18.19.
19. *Institutes* 4.17.1. *Short Treatise* in *Tracts*, 171–72; *True Partaking of the Flesh and Blood of Christ* (1561) in *Tracts*, 507.
20. See Zachman, *Image and Word*, 331. E.g., *Institutes* 4.17.3, from 1536; *Instruction in Faith* (1537), ed. and trans. Paul T. Fuhrmann (Louisville, KY: Westminster/John Knox, 1992).
21. *Institutes* 4.17.3; 4.14.3, from 1536.
22. Ibid., 4.17.1, from 1536.
23. Ibid., 4.17.3, from 1536.
24. Lyle D. Bierma, *The Doctrine of the Sacraments in the Heidelberg Catechism: Melanchthonian, Calvinist, or Zwinglian?* (Princeton: Princeton Theological Seminary, c. 1999), 9–20.

way were retained by him—unedited—in every edition of his *Institutes* after, evidence that he ever appreciated this aspect of the sacrament's "purpose."

However, this is not the only way Calvin speaks of the sacrament as a meal, even early on. For Calvin, the sacrament is not only an image or figure of God's promise to nourish us with the body and blood of Christ, but also a "seal" and a "pledge" of that promise. In saying this, Calvin moves beyond the thought of Zwingli, who determinedly uses these terms respecting Christ, not the sacrament.[25] In Calvin's thought, the sacrament is a "[seal] to seal the grace of God in our hearts, and to render it more authentic."[26] It is a "true and faithful pledge of our union with Christ," which is to say, it is a "pledge *by which* he communicates himself to us."[27] In Calvin's *Catechism of the Church of Geneva* (1545), one reads:

> **M:** Have we in the Supper only a figure of the benefits which you have mentioned, or are they exhibited to us in reality?
> **S:** Seeing that our Lord Jesus Christ is truth itself, there cannot be a doubt that he at the same time fulfils [sic] the promises which he there gives us, and adds the reality to the figures. Wherefore I doubt not that as he testifies by words and signs, so he also makes us partakers of his substance, that thus we may have one life with him.[28]

For Calvin, the Lord's Supper is a "seal" and "pledge" of grace. It is a "figure" of grace given continually and grace given *now*, sacramentally. That is, the Lord's Supper is an occasion—the sacramental occasion—when Christ's body and blood are truly presented, truly offered, truly communicated. In a confession composed for the "Reformed" churches of France, Calvin writes of the sacrament:

> [W]e hold that this doctrine of our Lord Jesus Christ, namely, that his body is truly meat, and his blood truly drink (John 6), is *not only represented and ratified in the Supper, but also accomplished in fact*. For there under the symbols of bread and wine our Lord presents us with his body and blood, and we are spiritually fed upon them, provided we do not preclude entrance to his grace by our unbelief.[29]

So for Calvin, the sacrament of the Lord's Supper is preeminently a meal, as an "analogy" and in "reality": In the moment of the Communion, we see with our eyes, grasp with our hands, and taste with our mouths, the promise that just as bread and wine sustain our bodies, Christ's body and blood sustain our souls.

25. Gottfried Locher, *Zwingli's Thought: New Perspectives* (Leiden: E. J. Brill, 1981), 323.

26. Calvin, *Confession of Faith for the Reformed Churches of France* (1562), in *Tracts*, 152; also in *Institutes* 4.14.3 and 7, from 1539 and 1543 respectively, where he identifies, then refutes "Zwingli's" view.

27. Calvin, *Second Defense of the Sacraments* (1556), in *Tracts*, 276 and 274 respectively.

28. Calvin, *The Catechism of the Church of Geneva* (1545), in *Tracts*, 91. Calvin is specifically distinguishing his view from Zwingli's. Locher says "the whole discussion of the sacraments in the Catechism of Geneva presents one single debate with Zwinglianism" (Locher, 321n34 and 324n46).

29. Calvin, *Confession of Faith* (1562), in *Tracts*, 157–58. Emphasis added.

But in the moment of the Communion, too, our very souls, feeding with the mouth of faith, are indeed truly nourished with their only sustenance: the very body and blood of Christ. The "reality," of course, is a profound mystery, but not beyond the bounds of further reflection, reflection that, for Calvin, is aided by consideration of the nature of figures, symbols, signs.

Of Signs and Things Signified

To further discern the mystery that transpires in the celebration of the Lord's Supper, Calvin—like Luther, Zwingli, and Bullinger (among others)—was drawn to Augustine's "theory" of signs and that which they signify, a theory founded on their being distinct but related. Each appropriated Augustine's teaching to different ends. To see Calvin's view, it is helpful to set it against a relief of his contemporaries' views.

In his earliest works on the Lord's Supper, Luther seemingly embraces an "Augustinian" understanding of the sacrament. He speaks of "the bread *eaten* and the wine *drunk*" as "the sign" of "fellowship and incorporation with Christ and all his saints."[30] By the Marburg Colloquy of 1529, however, he had abandoned this Augustinian model, effectively identifying the sign with that which it signified.[31] Zwingli, on the other hand, stringently distinguished sign and thing signified, since the first is physical and the second spiritual. In his conception, that which is physical could never bear that which is spiritual; so the only way in which a "sign" and a "thing signified" are related is that the one simply and only points to the other. Regarding the sacraments, for Zwingli, the thing signified is something already accomplished, already granted, and definitely *not* something accomplished or granted in or with the issuing of the sign. The sacrament is a sign of a past grace[32]; it is a "memorial" of that grace. For this reason, Zwingli's explication has been labeled "symbolic memorialism."[33] Given their diametrically opposed views of the relation between sign and thing signified, one easily sees why Luther and Zwingli could not but shout past each other at the Marburg Colloquy.

Though Bullinger is Zwingli's direct theological descendant, his nuance of the relation between sign and thing signified is different than Zwingli's, a nuance captured by the label "symbolic parallelism." Bullinger agrees with Zwingli that that which is physical cannot bear that which is spiritual, that the physical and the spiritual exist on nonintersecting planes. However, as may be inferred from

30. Ralph W. Quere, "Changes and Constants: Structure in Luther's Understanding of the Real Presence in the 1520's," *Sixteenth Century Journal* 16, no. 1 (1985), 48.

31. Quere, "Changes and Constants," provides a thorough, technical account of this movement in Luther's thought.

32. Brian Gerrish, "Sign and Reality: The Lord's Supper in the Reformed Confessions," in *The Old Protestantism and the New* (Chicago: University of Chicago Press, 1982), 119; Locher, *Zwingli's Thought*, 12 and 22.

33. The labels "symbolic memorialism," "symbolic parallelism," and "symbolic instrumentalism," are Brian Gerrish's now classic ascriptions, introduced by him in the article cited in note 32 above.

the label ascribed to his view, Bullinger (in contrast to Zwingli) allows that the thing signified can in fact be accomplished or granted *at the same time* that the sign is issued, though still completely *apart* from the sign itself. The two may occur in tandem, but only on parallel planes. So according to Bullinger, in the Supper, what is done "outwardly" (the nourishing of the body with bread and wine) simply points to that which is done simultaneously "inwardly" (the nourishing of the soul with Christ's body and blood).

Calvin, throughout his career, speaks akin to Zwingli and to Bullinger. Ultimately, however, his view of the relation between "sign" and "thing signified" is inflected to yet another end, namely, that the sign, though it is physical, can in fact be an instrument by which God grants the thing signified, though it is spiritual. For this reason, bread and wine are called Christ's body and blood, "because they are as it were instruments by which the Lord distributes them to us."[34] Calvin considers the sacraments to be a "means of grace" in the strong sense: they are "vehicles" by which God deigns to convey grace. For this reason, Calvin's view has been labeled "symbolic instrumentalism."

In passages where Calvin's nuance is keen, his language suggests he is following Bucer and Melanchthon. As noted before, by 1536, their efforts to conciliate the followers of Zwingli and Luther led them to fresh, mutually agreeable, expressions about the sacrament. One such expression is *exhibere,* an expression employed by Melanchthon and Bucer in the Wittenberg Concord (1536) and subsequently by Melanchthon in his revision of the Augsburg Confession (1541).[35] The easy English cognate is "to exhibit," but it means much more than "to present," as in "to show," as the English implies. It means "to present," as in "to offer," "to proffer," "to hand over."

Throughout his writings, Calvin demonstrates a fondness for the word *exhibere* and its derivatives, not least in the context of discussion about sacramental signs. In his excursus on the Lord's Supper in his commentary of 1 Corinthians 11, for example, Calvin writes, Christ is speaking in "a sacramental way" when he "applies to the sign the name of the reality signified."[36] Bread is called body, not because the bread simply "represents" or "stands for" the body, but "because it is a symbol by which the reality is held out to us (*exhibetur*)."[37] Without naming Zwingli and Bullinger, Calvin contrasts their view with his own:

> I do not accept the comparisons which some people make with secular or worldly things, for they are in a different category from the sacraments of our Lord. The statue of Hercules is called 'Hercules'; but it is nothing else but a bare, empty representation (*figura*). But . . . *the bread is the body of*

---

34. Calvin, *Short Treatise,* in *Tracts,* 171.
35. Joseph N. Tylenda, "Calvin and Christ's Presence in the Supper—True or Real?" *Scottish Journal of Theology* 27, no. 1 (1974), 65–75.
36. Calvin, *The First Epistle of Paul the Apostle to the Corinthians,* trans. John W. Fraser, ed. David W. Torrance and Thomas F. Torrance (Grand Rapids: Eerdmans, 1996; trans. copyright 1960: Oliver and Boyd), 245. Emphasis added.
37. Ibid.

> *Christ, because it bears indubitable witness to the fact that the very body, which it stands for, is held out to us (exhiberi); or because, in offering us that symbol, the Lord is also giving us His body at the same time.* . . . ; for Christ is not one to deceive us, and make fools of us with empty representations. Accordingly, it is clear as day to me that here the reality is joined to the sign; in other words, we really do become sharers in the body of Christ, so far as spiritual power is concerned, just as much as we eat the bread.[38]

Here as elsewhere, Calvin is emphatic (not unlike Bucer) that the signs are "not empty." They are "not naked."[39] For Calvin, the veracity of God is at stake. Unless we mean to call God a deceiver, we dare not suggest "an empty symbol is set forth by him."[40] While the sign and that which is signified must be distinguished, they must not be separated: "To distinguish, in order to guard against confounding them, is not only good and reasonable, but altogether necessary; but to divide them, so as to make the one exist without the other, is absurd."[41] For Calvin, a sacrament is a "true symbol," meaning it bears the "exhibition of the reality"[42]: "By the showing (*exhibitione*) of the symbol the thing itself is also shown (*exhiberi*)."[43] A sacrament's "nature" is to "bring and communicate truly to the receivers the thing signified by them."[44] In Calvin's estimation, there "is an inseparable tie between the sign and thing signified," such that it is "lawful" to say "that the body of Christ is given us 'under the bread,' or 'with the bread,'" because the thing denoted is not a substantial union of a corruptible meat with the flesh of Christ, but a sacramental conjunction."[45] With expressions such as "under" and "with" and especially "sacramental conjunction," Calvin's thought seemingly follows on that of Bucer, whose thought followed on that of Luther.[46] For each of them, Christ is the principal actor in the sacrament, who graciously, by means of the sign, holds forth to participants that which is signified, his very body as spiritual food for the spiritual journey.

---

38. Ibid. Emphasis added.

39. ". . . we are the last to teach that naked or empty figures are given, so there is nothing to prevent the true exhibition of the thing from having the figure annexed" (*Last Admonition to Joachim Westphal* [1557], in *Tracts*, 410).

40. *Institutes* 4.17.1, from 1539, as elsewhere.

41. Calvin, *Short Treatise*, in *Tracts*, 172. Also *Institutes* 4.14.15, from 1543.

42. Calvin, *True Partaking*, in *Tracts*, 519 and 508 respectively.

43. *Institutes* 4.17.10, from 1543.

44. Calvin, *Confession of Faith* (1562), in *Tracts*, 152.

45. *The Best Method for Obtaining Concord*, in *Tracts*, 576. In his *Institutes*, Calvin speaks of "signs" and "their mysteries" being "so to speak attached" (4.17.5).

46. Bucer adopted "sacramental union" from Luther's 1528 *Confession*. Calvin seemingly prefers the term "conjunction" to Bucer and Luther's "union." Also, Calvin's explicit, approving use of "with" and "under" here might be surprising, given their resonance with Luther's formulation "in, with, and under." In this particular treatise, his use is intentional given this resonance; after all, he is proposing the "best method for obtaining concord" *with Lutherans*. Notice that Calvin considers it permissible or "lawful," to us "with" and "under" but not "in." Calvin approves "with" and "under" given their "ambiguity" (*Best Method*, 576), but not "in," which suggests "contains," and thereby suggest a "local," even "corporeal," presence of Christ's body and blood. Calvin's preposition of choice is "under," as can be inferred from expressions in *The Best Method* and in other of his works quoted in this essay.

Calvin's pastoral summary is this: "If it is true that a visible sign is given us to seal the gift of a thing invisible, when we have received the symbol of the body, let us no less surely trust that the body itself is also given to us."[47]

The Work of the Holy Spirit

The question that follows is the "manner" or "mode" of the communion of Christ's body and blood in the Supper. With the Swiss, Calvin insists it is not a "corporeal" or "bodily" communion, thereby setting aside both Roman Catholic and Lutheran views. Rather, "for us the manner is spiritual because the secret power of the Spirit is the bond of our union with Christ."[48]

As noted before, Calvin firmly asserts that *the very, life-giving flesh of Christ* must be communicated to us if we are to enjoy the benefit of sharing the immortal life that is Christ's, and it is the Spirit, or Christ by his Spirit, who communicates it. Calvin writes,

> I myself maintain that it is only after we obtain Christ Himself, that we come to share in the benefits of Christ. . . . He is obtained, not just when we believe that He was sacrificed for us, but when He dwells in us, when He is one with us, when we are members of His flesh, when, in short, we become united in one life and substance . . . with Him. . . . Christ does not offer us only the benefit of His death and resurrection, but the self-same body in which He suffered and rose again. My conclusion is that the body of Christ is really (*realiter*), to use the usual word, i.e., truly (*vere*) given to us in the Supper, so that it may be health-giving food for our souls. I am adopting the usual terms, but I mean that our souls are fed by the substance of His body, so that we are truly (*vere*) made one with Him; or, what amounts to the same thing, that a life-giving power from the flesh of Christ is poured into us through the medium of the Spirit, even although it is at a great distance from us, and is not mixed with us.[49]

The person of the Spirit is the "medium" by whom the very substance of the flesh of Christ is communicated to us. But then that "medium" deigns also to use a "medium," namely, the sacrament, as an "instrument." Zwingli and Bullinger reject this view. To them, such a view grants undue efficacy to the sign and diminishes the *im*-mediate efficacy of the Spirit, who needs no "vehicle" by which to communicate Christ's body and blood to the soul.[50] To suggest the Spirit uses such a vehicle is to risk binding the freedom of the Spirit, and to attribute to the sacrament that which belongs properly to the work of the Spirit alone, namely, the increase of faith. It is, in short, to risk papism.[51]

47. *Institutes* 4.17.10, from 1539.
48. *Institutes* 4.17.33, 1559, with an appeal to Augustine.
49. Calvin, *Corinthians*, 246.
50. Gerrish, "Sign," 119–20, with reference to Zwingli's *Fidei Ratio* (1530). Also Locher, *Zwingli's Thought*, 12, 22, and 226.
51. Locher, *Zwingli's Thought*, 21.

Calvin agrees that "a serious wrong is done to the Holy Spirit, unless we believe that it is through his incomprehensible power that we come to partake of Christ's flesh and blood."[52] However, as we have seen, he also emphatically affirms that this communication is "accomplished in fact" "in the Supper." In a letter to Bullinger, Calvin forthrightly asserts that the Spirit's proper work of making us partakers of Christ is done "through the sacraments, as through instruments. . . . the Spirit is the author, the sacrament is the instrument used."[53]

Received by Faith

Calvin affirms that that which is offered in the sacrament can be received only in faith. In his own day and in every day since, Calvin has often been taken to mean that the presence of Christ in the sacrament is somehow "subjective," as if it were dependent upon the faith of the subject (or person) partaking. But this is not Calvin's meaning at all.

Christ's presence is divinely promised. Christ says "This is my body," and at the hand of the minister, who is his instrument, truly holds forth, by the signs of bread and wine, his own body and blood as spiritual food for the spiritual journey. The presence of faith does not make Christ present, just as the absence of faith does not make Christ absent. The "virtue" of the sacrament, having been instituted by God, remains.[54] Christ's body and blood are offered to all, truly and objectively, though only those with faith receive these gifts: "truly [Christ] offers and shows the reality there signified to all who sit at that spiritual banquet, although it is received with benefit by believers alone, who accept such great generosity with true faith and gratefulness of heart."[55] This is the "eucharist"— the thanksgiving—of the sacrament.

With respect to faith and the sacrament of the Lord's Supper, Calvin also says, "It is most true, that everyone receives from the sign just as much benefit as his vessel of faith can contain."[56] To Calvin, faith is not static, but "grows" and "increases" throughout life, and Christ, who dwells in us by faith, "in a manner grows up in us in proportion to the increase of faith."[57] So, the larger your faith, the larger your vessel; the larger your vessel, the larger your capacity for, literally, "possessing Christ," even in the sacrament.[58] This comes full circle in Calvin's thought, given that for Calvin the sacrament itself is an instrument by which the Spirit "increases faith."[59]

52. *Institutes* 4.17.33, 1559.
53. Cited in Paul Rorem, *Calvin and Bullinger on the Lord's Supper* (Nottingham: Grove Books, 1989), 33.
54. Calvin, *Confession* (1562), in *Tracts*, 158; *Catechism* (1545), in *Tracts*, 84.
55. *Institutes* 4.17.10, from 1539.
56. Calvin, "Exposition of the Heads of Agreement," in *Tracts*, 232.
57. Calvin, *True Partaking*, in *Tracts*, 534.
58. Ibid.; *Institutes* 4.17.12, from 1539: "the Spirit alone causes us to possess him completely."
59. *Institutes*, 4.14.8; *Catechism* (1545), 85.

Mystery

That we are made partakers of Christ's flesh and blood is a profound mystery, not least because Christ is in heaven, bodily. Such mystery is not lost on Calvin:

> Even though it seems unbelievable that Christ's flesh, separated from us by such great distance, penetrates to us, so that it becomes our food, let us remember how far the secret power of the Holy Spirit towers above all our senses, and how foolish it is to wish to measure his immeasurableness by our measure.[60]

We truly enjoy an "integral communion" of Christ, says Calvin, and

> whenever this matter is discussed, when I have tried to say all, I feel that I have as yet said little in proportion to its worth. And although my mind can think beyond what my tongue can utter, yet even my mind is conquered and overwhelmed by the greatness of the thing. Therefore, nothing remains but to break forth in wonder at this mystery, which plainly neither the mind is able to conceive nor the tongue to express.[61]

That this "integral communion" can take place *in the Supper* is likewise a profound mystery. In response to this sacramental mystery, Calvin, in the end, can but humbly confess:

> I rather experience than understand it. Therefore, I here embrace without controversy the truth of God in which I may safely rest. He declares his flesh the food of my soul, his blood its drink. I offer my soul to him to be fed with such food. *In his Sacred Supper* he bids me take, eat, and drink his body and blood under the symbols of bread and wine. I do not doubt that he himself truly presents them, and that I receive them.[62]

Sursum corda

To nourish our souls with the life-giving vigor of his flesh, Christ, "dwelling in us by his Spirit . . . raises us to heaven to himself."[63] This is so with respect to both the continual and sacramental communication of his body and blood.

So Calvin's liturgical summons to "lift up your hearts and minds" is, so to speak, a summons not to miss the mystery. It is a summons to exercise faith: to see that Christ—by his Spirit—raises our souls to himself in heaven to nourish us with the aliments of immorality, his very body and blood. "Don't fix your eyes *here*," says Calvin (with Farel before him, and Oecolampadius before Farel[64]), but set your minds on things above. Exercise your faith. *Assent* to the work of the Spirit, that you might here—in the sacramental act of communion—truly *experience* the *ascent* of your soul to Christ in heaven to be nourished by him there.

60. *Institutes* 4.17.10, 1559.
61. *Institutes* 4.17.7, from 1539.
62. *Institutes* 4.17.32, from 1543. Emphasis added.
63. Calvin, "Exposition," in *Tracts*, 240; also *Institutes* 3.1; 3.2.24; 4.17.12.
64. Elfriede Jacobs, "La Théologie de la Sainte Cène chez Farel," in *Actes du Colloque Guillaume Farel* (Lausanne, 1983), 164.

The *sursum corda* of the liturgy concerns not our volition (to ascend to heaven, as if this were our work), but our *disposition* toward the signs, which are called the "body and blood of our Lord." In the Supper, "Christ holds out his hand to us" to this end:

> to raise us upwards. For we must remember that our Lord descends to us, not to indulge our body, or keep our senses fixed on the world, but rather to draw us to himself, and hence the preamble of the ancient Church, 'Hearts upward,' as Chrysostom interprets.[65]

EARLY RECEPTION OF CALVIN'S DOCTRINE

The foregoing exposition of Calvin's doctrine of the Lord's Supper draws out a few themes explicitly, and several others implicitly. Together, they weave an impression of Calvin's sacramental theology that both identifies it with and distinguishes it from others within the Reformed tradition, the fiber of distinction being Calvin's "instrumental" view of the true communication of Christ's body and blood by the Spirit, *in the Supper, by means of* the gifts of bread and wine, received by faith as food for our souls. While "Calvin's view" cannot be equated with "The Reformed Tradition," it definitely takes its place in the tradition. This is evident in its early confessional appropriation and ongoing theological assimilation, a mere taste of which is offered here.

Confessional Appropriation

In the age of Reformation, statements of faith proliferated among Protestants. They set fence lines of faith, by which to mark certain beliefs "out" and others "in." In this sense, they are both polemical and apologetical. In some of the major Reformed confessions, certain apologetical expressions about sacraments in general and the Lord's Supper in particular demonstrate the appropriation of Calvin's robust sacramental thought.

We begin however, not with appropriation, but with anticipation, to offset yet again notions that Calvin's thought is fundamentally novel, to show that this "Calvinistic view" is actually older than Calvin's published thought itself.[66] In early 1536, several Swiss and south-German reformers gathered in Basel to prepare a confession of faith, in part as a ground for dialogue with Luther. The outcome was the First Helvetic Confession, with articles on the sacraments prepared by Bucer and Capito. Amid language that clearly strives to hold diverse "Reformed" views together, the confession declares that sacraments are "holy signs of sublime, secret things." They are "not mere empty signs, but consist of the sign and substance."[67] Therefore, "in the Lord's Supper, the Lord truly offers

65. Calvin, *Last Admonition* (1557), in *Tracts*, 443.

66. Gerrish, "Sign," 123.

67. Article 20. See Arthur C. Cochrane, ed., *Reformed Confessions of the Sixteenth Century* (Louisville, KY: Westminster John Knox, 2003), 107.

His body and His blood, that is, Himself, to His own." Given the institution of Christ, the bread and wine of the sacrament "are highly significant, holy, true signs *by which* the true communion of His body and blood *is administered* and offered to believers by the Lord Himself by means of the ministry of the Church." In short, "they present and offer the spiritual things they signify."[68] In Switzerland, the First Helvetic Confession was superseded by Bullinger's views, eventually codified in the Second Helvetic Confession, by which his (and Zwingli's) sacramental views held sway over those of Calvin.

Geneva was strongly tied to reform in France, and Calvin's views were soon appropriated there. In 1555 the first officially "Calvinist" congregation was established illicitly in Paris. Already burgeoning despite heavy persecution, reform in France continued, associated with Calvin. In 1557, one of Calvin's students, Antoine de Chandieu, prepared a confession of faith strikingly reflective of Calvin's thought.[69] In his article on the Lord's Supper, he employs Calvin's very locutions: though Christ is in heaven, "we believe that by the secret and incomprehensible power of his Spirit he nourishes and vivifies us with the substance of his body and of his blood." This mystery, he confesses, "surmounts the highest measure of our sense and even the natural order"; "it can be apprehended only by faith." To this point, his overall expression may be read to reflect Bullinger's thought as much as Calvin's. In a second article on the Lord's Supper, however, he declares—seemingly as only Calvin would—that

> in the Lord's Supper, as in baptism, God gives us really and in fact that which he sets forth to us; . . . consequently with these signs is given the true possession and enjoyment of that which they present to us. And thus all who bring a pure faith, like a vessel, to the sacred table of Christ, receive truly that of which it is a sign; for the body and blood of Jesus Christ give food and drink to the soul, no less than bread and wine nourish the body.

In 1559, the Reformed Church in France sought Calvin's assistance in preparing a confession of faith to present to the king. Calvin reluctantly agreed, but did not start fresh; he borrowed his student's confession and expanded on it. While Calvin simply reiterated Chandieu's two articles on the Lord's Supper verbatim,[70] his amendment to Chandieu's article on sacraments is telling: sacraments are not only seals of God's grace, but also "such outward signs as God works through them by the virtue of his Spirit, to the end that they figure nothing to us in vain." In short, Calvin effectively amends that these signs are not empty, but are instruments, employing the very language he once addressed

---

68. Article 22, Cochrane, *Reformed Confessions*, 108–9.

69. The confession is included in the *Ioannis Calvini opera quae supesunt omnia*, ed. Wilhelm Baum, et al., vol. 9 (Brunsvigae: A. Schwetschke and Son, 1863–1900): 715–30, hereafter *CO*. On Chandieu as author, see Jacques Pannier (*Les origins de la confession de foi et la discipline des églises réformées de France* [Paris: Relix Alcan, 1936], 83 and 92). The following translations are my own, but see The French Confession of Faith, 1559, Articles 34 and 36, in Philip Schaff, *The Creeds of Christendom*, vol. 3 (New York: Harper, 1882), 380.

70. See *CO* 9:751–52; also Article 36, Schaff, *Creeds*, 380.

to Bullinger on this point. Although the confession underwent further revision before ratification in 1559, Calvin's amendments remained, unaltered.

Not unlike the Reformed Church of France, the Reformed Church of the Low Countries emerged clandestinely until intense persecution invoked outright revolt. Strife was political as much as religious. In this context, Guido de Brès prepared an apology for Reformed Protestants in the region: the Belgic Confession, 1561, clearly modeled on the French Confession, 1559. Article 33 speaks of sacraments "instrumentally" as the French Confession before it: sacraments are "visible signs and seals of a thing inward and invisible, *by means of which* God works in us through the power of the Holy Spirit; so they are not empty and hollow signs to fool and deceive us."[71] Article 35 concerns the Lord's Supper. The first third concerns the perpetual reality that the sacrament is given "to represent" and "to testify." But the sacraments were not given "in vain": Christ "works in us all he represents by these holy signs," in a secret, incomprehensible manner. "Yet we do not go wrong when we say that what is eaten is Christ's own natural body and what is drunk is his own blood—but the manner in which we eat it is not by the mouth but by the Spirit, through faith." Finally, "this banquet is a spiritual table at which Christ communicates himself to us. . . . the sacraments are conjoined with the thing signified."[72] The Belgic Confession was ratified in 1619 at the Synod of Dort as an official confession of the Reformed Church in the Netherlands. Amid hints of Bullinger's thought, the confession ultimately upholds Calvin's doctrine of the Lord's Supper.

The opposite must be said of the Heidelberg Catechism, 1563. In this confession, one finds only hints of Calvin's robust doctrine of the Lord's Supper, though some interpreters assume that the catechism offers a concise, clear presentation of Calvin's thought. It does not. In fact, Bullinger's doctrine is preeminent, though, overall, influences on the confession's text must be understood to be varied since the confession was constructed in the Palatinate to be a good fence for making good neighbors of resident Melanchthonians, Calvinists, and Bullingerian-Zwinglians.[73] So, the catechism presents "those—and only those—dimensions of sacramental teaching that [they] could confess with one voice," dimensions such as

> the definition of the sacraments, the connection between the sacraments and Christ's sacrificial death, the parallelism between sign and signified, . . . and the Holy Spirit as the bond of union between Christ and the believer in the Lord's Supper.[74]

Conversely, the catechism conceals—in critical *silence*—certain dimensions of sacramental doctrine, such as the divisive issue of "the relationship between the signs of the sacraments and that which they signify."[75] For this reason, the

71. Schaff, *Creeds*, 424. Translation slightly adapted.
72. Ibid.
73. Bierma, *Heidelberg Catechism*.
74. Ibid., 7, 19–20.
75. Ibid., 7.

catechism is "shy about the notion of sacramental means."[76] It never declares, as Calvin does, that sacraments are instruments, or that "Christ, who instituted the Supper, works effectually by its means."[77]

In the same year the Heidelberg Catechism was issued for churches of the German Palatinate, the Thirty-nine Articles were issued for the Church of England, as the confessional statement of the Elizabethan Settlement. Reflective of the "Reformed" theology brought to the island already during the reign of Edward VI, its view on the Lord's Supper is "cautiously Calvinistic."[78] Sacraments are declared to be "effectual signs of grace . . . by which God works invisibly in us."[79] While this accords well with Calvin's view, and could be taken as an appropriation of it (or perhaps Bucer's), it also technically accords with Bullinger's view. The same may be said of its confession that "The body of Christ is given, taken, and eaten, in the Supper, only after an heavenly and spiritual manner. And the medium whereby the Body of Christ is received and eaten in the Supper, is Faith."[80] The strongest hint that this is to be taken according to Calvin is given in the article on baptism: Baptism "is . . . a sign of Regeneration or New-Birth, whereby, as by an instrument, they that receive Baptism rightly are grafted into the Church."[81] If the Thirty-nine Articles may be read as "cautiously Calvinistic," the brief Anglican Catechism (1549/1662) may be read as "clearly Calvinistic."[82] A sacrament is "an outward and visible sign of an inward and spiritual grace given unto us, ordained by Christ himself as a *means* whereby we receive the same, and a pledge to assure us thereof." The "sign of the Lord's Supper" is bread and wine; the "thing signified" is "the body and blood of Christ, which are verily and indeed taken and received by the faithful in the Lord's Supper."[83]

Calvin's doctrine of the sacraments perdured in especially the catechisms of the "Presbyterian Puritan" Westminster Assembly of the mid-seventeenth century. The Westminster Confession is not so clearly Calvinistic. Regarding sacraments as "means of grace," its "Calvinistic intention" must be "gleaned from incidental phrases that presuppose the instrumental view,"[84] phrases in which "grace" is said to be "exhibited."[85] In Article 29, on the Lord's Supper, Calvin's strong view is glimpsed in the use of such words as "sealing," "bond," and "pledge." Still, its discussion of the elements and that which they signify may be read to reflect a "parallel" rather than a strongly "instrumental" doctrine: "The outward elements . . . have such relation to him crucified, as that truly, yet sacramentally only, they are called by the name of the things they represent,

76. Gerrish, "Sign," 125.
77. Calvin, *Last Admonition*, in *Tracts*, 374.
78. Gerrish, "Sign," 126.
79. Schaff, *Creeds*, 502.
80. Ibid., 506.
81. Ibid., 504.
82. According to Gerrish, the catechism "expresses Calvin's intention exactly" ("Sign," 126).
83. Schaff, *Creeds*, 521. According to Schaff's introduction, exchanges about the sacraments were introduced in 1604.
84. Gerrish, "Sign," 126.
85. Article 27.3 and Article 28.6, in Schaff, *Creeds*, 661 and 663.

to wit, the body and blood of Christ"[86]; "worthy receivers," then, "outwardly partaking of the visible elements in this sacrament, do then also inwardly by faith, really and indeed, yet not carnally and corporally, but spiritually, receive and feed upon Christ crucified."[87] The Westminster Catechisms, however, are more clearly "instrumental," in averring that sacraments are "effectual means." So, "when the catechisms speak of feeding upon the body of Christ, they must surely mean a spiritual feeding that is *effected through* the outward eating of the bread."[88] That the Westminster divines intended Calvin's instrumental view is evident not least in the fact that, when the Larger and Shorter Catechisms speak of the functions of the Lord's Supper, "the Shorter Catechism restricts itself precisely to those functions that go beyond Zwingli's or Bullinger's" views[89]: Sacraments are ordained by the Lord, "wherein, *by sensible signs,* Christ and [his] benefits . . . are represented, sealed, and *applied*"; the Lord's Supper is "a sacrament, wherein, *by giving and receiving bread and wine,* . . . worthy receivers *are . . . made* partakers of his body and blood . . . to their spiritual nourishment and growth in grace."[90] In speaking this way, the Westminster Shorter Catechism accords with the Anglican Catechism (1549) and the Scots Confession (1560). The latter approaches "the full Calvinistic doctrine of the Lord's Supper in strikingly realistic language,"[91] even if Calvin's thought is not its only, or even primary, source.[92]

Calvin's doctrine of the Lord's Supper was appropriated into several confessions in the late-Reformation period and in the period immediately following. Only some have been surveyed here, though they are critical, given the extent to which they were trafficked throughout Europe, and, indeed, the world, in the post-Reformation period, and the extent to which they still have bearing in the Reformed tradition, broadly construed, today.

Theological Assimilation

Before the close of the sixteenth century, Protestant theological discourse began to shift to a new method that endured well into the late seventeenth century. At the risk of caricaturing this shift, it may be said that the discourse of the Reformers—most of whom were humanists trained in philology and a "historical-critical" method of approaching texts—is rhetorical, and the discourse of their successors analytical, syllogistic, logical. Early Reformers sought escape from the late-medieval scholastic method of theological discourse, or at least certain of its burdens; their successors returned to it, refreshed, not for the

86. Article 29.5, in Schaff, *Creeds*, 665.
87. Article 29.7, in ibid., 666.
88. Gerrish, "Sign," 127.
89. Ibid.
90. Question and Answer 92 and 96; Schaff, *Creeds*, 696 and 697. Emphasis added.
91. Gerrish, "Sign," 127. Richard L. Greaves, "John Knox, the Reformed Tradition, and the Sacrament of the Lord's Supper," *Archiv für Reformationsgeschichte* 66 (1975): 251.
92. Greaves ("John Knox") argues for the dominant influence of Bucer.

sake of the method itself, but for the sake of discerning truth. In 1580, Antoine de Chandieu, the student of Calvin who was instrumental in the formulation of the French Confession (1559), issued "an explicit and urgent call for a 'scholastic method' in Reformed theology," founded on Aristotelian logic.[93] Though Chandieu formally issued the call, some of his contemporaries were already shifting in this direction with him, taking "the ideas of the Reformers and, for the sake of preserving Protestantism from external attack and internal dissolution, [forging] a precise and detailed technical edifice of school-theology, now called Protestant orthodoxy or Protestant scholasticism."[94] They thus sustained "the historical progress of the Reformation . . . [and] clarified and developed the doctrines of the Reformers."[95] "Clarified and developed" are key words here, as they beg the question as to whether the Reformers' doctrine was "clarified and developed" beyond, or away from, their intent.

With respect to Calvin's doctrine of the Lord's Supper, this is a question Jill Raitt has asked of the works of Theodore Beza and, briefly, of Johannes Wollebius after him.[96] Beza was Calvin's specifically appointed successor in Geneva, and was bequeathed, among other responsibilities, the defense of Calvin's doctrine of the Lord's Supper.[97] According to Raitt,

> It is his development of the nature of the relation of the signs to the signified, hence of the recurrent problem of sacramental causality, which leads Beza to turn more and more to the method of the scholastics. In scholastic terminology, logic, and metaphysics he found the precision instruments he thought he required both to elucidate and to defend Calvin's doctrine of the Lord's Supper.[98]

Beza considered himself to be a faithful curator of Calvin's thought; but given his context, aim, and method, "he could not help being an innovator as well."[99] Raitt summarizes Beza's doctrine accordingly:

> [H]is main concern was to defend the real spiritual presence of Christ to the faithful communicant. . . . Beza insisted that Christ offered himself substantially in the Supper by the power of the Holy Spirit since the benefits of Christ cannot be separated from Christ himself. This is true also

93. Donald Sinnema, "Antoine De Chandieu's Call for a Scholastic Reformed Theology (1580)," in *Later Calvinism: International Perspectives*, ed. W. Fred Graham (Kirsville, MO: Sixteenth Century Journal Publishers, 1994), 159 and 168.

94. Richard A. Muller, preface to *Dictionary of Latin and Greek Theological Terms: Drawn Principally from Protestant Scholastic Theology* (Grand Rapids: Baker Book House, 1985), 7.

95. Ibid., 7.

96. Jill Raitt, *The Eucharistic Theology of Theodore Beza: Development of the Reformed Doctrine* (Chambersburg, PA: American Academy of Religion, 1972).

97. In the 1550s and early 1560s, Calvin was engaged in a pamphlet war initiated by the Gnesio-Lutherans Joachim Westphal and Tilemann Heshusius. Beza was appointed to respond to their continued attacks after Calvin was no longer able or inclined.

98. Raitt, *Eucharistic Theology*, viii.

99. Raitt, *Eucharistic Theology*, 9.

of the reception of Christ by the hearing of the word in faith, but in the Supper the power of the word is implemented and focused in the liturgy and individual communion, for the Holy Spirit creates and uses faith as a primary instrument and the word and sacraments as secondary instruments to unite the elect and Christ. So close is this union that the faithful become "bone of his bone and flesh of his flesh." This occurs, therefore, spiritually and mystically since it is by the power of the Holy Spirit and beyond human comprehension. With regard to the elements of bread and wine, these retain their nature as food and drink, but they are no longer destined merely to nourish naturally, but rather to feed the faithful with the bread of eternal life, the body and blood of Christ. They are changed, then, and they become and are rightfully called, the sacramental body and blood of Christ.[100]

All of Calvin's principal themes are present: union with Christ, the true communication of Christ *in the Supper*, the role of the Holy Spirit, faith, and mystery. He was faithful in summary. In "the defense of this doctrine, Beza increasingly defined the most difficult point," laboring to define the actual "mode of the conjunction of the signs with the signified, or of the bread and wine in their liturgical context, with the body and blood of Christ." He developed two terms, "analogy" and "relation" in an increasingly scholastic manner."[101] Calvin himself appreciated the sacrament as "analogy": as bread and wine nourish and delight the body, the body and blood of Christ nourish and delight the soul; but bread remains bread in order that that which is signified is *truly signified*.[102] As Raitt puts it, Beza pressed this point in the following direction: "Analogical signification is essential to the Supper which is eaten primarily by the faith-informed understanding: [not with the teeth, but with the mind]. The understanding, uplifted by faith, is then itself an instrument of the Holy Spirit for uniting the communicant with the whole Christ."[103] One wonders how Beza's emphasis on understanding accords with Calvin's emphasis that the partaking of Christ is not "by understanding and imagination," but is "true," by faith. Furthermore, does such a conclusion incline toward a confusion, or conflation, of the liturgical *sursum corda* and act of communion? That is, does Beza's understanding effectively diminish the communion, making the *sursum corda* not preparatory for the communion, but the communion itself? As discussed above (pp. 156–57), this does not seem to be the necessary end to which Calvin's "rhetoric" aims.

Beza's primary concern, however, is the *mode* of the "relation" that "analogy" implies. Calvin says the two are "conjoined"—nothing more. Beza turns "relation" into a philosophical category, the employment of which follows Calvin's trajectory: "The Supper is not an activity . . . which provides an occasion for a parallel activity of the Holy Spirit. The activity of the Spirit is *through* the activity

---

100. Ibid., 69.
101. Ibid., 69–70.
102. *Institutes* 4.17.14.
103. Raitt, *Eucharistic Theology*, 70.

and elements of the liturgy."[104] Beza posits a *relation* between the elements and Christ which is not physical, local, spatial, or temporal, but transcends these. So bread and wine *are not merely* bread and wine,

> nor are they changed substantially or joined with the body of Christ so that Christ can be said to be "under, with, or in" the bread. On the natural level, they remain bread and wine and as such nourish the body. But in the action of the Lord's Supper as declared by the words of institution, they are changed. They serve a new end and use through their relation to Christ, established by the Holy Spirit, and they become subservient efficient causes of the union of the faithful with Christ. They are food that nourishes eternal life.[105]

Explicating the "change" of the elements given their liturgical use, Beza amplifies a *pianissimo* motif in Calvin's doctrine. Emphasizing the Spirit, he keeps to Calvin, though he is wont to elucidate the Supper according to Aristotle's four causes to an extent that surpasses Calvin's.[106]

According to Raitt, if Beza's scholasticism enhanced Calvin's doctrine of the Lord's Supper, Wollebius' detracted from it. To paraphrase her conclusion: What places Beza nearer Calvin than Wollebius is Beza's emphasis on the "mystical." Wollebius explains everything in matter-of-fact propositions, with Scripture as tidy proof texts. He does not speak of the intimate union of the faithful with Christ, the purpose of the Lord's Supper as Beza (following Calvin) understands it, nor does he teach that the principal agent is the Holy Spirit, who effects that union. While Beza's method was often scholastic, he remained inspired by Calvin's doctrine of the Supper, and by that very doctrine was led frequently to the Scriptures to find its substance there. Wollebius, on the other hand, was more concerned to systematize, clarify, and catechize. The inspiration of the Spirit uniting believers to Christ in a fundamentally inexpressible union is, in Wollebius' work, replaced by a rather impersonal means for acquiring grace and merit.[107]

Wollebius' *Compendium of Christian Theology* (1626), on which Raitt bases her study, became a standard text for Reformed theologians of the seventeenth century and beyond. While its conclusions should not be taken to represent those of every Reformed treatise on the Lord's Supper in the era of Protestant scholasticism, its theological tenor at least suggests the fittingness of having Calvin open in one hand while reading the works of his (would-be) successors in the other.

For Calvin, the mystery of the sacrament is indeed worthy of reflection, deep theological reflection, even "scholastic" reflection, but ultimately it is a gift to be enjoyed. To quote him as before:

104. Ibid., 71.
105. Ibid.
106. Ibid.
107. Ibid., 73.

I rather experience [the mystery] than understand it. Therefore, I here embrace without controversy the truth of God in which I may safely rest. [Christ] declares his flesh the food of my soul, his blood its drink. I offer my soul to him to be fed with such food. In his Sacred Supper he bids me take, eat, and drink his body and blood under the symbols of bread and wine. I do not doubt that he himself truly presents them, and that I receive them.[108]

108. *Institutes* 4.17.32.

Chapter 8

Calvin's Doctrine
of the Lord's Supper

*Modern Reception
and Contemporary Possibilities*

TIMOTHY HESSEL-ROBINSON

INTRODUCTION

Tracing the history of the reception of any particular figure's doctrine is a
complex task. The task is even more complex when the doctrine has to do
with the practice of the Lord's Supper, because the Supper is a ritual practice
in which the Christian church claims to meet its risen Lord. Theology and
practice are inevitably intertwined. The doctrinal disputes about this rite that
have taken place in the history of sacramental theology have centered on the
precise nature of this meeting: what, exactly, occurs when the church gath-
ers around the table, or altar, set with bread and wine? As Sue Rozeboom's
first essay in this section makes clear, this was one of the liveliest questions
of the sixteenth-century Reformation, and John Calvin made a significant,
if not entirely novel, contribution in addressing it. As Rozeboom's essay also
makes clear, however, distinguishing Calvin's voice from other voices such as
Luther's, Zwingli's, Bucer's, Bullinger's, or others in the history of theologies
of the Lord's Supper requires a finely tuned ear. Calvin's is not the only, or
even the first voice of the Reformed tradition. Calvin's theology of the Lord's
Supper developed over time, and, as Paul Rorem points out, Calvin's views

Calvin

were "clarified and developed through dialogue" with colleagues and opponents alike.[1] As Rozeboom explains, Brian Gerrish has identified three operative notions of sacramental efficacy during the period: symbolic parallelism, symbolic instrumentalism, and symbolic memorialism.[2] Calvin's teaching has been placed within the symbolic instrumentalism category, but in many later Reformed communities any or all of the three views might be held without a critical awareness of their distinctions in practice.

Nevertheless, there have been numerous attempts to consciously reclaim Calvin's "true doctrine" of the Lord's Supper. In this essay, we will examine three instances of how Calvin's eucharistic theology has been received among the various heirs of the Reformed tradition since the beginning of the eighteenth century. Each of the figures or movements treated here comes from the United States. Obviously, Calvin's influence on this subject is not limited to the United States, and other case studies could have been selected from the U.S. context. However, the vast, global reach of Calvin's influence and the limitations of space necessitate making some hard choices. Jonathan Edwards, Alexander Campbell and the Disciples of Christ, and John Williamson Nevin provide illuminating snapshots of Calvin's impact ranging from intentional retrieval efforts to ambivalent adoption, from subtle influence to explicit reception. The logic for these choices is as follows: Edwards represents a transition between the Puritan and revivalist eras, each in their own way so influential for American culture and piety. The Disciples embodied both a frontier, revivalist impulse and an Enlightenment-inspired rationalist approach to religion in their quest for a restored apostolic order. A significant dimension of that apostolic order was the centrality of the Lord's Supper for the church. Finally, Nevin was a harsh critic of revivalism and rationalism, but shared the catholic and sacramental impulse of the Disciples. However, he drew on very different philosophical and theological influences while claiming to restore the true Calvinist doctrine of the church and its sacraments. Each drew on Calvin in distinctive ways and appropriated various dimensions of Calvin's theology for their own purposes. These brief glimpses of each figure's or movement's theology will reflect that diversity. The common thread in my treatments will be the way in which each of these figures has dealt with the issue of Christ's presence in the Lord's Supper. In the concluding section I will suggest some possibilities for retrieving dimensions of Calvin's theology of the Lord's Supper today, there engaging some recent appropriations of Calvin's eucharistic theology.

As I move to the heart of this essay, David Tracy's notion of a "classic" might be useful when thinking of Calvin's theology. Tracy articulates two senses of a "classic:" Classics are those texts "that have helped found or form a particular culture," and those texts that "bear an excess and permanence of meaning,

---

1. Paul Rorem, "Calvin and Bullinger on the Lord's Supper, Part 1: The Impasse," *Lutheran Quarterly* 2, no. 2 (Summer 1988): 155.

2. Brian A. Gerrish, "Sign and Reality: The Lord's Supper in the Reformed Confessions," *The Old Protestantism and the New* (Chicago: University of Chicago Press, 1982), 118–30.

yet always resist definitive interpretation."[3] As Rozeboom has pointed out, Calvin's full theology of the Lord's Supper is not contained in any single text, even the *Institutes*; thus we are not dealing with a discrete, "classic" treatise on the Eucharist. However, Calvin's teaching on the Supper can be viewed as a classic *doctrine*, of sorts. While it stands alongside other Reformed teachings on the Supper, Calvin's doctrine has played a significant role in shaping the practice and theology of Reformed churches. As to the many efforts to restore the "true" Calvinist doctrine of the Lord's Supper, they are evidence of Tracy's second point: the classic ultimately resists definitive interpretation. And so, the work continues.

JONATHAN EDWARDS (1703–1758)

Although Jonathan Edwards is not regarded as one of the great thinkers in the history of sacramental theology, nor did he write a systematic treatise on the Lord's Supper, there are good reasons to begin this study with Edwards. Besides his status as one of the most significant theologians of the Reformed tradition, Edwards also serves as a convenient transition point for the purposes of this book. Having lived in the first half of the eighteenth century, Edwards is variously considered to be either "the last Puritan" or the herald of the Great Awakening. Formed by New England Calvinist piety, Edwards devoted his enormous intellectual abilities to reconciling Reformed faith with Enlightenment thought. While he articulated a sophisticated, empirical account of religious experience and of genuine religious affections,[4] many of Edwards's views reflected those of the seventeenth-century North American Puritans. Like his Puritan forebears, his sacramental writings shy away from debating the subtleties of sacramental theology that so occupied the magisterial continental reformers. Brooks Holifield has noted that Puritans, while joining the sixteenth-century Reformers in rejecting both Roman Catholic and Lutheran views of the sacrament, added little to the substance of the discussion. Many Puritans tended to conflate Zwinglian and Calvinian themes to fit particular concerns or circumstances. Their sacramental views "represented the practical and pastoral application of a broad Reformed consensus."[5] The most significant Puritan contribution to Reformed eucharistic theology was a warm, affective, sacramental piety.

Edwards's major writings on the Lord's Supper emerged from controversy. After rejecting his grandfather's, Solomon Stoddard's, policies on admission to

3. David Tracy, *Plurality and Ambiguity: Hermeneutics, Religion, Hope* (San Francisco: Harper & Row, 1987), 12. For Tracy's fullest discussion of "classics" see *The Analogical Imagination: Christian Theology and the Culture of Pluralism* (New York: Crossroad, 1981), 99–153.

4. Jonathan Edwards, *The Works of Jonathan Edwards*, vol. 2, *Religious Affections*, ed. John E. Smith (New Haven, CT: Yale University Press, 1959).

5. E. Brooks Holifield, *The Covenant Sealed: The Development of Puritan Sacramental Theology in Old and New England, 1570–1720* (New Haven, CT, and London: Yale University Press, 1974), 27.

the Lord's Supper, Edwards produced *A Humble Inquiry into the Rules of the Word of God* to defend his actions.[6] Colonial Puritans struggled throughout the seventeenth century with the notions of covenant, election, regeneration, and sanctification received through their Calvinist heritage. While trying to maintain a pure and visible church, they had interpreted Calvin's teachings about election and regeneration in ways that caused anxiety about the assurance of their salvation and about their worthiness to commune. Following Calvin's admonition to careful self-examination in preparation for the sacrament, Puritans were scrupulous about their introspection before communing.[7] The "halfway covenant" was the uneasy arrangement by which New England's ministers determined to allow baptism for the children of baptized church members who could not produce clear evidence of "saving faith."[8] The communion table remained fenced, open only to the regenerate. Stoddard thought such a requirement caused unnecessary anxiety among otherwise sincere and upright believers, and presented a "stumbling block" to full communion realized at the Lord's table. Thus, Stoddard determined to welcome to the Supper anyone who demonstrated a basic knowledge of faith and who was living a fundamentally upright life, regardless of whether they could demonstrate an experience of saving faith. If the sacrament was the Word made visible, as Reformed doctrine held, then Stoddard believed the Supper was also a "converting ordinance," able to move communicants toward conversion and growth in grace. New England's leading divines attacked Stoddard's position, claiming he threatened to pollute the sacrament and the church. Still, Stoddard's practice became the settled policy in his Northampton parish until his grandson reversed it, inviting attacks from the parishioners. Like most conflicts between pastor and parish the Northampton crisis was not entirely theological: politics and personality played a role in Edwards's demise. However, there were some significant theological principles at stake for Edwards that had to do with the proper interpretation of Reformed faith.

Like Calvin, Edwards regarded the Lord's Supper as a seal of the covenant of grace. "'Tis a seal on Christ's part," he explains. The one who presides at the ordinance acts as Christ's "representative," declaring and confirming Christ's intention to honor the covenant made with the faithful through his death. Christ's action includes joining himself to his people. The Supper shows "his

---

6. For the history of the Stodderean and Northampton controversies, see Holifield, *The Covenant Sealed*; Thomas M. and Virginia L. Davis, eds., *Edward Taylor vs. Solomon Stoddard: The Nature of the Lord's Supper*, vol. 2, *The Unpublished Writings of Edward Taylor* (Boston: Twayne Publishers, 1981), 1–57; George Marsden, *Jonathan Edwards: A Life* (New Haven, CT, and London: Yale University Press, 2003), 341–74.

7. John Calvin, "Short Treatise on the Holy Supper of Our Lord Jesus Christ," in John Dillenberger, ed., *John Calvin: Selections from His Writings* (Garden City, NY: Anchor Books, 1971), 519–21. Holifield's *The Covenant Sealed* is an examination of the numerous sacramental manuals that were published to aid communicants in preparing for celebrations of the Lord's Supper.

8. In maintaining the boundaries of a "pure" or "visible" church, many Puritans required evidence of "saving faith" as distinct from mere external affirmations of Christian doctrine. Such faith was discerned internally, assuring the believer of his or her place among the elect.

readiness to receive them into that near relation, into vital union."[9] Edwards likened the covenant to a marriage and the Supper to a wedding feast. In part, the wedding feast imagery reflects an eschatological dimension in Edwards's understanding of the Supper: it points to "the marriage supper of the Lamb" which celebrates the consummation of creation and provides a foretaste of the coming heavenly banquet when the "resurrected church would continue to 'feast' on the 'body and blood of Christ.'"[10]

However, like many earlier Puritans, Edwards also drew on marital imagery to express the affective piety associated with Communion. A wedding involves two consenting parties and so the analogy had to be extended when describing what happens in the Lord's Supper. Not only is the covenant sealed by Christ, but also by the people. It is "a solemn declaration and open testimony and confirmation that they do make this part of the covenant, that they comply with the condition required of them . . . 'tis just in this ordinance as 'tis in the mutual tokens of consent and acceptance in marriage."[11] Calvin, too, explained that the sacraments are God's seal of assurance toward God's people, and the means by which "we in turn testify our piety towards Him."[12] Calvin also stressed that the benefits of the sacrament accrue only to those who receive it in faith, although the objective offering of Christ's body and blood is extended to all. Rozeboom earlier pointed out how Calvin's ideas have been repeatedly misunderstood or distorted as emphasizing the subjective aspect of the Supper. She shows that Calvin's sense of the objective reality of Christ's gift is clear and strong. However, because of his context, Edwards did not emphasize divine agency as strongly as Calvin did. Greatly concerned to maintain the purity of the rite and of the community by requiring professions of faith, Edwards and the anti-Stoddereans tip the balance between God's action and human response in favor of the latter.

There is a further dimension of the marriage analogy to which Edwards's understanding of presence is related. Earlier Puritans regarded the Supper as a place of intimate encounter between Christ and the believer, often drawing on the erotic imagery of the Song of Songs to describe this encounter. Viewing the eucharistic moment as a consummation of this spiritual marriage, opponents of Stoddard, such as Edward Taylor, naturally saw it as reserved for those who were assuredly a part of the covenant.[13] Edwards's sacrament sermons echo the language and imagery of those earlier Puritans, who spoke of the bridegroom's

9. Jonathan Edwards, "Sacramental Union in Christ," *The Works of Jonathan Edwards*, vol. 25, *Sermons and Discourses 1743–1758*, ed. Wilson H. Kimnach (New Haven, CT, and London: Yale University Press, 2006), 587.

10. William Danaher Jr., "By Sensible Signs Represented: Jonathan Edwards' Sermons on the Lord's Supper," *Pro Ecclesia* 7, no. 3 (1998): 264.

11. Edwards, "Sacramental Union in Christ," 588.

12. John Calvin, *Institutes of the Christian Religion* (1559), ed. John T. McNeill, trans. Ford Lewis Battles (Philadelphia: The Westminster Press, 1960), 4.14.1. Hereafter, *Institutes*.

13. See my articles "Language of the Feast: The Song of Songs in Edward Taylor's Eucharistic Theology," *Proceedings of the North American Academy of Liturgy* (2008): 90–113, and "Erotic Mysticism in Puritan Eucharistic Spirituality," *Studies in Spirituality* 19 (2009).

seductive allures on display at the feast. The Lord's Supper is intended to stimulate longing for Christ. In a sermon on the Song of Songs 5:1 Edwards told his congregation, "here we have that spiritual meat & drink Represented and offered to excite our hunger & thirst." Earlier in the sermon he dealt with spiritual appetites, explaining that the righteous person displays a deep hunger for Jesus Christ as the "bread which came down from heaven." Regenerated persons desire spiritual pleasures like the unregenerate desire carnal pleasures. However, their carnal appetites now constrained by grace, the former should place no restraint on their spiritual appetites: "there is no such thing as excess in Longings after Jesus." The righteous "may Indulge those appetites as much as they will in their thoughts & meditations & in their Practice they may drink yea swim in the Rivers of spiritual pleasure."[14] Edwards did not go as far as Taylor and others who were quite explicit about the erotic dimensions of their eucharistic experience, but it is evident that Edwards viewed the experience of Christ in the Supper as ecstatic, pleasurable, and intimate.

Such language belies a sense of something more than a memorial of remembrance. Edwards certainly regarded the Supper as a memorial feast that calls to mind Christ's atoning death; some statements in his controversy writings seem to indicate a purely memorial or spiritual sense of presence.[15] There is more to Edwards's understanding, though. David Rightmire interprets Edwards's notion of "representation" as "a recalling of things that once took place literally and naturally," rather than as an anamnetic "re-presenting of this reality in sacramental signification."[16] However, Edwards also speaks of the Lord's Supper as the place where Christ meets his followers as they gather in loving fellowship. As Christians sit at the feast of God they have communion with Christ:

> As in a feast they all have communion in the same fare with the host and
> with the other guests . . . Christ eats of the same feast with believers, and
> he eats with them . . . Christ sat with his disciples at this first sacrament,
> which For instance, signifies that he always has communion with them in
> the same spiritual blessings.[17]

14. Jonathan Edwards, "Sermon on Cant. 5:1 [1729]" in *Works of Jonathan Edwards Online*, vol. 44, *Sermons*, 2nd ser. (Jonathan Edwards Center, Yale University, 2008), http://edwards .yale.edu/archive?path=aHR0cDovL2Vkd2FyZHMueWFsZS5lZHUvY2dpLWJpbi9uZXdwaGlsby 9nZXRvbmplY3QucGw/Yy40MjoxNy53amVidVv (accessed June 7, 2009).

15. Danaher, 265; Jonathan Edwards, "A Humble Inquiry into the Rules of the Word of God, Concerning the Qualifications Requisite to a Complete Standing and Full Communion in the Visible Christian Church," in David Hall, ed., *The Works of Jonathan Edwards: Ecclesiastical Writings* (New Haven, CT, and London: Yale University Press, 1994), 174. Danaher states that Edwards was not trying to explain any particular notion of presence in *A Humble Inquiry*, passing lightly over the question as he tried to establish that the Supper is not a converting ordinance. Danaher argues that for a fuller understanding of this dimension of Edwards, one must examine his sacramental sermons.

16. David Rightmire, "The Sacramental Theology of Jonathan Edwards in the Context of Controversy," *Fides et Historia* 21 (January 1989): 57.

17. Edwards, "The Spiritual Blessings of the Gospel Represented by a Feast," in *Works of Jonathan Edwards*, vol. 14, *Sermons and Discourses 1723–1729*, ed. Kenneth P. Minkema (New Haven, CT: Yale University Press, 1997), 287.

Edwards repeatedly emphasized the communal dimension of the Lord's Supper. Christ is truly present, not in the elements of bread and wine, but in the loving communion of the faithful. Such an intimate encounter as is available at the Lord's Table cannot be offered to just anyone. Edwards's concern to ensure the purity of the rite, his efforts to establish a visible church, and his keen interest in the nature of genuine religious experience in the individual left the impression that he, like many earlier Puritans, promoted a more subjective view of the sacrament. Edwards maintained Calvin's objective sense of the Supper more effectively than many Puritans who preceded him, but his emphasis on maintaining the purity of the rite diverged somewhat from Calvin's understanding.

In some ways Edwards's reception of Calvin's theology of the Lord's Supper reflects his reception of Calvin's ecclesiology. According to Amy Plantinga Pauw, the Genevan Reformer and the New England revivalist each held a view of the church that displayed a "persistent tension between the ideals of inclusiveness and holiness."[18] This tension is evident in Edwards's warm language about the intimacy of the Lord's Supper as a place where Christ meets and nourishes his followers on one hand, and his efforts to ensure that the rite was not polluted by anyone unworthy to partake on the other.[19] As noted above, Edwards's emphasis on the purity of the Supper gave him a weaker sense of the objective offering of Christ at the Supper than in Calvin. The emphasis that Edwards had—with many other Puritans—on scrupulous self-examination and the requirement of "saving faith" at the Supper stands in some contrast to Calvin's approach toward the Lord's Supper and ecclesiology. On the one hand, Calvin is clear that "unbelievers" who partake of the Lord's Supper "profane the mystery." However, this occurs not through participation in the ritual of eating and drinking, but by "trampling underfoot the pledge of sacred union with God, which they ought reverently to have received."[20] That is, God's goodness and generous self-offering is what ensures the efficacy of the sacrament and this is offered to believer and unbeliever alike in the Supper, even though only believers receive the benefit.[21] Reflecting on what it means to be "worthy" to participate in the rite, Calvin says that if perfection is to be the standard of admittance then no one can participate. If one must be "pure and purged of sin" to partake, then "the door will always remain locked by that dread prohibition which decrees that they who eat and drink unworthily eat and drink judgment upon themselves."[22] Because God makes us worthy, faith and love rather than perfection are required to participate in the Supper. Calvin declares "this sacred feast is medicine for the

---

18. Amy Plantinga Pauw, "Practical Ecclesiology in John Calvin and Jonathan Edwards," in Thomas J. Davis, ed., *The American Legacy of John Calvin* (New York: Oxford University Press, 2010), 91–92.

19. Ibid., 97.

20. *Institutes* 4.17.33.

21. Calvin makes the following analogy: "Just as rain falling upon a hard rock flows off because no entrance opens into the stone, the wicked by their hardness so repel God's grace that it does not reach them." *Institutes* 4.17.33.

22. Ibid., 4.17.41.

sick, solace for sinners, alms to the poor." The tension named by Pauw remains in Calvin's writing on the church, but Calvin maintained a clearer sense that God ensures the efficacy of the Lord's Supper, as opposed to the individual's ability to demonstrate "saving faith" and the fruit of the Spirit. Edwards's ministry in Northampton might have ended more gracefully if he had more deeply appropriated Calvin's emphasis on divine agency in the Lord's Supper.

DISCIPLES OF CHRIST

The Christian Church (Disciples of Christ) presents a complex and ambiguous case study of engagement with Calvin's sacramental theology. Each of the four acknowledged early Disciples founders were formed in various branches of the Presbyterian Church; all of them were familiar with Calvinist theology, especially as it was mediated by the Westminster Confession; and their sacramental theology indicates this influence.[23] Alexander Campbell (1788–1866) and his father, Thomas (1763–1854), were Irish Presbyterians who migrated to the United States. Barton Stone (1772–1844), born in Maryland, was ordained as a Presbyterian. Walter Scott (1796–1861) was a member of the Church of Scotland before his emigration. However, arising within and influenced by early nineteenth-century revivalism, the Disciples were also shaped by the populism of the frontier and by the spirit of reason emerging from Enlightenment philosophy. Early Disciples were restorationists who aimed to do away with "human opinions" that divide Christ's body, vowing to rely solely on the Bible for guidance in matters of faith, morality, church organization, and worship. Such intentions echoed those of the sixteenth-century Reformers, the Puritans, and other previous restoration movements. Early Disciples saw themselves as restoring the purity and simplicity of the primitive apostolic church, or the "ancient order of things" as Alexander Campbell, the seminal thinker in early Disciples history, termed it.[24] Frequently railing against creeds, confessions, and other "human inventions," eighteenth-century Disciples rhetorically rejected formal theology as hierarchical, divisive, and unbiblical. They determined to rely solely on the Bible as their authority in all matters of faith and practice.

23. For example, Alexander Campbell argued that "sacrament" was not a biblical term, insisting that "ordinance" should be used instead. He used the term in a way similar to its use in the Westminster Confession, as synonymous with "sacrament." Both regarded the "ordinances" as means of grace, although many later Disciples would reject this view, associating sacramental language with magical formulas and priestly hierarchies. See Richard L. Harrison, Jr., "Early Disciples Sacramental Theology: Catholic, Reformed, and Free," in Kenneth Lawrence, ed., *Classic Themes of Disciples Theology* (Fort Worth, TX: Texas Christian University Press, 1986), 49–100; Mark Toulouse, *Joined in Discipleship: The Maturing of an American Religious Movement* (St. Louis: Chalice, 1992), 107–36; James O. Duke, "The Disciples and the Lord's Supper: A Historical Perspective," *Encounter* 50, no. 1 (Winter 1989): 1–28.

24. See E. Brooks Holifield, *Theology in America: Christian Thought from the Age of the Puritans to the Civil War* (New Haven, CT: Yale University Press, 2003), 291–305.

Such an approach would seem to leave little room for engagement with other systems of thought, such as Calvin's, or for extended formal reflection on the loci of theology. In fact, the ambiguity regarding the theological influence of Calvin on the early Disciples arises from the kind of theological reasoning implied in Campbell's statements: Campbell was not interested in developing theological positions based on critical, interpretive engagement with the sources of tradition, but rather on a direct, plain-sense reading of Scripture. He explained the Lord's Supper not by carefully evaluating the Reformer's positions, but by referencing the "apostolic witness" of the New Testament. However, while Campbell and others ostensibly rejected formal and speculative theology, his hermeneutic was explicitly shaped by Lockean epistemology, Baconian logic, and Scottish "common sense" philosophy.[25]

Campbell harshly critiqued Calvin at times and nineteenth-century Disciples wasted few opportunities to attack "Calvinism," often caricatured as a rigid, extreme predestinarian system that undermined evangelism and morality.[26] Campbell normally took aim at theological systems for being divisive, and he charged that Calvin had "renewed the speculative theology of Saint Augustine, and Geneva in a few years became the Alexandria of modern Europe." The result was "debates about forms and ceremonies" and "speculative strifes of opinion."[27] Campbell's severe tone toward Calvinism moderated over time and he often spoke admiringly of the magisterial Reformers, regarding his own movement as a continuation of the Reformation.[28]

The Lord's Supper was a central part of the Disciples reformation and what can be discerned about their sacramental theology generally conforms to their Calvinist heritage. Campbell explicitly appealed to the Reformers when they could bolster his arguments. For instance, he argues from Scripture and the early church fathers for weekly celebration of the Lord's Supper. To cap his argument, he quotes a polemical passage from Calvin to drive his point home: "And truly this custom, which enjoins communicating once a year, is a most evident contrivance of the Devil, by whose instrumentality soever it may have been determined."[29]

25. A fine summary of the empiricism of the Disciples is found in Samuel Pearson, "Faith and Reason in Disciples Theology," in Kenneth Lawrence, ed., *Classic Themes of Disciples Theology* (Fort Worth, TX: Texas Christian University Press, 1986), 101–29.

26. Paul M. Blowers and James O. Duke, "Calvinism," in Douglas Foster, Paul M. Blowers, Anthony Dunnavant, and D. Newell Williams, eds., *The Encyclopedia of the Stone-Campbell Movement* (Grand Rapids: Eerdmans, 2004), 110.

27. Alexander Campbell, *The Christian System*, revised edition (Nashville: Gospel Advocate Company, 1956; original publication, 1839), viii.

28. Blowers and Duke, "Calvinism," 109–11; James O. Duke, "The Nineteenth-Century Reformation in Historical-Theological Perspective: The First One Hundred Years," in James O. Duke and Anthony Dunnavant, eds., *Christian Faith Seeking Historical Understanding: Essays in Honor of H. Jack Forstman* (Macon, GA: Mercer University Press, 1997), 159–86.

29. Alexander Campbell, "On the Breaking of the Bread—No. IV," *The Christian Baptist* 3 (November 7, 1825), 25. The passages from the *Institutes* appear in 4.17.46.

While an argument about the frequency of celebration may appear to be simply a sign of his restorationist hermeneutic, frequent observance of the Supper indicated something fundamental about its character and about the nature of the church for Campbell. The "breaking of bread," as he preferred to call it, was a constitutive act. Like Calvin, he cited Acts 2:42 and Acts 20:7, arguing that sharing the Lord's Supper was the very purpose for which the early church met.[30] Campbell frames this custom in terms of obedience to a divine command, but his argument reveals a sacramental principle in his ecclesiology that would be developed by later Disciples thinkers. His vision of church and of ministry comes into focus around the Table and the act of "breaking the loaf." A primary dimension of this ecclesiology is its christological center. For all their antitheology rhetoric, slogans like "No creed but Christ!" established a "christological *à priori*: as Christ is one so the church of Jesus Christ is one."[31] Christ is the ground of Christian union and communion. This principle is represented at the Table through the symbol of one loaf. Campbell and Stone insisted on the necessity of a single loaf, representing both the one body of the Lord who suffered on the cross and the one "mystical or figurative" body of Christ composed of many members.[32] As ritual and symbolic action, the Lord's Supper continually represents to the church the work of Christ, while uniting believers to one another in the life, death, and resurrection of Christ. Campbell may have claimed scriptural precedent for his christocentric sacramental outlook, but it is a precedent he shared with Calvin.

The issue of Christ's presence in the Lord's Supper and the influence of Calvin's view on early Disciples are very difficult to adjudge. Campbell nowhere addresses the issue directly, but some of his statements about the nature of the Supper indicate a general congruence with Calvin's position of the real but spiritual presence of Christ. Of course, like the Puritans before him, Campbell's statements reflect various influences, often undistinguished and unattributed. Sometimes, Campbell appears to express a symbolic memorialism. However, like Calvin, Campbell regarded the ordinances as means of grace given by God for "our individual enjoyment of the present salvation of God."[33] Campbell's appreciation for the conveyance of a "spiritual presence through a sense-based act" derived from the Reformed tradition.[34] However, the closest Campbell comes to articulating a theology of real presence is when he writes, "every one

30. Campbell, *The Christian System*, 274–78. *Institutes* 4.17.44.
    31. Stephen V. Sprinkle, *Disciples and Theology: Understanding the Faith of a People in Covenant* (St. Louis: Chalice, 1999), 9.
    32. Barton W. Stone, "The Lord's Supper," *Christian Messenger* 3, no. 6 (June 1834):176; Campbell, *The Christian System*, 268.
    33. Campbell, *Christian System*, 148. Campbell regarded the following as ordinances: preaching, baptism, the Lord's Supper, observance of the Lord's day, fasting, prayer, confession of sins, and praise. All of these "contain the grace of God." The primary ordinances were preaching, baptism, and the Lord's Supper, indicating a Calvinist sense of the unity of Word and sacrament. However, Campbell does not develop this connection as fully as Calvin does.
    34. Harrison, "Early Disciples Sacramental Theology," 52.

that speaks or acts must feel himself specially in the presence of the Lord, not as on other days in other places . . . the Lord is indeed 'in the midst of the them' if they have met in his name and according to his word."[35] Overall, Campbell's position seems to fall somewhere between symbolic parallelism and symbolic instrumentalism.

A clearer statement of real presence comes from Robert Milligan (1814–1875), a conservative Disciples theologian who perpetuated Campbell's reasonable, empirical method. Milligan nowhere directly engages Calvin's thought, so it is difficult to know whether he actually studied Calvin. However, his reflections on the Lord's Supper echo Calvinian themes. For instance, Milligan asserted the necessity of divine accommodation to human limitation and the importance of symbolic mediation of the gospel: "God has from the beginning taught man by signs and symbols. . . . Our great Redeemer and Educator did not forget that we are still in the flesh, that we have bodies as well as spirits, and that while the word stands the former must ever be the medium of access to the latter."[36]

According to Milligan, the intended effect of the Supper is commemorative: "it is designed to keep ever fresh in our memories the first great fact of the Gospel '*that Jesus Christ died for our sins according to the Scriptures.*'" But Milligan sees Communion as more than a cognitive tool of recollection: "*It is intended also to be the medium of furnishing and imparting spiritual nourishment to the hungry and thirsty soul.*"[37] Although we are required to eat bread and drink wine, Milligan explains, it is not because they become the actual body and blood of Christ. Rather, they provide an analogy between physical and spiritual nourishment. Just as gazing upon a rich banquet of food does nothing to nourish the body, so simply remembering Christ's death does not nourish the spirit. Rather, the food must be "spiritually eaten, spiritually digested, and spiritually appropriated."[38] "Every ordinance of God is a medium of nourishment to the hungry soul," he writes, "but no other institution is so well and so directly adapted to this end as the Lord's Supper." Commenting on Jesus' words, "Take, eat," Milligan asks,

> Eat what? The bread, merely? Nay, verily, for he immediately adds, "*This is my body.*" We must then eat simultaneously of the commemorative loaf and of the bread of life; and while we literally drink of the symbolic cup, we must also at the same time drink spiritually of that blood which alone can supply the wants of the thirsty soul. Unless we do this the bread which we

35. Campbell quoted in Harrison, "Early Disciples Sacramental Theology," 52–53. At other times Campbell speaks of the Supper as a "memento" or a "commemoration" of Christ's death. While Harrison regards Campbell's eucharistic thought as heavily influenced by Calvin, others see the issue as more ambivalent. See Robert Howard, "Two Perspectives on the 'Banquet of Love': A Comparative Analysis of the Philosophical Bases of the Eucharistic Theologies of Alexander Campbell and John W. Nevin," *Discipliana* 59, no. 2 (Summer 1999): 50–54.

36. Robert Milligan, *Exposition and Defense of the Scheme of Redemption*, revised edition (St. Louis: Christian Publishing Company, 1885), 427–29.

37. Ibid., 429–30.

38. Ibid., 430.

eat can in no sense be to us the body of the Son of God, nor can the wine which we drink be in any sense the blood of the New Covenant which was shed for the remission of the sins of many.[39]

Thus, by the middle of the nineteenth century the most prominent Disciples leaders shared a general, if unofficial, consensus about the meaning of the Lord's Supper that substantially echoed the Calvinian dimensions of their Reformed heritage.

Twentieth-century British Disciple William Robinson (1888–1963) engaged Calvin more explicitly than earlier Disciples, locating the Stone-Campbell movement squarely within the Reformed tradition.[40] Like Campbell, Robinson noted that Calvin longed to reestablish the centrality of the Supper as normative for Sunday worship. Lamenting that the subjectivism of evangelical revivalism had elided the true sacramental character of the church, Robinson proclaimed that such subjective emphases were "no part of original Calvinism."[41] Robinson stressed the objective character of the sacrament, tying it to both Christology and ecclesiology. He emphasizes the sacramental character of the church as an incarnational community. As the body of Christ the church is "that concrete reality by which Christ becomes manifest in the world, and by which He acts in history."[42] The church represents God's work and presence in the world: "the whole work of creation and redemption—God's activity on and within the historical plane—is just *God's bid for fellowship*."[43] While Calvin did not regard the church as a continuation of the incarnation, such language echoes Calvin's sense of the church as a sign of God's merciful response to the fallen world.[44] Robinson sees God's presence represented in sacramental actions, but he stresses action over presence: "It was the *Real Action* of God in the sacraments which was central in early Christian thought, rather than the *Real Presence*."[45] He does not cite Calvin on this point, but this is a creative engagement and restatement of Calvin's emphasis on the objective character of sacramental action and on the importance of ritual action in representing God's work before the assembly. Sacramental efficacy depends on "the fact and nature of God's holy action," which includes the historical appearance of Jesus Christ. However, Robinson emphasizes that "this holy action was perpetuated and actualized in the dramatic

39. Ibid., 432.

40. While Robinson spent most of his career in England, he taught at the Butler University School of Religion in Indianapolis for several years in the 1950s. Robinson's ecclesiology and sacramental theology continues to be influential among many in the Stone-Campbell movement.

41. William Robinson, *A Companion to the Communion Service: A Devotional Manual* (London, New York, and Toronto: Oxford University Press, 1942), 7–8.

42. William Robinson, "The Nature and Character of Christian Sacramental Theory and Practice," *Shane Quarterly* (1941): 403.

43. Robinson, "The Nature and Character of Christian Sacramental Theory and Practice," 399; emphasis in original.

44. *Institutes* 4.1.17. Benjamin Charles Milner Jr. claims that the significance of Calvin's doctrine of the church is that it is "the history of the restoration of order in the world." Quoted in Charles Partee, *The Theology of John Calvin* (Louisville, KY: Westminster John Knox, 2008), 259.

45. Robinson, "The Nature and Character of Sacramental Theory and Practice," 406.

action of the sacraments."[46] Thus, both the fact and the form of the ritual are vital in representing this action.

JOHN WILLIAMSON NEVIN (1803–1886)

Bard Thompson and George Bricker exuberantly proclaimed of John W. Nevin's *The Mystical Presence,*

> Perhaps there is no comparable work in the history of American theology that sets out Calvin's doctrine of the Lord's Supper so accurately, completely, and appreciatively; no work that understands and expresses so well the theological status of context of the Eucharist in Reformed theology; no work that so perceptively recovers that forgotten side of Reformed theology; namely, its vigorous, almost Cyprianic sense of churchmanship; no work that more clearly anticipates the liturgical renaissance in American Protestantism.[47]

bio. of saint

Such flowery language borders on hagiography. That it comes from prominent and respected historians of liturgy and theology indicates the enthusiasm that Nevin generates among admirers of his work. While Nevin was known in his day, he was often dismissed for what were seen as his "Romish" tendencies; that is, his sense of continuity between creation and redemption, his broadly catholic view of the church, and his devoted sacramentalism. However, as indicated by Thompson and Bricker, Nevin's work gained prominence as the ecumenical and liturgical movements of the twentieth century made their way into Reformed churches. Nevin and the Mercersburg theology offer what some have called "a Reformed alternative" that is liturgical, sacramental, and catholic in character.[48]

For his part, Nevin understood his work simply to be a faithful reception and interpretation of Calvin's sacramental teaching. He appealed directly to Calvin as the ultimate authority, stating that "a proper view of the original doctrine of the Reformed Church" regarding the Eucharist should necessarily appeal to Calvin. Acknowledging that Calvin was neither the originator of nor the lone voice for the Reformed doctrine of the Eucharist, Nevin commended Calvin as the most skilled and authoritative interpreter of the doctrine. Engaging in his own bit of hagiography, Nevin wrote,

---

46. Ibid.
47. Bard Thompson and George Bricker, "Editor's Preface," in John W. Nevin, *The Mystical Presence and Other Writings on the Eucharist* (Philadelphia and Boston: United Church Press, 1966), 10–11.
48. E.g., Charles A. Jones III, "Mercersburg: A Reformed Alternative for the Twentieth Century," in Daniel Clendenin and W. David Buschart, eds., *Scholarship, Sacraments, and Service* (Lewiston, NY: Edwin Mellen Press, 1990), 160–77. For an account of Nevin's influence in his own time, see E. Brooks Holifield, "Mercersburg, Princeton, and the South: The Sacramental Controversy in the Nineteenth Century," *Journal of Presbyterian History* 54 (Summer 1976): 239–57.

His [Calvin's] profound far-reaching and deeply penetrating mind drew forth the doctrine from the heart of the Church, exhibited it in its proper relations, proportions and distinctions, gave it form in this way for the understanding, and clothed it with authority as a settled article of faith in the general creed. He may be regarded then as the accredited interpreter and expounder of the article for all later times. A better interpreter in the case, we could not possibly possess.[49]

Nevin regarded the doctrine of the Eucharist as "central to the whole Christian system."[50] Whatever one thinks of the Eucharist "is a plain index to what [one] will think of Christ, the church, and theology itself."[51] These three doctrines—incarnation, ecclesiology, and sacraments—are organically connected in Nevin's thought. James Hastings Nichols called the incarnation the "organizing principle" in Nevin's theology, foundational as it is for his ecclesiology, his eucharistic theology, and his soteriology.[52] Against a forensic transactional view of salvation, Nevin regards the incarnation of Christ as offering believers an invitation to participation in the divine-human life of Christ. Such participation is mediated to the church in the Lord's Supper.[53] In the incarnation, there is continuity between Christ's humanity and divinity.[54] Drawing on Paul's image of the first and second Adams, Nevin asserts that just as humanity is identified with Adam in his sin, so humanity is identified with Christ's perfect life resulting in a "mystical union" with Christ's glorified humanity.[55]

The incarnation is the source of the new humanity, the source of the Christian life. For Nevin, the church is the necessary womb of genuine piety, nourishing the life of its members through its outward forms as they manifest the objective character of God's revelation and saving action. Christian faith cannot exist outside of the church. He lamented what he called the "modern Puritan theory" that relied heavily on subjective experience for confirmation of the religious life. In an implicit critique of Edwards, Nevin states clearly that spiritual communion is not simply with the divine nature of Christ, or effected by the spirit moving one toward "holy affections." Rather, communion with Christ includes his whole person, the Word made flesh, and the whole human person, made known objectively in the church.[56] Thus, Nevin regarded "expressions of religious feeling" as inadequate:

49. Nevin, *Mystical Presence,* 30.

50. Ibid., 27.

51. B. A. Gerrish, "The Flesh of the Son of Man: John W. Nevin on the Church and the Eucharist," in *Tradition and the Modern World: Reformed Theology in the Nineteenth Century* (Chicago and London: University of Chicago Press, 1978), 52.

52. James Hastings Nichols, *Romanticism in American Theology* (Chicago: University of Chicago Press, 1961), 140.

53. Holifield, *Theology in America,* 476–77.

54. Nevin, *Mystical Presence,* 35.

55. Ibid., 166. Jack Martin Maxwell, *Worship and Reformed Theology: The Liturgical Lessons of Mercersburg* (Pittsburgh: Pickwick Press, 1976), 27.

56. Nevin, *Mystical Presence,* 34–35.

The life of the single Christian can be real and healthful only as it is born from the general life of the church, and carried by it onward to that end. We are Christians singly, by partaking (having part) in the general life of revelation, which is already at hand organically in the church, the living and life-giving body of Jesus Christ.[57]

Nevin viewed the church not as a voluntary association of individuals, but as a "divine organism, the locus of the continuing life of Christ."[58] As such, the church itself is sacramental, a sign of the new humanity effected by the incarnate Christ.

Christian faith is "grounded in the living union of the believer with the person of Christ," a union that is "emphatically concentrated in the mystery of the Lord's Supper."[59] For Nevin, a proper understanding of the incarnation is necessary to the right understanding of the Eucharist. The Lord's Supper communes believers with the whole of Christ's person, both his divinity and his humanity.[60] The communion is real and substantial; it is not merely a cognitive exercise in remembrance. Christ's own self is communicated to partakers, not merely his benefits. The two cannot be distinguished in terms of what is given in the Eucharist. By "sensible signs" are communicated "Christ's body and blood, with all his benefits." Nevin explains that the former is the "basis and medium" of the latter, but though "the visible and invisible are different" they may not be separated. He goes on: "They flow together in the constitution of one and the same sacrament. Neither of the two is a sacrament without the other."[61] Nevin is clear that Christ's body is neither "in nor under the bread" in a located sense, but that "the power of his life in this form is actually exhibited at the same time in the mystery of the sacrament."[62]

Thus, Nevin exuberantly reclaimed Calvin's doctrine of spiritual real presence. He claims that Calvin used the term "real" to indicate a "true" presence. Here Nevin is clarifying that the presence is not corporeal, but is substantial. His distinctions are worth quoting at length in order to see in his own words how he understood Calvin's doctrine:

> . . . a *real* presence, in opposition to the notion that Christ's flesh and blood are not made present to the communicant in *any* way; a *spiritual* real presence, in opposition to the idea that Christ's body is in the elements in a local or corporal manner; not real simply, and not spiritual simply—but real and yet spiritual at the same time. The body of Christ is in heaven, the believer on earth; but by the power of the Holy Spirit, nevertheless, the obstacle of such vast local distance is fully overcome, so that in the

57. Ibid., 24–25.
58. Gerrish, "The Flesh of the Son of Man," 52.
59. Nevin, *Mystical Presence,* 27.
60. Ibid., 181.
61. Ibid., 178.
62. Ibid., 178. Rozeboom explains in the preceding chapter, pp. 152–53 that the term translated "exhibit" in Calvin's work means "to offer" that which is signified. Nevin's use of the term follows Calvin's.

sacramental act—while the outward symbols are received in an outward way—the very body and blood of Christ are at the same time inwardly and supernaturally communicated to the worthy receiver, for the real nourishment of his new life.[63]

Nevin also criticized Calvin, attempting to correct what he viewed as the Reformer's "false psychology."[64] He thought that Calvin failed to distinguish the material laws of bodily existence from the animating life force, or what he called "the organic *law*, which constitutes the proper identity of a human body."[65] Nevin agreed that the action of the Holy Spirit facilitated a "real participation always" in the full humanity of Christ, but he thought Calvin represented the union poorly when he attempted to explain how, if the glorified Christ's body is now in heaven, two bodies could be joined over the vast separation of space. Nevin thought Calvin was so concerned with avoiding the suggestion of a local presence for Christ's body in the elements that Calvin mistakenly resolved the issue through "a special supernatural agency of the Holy Spirit, as a sort of foreign medium introduced to meet the wants of the case."[66] Such a move seems "somewhat fantastic" to Nevin. Had Calvin drawn on the organic law of Christ's human life, "his theory would have assumed at once a much more consistent and intelligible form."[67] Nevin's problems with Calvin were far outweighed by his authoritative exposition of the real presence of Christ in the Lord's Supper.

Nevin's work is remarkable itself for its analytical depth when surveying the history of the theology of the Lord's Supper. He was able to distinguish Calvin's original thought on the Supper from its later accretions. His whole project also stands out for its distinctive views, within Reformed theology of its day, on the catholic and sacramental character of the church. Gerrish includes *The Mystical Presence* as "among the classics of American theological literature."[68]

POSSIBILITIES FOR CONTEMPORARY RETRIEVAL

From this brief survey, it is evident that Calvin's doctrine of the Lord's Supper has been influential throughout its reception history, even if interpreted variously. Tracy's reminder that a "classic" bears an excess of meaning and eludes ultimate definition indicates that Calvin's theology of the Lord's Supper continues to hold generative possibilities for contemporary theology and practice. Many themes could be pursued here, but given the limitations of space, I will reflect on four: the sacramental character of creation, the sacramental character

63. Nevin, *Mystical Presence*, 38–39.
64. Ibid., 151.
65. Ibid.
66. Ibid., 154.
67. Ibid., 152.
68. Gerrish, "The Flesh of the Son of Man," 57.

of the church, sacrifice as a dimension of eucharistic meaning, and the role of the Holy Spirit.

Sacramental Character of Creation

The ecological crises of our present age have heightened awareness of the dualisms of matter and spirit that Christian theology and spirituality have often exhibited, and which have undergirded human abuse of the natural world. Theologies of the Lord's Supper have often contributed to and reinforced those dualisms, especially when they have suggested that the material elements of the rite are ancillary to its meaning. There are resources in Calvin's understanding of creation as well as his eucharistic theology that suggest a doctrine of the Lord's Supper that elucidates the sacramental character of the natural world. Such an outlook could be foundational for a liturgically formed ecological ethic.[69] For instance, Calvin understands the universe as irradiated by the splendor of God's glory; thus God's presence might be discerned in every element of the universe through the eyes of faith. Calvin describes the world with metaphors like the "theatre of God's glory," the "living image of God," and the "beautiful garment" in which God wraps Godself in order to become visible.[70] Indeed, Calvin's theology of creation is sacramental: God is revealed through material elements.

Jonathan Edwards also viewed the world in sacramental terms. For Edwards, the whole universe "shadows forth" the image of God, whose beauty and glory permeate all things: "*Everything* pointed to the real presence of Christ" according to Marsden.[71] Thus, Edwards's sense of Christ's presence in the Lord's Supper is rooted in his sacramental understanding of creation. The elements of public worship signify and evoke the spiritual presence in all things. The sacraments ritually celebrate and represent the conviction that the world is sacramental. Neither Calvin nor Edwards ever articulated a theology of the Lord's Supper in ecological terms, of course, but their doctrines of creation and the sacraments are suggestive.

Leanne Van Dyk frames her feminist reading of Reformed eucharistic theology within Calvin's view of "the entire created order as sacrament of God's

---

69. Efforts to develop such ecologically sensitive eucharistic theologies are increasingly common among Roman Catholic liturgical and sacramental theologians, but such reflections arising from the Reformed tradition remain scarce. See Kevin Irwin, "The Sacramentality of Creation and the Role of Creation in Liturgy and Sacraments," in Drew Christiansen and Walter Grazer, eds., *"And God Saw That It Was Good": Catholic Theology and the Environment* (Washington, DC: United States Catholic Conference, 1996), 105–46; Dorothy McDougall, *The Cosmos as Primary Sacrament: The Horizon for an Ecological Sacramental Theology* (New York: Peter Lang, 2003).

70. See Randall Zachman, *Image and Word in the Theology of John Calvin* (Notre Dame, IN: University of Notre Dame Press, 2007), 25–49. Also, Belden Lane, "Spirituality as the Performance of Desire: Calvin on the World as the Theatre of God's Glory," *Spiritus* 1, no. 1 (Spring 2001): 1–30.

71. Marsden, *Jonathan Edwards*, 353. Also, Belden Lane, "Jonathan Edwards on Beauty, Desire, and the Sensory World," *Theological Studies* 65, no. 1 (March 2004): 44–72.

presence and action."[72] The Reformed tradition has always affirmed that Christian liturgy, especially the sacraments, use material elements, "sensible signs," to mediate the sacred. Van Dyk picks up this theme, declaring, "The undiluted claim of a Calvinian understanding of sacramental grace is that these utterly ordinary elements are exactly what the Holy Spirit uses to unite us to Christ."[73] Calvin regarded the Lord's Supper as one of the divine gifts by which God graciously feeds and cares for God's children in a manner fitting our creatureliness. Van Dyk sees "natural connections" between feminist and womanist concerns and the sacraments because baptism and the Lord's Supper "are brimming with affirmations of community, relationality, bodies, feasting, transformation, healing, wholeness, inclusion, and hospitality."[74] While Van Dyk's appropriation of Calvin is not directed toward an ecological sacramental theology, the way she draws upon Calvin's theologies of creation and the sacraments point to such a possibility. God uses the things of the earth to convey God's goodness to us, and by affirming these common elements and experiences the sacraments can reveal God's intentions that humans treat the earth in which God's presence is revealed with greater care.

Sacramental Character of the Church

Calvin's famous dictum identifies the marks of the church as being the "Word of God purely preached and heard, and the sacraments administered according to Christ's institution."[75] This identification provides a good place from which to consider the sacramental character of the church. The church is sacramental in two ways. First, the practice of the Lord's Supper is central to the church's life. Consequently, this central practice informs the church's identity as a sign of God's presence and work in the world. Calvin's pronouncement came in response to what he considered defects in the church's liturgical life, especially in medieval Roman Catholicism, which elevated the Eucharist while diminishing the role of preaching. The Reformers viewed this as distorting both Word and sacrament. Calvin frequently stresses that the sacraments are the Word made visible, or that they are signs of what the Word accomplishes. As a result interpreters often see the sacraments as holding a subordinate place to the Word in Calvin's ecclesiology.[76] Second, viewed from another angle, Calvin's dictum insists that the Word and the sacraments belong together in a relationship of mutual complementarity. To be more precise, both preaching and the

---

72. Leanne Van Dyk, "The Gifts of God for the People of God: Christian Feminism and Sacramental Theology," in Amy Plantinga Pauw and Serene Jones, eds., *Feminist and Womanist Essays in Reformed Dogmatics* (Louisville, KY: Westminister John Knox, 2006), 206.

73. Ibid., 210.

74. Ibid., 209.

75. *Institutes* 4.1.9

76. E.g., Iain Torrance, "*Mysterium Christi* and *Mysterium Ecclesiae*: The Christological Ecclesiology of John Calvin," *The Greek Orthodox Theological Review* 43, nos. 1–4 (1998): 463–65.

sacraments manifest the presence of the true Word of God, bearing witness to the union believers enjoy with one another in Jesus Christ.

Calvin's identifiers offer a corrective to the ecclesiological distortions of many of his followers. Especially in North America, the long arms of revivalism, individualism, and antiformalism continue to reach into and shape Protestant worship life across the theological spectrum. Whether for pragmatic or dogmatic reasons, Reformed liturgy and theology have often regarded the sacraments as almost ancillary, with the preaching of the Word primary. However, the centrality of the Lord's Supper for the church in Calvin's thought is now more widely appreciated, as we will explore in several places below. Further, Calvin's marks of the church indicate a broad and inclusive understanding of the church in Calvin's thought, which can form the basis for ecumenical discussions about ecclesiology and sacraments.

theology-
functions
of church

Calvin's desire for frequent celebration of the Lord's Supper, although thwarted by Geneva's magistrates, also indicates something significant about his ecclesiology. Calvin, like Campbell and Nevin, saw the Lord's Supper gathering the body together. It is the means by which Christ demonstrates his union with his followers and their union with one another. In fact, this union with Christ is foundational for the existence of the church.

Calvin's doctrine of union with Christ has drawn a good deal of attention in recent years, and it could be treated as a separate theme in this section in relation to the Lord's Supper.[77] According to Martha Moore-Keish, Calvin often saw union with Christ as "both the content of the sacraments and a description of the Christian life."[78] Iain Torrance speaks of Calvin's ecclesiology as "rigorously Christological," by which he means that the church is a sign of God's radical commitment to creation confirmed in Christ. According to Torrance, Christ fulfills God's covenant with creation. Union with Christ through the Spirit—that is, becoming part of the body of Christ—is the means of responding to God's covenant-making initiative.[79] Gathering to share the Lord's Supper continuously represents the union that believers share with Christ. This eucharistic act also continuously represents to those gathered the sacramental character of the church in the world.

Sacrifice as a Dimension of Eucharistic Meaning

Other than the nature of Christ's presence in the Lord's Supper, few issues have been as controversial as sacrifice. Luther's most strident criticism was directed at the way that the Roman church had turned the sacrifice of the Mass into a

77. See Dennis Tamburello, *Union with Christ: John Calvin and the Mysticism of St. Bernard* (Louisville, KY: Westminster John Knox, 1994); J. Todd Billings, *Calvin, Participation, and the Gift: The Activity of Believers in Union with Christ* (Oxford and New York: Oxford University Press, 2007).

78. Martha Moore-Keish, "Calvin, Sacraments, and Ecclesiology: What Makes a Church a Church?" *Proceedings of the North American Academy of Liturgy* (2002): 120.

79. Torrance, "*Mysterium Christi* and *Mysterium Ecclesiae*," 461.

good work and then exploited it for profit. Like Luther, Calvin insisted that the Eucharist is neither a good work nor is the sacrifice of Christ in any sense repeatable.[80] Calvin maintained that the Lord's Supper is primarily a promise and a gift, thus "its essential nature is perverted by the pestilential belief that the mass is an offering to obtain forgiveness."[81] As a gift, the Supper should be "received with thanksgiving," whereas the sacrifice of the Mass purports to "pay a price to God, that he himself is to receive with satisfaction." Such a view displays "the most wretched ingratitude of humans," according to Calvin, for "Sacrifice differs from the Sacrament of the Supper as widely as giving differs from receiving."[82] Further, the idea that Christ's sacrifice must be repeated on the altar of Mass by a priest destroys the perfect sufficiency of Christ's death on the cross, accomplished once and for all for human salvation.[83] Finally, Calvin criticized the sacrificial aspects of Roman Mass for diminishing the corporate dimension of the Supper. As God's gift, the Lord's Supper is a meal requiring participation by the faithful. Being "distributed in a public gathering of the Church," it binds believers together as Christ's body. However, "the sacrifice of the mass dissolves this community and pulls it apart" as the priest supplants the role of the gathered community at the altar.[84] In what seems to be a clear statement rejecting any notion of the Eucharist as sacrifice, Calvin writes that God has provided "a Table at which to feast, not an altar upon which to offer a victim; He has not consecrated priests to sacrifice, but ministers to distribute the sacred banquet."[85]

However, Calvin did not give up the sacrificial dimension of the Lord's Supper entirely. The ways in which Calvin describes the Supper as a sacrifice, along with recent reappraisals of sacrifice by liturgical theologians, presents opportunities for Reformed Christians to reclaim and develop this aspect of the Lord's Supper.[86] Calvin distinguishes two kinds of sacrifice: The first is the sacrifice of "propitiation and expiation" by which Christ on the cross effected redemption. Such a sacrifice is unique and unrepeatable, and in no sense can this notion of

---

80. Brian Gerrish, *Grace and Gratitude: The Eucharistic Theology of John Calvin* (Minneapolis: Fortress, 1993), 146–49.

81. Gerrish, *Grace and Gratitude*, 148. *Institutes* 4.18.1.

82. *Institutes* 4.18.7.

83. Gerrish, *Grace and Gratitude*, 148–49.

84. *Institutes* 4.14.26; Gerrish, *Grace and Gratitude*, 150.

85. *Institutes* 4.18.12.

86. For example, Roman Catholic liturgical theologian Robert Daly proposes that the Christian sense of sacrifice should be viewed, not in terms of traditional Western atonement theory with its "monstrous implications," but rather in Trinitarian terms. According to Daly, both Catholics and Protestants since the time of the Reformation have mistakenly viewed sacrifice in a "history of religions" sense. A Trinitarian understanding begins by seeing sacrifice as "a mutually self-giving event that takes place between persons." Its primary thrust has to do with God's saving initiative, in the three persons of the Trinity, and in the Eucharist the church is caught up in the action of God, "the self-offering initiative of the Father in the gift of his Son . . . in the Spirit." This sense of sacrifice presents a more promising starting place for ecumenical and constructive dialogue than do Reformation-era polemics. Daly, "New Developments in the Theology of Sacrifice," *Liturgical Ministry* 18 (Spring 2009): 49–58.

sacrifice be applied to the Lord's Supper. The second is the sacrifice of praise and thanksgiving; the Lord's Supper can be regarded as a sacrifice in this second sense.[87]

As the Supper communicates the gift of God's salvation in Christ, so the church responds with offerings of grateful praise. Such sacrifices of praise are not confined to a ritual liturgical action, but take place whenever and wherever the Church's members offer themselves in loving, grateful service. The public liturgical action "enacts and confirms" this life of loving, sacrificial offering of selves. Such life offerings, the life of good works, are called "spiritual oblations" by Calvin, but they depend on the one sufficient redeeming sacrifice of Christ. Such a life of self-offering, "the sacrifice of praise," also belongs to the "very essence of the church" and to the essence of the church's liturgical life, according to Brian Gerrish:

> The Lord's Supper cannot be without a sacrifice of this kind. . . . From this duty of sacrificing, all Christians are called a "royal priesthood." In short the eucharistic sacrifice defines the church as a royal priesthood, whose sacred office is represented but not exhausted in the words and action of the holy banquet. The church is a priestly, eucharistic community. What makes it such is, of course, the expiatory sacrifice of Christ."[88]

This returns us to the nature of the church and its ministry. Todd Billings identifies Calvin's "participatory ecclesiology," which derives from the participation in Christ enjoyed by believers. In the self-offering of Christ, which makes believers partakers in his body, the church is also constituted as a society of mutual, active sharing with Christ, with one another, and with the world. Thus, writes Billings,

> The Lord's Supper is not a distant act performed by clergy offering up the body of God, acting *in persona Christi*. The Supper is a participation of the gathered believers in Christ and his body and blood; simultaneously, it is participation in the law of love and equity, tasting of the primal human communion which has been disrupted by sin.[89]

George Hunsinger sees possibilities for ecumenical rapprochement on the sacrificial dimension of the Lord's Supper, proposing that we view eucharistic sacrifice in connection with the Passover. "The paschal mystery is a mystery of substitution, participation, and exchange," he explains. Those redeemed by the propitiary death of the Christ, the Lamb, are made one with him through the sacramental meal. In the paschal meal "the sacrifice becomes a

---

87. See Joseph Tylenda, "Eucharistic Sacrifice in Calvin," *Theological Studies* 37, no. 3 (Summer 1976): 456–66.

88. Gerrish, *Grace and Gratitude*, 155.

89. Billings, *Calvin, Participation, and the Gift*, 173–74.

sacrament. The sacrifice is received and actualized in memory, communion, and hope."[90] Hunsinger further asserts that "the real presence of Christ is inseparable from his benefits and work." That is, Christ's presence in the Eucharist includes "the real presence of his expiatory sacrifice."[91]

Likewise, Calvin explains that the Lord's Supper is given to us "as a mirror in which we contemplate our Lord Jesus Christ crucified."[92] It represents to the faithful the all-sufficient death of Christ, making its benefits available: "the sacrifice of Christ is so shown to us there that the spectacle of his cross is set, almost visibly, before our eyes."[93] Hunsinger's explanation echoes Calvin's view:

> As he makes himself present in the Spirit, under the forms of bread and wine, the one sacrifice of Calvary is made present in its saving efficacy. It is present in its finished, perfect, and perpetual significance before God. It is not repeated but re-presented, not continued but memorialized, not supplemented but made available. It is not something the church manipulates but something in which it participates.[94]

The sacrificial dimension of the Eucharist is not wholly absent among contemporary Reformed churches, as evidenced by their liturgical texts. For instance, the Presbyterian Church (U.S.A.)'s *Book of Common Worship* includes the following phrase in its Great Thanksgiving: "With thanksgiving, we offer our very selves to you to be a living and holy sacrifice, dedicated to your service."[95] The eucharistic liturgy of the Reformed Church in America contains a similar phrase, preceded by this prayer: "We remember in this Supper the perfect sacrifice offered once on the cross by our Lord Jesus Christ for the sin of the whole world."[96] Thus, there are possibilities for further development and dialogue around this historically most contentious and misunderstood of eucharistic issues.

Role of the Holy Spirit

The Eucharistic liturgy of the Presbyterian Church (U.S.A.) includes the following epiclesis:

---

90. George Hunsinger, *The Eucharist and Ecumenism: Let Us Keep the Feast* (New York: Cambridge University Press, 2008), 176. Hunsinger's efforts to root reflection on sacrifice in the context of Passover also points to the Jewish roots of Christian faith and worship; while needing further reflection, this move begins to address the anti-Judaic supersessionism that is frequently expressed in Christian worship.

91. Ibid.

92. Calvin, "Short Treatise," 511.

93. *Institutes* 4.18.7.

94. Hunsinger, *The Eucharist and Ecumenism*, 176.

95. Presbyterian Church (U.S.A.), *Book of Common Worship* (Louisville: Westminster/John Knox, 1993), 71.

96. Reformed Church in America, "Order of Worship for the Lord's Day," http://images.rca .org/docs/worship/lordsday.pdf.

Gracious God,
pour out your Holy Spirit upon us
and upon these your gifts of bread and wine,
that the bread we break
and the cup we bless
may be the communion of the body and blood of Christ.
By your Spirit make us one with Christ,
that we may be one with all who share this feast,
united in ministry in every place.
As this bread is Christ's body for us,
send us out to be the body of Christ in the world.[97]

This invocation indicates a prominent role for the Holy Spirit in the Lord's Supper. This emphasis is consistent with Calvin's theology of the Supper, even if the Spirit's role was not prominent in his liturgy.[98] The contemporary prayer serves as a corrective to a lacuna in Calvin's liturgical compositions, as well as to the frequent neglect of the Holy Spirit in the history of Reformed worship. The role of the Spirit is a key to understanding Calvin's theology of the Lord's Supper, for it is the Spirit who is the vivifying power of the sacraments. Without the presence and work of the Spirit, the Lord's Supper is empty: "the sacraments can accomplish nothing more in our mind than the splendor of the sun shining on blind eyes." The sacraments are effective "only when the Spirit, that inward teacher, comes to them, by whose power alone hearts are penetrated and affections moved and our souls opened for the sacraments to enter in."[99]

This emphasis on the Spirit is essential to recovering a Trinitarian understanding of Christian sacramental worship. But the prominence of the Holy Spirit in Calvin's theology of the Lord's Supper also contributes to a better understanding of divine agency in the sacraments. The embedded theological understanding that dominates much Protestant sacramental practice is confused on this matter, often viewing the efficacy of the Lord's Supper as dependent on human action or response. Calvin's emphasis on the Holy Spirit as the crucial actor in the Lord's Supper, however, maintains the primacy of God's action in the sacraments.

Martha Moore-Keish connects this emphasis in Calvin's theology to God's sovereignty: "Divine sovereignty allows God to transcend natural boundaries to be present in the eucharist and the Holy Spirit is the specific way in which God is present, according to Calvin. The Holy Spirit is God's power and presence in the community of faith, particularly . . . in the sacraments."[100] It may seem that Calvin is dodging a hard question when he explains the presence of Christ as "the secret working of the Spirit," which he says is "too lofty for either my

97. *Book of Common Worship*, 72.
98. James White, *The Sacraments as God's Self-Giving* (Nashville: Abingdon, 1983), 60.
99. *Institutes* 4.14.9.
100. Martha Moore-Keish, *Do This in Remembrance of Me* (Grand Rapids: Eerdmans, 2008), 41.

Calvin

mind to comprehend or my words to declare."[101] However, he is convinced that the Spirit is the agent of divine sovereignty who effects the mystery of Christ's presence in the Supper. If the prospect that Christ is truly present to us while remaining in heaven seems implausible, Calvin instructs us to "remember how far the secret power of the Holy Spirit towers above all our senses, and how foolish it is to wish to measure his immeasurableness by our measure. What, then, our mind does not comprehend, let faith conceive: that the Spirit truly unites things separated in space."[102]

The emphasis on the Holy Spirit also points to a discussion of the social, communal dimension of Calvin's eucharistic thought. Moore-Keish touches on this, saying that Calvin stressed the role of the Spirit in the community, not simply within the hearts of individuals. "Calvin's eucharistic interest was social rather than metaphysical," she claims, meaning that he viewed the presence of Christ's true flesh to reside among the community gathered around the elements, rather than strictly in the elements themselves.[103] In making a similar point, Peter Leithart employs the image of "zoom" and "wide-angle" camera lenses. For too long, according to Leithart, discussions of Christ's presence in the Supper have used a zoom lens, focusing narrowly on what happens to the elements of bread and wine and how they become—or do not become—the body and blood of Christ. Pulling away for a wide-angle shot shifts the focus from the elements to the entire scope of ritual activity involving the elements and those who have gathered to partake of them as a community. Taking this view opens the door for an illuminating exploration of the anthropological dimensions of the rite. However, it also prompts reflection on what William Robinson called "the real action" of God's Spirit in the sacrament and in the whole community. "Through the zoom lens" writes Leithart, "the eucharist is presented as a miraculous puzzle of physics or metaphysics; through a wide-angle lens, the eucharist becomes a focal point for more theologically central issues: the relationships of the church's members to one another, creation, and God."[104]

101. *Institutes* 4.17.31, 32.
102. Ibid., 4.17.10
103. Moore-Keish, *Do This in Remembrance of Me*, 42.
104. Peter J. Leithart, "The Way Things Really Ought to Be: Eucharist, Eschatology, and Culture," *Westminster Theological Journal* 59 (1997): 159–61.

SECTION 5
CALVIN'S THEOLOGY OF CHURCH AND SOCIETY, AND ITS RECEPTION

Chapter 9

Church and Society

Calvin's Theology and Its Early Reception

JEANNINE E. OLSON

The contextual approach of this book is especially promising for this essay on
Calvin's theology of the church and society because Calvin was able to put many
of his ideas into practice in Geneva in the sixteenth century. [1] Thus not only do
we have Calvin's specific ideas about the church, how it should be organized,
and how society should function, but we have examples of how his ideas worked
out in practice. Just as his ideas were modified through the centuries, so too was
the application of his ideas to church organization and practice. Modifications
in Calvin's ideas were made in the name of Calvinism, often by those who considered themselves Calvinists!

There are a variety of books that examine related topics, such as Calvin's
doctrine of the church[2] or the influence of Calvin's thought and Calvinism on
society.[3] None of these works does what this essay does.

1. Thank you to Rhode Island College's Faculty Research Committee and the National Endowment for the Humanities.
2. Benjamin Milner Jr., *Calvin's Doctrine of the Church* (Leiden: E. J. Brill, 1970).
3. Max Weber's *The Protestant Ethic and the Spirit of Capitalism*; André Biéler's, *Calvin's Economic and Social Thought*, ed. Edward Dommen, trans. James Greig (Geneva: World Alliance
of Reformed Churches, World Council of Churches, 2006); originally published as *La pensée
économique et sociale de Calvin*, Publications de la Faculté des Sciences Economiques et Sociales de

This essay considers Calvin's thought on church and society, including the implementation of his thought in the arena where it first found practical application, Geneva. In Calvin's era, the church was such an integral part of European society that Calvin and others did not view the church and society as so widely separate as they are viewed by Western societies today. One must consider society when addressing Calvin's understanding of the church. Next, this essay explores the impact of Calvin's thought on church and society in the larger world up into the eighteenth century. For the Reformed tradition did indeed move out beyond Geneva within Calvin's lifetime, especially after 1555 and the defeat of his opposition in the city.

RECONSTRUCTION OF CALVIN'S THOUGHT ON THE CHURCH AND SOCIETY

This treatment begins with the fundamentals of Calvin's concept of the church, particularly as it applies to society.

Calvin's Augustinian View of the Church

Calvin follows Augustine, like Martin Luther and the other magisterial reformers of the sixteenth century in his understanding of the church. The church on earth is composed both of believers and nonbelievers, or as Calvin put it, the elect and the reprobate.[4] The church, however, was not only the church on earth. For Calvin and other reformers in the Augustinian tradition, the true church included all Christians both living and dead, on earth and in heaven.

The Augustinian view of the church fit the framework of sixteenth-century Christians, many of whom were members of state-recognized churches to which all local inhabitants belonged—as was the case of Geneva's church during Calvin's lifetime. It is difficult to imagine members of these state-recognized churches holding any other position on the nature of the church on earth than the inclusive position of Augustine. Augustine (354–430) lived, for most of his adult years, in a society in which one was expected to be Christian, especially after Emperor Theodosius made Christianity the official religion of the Roman Empire (380–381). Not all church members were necessarily Christian, however. Formal membership consisted of true and false members. Likewise in Geneva, church membership consisted of both the elect and the reprobate,

---

l'Université de Genève, vol. 13 (Geneva: Librairie de l'Université Georg, 1961). *John Calvin's Impact on the Church and Society,* ed. Martin Ernst Hirzel and Martin Sallman on behalf of the Federation of Swiss Protestant Churches (Grand Rapids: Eerdmans, 2009). *John Calvin Rediscovered: The Impact of His Social and Economic Thought,* ed. Edward Dommen and James Bratt (Louisville, KY: Westminster John Knox, 2007).

4. The scriptural basis lay most obviously in the biblical parable of the wheat and the tares (Matt. 13:24–30).

and for Calvin as for Augustine, only God knew the elect. Thus Calvin could describe the church in two ways:

> Holy Scripture speaks of the church in two ways. Sometimes by the term "church" it means that which is actually in God's presence, into which no persons are received but those who are children of God by grace of adoption and true members of Christ by sanctification of the Holy Spirit. Then, indeed, the church includes not only the saints presently living on earth, but all the elect from the beginning of the world. Often, however, the name "church" designates the whole multitude of men spread over the earth who profess to worship one God and Christ.[5]

Calvin then goes on in a positive tone, emphasizing unity and agreement among Christians, elaborating on baptism, the Lord's Supper, and the preaching of the Word. "By baptism we are initiated into faith in him; by partaking in the Lord's Supper we attest our unity in true doctrine and love; in the Word of the Lord we have agreement, and for the preaching of the Word the ministry instituted by Christ is preserved."[6]

Then comes an earthy assessment of actual church members: "In this church are mingled many hypocrites who have nothing of Christ but the name and outward appearance. There are very many ambitious, greedy, envious persons, evil speakers, and some of quite unclean life."[7] Calvin states that what is lacking is effective discipline: "Such are tolerated for a time either because they cannot be convicted by a competent tribunal or because a vigorous discipline does not always flourish as it ought."[8]

Finally, Calvin concludes that we must revere the church: "Just as we must believe, therefore, that the former church, invisible to us, is visible to the eyes of God alone, so we are commanded to revere and keep communion with the latter, which is called 'church' in respect to men."[9]

For Calvin, then, the church is the community of the faithful here below and above. As Calvin pointed out, the word "church" can be used in at least two ways: (1) to refer to the church on earth or (2) to refer to the church universal, the community of faithful both on earth and in heaven—in Augustine's terminology, the City of God.

The Anabaptist View of the Church as a Contrast to Calvin's

Not all sixteenth-century Christians agreed with Augustine's view of the church. The Anabaptists, or "rebaptizers," described a gathered church of the elect, those

5. John Calvin, *Institutes of the Christian Religion*, ed. John T. McNeill, trans. Ford Lewis Battles (Philadelphia: The Westminster Press, 1960), 4.1.7. Hereafter *Institutes*.
6. Ibid.
7. Ibid.
8. Ibid.
9. Ibid.

baptized at their own request, thus negating infant baptism. Anabaptists are a useful contrast to Calvin.

In addition to their disagreement about the baptism of infants, Calvin's view of the church ruled out a gathering of true Christians on earth as the Anabaptists would have it. Anabaptists believed in the need to separate themselves from evil in the world, which they defined broadly. As stated in the Anabaptist Schleitheim Confession of Faith adopted February 24, 1527, early on in their struggle for survival in an inhospitable Europe, "A separation shall be made from the evil and from the wickedness which the devil planted in the world, in this manner: simply that we shall not have fellowship with them [the wicked] and not run with them in the multitude of their abominations."[10] Separation for the Anabaptists meant avoiding "all popish and antipopish works and church services, meetings and church attendance, drinking houses, civic affairs . . ." among other things.[11]

Anabaptist separation from the world included avoiding the Catholic Mass, as Reformed Christians did, but Anabaptists also avoided church services of Protestants who practiced infant baptism (Lutheran and Reformed). Finally, cutting the Anabaptist community off entirely from civic responsibility, the Schleitheim Confession stated "it is not appropriate for a Christian to serve as a magistrate. . . ."[12]

The Anabaptist church of believers, baptized on their own recognizance, was not Calvin's idea of the church on earth, nor was the Anabaptist insistence on separation from the world. For Calvin, Christians were not called simply to separation but to the exercising of responsibility in the world, as later sections of this essay and the essay by David Little explore. From a historical standpoint, early in his career, before Calvin fully understood what Anabaptists stood for, he wrote a treatise against them for Guillaume Farel.[13] In 1544 Farel and the other pastors of Neuchâtel, a city north of Geneva, were struggling with the growth of Anabaptism in a nearby village. On February 23, 1544, Farel sent a poignant letter to Calvin requesting his help.[14] Farel asked specifically that Calvin respond to an Anabaptist booklet being circulated, which some take to

10. Michael Sattler, The Schleitheim Confession of Faith, in *The Protestant Reformation*, ed. Lewis Spitz (Englewood Cliffs, NJ: Prentice-Hall, 1966), 92.

11. Ibid.

12. Ibid., 94.

13. *Brieve instruction pour armer tous bons fideles contre les erreurs de la secte commune des anabaptists* (Geneva: Jean Girard, 1544). For a modern scholarly edition see John Calvin, *Brieve instruction pour armer tous bons fideles contre les erreurs de la secte commune des Anabaptists,* edited by Mirjam Van Veen, *Ioannis Calvini: Scripta Didactica et Polemica,* vol. 2 (Geneva: Librairie Droz, 2007). Calvin dedicated his treatise to the ministers of Neuchâtel: "Jean Calvin aux ministres des Eglises du Conté de Neuf chastel. [. . .] De Geneve. Le premier de Juing. 1544."

14. *Farellus Calvino,* letter 534 in *Calvini Opera* 11, 681–83 (Hereafter *CO*); also *Guillaume Farel à Jean Calvin, à Genève, de Neuchâtel,* letter 1332 in A.-L. Herminjard, *Correspondance des réformateurs dans les pays de langue française recueillie et publiée avec d'autres lettres relatives à la réforme et des notes historiques et biographiques,* vol. 9, 1543–1544 (Geneva: Georg & Cie, Libraires-Editeurs, 1897), 172–75.

have been Balthazar Hubmaier's *Vom dem Christlichen Tauff der gläubigen.*[15] However, W. Balke and Benjamin Farley consider the Anabaptist booklet to have been Michael Sattler's *Schleitheim Articles.*[16] Farel requested a response for the sake of the simple God-fearing folk and for posterity, although the booklet was not worth Calvin's attention on its own merits.[17]

Calvin's Conception of the "True Church"

So what then of other churches? Were they true churches? What, for instance, of the Roman Catholics?

Calvin does not exclude members of other churches from the true church. Consistent with his interpretation of Scripture and an Augustinian conception of the church, Calvin leaves the determination of true Christians up to God. Nevertheless, we are not left in a void. Calvin states "the Lord by certain marks and tokens has pointed out to us what we should know about the church."[18]

Calvin, like the Lutherans, felt that the church is found where the gospel is preached and the sacraments are rightly administered: "Wherever we see the Word of God purely preached and heard, and the sacraments administered according to Christ's institution, there, it is not to be doubted, a church of God exists. . . . 'Wherever two or three are gathered in my name, there I am in the midst of them.' [Matt. 18:20]."[19]

The preaching of the gospel and proper administration of the sacraments came to be called "marks of the Church." Calvin furthermore stated,

> Every congregation that claims the name "church" must be tested by this standard as by a touchstone. If in Word and sacraments it has the order approved by the Lord, it will not deceive; let us, then, confidently pay to it the honor due to churches. But again, if, devoid of Word and sacraments, it advertises the name of church, we must just as scrupulously beware such deceits.[20]

Calvin said further, "We recognize as members of the church those who, by confession of faith, by example of life, and by partaking of the sacraments, profess the same God and Christ with us."[21]

Calvin criticized many Roman Catholic practices as idolatrous—though individual Catholics were not necessarily excluded from the true church. Protestant

15. (Nuremberg: F. Peypus, 1525), in French titled, *Du Baptême chrétien des croyants*; Herminjard, *Correspondance des réformateurs*, vol. 9, 173n14; Rudolph Peter and Jean-François Gilmont, *Bibliotheca Calviniana*, vol. 1, 1532–1544 (Geneva: Librairie Droz, 159–60).

16. John Calvin, *Treatises against the Anabaptists and against the Libertines*, ed. and trans. Benjamin Farley (Grand Rapids: Baker Academic, 1982), 18, 25.

17. *Farellus Calvino*, 681–83.

18. *Institutes* 4.1.8.

19. Ibid., 4.1.9.

20. Ibid., 4.1.11.

21. Ibid., 4.1.8.

churches were easier to view in a positive light, however. Many churches that would eventually be considered "other Protestant denominations" were simply Christian churches in other geographic locations. It was not that Calvin did not wish for further reform of these other churches in some aspects of their practices. Sometimes it appears that diplomatic considerations, such as the need for support from German princes in negotiations with the King of France, overrode any inclination to speak out on what those reforms might be. It is enlightening to observe concern at the Colloquy of Poissy in France in 1561 that the Germans might be offended at the Reformed rejection of the Augsburg Confession as a possible compromise between the Reformed and the Catholics on the nature of the Sacrament of the Lord's Supper. According to Nicolas Des Gallars, a Reformed delegate, the Cardinal of Lorraine's request for the Reformed delegation to sign a Lutheran confession

> was done for a pollicy, to thintente, that if we denied so to do, he might set us at strife with the Germans, and make us to be hated of them. And if we did agre, then they as conquerors shoulde tryumph over us: and make a common iest of us, as of light and indiscrete persons, and so condemne our opinion.[22]

To the relief of the Reformed contingent, the Germans arrived after the crucial discussions of the Colloquy were over.

What then of individuals who were not in the church at all? In the tradition of the church fathers, Calvin states, "Away from her (the church), one cannot hope for any forgiveness of sins or any salvation."[23] He explains why. "God's fatherly favor and especial witness of spiritual life are limited to his flock, so that it is always disastrous to leave the church."[24] Calvin is speaking, then, not of people who have never heard the gospel, but of those who abandon the church. By comparing the church to a mother, Calvin emphasizes the nurturing and educative nature of the church. The church, like the sacraments, exists for us. In *The Theology of John Calvin*, Charles Partee labels book 4 of Calvin's *Institutes* as "the Faithful Community."[25] Quoting from Benjamin Milner, Partee asserts that "the special significance of Calvin's doctrine of the church is that we must think of the church 'as the history of the restoration of order in the world.'"[26] Partee elaborates, "The created order, which was disordered by the fall, is restored by the creation of the church. For Calvin the church is God's answer to the world's disorder."[27]

If Milner and Partee are correct that Calvin viewed the church as "God's answer to the world's disorder,"[28] then we have a clue to Calvin's activist stance

---

22. Nicolas Des Gallars, *A true report of all the doynges at the Assembly concernyng matters of religion lately holden at Poyssy in Fraunce. Written in Latine by Mayster Nicolas Gallasius, minister of the Frenche Churche in London, and then present, one of the disputers in the same, translated into English, by J. D., 1561,* (86).

23. *Institutes* 4.1.4.

24. Ibid.

25. Charles Partee, *The Theology of John Calvin* (Louisville, KY: Westminster John Knox, 2008), 258.

26. Ibid., 259; Milner, *Calvin's Doctrine of the Church,* 194–96, 4.

27. Partee, *Theology of John Calvin,* 259.

28. Ibid.

with regard to the church and society. Like the Anabaptists, Calvin wanted the church to be as pure as possible, but unlike the Anabaptists, he strove actively to reform society rather than to withdraw from it.

But for Calvin, church and government were complementary; each had its own jurisdiction, spiritual or civil, but responsibilities were intertwined. Calvin thinks that both church and state have a God-ordained place for "order" in response to the fall. Calvin said, "The magistrate ought by punishment and physical restraint to cleanse the church of offenses, so the minister of the Word in turn ought to help the magistrate in order that not so many may sin."[29] The observations of Milner and Partee move the discussion from Calvin's views on the church to Calvin's actions on behalf of the church and of society, as a pastor and member of the Venerable Company of Pastors of Geneva.

Organization of the Church in Geneva

Calvin's greatest opportunity to impact the organization of a church was when he was a pastor in Geneva. Calvin lived there from 1536 to 1538 and again from 1541 until his death in 1564. During this time, Geneva handled its own domestic and foreign affairs.

External to Geneva, the hold of the Holy Roman Empire over what was eventually to become Switzerland had weakened centuries before. In the early sixteenth century, Geneva was under the control of a prince-bishop of the House of Savoy to the south, but in a series of bold moves in the 1520s and 1530s, the Genevans drove the ruling prince-bishop out of town and adopted self-government. This political revolution facilitated religious reformation in the city. Independence from the Duchy of Savoy was achieved by the crucial Reformation years of 1535–1536, but the threat of a Savoyard comeback would remain until the early seventeenth century. Nevertheless, Geneva was more autonomous than an ancient Greek city. Geneva would not join the *Confederatio Helvetica* to become a part of Switzerland until 1815, after the major Napoleonic wars. Even today, the urbane French-speaking Genevans have their own spirit.

It is important to note that Calvin did not initiate the Reformation in Geneva. Already before Calvin arrived, Guillaume Farel and Pierre Viret had preached the gospel in Geneva. The Mass had been abolished, and the Roman Catholic priests, monks, and nuns had left town. The city had confiscated church lands and property and used the income to fund the social services that the religious orders had previously provided. New institutions had been established to keep the city running smoothly. The magistrates had initiated a system of compulsory public elementary education and organized a city hospital and social welfare system. All these changes had come about without the leadership of Calvin.

While this was going on, north, in Basel, Calvin was writing his *Institutes of the Christian Religion* (first published in 1536). That same year he made a trip to the Italian peninsula to visit the proto-Protestant Duchess of Ferrara. On his

29. *Institutes* 4.11.3.

return, he passed through Geneva, intending to move on; but there was more that needed to be done for the Reformed church and society of Geneva. Farel persuaded him to stay.

Calvin was received in Geneva initially as a lecturer on Scripture. Soon he became a pastor and a member of the Venerable Company of Pastors of Geneva, salaried by the city council. It did not take long for suggestions to come forth from the pastors. The government of the city, consisting chiefly of syndics and councils, was the legal body in control of local reform. Calvin and the pastors would have to work with four syndics and at least three councils: the Small Council, the Council of Sixty, and the Council of Two Hundred. The Small Council did most of the day-to-day governing, similar to what we might call today "the Genevan city council."

In January 1537, Calvin presented to the city council of Geneva on behalf of the pastors a program for the organization of the church in Geneva called the *Articles Concerning the Organization of the Church and of Worship*.[30] The germ of the Calvinist system of church discipline was evident in these proposals, which also requested that Psalms be sung in church, that the children be instructed and catechized, and that Communion be held monthly and not quarterly.[31] These latter requests on singing, education, and Communion appear benign, but proposals on church discipline were threatening to the magistrates, because of the suggestion of a system of oversight and excommunication that gave considerable power to the pastors. Specifically, the *Articles* asked the council to select reputable persons of "good life" to oversee the neighborhoods of the city. These representatives were to report defaulters to the ministers, who were to admonish the sinner to repent. If this was to no avail, "the minister appointed by those in charge of the case should announce publicly in the assembly what has been done to bring him to amendment and all with no result. . . . This is the time for excommunication." In such case, he is to be

> expelled from the Company of Christians and left in the power of the devil for his temporal confusion, until he give good evidence of his penitence and amendment . . . he is to be barred from the communion of the Supper and denounced to other believers that they have no intimate dealings with him. But he is never to omit coming to receive teaching, in order to prove whether it will please the Saviour to touch his heart and turn him to the right path.[32]

A reason for excommunication from the church was the hope of encouraging repentance of sinners. Another reason was a desire to avoid contamination of the Lord's Supper by those who "manifest by their misconduct and evil life

30. *Articles Concerning the Organization of the Church and of Worship at Geneva Proposed by the Ministers at the Council, January 16, 1537*, in *Calvin: Theological Treatises*, The Library of Christian Classics, trans. J. K. S. Reid (Philadelphia: Westminster Press, 1954), 48–55.

31. Ibid., 49–50, 53–54.

32. Ibid., 52.

that they do not at all belong to Jesus" so that "this Holy Supper, ordained and instituted for joining the members of our Lord Jesus Christ with their Head and with one another in one body and in one spirit, be not soiled and contaminated and our Lord be not gravely dishonored."[33] Here is a desire for purity similar to the Anabaptists.

The *Articles* proposed a matrimonial commission to resolve sexual and marital issues, filling in for the absence of Roman Catholic canon law. The magistrates on the council were advised to pick from their members to decide matrimonial issues. This foreshadowed the consistory. The councilors were joined by ministers "to secure that what is done is in accordance with the Word of God."[34]

The magistrates of Geneva put very few of these proposals into effect, even the innocuous suggestion that Communion should be offered every month rather than quarterly.[35] As for excommunication, this was a prerogative that other Protestant city councils reserved for themselves. Although the *Articles* might not have clearly stated who was doing the excommunicating, the pastors had a large role.[36] The council was not receptive to requests from the pastors that were interpreted as interfering with council prerogatives. The magistrates had no intention of turning over their hard-won responsibilities to the pastors. Magistrates controlled the hour and place of worship. The council approved of changes in scheduling, liturgy, and personnel.

The magistrates guarded their prerogatives over the church. The council transferred pastors to less desirable country churches without always consulting with the Company of Pastors, such as happened to Nicolas Des Gallars in 1553. The council fired pastors, such as Nicolas Colladon, who on August 26, 1571, criticized from the pulpit the magistrates of Geneva. Colladon disagreed on financial policy, was deposed in September 1571, and in January 1571 began teaching in the Academy of Lausanne, finishing his life as rector there.[37]

Those who accuse Geneva of being a theocracy under Calvin (or of the Company of Pastors) know little of how the city worked. The highest office that Calvin ever held in Geneva was moderator of the Company of Pastors. He was not a citizen. He did not become a "bourgeois" until within five years of his death.

The Expulsion

Clearly what Calvin, Farel, and the pastors could do in Geneva was limited in the early years. In 1538, Calvin and Farel were in trouble with the city council, which had different priorities than the pastors. The council felt it expedient to please the city of Bern in order to help perpetuate an alliance the two cities had

33. Ibid., 50.
34. Ibid., 55.
35. Ibid., 50.
36. Ibid., 52.
37. Archives d'État de Genève, Registres du Conseil, vol. 66, January 7, 1571 to January 4, 1572, folios 104–122 verso. Hereafter, AEG, Reg. Conseil.

forged when Geneva broke from the House of Savoy in 1526. This was due to Geneva's need of Bern's military protection. Bern encouraged Geneva and Lausanne to imitate the Bernese church and adopt the Bernese rite, but Calvin and Farel were unwilling to adopt practices abolished by Farel: the use of unleavened bread, baptismal fonts, and the observance of Christmas and other religious days, which some associated with Roman Catholicism. In addition, the magistrates told the pastors they could not exclude people from Communion. Farel and Calvin were told not to preach. On Easter, they preached anyway, refusing to administer Communion in the atmosphere of discord. With this defiance, the magistrates gave three pastors three days to leave town: Calvin, Farel, and the blind and aged Courrault.

Calvin and Farel left Geneva, attempted to return, and went their separate ways, Calvin to Basel and Farel to Neuchâtel, where he served as pastor the rest of his career. Martin Bucer invited Calvin to Protestant Strasbourg. There Calvin was pastor to a congregation of French-speaking refugees, preached in the Cathedral, lectured at the newly-founded academy of Johann Sturm, and attended ecumenical meetings of representatives from other churches. Scholars credit this sojourn in Strasbourg as important in forming Calvin's opinions on church office and the organization of the church. Calvin profited from the example of Bucer and the church in Strasbourg, but he also developed ideas of his own.[38]

The city council of Geneva invited him back in the fall of 1540. Calvin did not want to return. He suggested they call Pierre Viret, who arrived in Geneva January 10, 1541. Under Viret's influence, the Small Council moved to establish a consistory. The Genevan Council of Two Hundred blocked it. Nevertheless, Viret's presence in Geneva encouraged Calvin to return there.[39]

The *Draft Ecclesiastical Ordinances*

In September 1541, Calvin took precautions when he returned to Geneva. He appeared to have assured his ecclesiastical goals and left his wife behind in Strasbourg with her children temporarily. Upon arriving in Geneva, he appeared before the city council, which organized a committee consisting of pastors and city councilors who composed the *Draft Ecclesiastical Ordinances*.[40] Having been trained in law at Orleans and Bourges, Calvin also rewrote the Genevan civil laws.

The *Ecclesiastical Ordinances* organized the church of Geneva and established institutions replicated by Reformed churches as they spread worldwide. The

38. For a balanced view on the influence of Strasbourg see Harro Höpfl, *The Christian Polity of John Calvin* (Cambridge: Cambridge University Press, 1982), 89–90.

39. For the role of Pierre Viret in the recall of Calvin to Geneva see Michael W. Bruening, "Pierre Viret and Geneva," *Archive for Reformation History* 99 (2008): 182–85.

40. *Ordonnances ecclésiastiques, 1541*, in *Registres de la Compagnie des Pasteurs de Genève au temps de Calvin*, published under the direction of the Archives of the State of Geneva, vol. 1, 1546–1553, ed. Jean-François Bergier (Geneva: Librairie Droz, 1964), 1–13.; for an English translation see *Draft Ecclesiastical Ordinances*, in Reid, ed., *Calvin: Theological Treatises*, 58–72.

Ordinances describe four offices of the church: pastors in lieu of priests, doctors (professors), elders, and deacons who worked with the poor, an organizational scheme that departed from the Roman Catholic hierarchical system of church office—popes, cardinals, archbishops, bishops, priests, and deacons who were liturgical assistants.[41] Calvin did not label the pastors "clergy." He considered the four offices God-given, as evidenced by the beginning sentence of the *Draft Ecclesiastical Ordinances*: "There are four orders of office *instituted by our Lord for the government of his Church*."[42]

The *Ecclesiastical Ordinances* proposals added considerably to the abortive requests of the 1537 *Articles Concerning the Organization of the Church and of Worship*. The 1541 *Ordinances* was a mature document, drafted by a committee that included Calvin, pastors, and city councilors, which increased its likelihood of passage. It included not only the fourfold vision of church office, but also definite organizational guidelines. These provisions were discussed, altered by the city magistrates and councils, and passed on November 20, 1541, as law, becoming part of the governing structures of Geneva.[43]

Central to both the *Articles* and the *Ordinances* were the disciplinary guidelines. The 1541 *Ordinances* placed the responsibility for surveillance under twelve elders, chosen from the councils of the city. Until 1555, the councils consisted of Genevans rather than French immigrants. Elders were to be from "every quarter of the city to keep an eye on everybody."[44] They were to meet with the pastors weekly, Thursday mornings, to interview, admonish, and excommunicate recalcitrant sinners. This meeting was called the consistory. It also took over cases involving sex and marriage, fulfilling the 1537 request for a matrimonial commission.

Convening the pastors and elders weekly was an ingenious move. The consistory meetings regularly brought together government leaders, mainly Genevans, and the pastors, who, during Calvin's time were mainly French. The elders' attendance was often better than the pastors'. Elders were paid for attendance, while the pastors were not.

The office of pastor was the first listed in the *Draft Ecclesiastical Ordinances*. The pastors' duties and responsibilities were described, as was the screening process through the Company of Pastors before prospective pastors were presented for city council affirmation. The *Ordinances* list infractions that were "quite intolerable" in a pastor, including drunkenness but also "games forbidden by law and scandalous, dances, and similar dissoluteness."[45]

Not just pastors were limited in their behavior. Anyone could be brought before the consistory. Everyone was expected to dress soberly although nothing

41. I have commented on Calvin's four offices in "Calvin and Social-Ethical Issues" in Donald K. McKim, ed., *The Cambridge Companion to John Calvin* (Cambridge: Cambridge University Press, 2004), 153–72.

42. *Draft Ecclesiastical Ordinances*, in Reid, ed., *Calvin: Theological Treatises*, 58; emphasis added.

43. Ibid., 56–58.

44. Ibid., 64.

45. Ibid., 60–61.

is said about modest dress in the *Draft Ecclesiastical Ordinances.* Conservative (sometimes austere) clothing was a mark of the early Reformed tradition. Perhaps the making of watches did well in Geneva in early modern times because other ornamentation, such as jewelry, was discouraged. Although drunkenness was frowned upon, drinking alcoholic beverages was not questioned. These Reformers were not teetotalers. Genevan pastors received part of their pay in wine. The hospital gave wine to the sick to help them get well.

The *Draft Ecclesiastical Ordinances* stipulated that the pastors were to meet together weekly. In addition, in order to keep the "discipline in operation," every three months the ministers were to "take special notice whether there be anything to discuss among themselves, to remedy it as soon as possible."[46] A quarterly meeting for group self-examination became characteristic of groups in Geneva. Such meetings were called a *grabeau.* We know very little about what went on, perhaps confession and mutual admonishment.

The deacons, in Calvin's vision of the office, were to deal with the poor. The *Draft Ecclesiastical Ordinances* also permitted deacons to give the wine chalice to the communicants as in the early church.[47] "The ministers are to distribute the bread in proper order and with reverence; and none are to give the chalice except the colleagues or deacons with the ministers."[48] In Geneva during Calvin's lifetime, the names listed to give the chalice in the documents I have studied from the 1550s were those of elders. Perhaps they were "the colleagues" noted in the above quotation.

For Calvin there were two grades of deacon based on Paul's letter to the Romans: (1) those "who distribute the alms" and (2) those who devote "themselves to the care of the poor and the sick."[49] Calvin's broad interpretation of Romans 12:6–8 is the basis for Calvin's "double diaconate." "Having gifts that differ according to the grace given to us, let us use them: . . . he who contributes, in liberality [designating the first grade of deacon]; he who gives aid, with zeal [designating the second grade of deacon]."[50]

It probably was no coincidence that the double diaconate fit the actual poor relief system of Geneva in 1541. Calvin considered the trustees of the city hospital to be the first grade of deacons, even though the title of deacon for the trustees did not catch on in Geneva's legal documents of Calvin's era. Genevans called the trustees procurators. Procurators met weekly as a governmental committee to oversee the welfare system of Geneva, centered in the city hospital. The

46. Ibid.
47. *Constitutions of the Holy Apostles* 8.2 in *Ante-Nicene Fathers,* vol. 7, *The Fathers of the Third and Fourth Centuries: Lactantius, Venantius, Asterius, Victorinus, Dionysius, Apostolic Teaching and Constitutions, Homily, and Liturgies.* American repr. of Edinburgh edition, ed. A. Cleveland Coxe (Grand Rapids: Eerdmans, n.d.), 491.
48. *Draft Ecclesiastical Ordinances,* 67.
49. *Institutes* 4.3.9.
50. For an elaboration on the double diaconate see Elsie McKee, *John Calvin on the Diaconate and Liturgical Almsgiving* (Geneva: Librairie Droz, 1984), 195.

second grade of deacons consisted of the administrator of that hospital and others who worked directly with the poor, potentially even women, whom Calvin allowed this one office. "Women could fill no other public office than to devote themselves to the care of the poor," said Calvin in his *Institutes*.[51]

There were to be other deacons in Geneva. After the *Ecclesiastical Ordinances* were passed, Geneva became overwhelmed by refugees pouring into the city in flight from persecution from Catholic countries that considered Protestants heretical. By 1545 the population of refugees in Geneva had reached the point where they were about to be expelled, shipped up Lake Geneva by boat. Then a wealthy man died with Calvin at his bedside. The dying man willed his wealth to the poor of Geneva and of Strasbourg and this money apparently saved the refugees.[52] Along with other gifts, it provided the basis for the first refugee fund in Geneva, the *Bourse française*.[53] This French fund was followed by an Italian fund, a fund for English refugees during the Marian exile of the 1550s, and a fund for German-speaking refugees. In each case, the more prosperous within each ethnic group of refugees contributed to the poor. I have discussed these refugee funds and welfare in Geneva elsewhere.[54]

There remains one office of the church in the *Draft Ecclesiastical Ordinances*, that of doctor, defined not as a medical doctor but as a doctor of the church, a professor, reminiscent of medieval terminology for scholars such as Thomas Aquinas (1224 or 1225–1274). The section of the *Draft Ecclesiastical Ordinances* that dealt with "doctors" was called "the order of the schools." It provided for two lecturers in theology, one in Old Testament and one in New Testament, roles that Calvin and Farel had already undertaken in Geneva.[55] Their lectures, in a sense, were the foundation of the Genevan Academy. They were in Latin as were lectures in universities of the era. Therefore, the *Draft Ecclesiastical Ordinances* recommended foundation of a Latin school, the *collège*, to prepare young

---

51. *Institutes* 4.3.9. For an elaboration on this see Jeannine Olson, "John Calvin's One Public Office for Women, the Care of the Poor: Widows, Wet Nurses, and Welfare among French Refugees and in the Reformed Tradition," in *Mythes et réalités du XVIe siècle, Foi, Idées, Images: Études en l'honneur d'Alain Dufour*, ed. Bernard Lescaze and Mario Turchetti (Alessandria: Edizioni dell'Orso, 2008), 51–69.

52. AEG, Reg. Conseil, vol. 40 (February 8, 1545–February 7, 1546), dated January 5, 1541, folio 161.

53. Jeannine Olson, *Calvin and Social Welfare: Deacons and the* Bourse française (Selinsgrove, PA: Susquehanna University Press; London and Toronto: Associated University Presses, 1989), 33.

54. Some publications on social welfare in Geneva include "Calvin, Social Justice and Diakonia, a Comparative Perspective," *Seminary Ridge Review* 7, no. 2 (Spring 2005): 32–49; "The Crisis of the Advent of Catholicism in a Protestant State: Changing Structures in Social Welfare," in *The Identity of Geneva: The Christian Commonwealth, 1564–1864*, ed. John Roney and Martin Klauber (London: Greenwood Press, 1998), 155–68; "La Bourse Française de Genève: les années d'origine," *Revue de Vieux Genève* (1987): 16–20; "The Bourse Française: Deacons and Social Welfare in Calvin's Geneva," *Pacific Theological Review* 15, no. 2 (Winter 1982): 18–24; "Calvin and the Diaconate: Genevan Origins," *Liturgy: Journal of the Liturgical Conference* 2, no. 4 (Fall 1982): 78–83.

55. *Draft Ecclesiastical Ordinances*, 62–63.

men "for the ministry as well as civil government," reminiscent of Luther's recommendations on education.[56]

At the *collège,* the boys studied in Latin and learned Greek. The Academy taught Hebrew. The Academy originally used church buildings for lecture rooms. The *collège* came into formal existence almost twenty years after the drafting of the *Ecclesiastical Ordinances.* The project waited until those who were opposed to Calvin, called *enfants de Genève* or Libertines, were condemned in May 1555 of trying to destroy the ecclesiastical discipline, namely, the *Ordinances* of 1541. Their property was confiscated and used to build the *collège* (1558–1562). "Genevan Academy" is a term often used popularly to encompass both the *collège* and the Academy.

Calvin's Attitude toward Society and Financial Matters

The Genevan Academy and social welfare system were costly, but Calvin felt the church and the government had an obligation for social and economic life. Calvin and the other pastors repeatedly pressured the city council to protect the poor and to pass laws to favor social welfare.

None of the magisterial Reformers considered poverty a virtue. It certainly was not a blessing. Although little socialism was practiced in Europe at this time, there was a sincere desire on the part of many Reformers, both Catholic and Protestant, to alleviate poverty. Calvin thought that giving should be voluntary but generous, yet responsibility could not all lie with the church. There was no income tax in sixteenth-century Geneva, and professors' and pastors' salaries were expensive. Magistrates and pastors appealed for donations, and notaries were required to remind testators to include Geneva's welfare institutions and schools in their wills.

Calvin opposed hoarding, speculation, and profiteering on commodities that were essential, especially food.[57] The welfare system that evolved in the city during his lifetime was a living testimonial to the commitment of his generation to provide for the poor. It was based almost exclusively on freewill donations beyond what the city was willing to provide. Calvin and the other magisterial reformers believed Christians were stewards of God's gifts. Good stewardship of God's gifts committed one to a generous and open spirit toward the less fortunate, but stewardship was not haphazard. Indeed, some donors appear to have pledged a specific monthly amount for the poor.[58]

Calvinism is characterized more by a struggle against poverty than by a justification of lending money at interest or of keeping one's profits to oneself.

56. Ibid., 63; Martin Luther, "To the Councilmen of All Cities in Germany That They Establish and Maintain Christian Schools," in *Luther's Works,* ed. Jaroslav Pelikan, American Edition, vol. 45 (St. Louis and Philadelphia: Concordia and Fortress Press, 1962), 339–78.

57. William Innes, *Social Concern in Calvin's Geneva* (Allison Park, PA: Pickwick Publications), 244.

58. See, for instance, "Donors to the *Bourse française:* 1550–1559," in Olson, *Calvin and Social Welfare,* 120–26.

Calvin did not see material possessions or success as a sign of God's blessing for personal merit, and one finds no special Protestant work ethic in Geneva, although eliminating saints days and religious holidays such as Christmas meant Genevans had less time off than their Roman Catholic neighbors.

As for Calvinism and capitalism, Calvin's Geneva seems relatively unsophisticated economically. Genevans had not yet adopted double entry bookkeeping from Italy. Protestants allowed the lending of money at interest, but Luther and Calvin wanted to control the rates even though the sixteenth century was an inflationary one. Genevan pastors wanted interest on loans to be reasonable, lower than the market would bear. After returning to Geneva in 1541, Calvin worked with the city council to keep interest no higher than 5 percent. By November 12, 1557, it was raised to 6.67 percent. There were Genevan pastors who lent money above the legal rate of interest although that was one of the crimes "intolerable in a minister" in the *Draft Ecclesiastical Ordinances*.[59]

Calvin opposed slavery and exposited this view in his sermons and commentaries on Scripture.[60] In later centuries, particular leaders of the Reformed tradition championed the abolitionist cause.

Calvin, Democracy, and Resistance Theory

Like ancient philosophers, Calvin acknowledged three forms of government: (1) monarchy, rule by one, (2) aristocracy, government composed of people of note, and (3) democracy, popular government in which every person has power. But there were dangers in each of these. Calvin stated, "The fall from kingdom to tyranny is easy [leaving France unnamed]; but it is not much more difficult to fall from the rule of the best men to the faction of a few; yet it is easiest of all to fall from popular rule to sedition."[61] Thus no form of government was safe. However, "I will not deny that aristocracy, or a system compounded of aristocracy and *politia* far excels all others."[62] Ford Battles translated *politia* as democracy in his popular translation into English of Calvin's 1559 edition of his *Institutes*.[63] Mario Turchetti maintains that if Calvin had wanted to say democracy he would have used that term as he had before, *démocratie*, in French.[64] *Politia* can be more accurately translated as republic (republicanism) or as government based on a constitution (constitutionalism). Battle's translation of *politia* as democracy can lead to erroneous conclusions about what Calvin meant.

In light of his context, it is no surprise that Calvin favored aristocracy. Once Calvin left France, he lived in Basel, Geneva, and Strasbourg ruled by the

59. *Draft Ecclesiastical Ordinances*, 60–61; W. Fred Graham, *The Constructive Revolutionary: John Calvin and His Socio-Economic Impact* (n.p.: Michigan State University Press, 1987), 120.

60. Biéler, *La pensée économique et sociale de Calvin*, 171.

61. *Institutes* 4.20.8.

62. Ibid.

63. Ibid.

64. Turchetti, "The Contribution of Calvin and Calvinism to the Birth of Modern Democracy," in Hirzel and Sallmann, eds., *John Calvin's Impact on Church and Society*, 195–97.

bourgeoisie—the established, notable, and wealthy families. While not holding noble titles, these families constituted an aristocracy of sorts.

Whatever the form of government, Calvin was concerned that those who rule check and restrain each other. "Men's fault or failing causes it to be safer and more bearable for a number to exercise government, so that they may help one another, teach and admonish one another; and, if one asserts himself unfairly, there may be a number of censors and masters to restrain his willfulness."[65] Calvin was referring to the *grabeau*, the regular meeting of Genevan committees, civil and ecclesiastical, for mutual criticism and correction.

In an age when absolutist monarchy was about to gain the ascendancy in continental Europe, Calvin was no democrat, but he was no autocrat either. He preferred rule by the knowledgeable few rather than by the many. In the case of the church, this ruled out repeated popular election of officers. After the initial election in a congregation, incumbent church officers selected those men whom they wanted to fill vacancies. Calvin opposed Jean Morély, a creative thinker and author of the *Treatise on Christian Discipline and Polity*.[66] Morély advocated democratic procedures and congregational autonomy.

Asking whether or not Calvin was a democrat is altogether different from asking whether or not Calvin inadvertently contributed to the growth of democracy. Elements of his thought and actions argue in favor of his positive contribution: for instance, the place of "conscience" in his theology and his commitment to a collective approach to church governance.[67]

On the side of Calvin's contribution to democracy, the *Draft Ecclesiastical Ordinances* are riddled with what a modern Master of Business Administration might call team-building, as are the organizational structures of many Presbyterian and other churches in the Reformed tradition today. Group decision-making in Reformed churches expanded over the centuries from the pastors, elders, and deacons to include entire congregations. Just as the Reformers insistence on everyone being able to read the Bible inadvertently served as an equalizing force in society (which was not the original intent), so too might have Calvin's political legacy been democratic by extension. Some think that democratic procedures in Reformed churches became a model for modern secular governments.

One can argue convincingly that Calvin's thought influenced modern constitutionalism because of his belief in natural law, equity, inherent rights of the individual, and the central role of conscience. Significant weight has been placed on Calvin's "doctrine" of freedom of conscience, evolved from Luther's

---

65. *CO* 4.20.9.

66. For Morély's biography and theology see Philippe Denis and Jean Rott, *Jean Morély (ca 1524–ca 1594) et l'utopie d'une démocratie dans l'Eglise* (Geneva: Librairie Droz, 1993).

67. On the issue of Calvin's contribution to democracy there has been a divergence of opinion. See Robert Kingdon and Robert Linder, ed., *Calvin and Calvinism: Sources of Democracy* (Lexington, MA: D. C. Heath and Company, 1970); Turchetti, "The Contribution of Calvin and Calvinism to the Birth of Modern Democracy," in Hirzel and Sallmann, eds., *John Calvin's Impact on Church and Society* (2009), 195–197.

Christian freedom. However, for Calvin and others during his era, freedom of conscience was limited. It did not extend to Anabaptists or antitrinitarians and certainly not to Servetus, who was burned at the stake in Geneva in 1553 for his unorthodox beliefs.

Nevertheless, the concept of freedom to act according to conscience contributed to resistance theory, the power of the people to resist an unjust government. Calvin asserted in the final pages of his *Institutes* that magistrates, but not private individuals, have a right to restrain unbridled despotism.[68] To many, such as Charles Partee, Calvin seems too cautious, but Calvin was writing what was possible to write in turbulent times before the French Wars of Religion. Calvin's was not full-blown resistance theory. He did not want to antagonize French monarchs. It remained for his successors to speak more boldly.

HIGHLIGHTS IN THE HISTORY OF RECEPTION UP TO THE EARLY EIGHTEENTH CENTURY

Well before the building of the *collège*, the reception of Calvin's ideas passed from Geneva to Europe. Expansion into the rest of Europe was accomplished through (1) missionary pastors; (2) religious books such as Bibles, Psalters, and catechisms; and (3) eventually through the alumni of the Academy.

Calvin's Ideas and Practices Modified

The context of Reformed congregations changed as the Reformed tradition spread into Catholic countries. They had no church buildings and no government support. Members of congregations supported pastors, their own poor, and sometimes others. They provided safe havens for refugees moving from one Reformed congregation to another to escape persecution.

In France, the newly formed Reformed churches accepted Calvin's theology and benefited from the example of the Genevan church, but because of local needs they could not replicate it. Because of contextual challenges, they departed from Calvin's polity and the Genevan fourfold system of church office. Which adjustments needed to be made could be a matter of controversy. With the growth of congregations in France, demand for pastors exceeded supply. Congregations responded (1) by requesting pastors from the Company of Pastors of Geneva, and when the Company could not fill all congregational requests, (2) by sending their own men to study in Geneva, expecting them to return and serve as pastors in their communities of origin, and (3) by giving deacons more responsibility, such as teaching the catechism. This role for deacons did not fit into Calvin's description of deacons in the *Institutes*.[69] However, in the early

---

68. *CO* 4.20.31.
69. *Institutes* 4.3.9.

church, deacons taught catechism.[70] One common denominator among these new Reformed churches was a concern for discipline.

Discipline had two meanings in Reformed churches: (1) "The discipline" was their organizational structure, written down in what was called a "discipline" (a church order or constitution), but (2) "discipline" also referred to "moral discipline," obedience to the Ten Commandments and the attempt to enforce conformity through church courts called consistories. As Calvinism spread, "discipline" was a distinguishing feature of the Reformed churches. Concern for discipline guaranteed the establishment of consistories along with officers to enforce discipline in many Reformed churches. In France, churches in the houses of the nobility were the exception.[71]

The composition of French consistories differed from the Genevan consistory, which consisted of pastors and elders. Many consistories in France also included deacons. Glenn Sunshine points to the Reformed church of Poitiers, whose consistory exceptionally contained no pastors, only elders and deacons.[72]

Unlike Geneva, consistories of Reformed churches in countries where they did not have state support were responsible for more than discipline. They functioned also as church councils and boards of trustees, administering the church's affairs, arranging for services, and paying for salaries and repairs without forgetting the poor in their midst.

With regard to church finances, the Genevan Company of Pastors preferred that deacons take charge, or if not, someone other than pastors. The Company stated in a letter to churches of Normandy:

> We add yet this word, that it seems to us that in such a case, and generally, it is good that those who are committed to administer the Word are not embroiled in investments or receipts, but that one keeps them soberly and honestly, either by the means of the deacons (which really would be the better) or by other means, according to the circumstance of time and place.[73]

In Geneva, church finances were the responsibility of city councilors, who paid pastors and maintained church buildings, but as the Reformed church spread into other countries where Protestantism was in the minority, such as France, there was no support from governments hostile to Protestant churches. Minority churches survived on freewill offerings. In many congregations, elders

70. "Deacons and Deaconesses in the Bible and the Early Church: The First to the Fourth Centuries," in *One Ministry Many Roles: Deacons and Deaconesses through the Centuries* (St. Louis: Concordia Publishing House, 1992), 34.

71. Glenn Sunshine, *Reforming French Protestantism: The Development of Huguenot Ecclesiastical Institutions, 1557–1572* (Kirksville, MO: Truman State University Press, 2003), 146.

72. Ibid., 127–28.

73. From a *Lettre de la Compagnie des Pasteurs de Genève aux Églises de Normandie* (Letter of the Company of Pastors of Geneva to the churches of Normandy), November 30, 1564, in *Registres de la Compagnie des Pasteurs de Genève*, vol. 2, 1553–1564, ed. Robert Kingdon (Geneva: Librairie Droz, 1962), 140.

had a significant role in handling church finances. Thus, polity practices related to church finance varied from place to place. As Reformed churches spread to New England through the Puritans and Separatists, boards of trustees were to hold church property and to handle finances.

Maintaining Connections among Reformed Churches

Although ultimately concentrated in the South of France, Reformed congregations in France sprang up in disparate locations but became one French Reformed church. Unity was accomplished in two ways: (1) Representatives of these churches, early in their development, met together in national synods, the first, in Paris in 1559.[74] They adopted a discipline, a common confession of faith, and a pyramidal set of judicatory levels between individual congregations and national synods, initially provincial synods. (2) After the first election of congregational officers, pastors and church leaders already in office selected new officers rather than giving individual congregational members a larger voice. Undemocratic as the selection of leadership by those officers already in place seems, it kept individual congregations from spinning off independently in different directions. (Before judging procedures of early French Reformed churches harshly, reflect on modern organizations that present one slate of officers for election.)

Education in Reformed Churches, the Office of Doctor

Calvin's *Ecclesiastical Ordinances* stated that four offices were instituted by God.[75] Nevertheless, as Reformed churches spread, most did not maintain four offices. The office most slighted, as Reformed churches developed, was that of doctor. This was true in France, although during the 1560s French Protestants seem to have had a theological faculty, which included Nicolas Des Gallars, in Orléans, the center of the Protestant cause during the first wars of religion. The Reformed also established academies for young men in France. Likewise in Scotland, the office of doctor dropped out of the organizational structures of the Scottish kirk, leaving pastors, elders, and deacons.

However, the dropping of this office by many Reformed churches did not mean education was emphasized less. Congregations continued to demand an educated clergy able to preach from biblical texts and competent in biblical languages. Reformed churches insisted that children be able to read the Bible in their own language, and, of course, those who read the Bible could read other material, too. In Scotland, pastors were responsible for making sure someone taught the children in their congregations.

---

74. A list of national synods of the Reformed Church of France and their dates can be found in Sunshine, *Reforming French Protestantism*, xi.

75. *Draft Ecclesiastical Ordinances*, 58–72.

The Third Mark of the Church in the Belgic and Scots Confessions

As the Scots were adopting the Presbyterian kirk in the late 1550s and early 1560s, Reformed preaching was spreading to the Low Countries north of France. Unlike Calvin, other Reformed confessions such as the Belgic Confession of Faith (1561) and the Scots Confession (1560), recognized "discipline" as a third mark of the Church. As the Belgic confession says,

> The true church can be recognized if it has the following marks: The church engages in the pure preaching of the gospel; it makes use of the pure administration of the sacraments as Christ instituted them; it practices church discipline for correcting faults. In short, it governs itself according to the pure Word of God.[76]

Modifications in Reformed Church Order in the Colonies, Java

By the seventeenth century, Christianity was spreading from Europe to outlying trading ports such as the island of Java, eventually a colony of the Netherlands. Ministers sent there drafted the *Batavische Kerkenordening* or Church Order of Batavia (Jakarta) in 1624. It followed the Church Order of the Synod of Dort (1618–1619), with modifications. Besides the four offices of the church (pastors, teachers [doctors], elders, and deacons), the Batavia Church Order allowed limited ministerial capacity to "visitors of the sick" and school teachers. In rural areas, their responsibilities expanded to most churchly duties. They often led worship but were prohibited from writing sermons. They could read sermons by ordained pastors.[77]

The Reception of Calvinism in England

England was heavily influenced by Calvin's theology in the sixteenth and seventeenth centuries. But English monarchs preferred bishops to presbyteries, so the ecclesiastical structure of the Church of England remained hierarchical.

The Church of England adopted Archbishop Thomas Cranmer's *Book of Common Prayer,* a liturgy with beautiful but set wording, providing little room for spontaneity or extemporaneous prayer, leaving dissatisfied those who wanted to purify the Church of England from "popish practices." Many of this persuasion were Marian exiles, people who left England when Queen Mary Tudor (1553–1558) brought the Roman Catholic Church back. These exiles lived in Protestant cities in Europe, including Geneva. Returning to England

---

76. *A Confession of Faith Commonly Known as the Belgic Confession* (Grand Rapids: Faith Alive Christian Resources, 1988), article 32.

77. Yudha Thianto, "Elements of Calvin's Theology and Practice in the Establishment of Reformed Churches in Java in the Seventeenth Century," (unpublished paper delivered to the Calvin Studies Society, Grand Rapids, MI, April 18, 2009), 3, 6–7, 12–14.

under Elizabeth I (1558–1603), they desired a church resembling continental Reformed churches. Eventually called Puritans, they were frustrated with clerical dress, vestments, baptismal fonts, the *Book of Common Prayer,* inadequate sermons, altars (instead of tables for Communion services), and the relative lack of church discipline.

Calvin, however, did not rail against differences between the Church of England and that of Geneva. He allowed for bishops, as long as they governed collegially. Some bishops supported the Reformed cause. Calvin's successor, Theodore Beza, was outspoken in his negative opinions of bishops, voicing this to the Scots, who opposed bishops.[78] A Marian exile, Edmund Grindal, became bishop of London (1559–1570) under Elizabeth I. Tolerant toward Puritans and nonconformity, Grindal helped restore the Stranger Churches (repressed under Mary Tudor). Under him as superintendent, they were allowed Reformed worship and discipline. Grindal became Archbishop of York (1570) and Canterbury (1576). He was deposed by Elizabeth I for protecting Reformed practices, such as prophesying and gatherings of preachers to expound on Scripture, often with a lay audience. Prophesying sometimes lasted all day, sometimes accompanied by fasting, followed by a Communion service and meal to conclude the day's activities.[79]

New England, the Weber Thesis, and Church Organization

In parts of England the Puritans created a church within a church, in effect, with Reformed discipline, home conventicles, and endowed lectureships to ensure adequate preaching. Attempts to work through Parliament to remedy a church only "halfly reformed" failed. Some broke with the Church of England entirely and became Separatists, a precarious stance. Some moved to the Low Countries and later, beginning in 1620, as Pilgrims to New England. Puritans followed the same trajectory to the Massachusetts Bay Colony, where they imposed limits on the accumulation of excessive profit and the lending of money at high rates. Some merchant families even moved to Rhode Island to escape Puritan economic restrictions. Yet Max Weber looked to Calvinists of England and colonial America for the eventual legitimization of modern capitalism.

Puritans organized the church in New England with more congregational autonomy than Calvin condoned and modified Calvin's Augustinian view of the church considerably by limiting membership. (These New England churches came to be called Congregationalist. They joined with other Reformed Christians in the twentieth century, becoming the United Church of Christ.)

In the words of the "Cambridge Platform" of 1648, a recognized standard of Congregationalism in Massachusetts,

78. Patrick Collinson, *The Elizabethan Puritan Movement* (1967; repr., Oxford: Clarendon Paperbacks, 1998), 110.
79. See the chapter on prophesying in Collinson, *The Elizabethan Puritan Movement,* 168–76.

The doors of the Churches of Christ upon earth, do not by God's appointment stand so wide open, that all sorts of people good or bad, may freely
enter therein at their pleasure; but such as are admitted thereto, as members
ought to be examined and tried first, whether they be fit and meet to be
received into church-society, or not. . . . The officers are charged with the
keeping of the doors of the Church, and therefore are in a special manner
to make trial of the fitness of such who enter. . . . A personal and public
confession, and declaring of God's manner of working upon the soul, is
both lawful, expedient, and useful.[80]

Calvin and the pastors of Geneva had required no such personal public confession of church members.

The Cambridge Platform considered the ordinary offices of the church to
be that of elder and deacon. Elders consisted of pastors, teachers, and "ruling
elders." "Of *Elders* (who are also in Scripture called *Bishops*), some attend chiefly
to the ministry of the word, as the *Pastors & Teachers. Others*, attend especially
unto *Rule*, who are therefore called *Ruling Elders*."[81]

Deacons were in charge of the temporal goods of the church until civil law
in America required trustees to hold and transfer property in many regions.
Deacons were to receive the offerings and keep the treasury of the church.
The Cambridge Platform provided for "*ancient widdows* [sic] (where they may
be had) to minister in the church, in giving attendance to the sick . . . &
others."[82] The office of widow appears to have remained theoretical in New
England.

Deacons, in time, took on responsibilities that could conceivably have been
those of elders in the governance of Congregational churches. This pattern of
elevating the deacon to a governance role at the expense of the office of elder was
to be true also of other denominations within the Reformed tradition, such as
American Baptists. Where elders and deacons sat on the same governing body,
one office could be subsumed by the other. In France, deacons tended to lose
out to elders.[83]

Some Calvinists were opposed to the slave trade, but in the eighteenth century, Rhode Island's merchants were heavily involved in the trade. Samuel Hop-
kins, pastor of Newport's First Church (Congregational), rose up before his
slave-holding congregation and called on them not to include slave owners and
traders in their membership. In 1784 his congregation voted not to tolerate the
slave trade and slavery within their congregation.[84]

---

80. "The Cambridge Platform," in *Creeds of the Churches*, ed. John Leith, 3rd ed. (Atlanta: John
Knox, 1982), 394–95.

81. "The Cambridge Platform," in Williston Walker, *The Creeds and Platforms of Congregationalism* (New York: Charles Scribner's Sons, 1893), 211.

82. "The Cambridge Platform," in Walker, 214.

83. "The Loss of the Diaconate" in Sunshine, *Reforming French Protestantism*, 138–42.

84. Richard H. Taylor, "Embracing God's Hospitality: Celebrating Over Two Hundred Years
of Ministry Together: The Rhode Island Conference of the United Church of Christ" (Mimeo-
graphed, 2006), 12.

CONCLUSION

As André Biéler commented, the Calvinist reform was integral to society.[85] It remained so after Calvin's death. Calvin and the pastors of Geneva had created institutions that endured by delegating responsibilities to others. Their ideas did not die with them, but as Calvin's theology and institutions spread beyond Geneva, they were modified.

In New England, Puritans honored Calvin's concern for avoiding contamination of the Lord's Supper, but their limits on membership and halfway covenants compromised Calvin's all-encompassing Augustinian conception of church membership. On the other hand, like Calvin, Puritans were champions of education and founded elementary schools while prodding governments to act.

Looking to the worldwide Reformed churches, there were changes from Calvin and from the *Draft Ecclesiastical Ordinances*. Often the office of doctor was dropped, but the essence remained: education, discipline, social concern (which all led to schools), consistories, and social welfare. Over time the privileging of the shamefaced poor declined, those "worthy of special charity."[86]

Discipline remained a constant in Reformed churches for centuries, and it has been given considerable attention, especially after Robert Kingdon, Thomas Lambert, and Isabella Watt began publishing the Genevan Consistory records.[87] Genevan life in the sixteenth century has been seen as repressive by some scholars, who are repulsed by efforts to enforce moral conformity such as Communion tokens used in some Reformed churches to exclude those not approved to partake.[88]

However, there is a positive dimension to the careful observation of personal conduct, so characteristic of early-modern Reformed churches. The battered spouse and the neglected child may have been less likely to slip through the cracks of society's obliviousness in Calvin's Geneva, but history is not written by the losers. We read little of their point of view.

Eventually discipline grew lax, but insistence on moral rectitude among church members remained a feature of Reformed churches beyond the early modern period. There are those who hope that the "discipline" can be recovered today, but more enduring than moral discipline in Reformed churches has been the concern for the disadvantaged. Some consider this concern and action to improve the lot of the disadvantaged as the most positive contribution of Calvin's theology of church and society in the modern world.

---

85. Biéler, *La pensée économique et sociale de Calvin*, 1.
86. *Draft Ecclesiastical Ordinances*, 65.
87. *Registres du Consistoire de Genève au temps de Calvin*, 3 vols. (1542–1548), (Geneva: Librairie Droz, 1996–2007).
88. An example of a negative approach to the consistory of Calvin's Geneva is the otherwise useful work of François Wendel, *Calvin: Origins and Development of His Religious Thought*, Philip Mairet, trans. (Grand Rapids: Baker Book House, 2002), 84–86.

Chapter 10

Calvin's Theology
of Church and Society

*Modern Reception
and Contemporary Possibilities*

DAVID LITTLE

CALVINISM, CONSTITUTIONALISM,
AND RELIGIOUS FREEDOM: AN AMERICAN DILEMMA

When it comes to Calvin's influence on modern society, no figure has been more visible, or more controversial, than the German sociologist, Max Weber (1864–1920). He is best known for his essay, *The Protestant Ethic and the Spirit of Capitalism*, first published in 1904–1905,[1] where he argued that Calvin's deep, theologically grounded commitment to "innerwordly" reform, based on a rejection of monasticism and the sanctification of methodical, worldly pursuit of profit, contributed decisively to the eventual legitimation of modern capitalism, originating, as Weber believed, in seventeenth-century England and Colonial America. That essay generated a huge, ever-growing array of criticisms

---

1. Max Weber, *Die protestantische Ethik und der Geist des Kapitalismus*, *Archiv fur Sozialwissen-schaft und Sozialpolitik*, vols. 20 and 21, 1904–1905. Several English translations exist starting with one by Talcott Parsons (New York: Charles Scribner's Sons, 1958); the most recent is by Stephen Kalberg: *The Protestant Ethic and the Spirit of Capitalism with Other Writings on the Rise of the West* (New York: Oxford University Press, 2008).

and defenses by sociologists, anthropologists, economists, historians, and theologians, including several Calvin scholars.[2]

But whatever the merits of Weber's thesis about Calvinism and capitalism,[3] the scholarly preoccupation with the *Protestant Ethic* has detracted from Weber's wider interests in the development of what he called "legal rational authority," of which the premises of modern capitalism are but one example. This form of authority assumes a set of formal, impersonal (typically bureaucratic) rules variously applicable to distinct social spheres,[4] such as economic life, the functions of government, and scientific endeavor. A legal-rational social order consists of institutions that have each achieved, respectively, a relative degree of autonomy on the basis of "functionally specific" norms and ideals. As such, it contrasts with a "traditionalistic" social order, in which one institution, whether religious, political, or familial, dominates all others on the authority of the past, or with a "value-rational" social order, in which the rules for all spheres of social activity are regulated by one overarching authority, frequently religious in character.[5]

In his introduction to *The Protestant Ethic*, added later, Weber emphasizes this broader interest, together with his conclusion that legal-rational authority, comprehensively understood, is unique to the West, in part, he implies, because of the Calvinist influence. An aspect of special importance to Weber is the rise of the modern constitutional state. He writes that the very idea of the state as we know it, understood as "a political association operated according to a rationally enacted written constitution and rationally enacted written laws, and administered by civil servants possessing *specialized* arenas of competence and oriented to rules and laws, [came into existence] with these distinguishing features only in the West, even though there are rudimentary developments elsewhere."[6] Our contemporary phrase, "rule of law," nicely summarizes what he has in mind.

Though he never pursued it, Weber's hint of a close connection between Calvin's thought and the rise of modern constitutionalism needs further investigation. Calvin's whole notion of Reformed theology was shaped by his passion to "reform" the structures of church and state in keeping with his understanding of the rule of law. He received legal training in a milieu strongly sympathetic to the development of constitutionalism, and, throughout his adult life, he was exposed to and helped direct a kind of constitutional government in

---

2. See Kalberg's edition of Weber, *The Protestant Ethic*, for the most up to date and comprehensive overview of the vast array of conflicting opinions and arguments on this subject and for a thoughtful appraisal of where things stand at present.

3. My book, *Religion, Order, and Law: A Study in Pre-Revolutionary England* (Chicago: University of Chicago Press, 1984) reframes and partially defends Weber's famous thesis. I am critical of Weber for overemphasizing the psychological aspects of Calvin's theology and underplaying the institutional dimensions which are, in fact, profoundly relevant to Weber's general interests; see 23.

4. See Max Weber, *Economy and Society*, vol. 1, ed. Guenther Roth and Claus Wittich (New York: Bedminster Press, 1968), 217–20.

5. Ibid., 24–26.

6. Kalberg, Weber, *The Protestant Ethic*, 208. I have somewhat modified Kalberg's translation. Weber's word, "enacted," appearing twice in this passage (*gesatzter, gezatztem*), carries the idea of *written* law. (Original italics.)

sixteenth-century Geneva. Not surprisingly, his influence in Britain, Holland, France, New England, and other places is closely bound up with constitutional reform. Calvin was, above all, a political theologian.

It is of great interest that Weber first publically presented his ideas on Calvinism and capitalism as the result of having read a book on the origins of declarations of rights and their place in modern constitutional history by his friend and colleague, Georg Jellinek.[7] By demonstrating the significance of "religious influences [on] the genesis of 'human rights,'" writes Weber, Jellinek shows "the importance of religious elements in areas where one would not expect to find them."[8] Indeed, Jellinek's central conclusion is that "the idea of legally establishing inalienable, inherent and sacred rights of the individual is not of political but religious origin. What has been held to be a work of the [French] Revolution was in reality a fruit of the Reformation and its struggles."[9]

This commitment to a set of inalienable individual rights, was, on Jellinek's account, a prominent feature of a movement on the part of all thirteen of the original American colonies to incorporate declarations of rights into their respective constitutions. While there remained differences, especially in respect to the right to religious liberty and the separation of church and state, eleven of the thirteen colonies had adopted state constitutions before the outbreak of the French Revolution, and two of them retained their original charters. Connecticut's dated from 1662 and Rhode Island's from 1663, making these two documents "the oldest written constitutions in the modern sense."[10]

Jellinek exerts considerable effort proving that it is this strong constitutional impulse among the American colonies, expressing as it did a commitment to the rule of law and to the robust protection of individual rights, that was the foundation of modern constitutionalism, apparent in both the American and the French cases. As he sees it, the founding document of the American republic, along with the Bill of Rights, was a direct consequence of the colonial experience,[11] and the French *Declaration of the Rights of Man and Citizen* was not, as hinted above, the product of the French Revolution or Rousseau and other French Enlightenment figures, but was also drawn, often word for word, from the declarations of rights of the American colonies.[12]

Perhaps most important of all, Jellinek contends that the early American documents were remarkable innovations. Although they selectively incorporated

---

7. Georg Jellinek, *The Declaration of the Rights of Man and Citizen: A Contribution to Constitutional History* (Westport, CT: Hyperion Press, 1979), first published in German in 1895. The importance of this book to Weber as an inspiration for a public lecture in 1897 is mentioned by Wolfgang Schluchter in his *Rationalism, Religion, and Domination: A Weberian Perspective* (Berkeley: University of California Press, 1989), 556n39.

8. Marianne Weber, *Max Weber: A Biography* (New Brunswick: Transaction Publishers, 1995), 476.

9. Jellinek, *Declaration of Rights*, 77.

10. Ibid., 22.

11. Ibid., 85–86.

12. Ibid., chap. 2, "Rousseau's 'Contrat Social' was not the Source of the [French] Declaration," and chap. 5, "Comparison of the French and American Declarations."

aspects of English common law, they were anything but carbon copies. "A deep cleft separates the American declarations from . . . English enactments," such as the Magna Carta (1215) and the Petition of Right (1628).

> The English statutes are far removed from any purpose to recognize general rights of man, and they have neither the power nor the intention to restrict the legislative agents or to establish principles for further legislation. According to English law, Parliament is omnipotent and all statutes enacted or confirmed by it are of equal value. . . . The American declarations, on the other hand, contain precepts which stand higher than the ordinary lawmaker. In the Union, as well as in the individual states, there are separate [arrangements] for ordinary and for constitutional legislation, and the judge watches over the observance of the constitutional limitations by the ordinary legislative power. . . . The declarations of rights even at the present day are interpreted by the Americans as practical protections of the minority.[13]

However, for all of its importance, one thing Jellinek's essay does not elaborate on is some of the deep and abiding tensions in American constitutionalism. One of those tensions concerns the constitutional protection of individual rights, and particularly the right of religious freedom.[14] That issue has caused controversy from the beginning of the colonial period right up to the present. If Jellinek is correct that the idea of constitutionally establishing inalienable individual rights, including rights of conscience, goes back to the "struggles" of the Reformation, then perhaps it is worth inquiring whether some of the key conflicts in the subsequent constitutional interpretation of rights can be traced back there, too.

In the process, then, of testing the proposition that modern constitutionalism, as an expression of legal rational authority, in Weber's sense, was influenced by Calvinism, we want also to explore the possible influence of Calvinism on some of the underlying tensions of constitutional interpretation, especially regarding religious freedom. We begin with some thoughts on Calvin's approach to constitutionalism, both in church and state; then we consider the political and legal effects of that approach as mediated, principally, by Calvin's heirs, the American Puritans; and, finally, we reflect on the deep and persistent dilemma in American constitutional history concerning religious freedom that was, as we shall try to show, inspired to an important degree by the Calvinist legacy.

CALVIN AS CONSTITUTIONALIST

Though more must be said in support of Jellinek's thesis concerning the Puritan contribution to the rise of modern constitutionalism, it is important to examine

---

13. Ibid., 46–47.
14. Though Jellinek does mention that the degree of constitutional protection of freedom of conscience "differed in different states" (note 30, page 46).

first the thought of John Calvin, regarded by English and American Puritans "as the pioneering force behind their Reformed faith" and also as an important source of their general theological and political outlook.[15] As I have put it elsewhere, Calvin's thought constituted a kind of grammar for Puritan rhetoric.[16]

As it happens, Calvin strongly supported most of the basic features of modern constitutionalism: a written code understood as "fundamental" in being antecedent to the government and subsequently "unalterable by ordinary legal process"; attribution of political and legal authority, including limits on and division of power by means of a "self-conscious," "direct and express" act by "the people" whom the government is taken to represent; the conviction that any act of government outside the enumerated limits is an exercise of "power without right" and properly subject, if need be, to coercive restraint; "an honest, able, learned, and independent judiciary"; and the codification of a set of inalienable individual rights, whose enforcement is considered to be a critical condition of legitimate government.[17]

"Every commonwealth rests upon laws and agreements"[18] preferably written, wrote Calvin, agreements that are regarded as fundamental to the protection of the "freedom of the people,"[19] a term he used repeatedly. Written law is "nothing but an attestation of the [natural law], whereby God brings back to memory what has already been imprinted in our hearts."[20] The structure of government should, on his view, be polyarchic rather than monarchic.

> It is very rare for kings so to control themselves that their will never disagrees with what is just and right, or for them to have been endowed with such great keenness and prudence, that each knows how much is enough. Therefore, men's fault or failing causes it to be safer and more bearable for a number to exercise government.[21]

As McNeill summarizes Calvin's position: "Kingship by hereditary right does not seem to be in accordance with liberty; a well-ordered government is one derived from the general vote [of the people]."[22]

Moreover: "Certain remedies against tyranny are allowable, for example when magistrates and estates have been constituted, to whom has been committed the care of the commonwealth; they shall have power to keep the prince to his duty and even to coerce him if he attempt anything unlawful."[23] Even though Calvin here denied any right of coercive restraint to "private individuals," he welcomes

15. James Calvin Davis, *The Moral Theology of Roger Williams* (Louisville, KY: Westminster John Knox, 2004) 18 and 17. Cf. Little, *Religion, Order, and Law*, chaps. 3 and 4, and 257–258.

16. Little, *Religion, Order, and Law*, 33.

17. Charles Howard McIlwain, *Constitutionalism: Ancient and Modern* (Ithaca, NY: Cornell University Press, 1966), 9, 14, 21, 76, 81, 117, 139–40.

18. John Calvin, *Homilies on I Samuel*, 10, cited in Herbert D. Foster, "Political Theories of Calvinists," in *Collected Papers of Herbert D. Foster* (privately printed, 1929), 82.

19. John Calvin, *Institutes of the Christian Religion*, John T. McNeill, ed., Ford Lewis Battles, trans. (Philadelphia: Westminster Press, 1960), 4.20.31.

20. John Calvin, *Commentary on the Psalms* chap. 119, cited in Foster, *Collected Papers*, 82.

21. *Institutes* 4.20.8, from 1536.

22. *Institutes* 4.20.31, from 1536, p. 1518n.54.

23. John Calvin, *Homilies on I Samuel*, 8, cited in Foster, *Collected Papers*, 82.

duly authorized restraint on the part of "constitutional magistrates," as he calls them.[24] They are

> any magistrates of the people, appointed to restrain the willfulness of kings (as in ancient times the ephors were set against the Spartan kings, or the tribunes of the people against the Roman consuls, or the demarchs against the senate of the Athenians; and, as things now are, such power as the three estates exercise in every realm where they hold their chief assemblies), I am so far from forbidding them to withstand, in accordance with their duty, the fierce licentiousness of kings, that, if they wink at kings who violently fall upon and assault the lowly common folk, I declare that their dissimulation involves nefarious perfidy, because they dishonestly betray the freedom of the people, of which they know that they have been appointed protectors by God's ordinance.[25]

Finally, Calvin affirmed a set of basic, inalienable rights taken to undergird any licit founding agreement and to constitute an imprescriptible limit on governmental power.[26]

Calvin, of course, did not invent constitutionalism. The Geneva of his time already exhibited some essential characteristics, such as a form of representative government based on "the general voice of the people." Just as important, Calvin was keenly influenced by conciliarism, a Catholic movement that originated in the Middle Ages, and reached its peak of influence in the fifteenth century, opposed to papal monarchy. It was premised on three principles underlying the constitutional impulse: the mutual autonomy of church and state; representative government, based on the ideas that "the will of the people is the supreme law," and that the natural rights of all should be protected in church and state; and the importance of national representation. Calvin's distinctive contribution was to reformulate these principles in a compelling theological framework able to inspire an energetic social movement leading to broad institutional reform.

Calvin's emphasis on what Josef Bohatec has called, the "original natural rights of freedom," calls for special comment, since they play such an important part in Calvinist constitutionalism.

> [From among these natural rights,] liberty and property stand out. . . . God has equipped rulers with full authority that the rights of each individual to person and property not be denied, for these rights are goods bestowed by God. The authorities protect these rights through laws, which therefore must be made firm and durable; continually changing established public

---

24. *Institutes* 4.20.30–31. Calvin did publicly support a private right of rebellion shortly before he died. See Willem Nuenhuis, "The Limits of Civil Disobedience in Calvin's Last-Known Sermons, *Ecclesia Reformata: Studies on the Reformation,* vol. 2 (New York: Leiden and Köln: E. J. Brill, 1994), chap. 4.

25. Ibid., 4.20.31.

26. Josef Bohatec, *Calvins Lehre von Staat und Kirche mit besonderer Berücksichtigung des Organismusgedankens* (Scientia Aalen: 1961), esp. chaps. 1–3, 1–116 for an extensive, fully documented, and enlightening discussion of the role of "subjective rights" in Calvin's moral and political thought. (The subsequent translations are mine.)

law is a mark of arbitrariness, which every form of reasonableness rules out. In short, the subjective rights of freedom have no strong security if they are not supported by the authorities and legislation. This individual sphere of freedom . . . yet belongs to the enjoined rights and duties associated with the second table of the Decalogue. [27]

In addition, Calvin gives considerable prominence to what may be called a "natural right of confession"[28] or of conscience, meaning, ideally, that fundamental, sacred beliefs ought not to be subject to coercive regulation, and as such stand beyond the jurisdiction of the state. Even under the conditions of human sin and ignorance, Calvin writes, "this tiny little spark of light remained" recognizing "conscience to be higher than all human judgments."[29] "[H]uman laws," he continues, "whether made by magistrate or church, even though they have to be observed (I speak of good and just laws), still do not of themselves bind conscience."[30] This last remark is of special consequence because it reveals the radical implications of at least one side of Calvin's thought. The statement not only reserves the right of individual conscience, ultimately, to stand in judgment on the worth and justice of human laws, but also suggests that only worthy and just laws require obedience. Though Calvin by no means consistently adopted such a permissive view, part of him is strongly drawn to a very high doctrine of the sovereignty of conscience.

The doctrine is directly related to a critical distinction he draws between two forums or tribunals, the "internal forum" or conscience and the "external forum" or civil authority.[31] The first concerns personal, inward deliberation regarding fundamental belief and practice that is regulated by "spiritual power," and the second concerns "external" or public deliberation regarding "outward behavior"—the needs of "the present life," such a food, clothing and the laws of social cooperation—that are regulated by the "power of the sword."[32] Calvin sometimes speaks of these as "two worlds," over which different kings and different laws have authority, requiring that they "always be examined separately."[33] The idea is that the "outward" sphere of social order, underwritten by the threat of force, is sharply set apart from the sphere of conscience, and, as such, delimited by it. Calvin says as much in his commentary on the thirteenth chapter of the Letter to the Romans. The proper jurisdiction of a well-ordered government is defined exclusively by the "part of the law that refers to human society," or the second table of the Decalogue, whose basic principle, says Calvin, is that "all individuals should preserve their rights." "There is no allusion at all [in Paul's discussion of political order] to the first table of the law, which deals with the worship of God,"[34]

27. Ibid., 94–95.
28. Ibid., 114–15.
29. *Institutes* 4.10.5.
30. Ibid.
31. Ibid., 3.19.15.
32. Ibid. The phrase "power of the sword" occurs at 4.11.8.
33. Ibid., 3.19.15.
34. John Calvin, *Epistles of Paul the Apostle to the Romans and the Thessalonians*, trans. Ross MacKenzie, ed. David W. Torrance and Thomas F. Torrance (Grand Rapids: Eerdmans, 1976), 286, Comm. on Rom. 13:10.

and Calvin accentuates the same point elsewhere: Since "the whole of [Paul's] discussion concerns civil government [, those] who bear rule over . . . consciences attempt to establish their blasphemous tyranny . . . in vain."[35]

Sometimes, especially later in his life as he saw the effects of arbitrary political power in France and elsewhere, Calvin explicitly called to account magistrates who failed to protect second-table rights. He spoke of an "inborn feeling" human beings have "to hate and curse tyrants" who subvert "the common people and their money" or exercise "sheer robbery, plundering houses, raping virgins and matrons, and slaughtering the innocent,"[36] all of which, he says, amounts to a "betray[al of] the freedom of the people."[37]

The distinction between the internal and external forum, between conscience and state, underlies Calvin's doctrine of the Christian church. On Calvin's view, the church is the context of the "liberation of the conscience,"[38] wherein regenerated persons no longer need be coerced or compelled to do the right thing, but, inspired and guided by the "law of the spirit" as manifest in Scripture, are, ideally at least, able to grasp and to do the will of God of their own accord. Thus "released from the power of all men,"[39] the church takes charge of its own affairs based on an ideal of active member participation, assuming, in principle, that individuals must be able, independent of all civil restraint or liability, to exercise conscience by choosing freely whether or not to associate with and contribute to the church and its mission. There is, writes Calvin, "a great difference and unlikeness . . . between ecclesiastical and civil power." Unlike the state, the "church does not have the right of the sword to punish or compel, not the authority to force; not imprisonment nor the other punishments which the magistrate commonly inflicts." "The church does not assume what is proper to the magistrate; nor can the magistrate execute what is carried out by the church."[40]

There are two important implications of Calvin's doctrine of the church for the development of constitutionalism. One is that the sharp differentiation between church and state strongly underscores the obligation of the state to defer to and to protect the prior rights of conscience of all citizens, along with their other natural rights, thereby providing a telling example of the limitations on state power so central to the idea of constitutionalism. The other is that, in Calvin's hands, the structure of the church itself is extensively reworked in constitutional terms.

---

35. Ibid., 283, Comm. on Rom. 13:5. Calvin is here presupposing a distinction between the two tables of the Decalogue or Ten Commandments. The first four commandments refer to divine-human relations and the second six to human relations. Later in his career, Calvin reverses his claim here that civil government should enforce only the second table. However, there is reason to wonder how secure Calvin is in this unequivocal statement. In a preceding comment on Romans 13:8 (p. 285), he admits that Paul "makes no mention of the worship of God, although," Calvin adds, "he should not have omitted this." The countervailing comment suggests a rather deep ambivalence in Calvin's position.

36. *Institutes* 4.20.24.

37. Ibid., 4.20.31.

38. Words contained in the heading to ibid., 2.7.14.

39. Ibid., 3.19.14.

40. Ibid., 4.11.3.

The theme of "constitutionalizing" the church was at the heart of Calvin's whole career in Geneva. Early on, outraged city authorities expelled him for proposing an organizational plan that, they believed, unacceptably expanded the independence of the church at the expense of civil authority. When he returned in 1541, he drafted and got accepted the *Ecclesiastical Ordinances of the Church of Geneva*, which, although much modified compared to his earlier proposal, still retained a significant degree of institutional autonomy for the church.[41] Beginning with the words, "If we will have a Church well ordered and maintained we ought to observe [the following] form of government,"[42] the document details the offices, powers, and responsibilities of the church officials and members, also describing the role of the civil authority in church affairs.

In commenting elsewhere on the constitution of the church, he employs the term, *adminstratio spiritus*. By that he means that the offices of authority in the church have no intrinsic status or superiority, since Christ alone is the real authority. All offices are established and assessed with respect to their special service or "function" in the edification of the body of Christ. Though ministers be "of inferior rank" they are to be honored because they speak the Word of God, and officials are not to be regarded "so much higher in honor and dignity [as] to have lordship over [their] colleagues."[43] Calvin invoked the model of the early church as authoritative. Contrary to the practice of the Roman Catholics, the office of bishop "was not in one man's possession to do whatever he pleased, but in the hands of the assembly of elders, which was to the church what the Senate was to the city."[44] In addition, all official functions had finally to be certified "by the general voice" of the people. This reference to consulting the general voice is especially important for Calvin, so as "not to diminish any part of the common right and freedom of the church." He quotes Cyprian favorably: "A priest should be elected publicly in the presence of all the people, and . . . should be approved as a worthy and fit person by public judgment and testimony."[45]

To be sure, Calvin does not support unconditional democracy. "Pastors ought to preside over the election in order that the multitude may not go wrong either through fickleness, through evil intentions, or through disorder."[46] As with civil government, he favors a plural or polyarchic system for the church, one "compounded of aristocracy and democracy."[47] He means an aristocracy of excellence,

41. See François Wendel, *Calvin: Origins and Development of His Religious Thought* (New York: Harper & Row, 1963), 79.

42. John Calvin, *Draft Ecclesiastical Ordinances September & October 1541*, in *Calvin: Theological Treatises*, J. K. S. Reid, ed. (Philadelphia: Westminster Press, 1954), 58.

43. *Institutes* 4.4.2.

44. Ibid., 4.11.6.

45. Ibid., 4.3.15.

46. Ibid.

47. Ibid., 4.20.8. See also chap. 9, p. 207 above for Olson's observation about Battles' translation. But whatever translation one accepts, it is important to emphasize that for Calvin "a well-ordered government is derived from the general vote of the people," as stated in Calvin's Comm. on Micah 5:5. John T. McNeill, "John Calvin on Civil Government," in *Calvinism and the Political Order*, ed. George L. Hunt (Philadelphia: Westminster Press, 1965), 38.

not inherited status, and a practical example of combining aristocracy with democracy is that the nominees to be voted on in a church election would be selected by "experienced predecessors in office."[48] In short, Calvin clearly found "safety in plurality, and in the consequent opportunity of mutual admonition and the pooling of wisdom. Even the "best men" [had] to pass the test of the ballot box."[49]

But if Calvin is unquestionably an apostle of constitutionalism, his interpretations, particularly of church-state relations and the defense of the rights of conscience, are very complicated, if not contradictory.[50] Having said that the jurisdiction of the state pertains exclusively to the advancement and protection of second-table rights, and that political authorities who attempt to "bear rule over consciences" are "blasphemous tyrants," Calvin frequently advocates policies sharply at odds with these prescriptions. However much governments should, in theory, stick to the second table, Calvin in one place confidently (and somewhat surprisingly) invokes "secular writers" to the effect that "no government can be happily established unless piety is the first concern; and that those laws are preposterous which neglect God's right and provide only for men."[51] However distinct are the "two worlds"—the inward and outward forums—over which "different kings and different laws have authority," Calvin can be found solemnly stating that "civil government has as its appointed end, so long as we live [in the world], to cherish and protect the outward worship of God, to defend sound doctrine of piety and the position of the church."[52] And however reluctant his initial acquiescence in accepting the compromise church-state arrangement in Geneva, one which permitted extensive entanglement of the laws of spirit and sword, he did endorse that arrangement with what appears, as time went by, to be increasing relish.

While this deep inconsistency in Calvin's thought can in part be explained by the understandable difficulties of finding the right balance between freedom and order during a period of enormous social turmoil, an additional consideration is a deep theological lack of resolution in Calvin's mind as to how reliable, how trustworthy, is the management of the temporal order, including the exercise of political authority, without correct religious direction. Calvin is of two minds on this matter. Sometimes, he attributes a limited, but significant, "natural" moral capacity to unregenerate people, including rulers, who, "guided by nature, have striven toward virtue throughout life." Such people "warn us against adjudging [human] nature [to be] wholly corrupted."[53] Not only is their understanding

48. Ibid., 37.
49. Ibid., 38.
50. I mention here the conflict in Calvin's thinking concerning whether the state should or should not regulate "first-table affairs," or matters of conscience, but there are other critical points of conflict, e.g., whether or not governments should be disobeyed and changed; cf. *Institutes* 4.20.8 and Comm. on Romans 13:3, p. 282 with *Institutes* 4.20.31, taking account of footnote 54, which concerns Calvin's use of near revolutionary language.
51. *Institutes* 4.20.9.
52. Ibid., 4.20.2.
53. Ibid., 2.3.3.

relatively intact, particularly as regards complying with the "earthly" or "outward" demands of the second table, but their will—the capacity to choose and act aright—is, too.[54]

On other occasions, however, Calvin expresses deep, virtually unqualified, distrust of natural moral capabilities, especially the ability of the unregenerated will to attain even a small degree of righteousness without direct divine assistance. This aspect of his thought leads him to conclude that only proper Christians, those living by orthodox doctrine, have any hope of recovering a "sound will" and thereby the capacity, not only to know the good and the right, but to choose and to act accordingly. Anyone else, Calvin often insists, is in a state of "total depravity," meaning a condition that is pervasively "confused, mutilated, and disease-ridden." This side of Calvin's thought, the side that caught hold in Geneva during his life, plays down natural moral competence even in "outward," second-table matters, and instead raises the status and emphasizes the indispensability of the Calvinist church as the repository of true righteousness. On that understanding, it is the church, duly promoted and protected by the state, whose guidance becomes a necessary condition for upholding law and order. Without it, chaos and violence are the likely result.

CALVIN'S UNSTABLE LEGACY: RELIGION, CONSTITUTION-MAKING, AND AMERICAN PURITANISM

According to Charles Howard McIlwain, a leading historian of the subject, critical precedent for modern constitutionalism was established by the "North American colonies of Great Britain,"[55] which makes all the more significant the Puritan contribution. Clearly, the idea of "written constitutions creating, defining, and limiting governments," which subsequently became "the general rule in almost the whole of the constitutional world,"[56] gained strong, early expression in the founding documents of Puritan New England. Several of the key features of constitutionalism, mentioned above, were there: a written code understood as fundamental law antecedent to the government and based on a "self-conscious," "direct and express" act by "the people" whom the government is taken to represent; attribution of political and legal authority, including limits on and division of power, such that any act of government outside the enumerated limits is an exercise of "power without right" and properly subject, if need be, to coercive restraint; an independent judiciary; and the codification of a set of inalienable individual rights, whose enforcement is regarded as a critical condition of legitimate government.

Incipient constitutionalism was at work from the earliest origins of the government of the Massachusetts Bay Colony, well before the founders had left

---

54. See my essay, "Calvin and Natural Rights," *Political Theology* 10, no. 3 (July 2009): 411–30.
55. McIlwain, *Constitutionalism*, 14.
56. Ibid.

for the new world. The Charter of the Massachusetts Bay Company, which elaborated the form of government for the new colony, was modified by the Cambridge Agreement, adopted on August 26, 1629, in Cambridge, England, by the stockholders or "freemen" of the company. The agreement, calling as it did for the founders to expand control over their own affairs, gave considerable impetus to the notion of constitutional self-government.

Though the government in Massachusetts Bay took time to evolve from corporation to commonwealth, and when completed was more oligarchy than democracy—given the fear on the part of some of untrammeled popular control[57]—the Puritan authorities nevertheless "left out of their foundations two principles of government, the feudal and the hereditary, upon which democracy had always found it difficult to [develop]." The apprehensions about democracy of some leaders were also partially counterbalanced by other leaders who affirmed the merits of elections as a necessary restraint on arbitrary government.[58] Moreover, by the time the revised Code of 1648 had been adopted, there was significant movement toward drawing a distinction between the judicial and legislative aspects of lawmaking, and of confining the judicial function to the interpretation and enforcement of "a relatively stable corpus of statutory written law,"[59] including the fundamental codes that amounted to constitutions.

Of particular importance was the Body of Liberties of the Massachusetts Colony in New England, which was adopted into law by the General Court in 1641, and which amounted to an exceptionally lengthy bill of rights. Though its author, Nathaniel Ward (1578–1652), prominent pastor and lawyer, incorporated provisions drawn from English statutes and precedents, the Body of Liberties was anything but a simple reiteration of tradition and custom. It redefined and restructured the traditional rights of English subjects in the light of Puritan Christianity, adding modified portions of biblical law, and some "daring rights proposals"[60] from left-wing English Puritan pamphleteers. Above all,

> what was new . . . was to have these widely scattered traditional common law rights (and many rights besides) compiled in a single source, generally available to all subjects of the community regardless of the court in which they appeared, and generally binding on all officials and citizens at once.[61]

Although the grounds on which these rights were believed to rest are not mentioned in the document itself, Ward makes clear in a pamphlet written four years later that, in his view, the enumerated rights are founded on a combination

---

57. As one leader, John Cotton, put it: "If the people be governors, who shall be governed?" "A Letter from Mr. Cotton to Lord Say and Seal" (1636), Morgan, ed., *Puritan Political Ideas*, 163. Cf. John Winthrop's opposition to democracy, cited in Francis J. Bremer, *John Winthrop, America's Forgotten Founding Father* (Oxford: Oxford University Press, 2003), 355.

58. See John Witte Jr., *Reformation of Rights: Law, Religion, and Human Rights in Early Modern Calvinism* (Cambridge: Cambridge University Press, 2007), 317.

59. George Lee Haskins, *Law and Authority in Early Massachusetts: A Study in Tradition and Design* (New York: MacMillan & Co., 1960), 119–20.

60. Witte, *Reformation of Rights*, 280.

61. Ibid., 286.

of "God's rule," experience, public deliberation, and the "light of nature," all of which assume a universal set of moral "essentials," where, beyond local differences and variations in the form of government, "rule and reason will be found all one."[62]

There was, however, one part of the Body of Liberties that generated a particularly strong division of opinion: the rights pertaining to religious belief and practice, namely, section 95, articles 1 through 11, identified as "A Declaration of the Liberties the Lord Jesus hath given to the Churches." According to these articles, all members of the colony have "full liberty" to practice religion according to conscience, though only so long as they "be orthodox in judgment," and, "every church has full liberty to elect church officers," "provided they be able, pious and orthodox."

The special conditions on religious rights, permitting free exercise but only in conformity with orthodox scriptural and doctrinal interpretation, points to what Cotton himself called the "theocratic" character of the Massachusetts Bay Colony, namely, a state governed by officials regarded as divinely guided.[63] This attitude led officials of the colony, like John Winthrop, John Cotton, and Nathaniel Ward, to oppose ideas of religious toleration and liberty of conscience, ideas that had the effect, as Ward put it, of hanging the Bible on the Devil's girdle, and, consequently, of undermining social order.[64]

While leaders like Cotton argued that church and state should not be "confounded," as they serve different ends and jurisdictions,[65] the two spheres should nevertheless be "close and compact and co-ordinate one to another,"[66] precisely so as to prevent the kind of heterodoxy in thought and practice and consequent disruption of social order that Nathanial Ward warned of. As one contemporary divine put it, "the interest of righteousness in the commonwealth and holiness in the churches are inseparable. The prosperity of church and commonwealth are twisted together. Break one cord, you weaken the other also."[67]

"Twisted together" church and state most certainly were. Although magistrates were precluded from holding church office, and church officials from holding civil office, only church members might vote in civil elections. In addition, churches and clergymen received direct public support through taxes and other donations, and religious beliefs and practices were extensively and harshly regulated by laws covering blasphemy, irreverence, profanity, idolatry and

---

62. Nathanial Ward, "The Simple Cobler of Aggawam" (1645; first published in 1647), in Perry Miller and Thomas H. Johnson, eds., *The Puritans: A Sourcebook of Their Writings*, vol. 1 (New York: Harper Torchbook, 1963), 236. (I have modernized and here and there "translated" some of the archaic words and forms of speech.)

63. Cotton actually uses the term to describe what in his mind is "the best form of government in the commonwealth, as well as the church," in Morgan, ed., *Puritan Political Ideas*, 163.

64. Miller and Johnson, eds., *The Puritans*, vol. 1, 230.

65. Morgan, ed., *Puritan Political Ideas*, 162–63, 164–65.

66. Ibid., 163.

67. A statement by Urian Oakes, pastor and president of Harvard, cited by Witte, *Reformation of Rights*, 310.

"schismatic" activity. Ministers were regularly called upon to provide instruction on the pertinence of God's law to new legislation.[68]

However, not all Puritans agreed with the official Massachusetts Bay position on religious rights, and especially with the meaning of "full liberty" when it came to avowing and practicing one's faith. The task of articulating and mobilizing the "other side" of Calvinist legacy on the constitutional protection of religious freedom, fell to one Roger Williams (1603?–1683), who himself was in trouble with the Bay authorities almost from the time he set foot in New England in 1631.

After being forced to move from one church to another because of his controversial views, Williams was indicted for continuing to oppose laws enforcing religion, as well as other official beliefs and practices he found offensive, such as the assumption that colonial lands belonged to the English monarch and not, as he thought, to the Native Americans, or that the English flag was legitimate even though it prominently displayed a Christian cross at its center thereby, in Williams's view, hopelessly confusing civil and spiritual spheres. Predictably, Williams was found guilty as charged, and condemned to return to England for punishment. However, he eluded the authorities and, with the help of Narragansett Indians he had befriended, found his way to territory that, under his leadership, would eventually become the Rhode Island colony.

In 1643 Williams acquired a minimal patent from Parliament for the towns of Providence, Portsmouth, and Newport, which by 1647 was expanded into a fuller constitutional document which "gives us power to govern ourselves and such others as come among us, and [to establish] such a form of civil government as by the voluntary consent, etc., shall be found most suitable to our estate and condition." In words somewhat to the left of the Bay colony, the document goes on to specify without apology and without reservation that the form of government will be "democraticall," which is to say, "a government held by the free and voluntary consent of all, or the greater part of the free inhabitants," assuring "each man's peaceable and quiet enjoyment of his lawful right and liberty. . . ." And it continues in language largely reminiscent of the Bay charter and Body of Liberties to outline a representative political system together with legal institutions carefully regulated by due process, including extensive rights and liberties against arbitrary injury, trial, imprisonment, loss of property, and so on.[69]

Where the Rhode Island colony differed most sharply from Massachusetts Bay and other colonies was in the treatment of religion, a point articulated most eloquently in the charter of 1663 that Williams and his associate, John Clarke, were able to acquire from King Charles II. It is this document that Jellinek called, one of the two "oldest written constitutions in the modern

---

68. I am drawing here on Witte's excellent summary of the church-state arrangement in the Bay colony; *Reformation of Rights*, 310–12.

69. The Forum at the Online Library of Liberty, "1647: Acts and Orders (Rhode Island)," Liberty Fund, Inc., http://oll.libertyfund.org/index.php?option=com_content&task=view&id=1040S&Itemid=264, 7.

sense."[70] The charter commends the aspirations of the colonists "to hold forth a lively experiment, that a most flourishing civil state may stand and best be maintained . . . with the full liberty in religious concernments . . . and . . . in the free exercise and enjoyment of all . . . civil and religious rights. . . ." It then declares, in a radical departure from the Bay colony's understanding of "full liberty," that

> no person within said colony, at any time hereafter, shall be [in] any wise molested, punished, disquieted, or called into question, for any difference of opinion in matters of religion, and do not actually disturb the civil peace, . . . but that all and every person and persons may . . . freely and fully have and enjoy . . . their own judgments and consciences in matters of religious concernments, . . . they behaving themselves peaceably and quietly . . ."[71]

For Williams and the Rhode Islanders, the Massachusetts Bay authorities, while expressing commitment to the ideas of freedom of conscience and separation of church and state, had grossly distorted the meaning of those terms. The conscience and the civil authority—the "inner" and "outer forum"—are, at bottom different realms governed by different laws, the one by the "law of the spirit," the other by the "law of the sword."

Williams strictly adhered to Calvin's comments on Romans 13 that civil authority pertains exclusively to second-table matters: the law of the sword, administered by temporal governments and backed by physical coercion, applies *only* to "the bodies and goods" of human beings, to their "outward state," while the law of spirit applies to the inner life, a life that operates according to the standards of reason and sentiment. To try to convince a person of the truth of something by threatening injury or imprisonment is to make a mistake about how the mind and spirit work.

> All lawful magistrates in the world, both before the coming of Christ Jesus, and since (excepting . . . the church of Israel) are but derivatives and agents [of the people who appointed them] immediately derived and employed as eyes and hands, serving . . . the good of the whole. Hence they have and can have no more power than fundamentally lies in [the people] themselves, *which power, might or authority is not religious, Christian, etc., but natural, humane, and civil.*[72]

Here is an unqualified endorsement of a secular, religiously tolerant constitutional theory justified on multiple grounds: biblical, rational or natural, and experiential. And Williams meant what he said. All these sources point to a set of "common rights" assuring the "peace and safety of all citizens," even atheists and

---

70. See above, note 10.
71. Yale Law School, Lillian Goldman Law Library, "Charter of Rhode Island and Providence Plantations—July 15, 1663," The Avalon Project, http://avalon.law.yale.edu/17th_century/ri04.asp.
72. Williams, *Complete Writings of Roger Williams* (New York: Russel and Russel, 1963) vol. 7, 178, vol. 3, 398.

people altogether indifferent or hostile to religion.[73] Beyond that, he was fully prepared to grant equal freedom to religions like Judaism, Islam, and Roman Catholicism, so long, of course, as adherents were willing to accept citizenship on Williams's general terms. It is "known by experience," he said, that "many thousands" of Muslims, Roman Catholics, and Pagans (meaning Native Americans) "are in their persons, both as civil and courteous and peaceable in nature, as any of the subjects in the state they live in."[74] Such people, whatever their religious identity, may be trusted because there exists a "natural" moral law universally available as the proper basis for protecting the "common rights, peace and safety" of all citizens.[75] In fact, just because of such widely distributed common moral essentials, "civil places need not be monopolized [by] church members, (who are sometimes not fitted for them), and all other [people] deprived of their natural and civil rights and liberties."[76]

RELIGION AND CONSTITUTION:
AN AMERICAN DILEMMA

Several generalizations about the American colonial experience are by now well confirmed. One is that the Massachusetts Bay charter "approximated a popular constitution more closely than any other instrument of government in actual use up to that time in America or elsewhere in modern times,"[77] and as such served as a special inspiration for other colonial constitutions, and indirectly for the American constitution. Another is that the documents elaborating and safeguarding inalienable individual rights, such as the Massachusetts Bay Body of Liberties, were "the culmination of an extraordinarily creative period" of legal and constitutional thought, and "were widely copied by other colonies, or used by them as models in framing their own laws."[78] The tradition was particularly important in the proliferation of written rights guarantees throughout the colonies by the end of the seventeenth century as well as in the elaboration of colonial declarations of rights in the 1770s and 1780s.[79] The experience of the colonists with state bills of rights would come to have an important impact on

73. Ibid., vol.7, 181.
74. Cited in Davis, *The Moral Theology of Roger Williams*, 94. It is true that Williams, worryingly, advocated that Catholics should wear some overt identification. Nevertheless, Williams's commitment to an extraordinary degree of tolerance for Catholics should not be overlooked. See note 7, 159 in Davis.
75. Davis, *The Moral Theology of Roger Williams*, 363.
76. *Complete Writings of Roger Williams*, vol. 4, 365.
77. C.H. McIlwain, *Constitutionalism and the Changing World: Collected Papers* (Cambridge: Cambridge University Press, 1939), 241, cited in Bernard Bailyn, *The Ideological Origins of the American Revolution* (Cambridge, MA: Harvard University Press, 1967), 190. McIlwain is here correctly citing the Massachusetts Bay charter as the predecessor to the charters of Connecticut and Rhode Island, which Jellinek calls, "the two oldest written constitutions in the modern sense."
78. Haskins, *Law and Authority in Early Massachusetts*, 136ff., 120, cited in Bailyn, *Ideological Origins*, 194.
79. Jellinek, *Declaration of the Rights of Man*, 24ff.

the debate at the end of the eighteenth century over whether or not to adopt a bill of rights at the federal level. Finally, Roger Williams was responsible both for enshrining an expanded and influential understanding of the right of religious freedom,[80] and, by advocating that understanding, for laying the foundations of a lasting controversy over the interpretation and application of that right in American life.

Although the other colonies, except for New York, did not immediately follow the lead of Rhode Island in adopting expansive language in favor of religious freedom and equality, they had done that, to varying degrees, by the end of the 1780s. Thanks to the adoption in 1776 of the Virginia Declaration of Rights, drafted by George Mason, and in 1786 of the Statute of Religious Freedom, proposed by Thomas Jefferson, and supported by James Madison, Virginia exemplified a particularly permissive interpretation of the rights of conscience. It abolished the Anglican establishment and proclaimed that all human beings without qualification are "equally entitled to the free exercise of religion." Besides Rhode Island, Pennsylvania, Delaware, and New Jersey never had established religions, North Carolina disestablished by 1776, and the establishments in Georgia, South Carolina, and Maryland were controversial and soon removed.

At the same time, government support for religion was a significant factor in several states during and after the drafting and adoption of the U.S. Constitution. Vermont did not relinquish its system of establishment until 1807, Connecticut, until 1818, New Hampshire, until 1819, and Massachusetts, until 1833. Numerous other states, including Pennsylvania and Delaware, imposed religious tests for public office, which often excluded Catholics, Jews, and sometimes atheists.[81] For example, all appointed and elected officials in Delaware were required to profess "faith in God the Father, and in Jesus Christ His only son, and in the Holy Ghost, one God blessed forever."[82] States also frequently enforced religiously preferential laws, such as Massachusetts laws making exposure to a Calvinist doctrinal centerpiece, the Westminster Catechism, mandatory in public schools, and outlawing theatre-going, blasphemy, and disturbing the Sabbath.[83]

This deep ambivalence toward public support of religion set the stage for intense debates across the colonies during the process of ratifying the new constitution in 1787–1788, and for related controversies over a bill of rights, particularly in regard to safeguarding freedom of religion. Though article 6 of the U.S. Constitution, that "no religious Test shall ever be required as a Qualification to any Office or public Trust under the United States," was adopted with relative

80. We may thank, among others, Jellinek, *Declaration of the Rights of Man*, Martha Nussbaum, *Liberty of Conscience: In Defense of America's Tradition of Religious Equality* (New York: Basic Books, 2008), and Isaac Kranmick and R. Laurence Moore, *The Godless Constitution: A Moral Defense of the Secular State* (New York: W.W. Norton & Co., 2005) for highlighting Williams's importance.

81. Nussbaum, *Liberty of Conscience*, 84–85.

82. Kramnick and Moore, *Godless Constitution*, 30.

83. Ibid., 119–20.

ease by the delegates to the constitutional convention, the reactions of the state conventions were a different matter. The "no religious test" clause was seen by many state delegates to constitute a fatal defect in the document they were being asked to accept. "In New Hampshire the fear was of 'a papist, a Mohomatan, a deist, yea an atheist at the helm of government.'" Without a religious test, "to whom," asked a North Carolina delegate derisively, "will [officeholders] swear support—the ancient pagan gods of Jupiter, Juno, Minerva, or Pluto?" Delegates from other states were horrified "that Popery and the Inquisition may be established in America." [84]

On the other hand, there was also strong countervailing support from clergy and others. A Virginia Baptist minister hailed article 6 for dissociating religious faith from governmental support, as did a clergyman from North Carolina who urged that religion stand on its own "without any connection with temporal authority." A minister called on the New Hampshire convention to stand behind the ban on religious tests since "civil authority could not interfere without infringing upon the rights of conscience."[85]

In the end, of course, article 6 would be ratified in 1788, along with the other original seven articles of the Constitution, despite widespread objections to it. However, another controversy plagued the state ratification process, one that also bore in an important way on the interpretation of religious freedom. That was the question of including a bill of rights in the Constitution, after the pattern of the states. Among the drafters, the federalists, supported at first by James Madison, opposed such a declaration because they thought it both unnecessary and dangerous: unnecessary because there was by now a broad enough consensus in favor of rights, including state constitutional guarantees, and dangerous because such a declaration might suggest that rather than being the prior, natural endowment of all citizens, antecedent to and a limitation on government, rights are rather the creation of government, and as such wholly subject to its control. Madison was also skeptical of bills of rights as little more than "parchment barriers," unable to withstand "overbearing majorities" at times of testing.[86]

Federalist arguments against bills of rights met with strong dissent from antifederalists like Thomas Jefferson and George Mason, but also from a large contingent of religious agitators. "No single issue" in regard to the interpretation of state bills of rights had "caused so much discussion or legislative action as freedom of religion." "All citizens could expect equal treatment under the bills of rights except those whose religious convictions placed them in the minority."[87] In other words, what was regarded as widespread mistreatment of religious minorities in many of the states elevated the importance of specifying and protecting personal rights over against the whims of legislative majorities.

---

84. Ibid., 32–33.

85. Ibid, 38–39.

86. Cited in Robert Allen Rutland, *The Birth of the Bill of Rights, 1776–1791* (Chapel Hill: University of North Carolina Press, 1955), 81–82.

87. Rutland, *Birth of the Bill of Rights, 1776–1791*, 82.

Such experience converged with Jefferson's arguments in favor of placing greater trust in explicit constitutional safeguards than in the discretion of state representatives.

Of course, the need to protect individuals against overweening government was a key tenant of the antifederalist case. Eventually deviating from federalist opposition to a bill of rights, Madison came to embrace that tenet as expressed by Jefferson and others. He remarked that "the great mass of people who opposed [the Constitution], disliked it because it did not contain effectual provisions against the encroachments on particular rights, and those safeguards *which they have been long accustomed to have*, interposed between them and the magistrate."[88] He came to agree that the threat to private right was "*chiefly* to be apprehended . . . from acts in which the Government is the mere instrument of the major number of the constituents," and therefore that a bill of rights might, after all, serve well to "counteract the impulses of interest and passion."[89] Madison was particularly drawn to an insight of Jefferson's he had earlier overlooked: that "independent tribunals of justice [and ultimately the Supreme Court] will consider themselves in a peculiar manner the guardians of those rights . . . [and] resist every encroachment upon rights expressly stipulated . . . by the declaration of rights."[90] In a word, Madison eventually became a vigorous proponent of one of the key features of modern constitutionalism: an independent judiciary with special responsibility to protect constitutionally guaranteed inalienable individual rights against the whims of legislative majorities.

Madison's conversion and consequent role as legislative champion of the ten amendments to the Constitution—the "Bill of Rights"—was, of course, of enormous importance in their final ratification by the end of 1791. He played a particularly significant part in drafting the first two clauses of the First Amendment—"Congress shall make no law respecting the establishment of religion, or prohibiting the free exercise thereof"—clauses that defined the constitutional limits within which Americans would struggle ever after to work out the meaning of the right to religious freedom.

Of special interest is the fact that Madison was not satisfied with protecting the rights of conscience simply at the federal level, which is what the religion clauses of the First Amendment did. Once the two clauses had been adopted by Congress, Madison moved on to an additional proposal he believed to be "the most valuable amendment in the whole list," a provision prohibiting state laws from "infring[ing] the equal rights of conscience." Although the measure is aimed at safeguarding free exercise, it could reasonably be understood to outlaw state establishments of religion, particularly because of Madison's own strong support for the Statute for Religious Freedom, which had done just that in

88. Cited in ibid., 201. Emphasis added.
89. Cited in ibid., 193.
90. Cited in ibid., 202.

Virginia.[91] In any case, the proposal clearly meant to apply federal law directly to the states, and, if adopted, would have radically altered the status quo, which largely exempted state laws on religion from the reach of the First Amendment.

The fact that Madison's proposal was defeated and set aside meant that at least up until the Civil War that wing of the Calvinist tradition favoring the civil indispensability of religion and the desirability of governmental regulation was able to gain headway by taking advantage of sympathetic state legislators.

In 1811, a resident of New York named Ruggles (no full name available) was convicted of uttering in public "these false, feigned, scandalous, malicious, wicked and blasphemous words, to wit, 'Jesus Christ was a bastard and his mother must be a whore.'"[92] The judge in his supporting opinion asserts that the "maliciously reviling" of Christianity is an offense "punishable at common law . . . because it tends to corrupt the morals of the people, and to destroy good order [,]" and because it affects "the essential interests of civil society."

There were changes through the second half of the nineteenth century and into the first part of the twentieth, but they were minor. Blasphemy prosecutions declined, as did restrictive standards for witness competency based on religious affiliation. On the other hand, convictions for taking the name of God in vain continued, despite challenges that such convictions violated rights of religious liberty. Sunday laws were still enforced, and even expanded, and up into the 1920s the practice of reading the King James Bible in public schools was judged constitutional, despite the appeal of Catholics and others to be exempted on conscientious grounds.[93]

Perhaps the most famous expressions of majoritarian religious dominance were exemplified in several cases involving Mormons, focusing particularly on their practice of polygamy. In *Reynolds v. United States* (1879) and *Davis v. Beason* (1890), the Supreme Court upheld convictions, respectively, for bigamy and for seeking to register as a voter while knowingly belonging to the Mormon church. In both cases, the court rejected free exercise arguments out of hand. In *Reynolds*, Chief Justice Morrison Waite ruled that while Congress might not, under the First Amendment, regulate "mere opinion," it was free to limit action as it saw fit.[94] In *Davis*, Justice Stephen Field would not even consider Mormon beliefs religious:

> To call their advocacy a tenet of religion is to offend the common sense of mankind . . . The term 'religion' has reference to one's views of his relations to his Creator, and to the obligations they impose of reverence for his being

91. Martha Nussbaum, in *Liberty of Conscience* (100), reads Madison's words that way, though she does not mention what seems to me the most compelling reason to draw the inference, namely, Madison's support for the Virginia Statute for Religious Freedom. Jefferson grounded that document in universal appeal, "the natural rights of mankind," a foundation, he said explicitly, that overrides all legislative acts (in Virginia and elsewhere, one would assume).

92. Michael S. Ariens and Robert A. Destro, *Religious Liberty in a Pluralistic Society* (Durham, NC: Carolina Academic Press, 1996), 113. *People v. Ruggles* 8 Johns 290 (N.Y. 1811).

93. Ariens and Destro, *Religious Liberty*, 147–50.

94. Ibid., 190.

and character, and of obedience to his will. It is often confounded with the cultus or form of worship of a particular sect, but is distinguishable from the latter.[95]

The court took similarly dismissive attitudes toward the claims of conscience of pacifists during World War I and after.[96]

These decisions, and many like them, were left unchallenged well into the twentieth century, mainly because the Supreme Court took the position that the First Amendment applied only to federal and not to state law. States, on this reading, were free to interpret the right of religious freedom very narrowly, as they did in the New York and Pennsylvania cases just cited, thereby allowing what looked like a form of majority religious establishment at the state level.

The Fourteenth Amendment, adopted after the Civil War, offered the opportunity of "incorporating" the First Amendment into its provisions, which assured due process and equal legal protection for all citizens. That would have transferred final authority from the states to the Supreme Court, and made possible wider and more robust protection of conscience, particularly in regard to minority beliefs.

However, in its wisdom, the court refrained from taking advantage of that opportunity until 1940, when in a landmark case, *Cantwell v. Connecticut*, a Jehovah's Witness was exempted from a local licensing law regulating public speaking and soliciting because it was held to restrict unduly the free exercise of religion.[97] In arriving at its decision, the court modified Waite's opinion in *Reynolds*, arguing that in some circumstances actions as well as beliefs are protected under the First Amendment, thereby expanding the meaning of free exercise. Accordingly, *Cantwell* "opened the modern era of free exercise jurisprudence"[98] moving closer to the ideals of Roger Williams and the liberal side of Calvin's legacy, which, as we have seen, gave special priority to the rights of conscience.

Two subsequent cases illustrate the outlines of "free exercise jurisprudence" with particular force. One is *Sherbert v. Verner*,[99] involving a Seventh-Day Adventist named Adell Sherbert. She was denied unemployment benefits under the South Carolina Unemployment Act for declining to work on Saturday, as required by her employer, a textile manufacturer, because of her religious beliefs concerning the Sabbath. According to the statute, a person is not eligible for compensation where suitable work is rejected without good cause. State authorities ruled that an appeal to conscience based on religion does not qualify as a good cause, and the judgment was upheld by the South Carolina Supreme Court.

Justice William Brennan, writing for a (7–2) majority of the U.S. Supreme Court, overruled the lower court in favor of Sherbert. It is a decision that has

95. Idaho Rev. Stat. 501 (1887), 341–342.
96. John Witte Jr., *Religion and the American Constitutional Experiment*, 2nd ed. (Boulder, CO: Westview Press, 2005), 129–31.
97. See ibid., 137.
98. Ibid., 177.
99. 374 U.S. 398 (1963).

been called, "a major achievement, suggesting a test that shaped legal reasoning for decades."[100] Among other things, Brennan asks if "any incidental burden on the free exercise of appellant's religion may be justified by a 'compelling state interest.'" That means that should the circumstances dictate, the state would be under obligation to override appeals of conscience as a basis for exemption from generally applicable laws in face of an urgent need to protect the "outward" affairs of the social order, namely public order, health or safety. However, he finds no such compelling state interest in this case.[101] Moreover Brennan added another concern about the South Carolina law. It explicitly exempted employees with scruples against Sunday employment from working on Sunday during times of national emergency, thereby constituting discrimination against those whose religious scruples, like Sherbert's, dictate a different day of rest.

This decision has two important consequences. One is to enshrine a doctrine of the sovereignty of conscience by holding that the state should normally defer to the right of religious free exercise, including actions, unless there is an overriding "compelling state interest." The idea that the state should not "burden" conscience except for very good reason implies that freedom of conscience is one of those individual entitlements that is part of the "fundamental" law antecedent to the state, for whose protection the state is solemnly accountable. The other is that in executing its responsibility to safeguard the right of conscience, in part by showing cause for any infringements, the state must give special consideration to the threat of majoritarian domination. The fact that in *Sherbert* state law allowed a conscientious excuse for not working on Sunday, while denying the same excuse to those who regard Saturday as the Sabbath, clearly privileged majority religion and seriously disadvantaged a minority without cause.[102]

The second significant case is the landmark ruling in 1990 by the U.S. Supreme Court, *Employment Division, Department of Human Resources of Oregon v. Smith*,[103] which, in a 6–3 decision, effectively overturned *Sherbert.* The Court was sharply divided, with the majority rejecting *Sherbert* principles, and the minority, abetted by a fourth concurring justice, defending them. The conflicting opinions thereby dramatically reflect the two sides of the American dilemma over religious freedom we have been analyzing throughout. Furthermore, the widespread negative reaction to the decision, implying strong agreement with the minority opinion, vindicates Martha Nussbaum's observation that "subsequent developments show the *Sherbert* approach currently has the overwhelming support of the American people."[104]

---

100. Nussbaum, *Liberty of Conscience*, 139. The court ruled similarly in a number of subsequent cases: *Thomas v. Review Board*, 450 U.S. 707 (1981); *Hobbie v. Unemployment Appeals Comm'n of Florida*, 480 U.S. 136 (1987); and *Frazee v. Illinois Department of Employment Security*, 489 U.S. 829 (1989).

101. Ariens and Destro, *Religious Liberty*, 205–6.

102. Nussbaum, *Liberty of Conscience*, 139.

103. 496 U.S. 913 (1990). Ariens and Destro, *Religious Liberty*, 240–53.

104. Nussbaum, *Liberty of Conscience*, 139.

The Court denied unemployment compensation to two members of the Native American Church, who had been fired from their jobs with a private drug rehabilitation center because they ingested peyote for sacramental purposes in a religious ceremony. Under the religious free exercise clause of the First Amendment to the U.S. Constitution, the defendants claimed a right of exemption from a state law that criminalized all use of controlled substances, including peyote, except if prescribed by a physician. The Court majority argued that there is absolutely no constitutionally required protection from generally applicable laws.[105] Whatever religious exemptions are allowed must be left to state legislatures, who are fully entitled to ignore and override any conscientiously held beliefs of citizens, so long as the laws passed do not specifically single out one individual or group for discriminatory treatment. There is an admission that failing to give constitutional protection to "religious practices that are not widely engaged in"—namely, by minority religions like the Native American Church—"will place them at a relative disadvantage." Nevertheless, that is an "unavoidable consequence," since otherwise "anarchy" would result from a system where "each conscience is a law unto itself or in which judges weigh the social impact of all laws against the centrality of all religious beliefs."[106]

A storm of protest from religious groups, as well as from other nongovernmental organizations and civil libertarians, arose over the *Smith* decision. Opposition forces gathered momentum and eventually coalesced around the Religious Freedom Restoration Act (RFRA), passed by Congress in 1993. The act declared that the government "may substantially burden a person's exercise of religion only if it demonstrates that application of the burden to the person, (1) is in furtherance of a compelling governmental interest; and (2) is the least restrictive means of furthering that compelling governmental interest."[107] The act held until 1997 when the Court partially overturned it in *City of Boerne v. Flores* for transgressing Congress's authority by trying to tell the Court how to rule on religious freedom issues. Still, widespread disagreement with *Smith* continues to exist, and there is some indication the Court may be moving away from it.[108]

The dissenters in the *Smith* case took strong exception to the majority arguments. They held that the two-fold test of RFRA—determining the least restrictive means in support of a compelling state interest—epitomizes "the First Amendment's command that religious liberty is an independent liberty, and that it occupies a preferred position," and that it is the responsibility of the Court "to strike sensible balances between religious liberty and a compelling state interest."[109] The dissenters also added that were the protection of religious

105. Ariens and Destro, *Religious Liberty*, 244.
106. Ibid., 244–45.
107. Ibid., 255.
108. Garrett Epps, *To an Unknown God: Religious Freedom on Trial* (New York: St. Martin's Press, 2001), 239, 240.
109. Ariens and Destro, *Religious Liberty*, 245–46.

liberty rights left to the legislative process, that would contradict the clear purpose of the First Amendment, which is "precisely to protect the rights of those
whose religious practices are not shared by the majority, and may be viewed
with hostility."[110] They concluded, "The history of our free exercise doctrine
amply demonstrates the harsh impact majoritarian rule has had on unpopular or
emerging religious groups such as the Jehovah's Witnesses or the Amish," and,
it might be added, the Native American Church.[111]

CONCLUSION

In two respects, Jellinek and Weber were surely right. Jellinek's conclusion,
embraced by Weber, that the development of modern constitutionalism, critically including the idea of inalienable individual rights, was "not of political but
religious origin," that it was the "fruit of the Reformation and its struggles," is
vindicated. We believe we (and others[112]) have shown that while Calvin certainly did not "invent" modern constitutionalism, particularly as manifested in
the American experience, he provided a compelling and practically influential
theological framework within which his heirs, the Puritans, formulated and promoted it on American shores.

Also, the "elective affinity" (a favorite phrase of Weber's) between Calvinism
and constitutionalism lends strong support to Weber's general thesis, stimulated
by Jellinek, in favor of the distinctive impact of Calvinism on the rise of "legal
rational authority," understood here not in regard to the emergence of modern
capitalism, but of the modern constitutional state. Weber's idea of legal rational
authority is precisely exemplified by constitutional government. In some ways,
the affinity between Calvinism and the idea of a modern constitutional state
can be demonstrated in a more straightforward way than the affinity to modern
capitalism.

But there is one crucial difficulty in this picture, which neither Jellinek nor
Weber expanded on and which importantly complicates things: the *meaning*
of the constitutional right to religious freedom. According to our analysis, the
abiding controversy over this issue is an important part of the "Reformation
struggles" Jellinek refers to, especially in the Calvinist tradition. The position
of Roger Williams, which was also Madison's and Jefferson's view, elevates the
equal rights of conscience thereby encouraging religious pluralism and diversity
and discouraging the entanglement of religion and state. From Jellinek's and
Weber's point of view, that is a strong form of legal rational authority in that
it supports the sharp differentiation of religious and civil authority as a means
of protecting equal rights. One part of Calvin's thought, as we saw, also favors
that view.

110. Ibid., 247.
111. Ibid.
112. Especially Witte, *Revolution of Rights*.

But the problem is that Calvin, and the tradition he helped to inspire, is profoundly conflicted on this subject. While there is support in Calvin, and in some of his Puritan heirs, for Williams's view, there is also much against it. There is a strong tendency, both in Calvin's Geneva and in seventeenth-century Massachusetts Bay (and elsewhere), to embrace extensive, state-supported restrictions on religious freedom, a tendency that actively works against central features of legal rationality. The fact that the American constitutional tradition, partly following, as it does, from colonial Puritanism, so clearly continues to manifest this deep dilemma, attests to the power of the Calvinist influence.

Contributors

J. Todd Billings is Associate Professor of Reformed Theology at Western Theological Seminary in Holland, Michigan. He is also the author of numerous articles and three books, including *Calvin, Participation, and the Gift* (Oxford), for which he won a 2009 Templeton Award for Theological Promise.

I. John Hesselink is Albertus C. Van Raalte Professor of Systematic Theology Emeritus at Western Theological Seminary in Holland, Michigan. He is the author of numerous publications on the thought of John Calvin, including *Calvin's Concept of the Law* (Pickwick) and *Calvin's First Catechism: A Commentary* (Westminster John Knox).

Timothy Hessel-Robinson is Alberta H. and Harold L. Lunger Associate Professor of Spiritual Disciplines and Resources at Brite Divinity School at Texas Christian University. In addition to a number of articles, he is the author of *The Reverend Edward Taylor's Sacramental Meditations on the Song of Songs* (Edwin Mellen) and the editor of *Spirit and Nature: The Study of Christian Spirituality in a Time of Ecological Urgency* (Pickwick).

Michael S. Horton is J. Gresham Machen Professor of Systematic Theology and Apologetics at Westminster Seminary California. He is the editor-in-chief of *Modern Reformation* magazine. His most recent books are *The Christian Faith: A Systematic Theology for Pilgrims on the Way* (Zondervan) and *People and Place: A Covenant Ecclesiology* (Westminster John Knox).

Mark Husbands is Leonard and Marjorie Maas Associate Professor of Reformed Theology at Hope College in Holland, Michigan. He is the author of numerous articles and chapters in dogmatic theology, and has edited or coedited seven books, including *Justification: What's at Stake in the Recent Debates? Essays Catholic and Critical,* and *Ancient Faith for the Church's Future.*

David Little is retired Professor of the Practice in Religion, Ethnicity, and International Conflict at Harvard Divinity School, and Faculty Associate at the Weatherhead Center for International Affairs at Harvard University. He is the author of many publications including *Religion, Order, and Law: A Study in Pre-Revolutionary England* (University of Chicago Press).

Suzanne McDonald is Assistant Professor of Religion at Calvin College in Grand Rapids, Michigan. She has authored numerous articles as well as the book *Re-Imaging Election: Divine Election as Representing God to Others and Others to God* (Eerdmans).

Jeannine E. Olson is Professor of History at Rhode Island College in Providence, Rhode Island. She is the author of three books, including *Calvin and Social Welfare: Deacons and the* Bourse française (Associated University Presses) and *Deacons and Deaconesses through the Centuries* (Concordia Publishing House), which received an Award of Commendation of the Concordia Historical Institute.

Sue A. Rozeboom is Assistant Professor of Liturgical Theology at Western Theological Seminary in Holland, Michigan. She obtained a Ph.D. in Liturgical Studies at the University of Notre Dame, having prepared a dissertation on Calvin's theology of the Lord's Supper. With Cornelius Plantinga Jr., she is coauthor of *Discerning the Spirits: A Guide to Thinking about Christian Worship Today* (Eerdmans).

Carl R. Trueman is Paul Woolley Professor of Church History at Westminster Theological Seminary in Philadelphia. He is former editor of *Themelios* and has authored numerous books, the most recent of which is *Histories and Fallacies: Problems Faced in the Writing of History* (Crossway).

Index

CPSIA information can be obtained at www.ICGtesting.com
Printed in the USA
BVOW02s0233150115

383365BV00006B/104/P